Archaean Hills

ADIRONDACK
MTS.

I R I E S

M T S.

A P P A L A C H I A N

ATLANTIC

OCEAN

OF THE UNITED STATES

THE CONTINENT IN OUR HANDS

Charlton Ogburn

THE CONTINENT
IN OUR HANDS

William Morrow & Company, Inc.
New York 1971

For Nyssa and Holly, who have made it better

Grateful acknowledgment is made by the author to *The Washington Post* and to *National Parks & Conservation Magazine* for permission to draw upon his article, "The Continent in Our Hands," which appeared in *Outlook*, issue of October 5, 1969, and *National Parks & Conservation Magazine,* issue of May 1970; also to *Holiday* for permission to reprint excerpts from "Virginia: A State That Has—Well Almost—Everything," which appeared in their September/October 1970 issue, © 1970 The Curtis Publishing Company. Base Map appearing on endpapers and between pages 172–173 © 1958, Jeppesen & Co., Denver, Colo., U.S.A., All Rights Reserved.

CONTENTS

*Maps of the author's trip appear between
pages 15–16, 77–78, and 203–204.
Topographical map of the United States appears
between pages 172–173.*

". . . for the Continent is of
a huge and unknown greatness."

——Richard Lane to
Richard Hakluyt, 1585

PROLOGUE:

BY WAY OF
EXPLANATION

Why would anyone let himself in for driving ninety-six hundred miles in twenty-two days? I suppose I need not have. However, I had been asked to do a piece of work I did not like to turn down and felt I could not adequately perform without a better acquaintance with the physiography of the country, of which circumstances had kept me from seeing little beyond the Atlantic States for a good many years. And the deadline for completing what I had to do was such that three weeks was the most I felt I could spare away from the desk.

To make the tour feasible, economically as well as otherwise, I had a miniature bus fitted out with counter, icebox, two-burner stove, sink, cabinets, rear seats facing each other across a table, which all let down to form a bunk, and an erectable top to permit standing up while washing or pulling on trousers. The vehicle, which looks large end-on, reminding one of some kind of fat larva, magnified, had served me very well on other, shorter expeditions, and I had learned to live in comfort in it, insofar as doing so does not depend on plumbing. However, I have to admit that the trip had no sooner occurred to me as a possibility than it struck me as of very doubtful rationality. On this point the opinion of others was not reassuring.

I did not know whether I could manage all that driving in the time allowable, even when I computed the essential mileage at only 7,500. I could not imagine what the physical effects would be, with the enforced inactivity, or how I should take to so long a stretch of unbroken solitude. With the two girls in school to look after, my wife could not go, and no one else I knew could, or would, either—which may have been just as well; two men (and it had to be assumed that the other would have been a man) confined together at close quarters for three weeks would probably become a trial to each other well before the time was up. There was also the question of whether, if the excursion came down to a test of endurance, I should get much out of it. Yet from the moment of first thinking of it I was committed.

"As age triumphs," Charles de Gaulle wrote from his country home at the age of seventy, "nature comes closer to me." * It is doubtless true for many of us. While I cannot yet speak with authority of age's triumph, I do think that as we grow older we are drawn to what is timeless and look to Nature for more. What we seek, I believe, goes beyond the aesthetic and sensuous delight of its beauties, sounds and fragrances, beyond the charm and encouragement of shared life with an irrepressible array of exquisitely contrived plants and animate creatures; beyond even those things. We turn to Nature, unless I am greatly mistaken, for a sense of ultimate truths in its great and intricate harmonies and, I should add, in recognition of the need of those who feel an unappeasable inadequacy in themselves, an intimation of that to which, without compromise of one's critical judgment or manhood, one may pay homage.

For myself, I have found that my susceptibility to Nature, which began in boyhood as an ardor for birds, has grown broader with the years. It has come to embrace the earth itself—earth and rocks, to which everything owes its origin. I have fallen under their thrall, so much so that I even set out some time ago to see what I could learn of them from the thorny texts of geology. To find the meaning that anything may have for you, you have to delve into it. From trying to understand the earth-history manifested in the Eastern regions I was familiar with, I turned also to look out, figuratively, across North America in an effort to visualize its mighty features and the processes, microscopic and stupendous, that brought them into being. How could I not feel the strongest desire to see the great sculpture itself?

But one may have the best reason to seize a chance to go out and

* Sources of quotations are listed by page number at the end of the book.

discover the continent for oneself without necessarily yearning to do it in three weeks—even with an allowance for expenses. Yet it was this limitation of time as much as anything that made the idea of the trip irresistible to me. There was the adventure of it; but more than that it promised the nearest thing I could think of to a total immersion in the country as a whole. In what other way could one encompass so much of the continent at close range in one uninterrupted exposure? (Not by a longer trip. If three weeks' steady travel and absorption in the passing scene did not exhaust one's powers, I felt sure that four would.) From such a concentrated, comprehensive view one ought to have as vivid an impression as anyone could of the country as it truly is.

And, as it fell out, I think I had. Many others have seen incomparably more of America than I have and know it far better. But I cannot believe anything could quite equal the effect of having it unreeled before one in a single, unbroken sequence, from coast to coast and back again and from Texas to Canada, when one is traveling alone and living under, eating under, going to bed and awakening under the visual impact the country is capable of making and being almost altogether subject to it. It was an experience I should not have missed for the world; and the chance to bear witness to it—I should not have missed that either, if I could help it, having, with respect to the standing of my account with the earth, with life, a sense of heavy imbalance on the debit side and of the need to make a return however possible.

This suggests a way of dealing with the bothersome question of why anyone should attend my struggles to do justice to what I have seen. It is a question that grows insistent as I come actually to make a beginning and feel less confident that having the country all at once, as it were, brings out anything about it not evident from partaking of it piecemeal over a course of time. The answer to it is this: if by pilgrimages and other appropriate observances we acknowledge our duties to that which we owe all that is and thus gain merit, the reader who follows this recital, which will lead past many of the greatest of the works of Creation that make the continent what it is, may legitimately expect, I think, a very significant accrual to his credit. If he stands to gain less than a Madrasi from a trip to the Ganges or a Japanese from an ascent of Fuji No Yama—"Peerless Mount"—it is only because the physical effort required will be less.

One thing more. Even a traveler whose primary concern is with the natural features of the country and who therefore shuns centers of population can hardly fail to be constantly provoked by what he sees or is reminded of to reflect on the character of our people's involvement with the land. He may well even be moved, as I have been, to learn more about the background of that involvement. As much as he may be affected by the natural magnificence of the continent we have made ours, he is likely to ponder long all that seems to be at stake in the meaning it has for us, or may come to have for us, and we for it.

1

PIEDMONT AND APPALACHIANS

The truth is that leaving home, and those who make it home, is an unhappy business. Regardless of how much one may enjoy travel, the heart grows heavier as the time approaches. Or it does so with me. I drag about, cast down by forebodings and remorse and a sense of life's irremediable sadness. I do not know why it should have to be as it is, when it is part of the day's work and when it is not as if one were off for years, as the whalers were. Still, it is all I can manage, finally, to climb up behind the steering-wheel, exchange good-byes and futile, last-minute injunctions, and set the bus off down the driveway. I say this not in a spirit of confession; that, I shall try to keep to a minimum. My aim is to show, when I say that even I am transported by it, what an exhilaration there is in being abroad early in the morning of a sunny second day of May with the continent before one. The continent—in all its splendors, many renowned, many I have doubtless never heard of, all new to me or to be seen with new eyes, and with nothing asked of me but to take in as much of it as I can! Think of it! Life does not come up with many such offerings. For one thing, there are not many continents. And not only is the sky blue and as innocent in its spotless clouds as if it had never looked down on guile or malevolence, but beneath it, to start me off, lies a green and billowing land as fair as any you may hope to find this side of the ocean.

From where we live in the woods above Difficult Run, fifteen miles inland of the last rapids of the Potomac above Washington, the Virginia Piedmont rolls away westward and southward. It might have been designed expressly to satisfy the needs of the human spirit. Northerners with the means to live anywhere have been coming here for generations; those, that is, for whom the good life calls for land and horses. With tree-lined streams in the valleys that divide its low hills, with meadows interspersed with woods, it combines the spaciousness of distant vistas rimmed by the Blue Ridge with the intimate security of closed-in dales. It comes as near as any landscape could, I should think, to the Arcadian idyll to which the West has been drawn since Virgil's time. White board fences undulating away with the rise and dip of the land, a Georgian mansion back from the highway, horses grazing and Angus cattle black as holes punched in the greensward placidly chewing their cuds: it makes one think of the Roman manors of fourth-century Britain or of eighteenth-century England of the landscape painters; it is indeed a recurrent theme of civilization. As a matter of fact, everything about Virginia that is particularly Virginian *is* eighteenth-century England.

In traveling—perhaps the reader has found it so too—one is forever engaging mentally in fission. One subdivides, leaving one of oneself behind to take up life in some scene one is having to leave, some pastoral vale or snug village in which one can see oneself settling and being happy forever. Without this device I could scarcely put the Virginia Piedmont behind me, either its country mansions, which can in fact be quite modest, or the old town-houses of Leesburg, Middleburg, Warrenton, or Culpeper, compactly built of stone or brick now weathered and seasoned with time. These are houses at peace with themselves, sure of what they are, unlike the ramblers and split-levels, restless and uneasy in their dispro-portions and the disharmonious styles they combine, that cluster over the landscape around where I actually do live. These old houses have acquired a life and being of their own from the slow absorption of the lives lived within them. And it should not be too hard a fate to invest a house with one's life, creating a living guardian of lives to come. Or so it seems to me under the sway of a kind of homesickness I have become subject to, a nostalgia for a continuity such as I and probably most other Americans born in this century have never known. Perhaps we should find if we had it that it would pall on us. Still, those who have endured five decades or more of accelerating change—as much change, almost, as mankind has had to accommodate itself to in all preceding history—may be permitted a waning of enthusiasm for a civilization that seems to grow more fragmented as it grows more uniform and be forgiven an instinct to reach out for an alternative.

Be that as it may, however, no one acquainted with the Washington metropolitan area's rate of growth would look for permanence and stability within an hour's drive or more of the central city. Within that radius, everything will have to go that stands in the way of new highways, garish new gasoline stations. . . .

But never mind—for the moment. I am not going to think about it. One lives only once, and there is the country itself to be enjoyed, even if enjoying a trip through America means cultivating selective vision—wearing blinders. And all is not yet lost. Indeed, it is astonishing, I am to find, how much remains of an America to be gloried in. So, the little bus rumbles on, and thinking only of the Piedmont's perfect balance of sky, woods, and meadows, where next month the Viper's bugloss will form fairy fir forests eighteen inches high, of dusty blue, and the daisies trail a Milky Way to the hilltops, I am scarcely able to believe my own good fortune. *Early May:* what a lovely radiance is in the words!—but no more than that which bathes the landscape around me, glistening on the leaves of Black oak and Black tupelo. I am in favor of trees with glossy leaves on which the sunlight sparkles. They have my approbation, as have the grackles, black as Angus cattle, flying off in pairs. The Appalachians, the Mississippi, the Great Plains, the Western Cordillera, the Pacific: all ahead! Imagine being rewarded for doing this. I have ceased to think of the amount of driving and have even forgotten my anxieties about the undertaking that has led to the excursion. The only reminder of them—and I must say it is a not inconsiderable one—is a black object on the motor housing beside me. (The motor is between the driver's and the other front seat.) It is squat, like a toad, and is a tape recorder. It is to be the repository of my observations, which there will be no time to stop and enter in a notebook. I am unused to the device and intimidated by it, fearful of wasting its time should I set its reels in motion and find myself tongue-tied and feeling a complete jackass when I try to speak into the microphone in the sole company of the taciturn and superior instrument.

An hour and a half gone, Culpeper to the rear, and there is a roadside park with gravel lanes. To make the hours behind the wheel supportable—and there are to be a great many more of these than might seem necessary since fifty-five is a fair speed for the wind-resistant, under-powered little bus as it is for me too unless I am to give my attention undeviatingly to the highway—it has come to me that I must get out every two hours, anyway, to work my limbs and stir up my circulation. So it is into the park and out for a jog. There are cars in two of the other picnic spaces, and I am afraid that to the couples in them I am not a man in holy orders, an acolyte of the continental mysteries and of the millions and billions of years of geologic time, whom prosaic mortals may not presume to judge, but a balding, middle-aged eccentric, a nut.

Later witnesses of my exercising are to have even more reason to think so, for after providing myself with rocks at the first stop in the mountains I do my jogging with one in each hand, to get the most benefit for the time spent. But really there is no alternative if one is to escape the stupor of stultification from long sessions at the wheel. Moreover, refreshments taste better for being earned, and if a meal does not follow a run, I generally see to it that coffee or tea does. For the first stop of the day there is coffee in a vacuum bottle, prepared at breakfast. Thereafter, I set water on to boil when I start out for a run and I am back in time to put in coffee powder or tea-bag; I run about a third of a mile at a stop. Of course, there is no time for sitting over a beverage; I drink it from the bottle through a straw as I drive. I am ashamed to admit how much eight ounces of hot coffee and a doughnut or of tea and a graham cracker spread with peanut butter add to my appreciation of the finer things of life, such as a new and felicitous landscape through which I am swinging along.

Such a prodigality of space as there still is here, even in the long-settled East! The cornucopia of the gods has poured forth this supreme gift, this plenitude of well-favored land. But seeing the towns straggle out across it, spoiling more than they utilize, you would think this was taken only as a license to waste it. You wonder if the American people understand what it means not having to skimp and scrape over every half-acre, not eternally to be cramped. Do they appreciate having room in which to expand, not to expand the apparatus of civilization, but to expand in spirit—room enough to feel unconfined? It cannot be that they do or they would never stand for the national treatment of the land as a mere marketable commodity to go to the highest bidder for whatever use, or very nearly, he cares to make of it. They would not put up with couples whose heedless breeding we can thank for the more than a million and a half annual excess of births over deaths in the United States. They would look a great deal more critically than they give any evidence of doing at a policy of admitting nearly half a million immigrants to the country every year—estimable persons, every last one of them, for all I know, but persons who might yet devote their talents and energies (is it brutal to suggest?) to bringing about in their own countries what they seek to possess in this.

But that is part of what I am not going to dwell on. There is the world about me, and all the mornings ahead, if I am lucky, to make the most of without fretting over what I cannot help.

And there are these hills, which give rhythm to the land—and which are growing more abrupt with the approach of the mountains. The larger streams have cut through to bedrock and pour over boulders. Rock ledges now protrude through the red soil, worn and rounded. These facts I confide, in accents portentous and unnatural, to the tape recorder, which has been awaiting my discourse with an air of ironical patience. Rocks have become, for me, in my immersion in geology, just about the nub of everything. In rocks the whole visible earth began and, as the rocks are slowly worn away and as slowly reconstituted, it is eternally in process of beginning anew. My head is full of them. Every outcropping has come to have in my eyes the character, in a manner of speaking, of a preceptor and guru with an eons-spanning and awful story to tell—one which I, a most unworthy disciple, am likely to have difficulty getting straight even with the help of the authorities.

In the Piedmont, the testimony of the rocks is especially complicated. Those that give it its topography are said to be the roots of vanished mountains. Mountain chains, it seems, do have roots, like teeth, and these, when the chains are first formed, may descend as far as thirty or forty miles into the earth. The continents may evidently be likened to ice floes basically of granite, some twenty miles thick in the main, floating on the layer of basalt that is the earth's integument, and their lower surface appears to be something of a mirror image of their upper; where mountains rise they have foundations that go down. It is the great depths to which

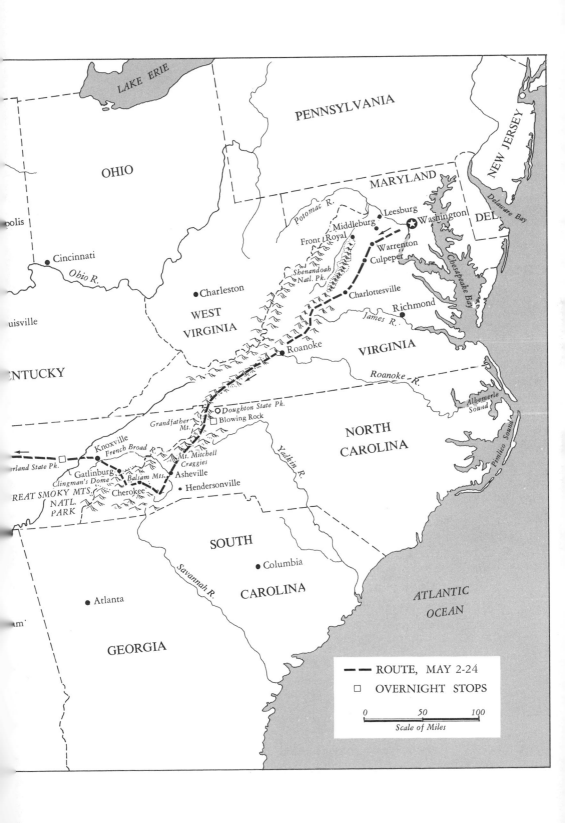

LAKE ERIE

PENNSYLVANIA

OHIO

MARYLAND

NEW JERSEY

DEL.

Delaware Bay

Potomac R.

Leesburg

Washington

Middleburg

Front Royal

Warrenton

olis

Cincinnati

Culpeper

Ohio R.

Charleston

Shenandoah
Natl. Pk.

Charlottesville

Chesapeake Bay

WEST
VIRGINIA

Richmond

uisville

James R.

VIRGINIA

Roanoke

ENTUCKY

Roanoke R.

Albemarle
Sound

Doughton State Pk.

Grandfather
Mt.

Blowing Rock

Knoxville

French Broad R.

Mt. Mitchell
Craggies

NORTH
CAROLINA

Yadkin R.

Pamlico Sound

erland State Pk.

Gatlinburg

Clingman's Dome

Balsam Mts.

Asheville

REAT SMOKY MTS.
NATL.
PARK

Cherokee

Hendersonville

am

SOUTH

Columbia

Savannah R.

CAROLINA

ATLANTIC
OCEAN

Atlanta

GEORGIA

— — ROUTE, MAY 2-24

☐ OVERNIGHT STOPS

0   50   100

Scale of Miles

mountain ranges like the Appalachians, the Rockies, the Andes, and the Alps descend that give them their longevity. As they wear down, they apparently continue to rise, like melting icebergs. But with the mountains of which the Piedmont's hills are the remains, the process must be at an end, the reserves used up.

One wonders how long ago those mountains towered here, the epitome of mountains in their day, perhaps, their jagged, gale-raked pinnacles piercing the clouds. Some of the rocks of the Piedmont were crystallized in the furnace of the earth's depths about three hundred million years ago. That means that mountains may have arisen here as the Appalachians were rising, when, according to a theory derided for half a century but now generally accepted, the continents were all joined in a single land-mass. But long before that, 850 million years ago, in a totally unrecognizable pre-Paleozoic world, there was mountain-making in the Piedmont, perhaps volcanic. Yet any Mauna Loas or Aleutian-like chain of fuming cones that arose here in that inconceivably remote past were still in an inconceivably distant future when an earlier surge of mountain-making took place here, of which the billion-year-old "Baltimore gneiss" is a legacy. Rocks from the crest of the Blue Ridge have been found to be of a similar age and could well have belonged to the same range. That does not mean that the Blue Ridge was standing a billion years ago. What it does mean, presumably, is that when the Blue Ridge was elevated, some of the ancient basement of the continent, as the geologists call it, came up with it.

I do not quite know why, but the idea of the continental basement has taken hold of my imagination. Every continent has such a basement, a floor underlying its surface features (apart from its newer margins) composed of the planed-down bases of ancient mountains and remains of ancient lava-flows—all hard, resistant rock. Where the continental basement is at the surface, as it is over a part of every continent, it is called a shield, because of its broadly convex form. In North America it is at the surface over the larger part of Canada—all that part north of the necklace of waterways formed by the St. Lawrence River, the Great Lakes, Lake Winnipeg, Lake Athabasca, Great Slave Lake and Great Bear Lake—and is known as the Canadian Shield. To the south and west, the basement slopes gently downward, passing under deepening layers of newer rock formed of the sediments that settled in the seas that repeatedly advanced upon and withdrew from the continent below the shield during the Paleozoic (the "Early-Life") era. The basement rocks can, however, be seen where for some reason they have bulged up, not only in the Blue Ridge, but to produce the Ozark Mountains, the Black Hills of South Dakota, and the Central and Southern Rockies.

The Canadian Shield contains the oldest known rocks of the continent: a pink gneiss from a detached portion of the Shield south of Lake Superior in Minnesota has been found to be three and a half billion years old. And on the other side of Superior, running down to the lake from the north, are hills that I have learned are the continent's oldest: its oldest highlands, formed of its oldest rocks. The Archaean Hills, I call them, having been unable to discover from any geography, map or agency of the Canadian government that they have any other name. I have come to think of them as the ultimate goal of my trip. Something must happen to one who stands before those eminences that look beyond the millennia of human history as I look beyond an object inches from my nose when I lift my gaze to the far horizon; so I feel at least to the degree of having to recognize what an irrational notion it is.

No special revelation of the true inwardness of things can be expected of a pilgrimage to my Archaean Hills, admittedly. Yet I feel that no one will be quite the same after having tried to work his way back through geologic ages. You goad a refractory imagination to come up with the feeling of the crushing vastness of time of which the continent today is the outcome and of the reality of the generations of mountain chains that reigned, unseen by any eye, for eons endless in human terms to augment the continental basement by their gnarled stumps. And the imagination does respond with flickering suggestions of what the words represent. The soul draws back from the presentiments, it is true. Think of finding yourself pressed against an icy crag of the mountain whence came that pink gneiss, in a world empty of any living thing—forgetting there is also no oxygen in the air to sustain you long enough for your plight to sink home. Yet there is the knowledge that all you are, every atom you contain in your sinews, nerves, and brain, all that every other living creature is, and every feature of the earth today, was in existence in the waters and minerals of that remote and bitterly inhospitable world. (Yes, additional material has filtered in from space since then, but it hardly affects the issue.) You are kin to all that is and that has been. A common origin and skein of interrelationships binds the earth and its offspring together, in a single composition—and on what a scale of time and immensity!

From the realms of geology you return awed and enlarged within yourself by the scope of the creation of which man is inseparably part and product—and moved as never before, perhaps, by man's uniqueness. That life should have come to pass among the seething lavas, harsh rocks, barren waters and impalpable gases lethal to animals that was all the planet offered is astonishing enough. But to encounter man as the outcome of the insensate forces that lift mountains and send the oceans over continental lowlands, that pour the sun's heat on the earth and draw the ocean's water into clouds—that is truly cause to marvel! How could it ever be that there is man—man in his ability to re-create the mountains of a billion years ago from their mangled remains, man in his awareness of himself, in his fancies, dreams and yearnings, in his humanity? Imagine yourself condemned by hideous mischance to a world in which mankind is a hundred and fifty million years in the future . . . and after months, if you have managed to cling to existence and to sanity, suddenly there before you is another human being! With what tears of joy would you rush to embrace him! How like an angel indeed would your fellow man appear—and how different from your fellow man in the ten thousand motorcars jamming a highway, your fellow man multiplied ten million-fold in festering cities, from the billions of the race mindlessly multiplying which threatens to deplete life on earth as the most ruthless geological force never did.

The landscape of the Piedmont grows bolder and more exhilarating. From the fields, the woods have drawn back, crowding together, to the safety of the hills. These are bigger and steeper— the foothills of the mountains. Dark, reserved, the Appalachians rise before you, a sea frozen in tumult. Nature must be deeply attached to the form of waves. Not only do the running waves of the ocean and the standing waves of streams have this form, and sand dunes, but it is the form to which mountains of all origins tend, whatever their inherent shape.

Like the woods taking to the hills, you feel as the road begins to wind, climbing into the mountains, that you are making good an escape. The forest stands closer on the steep slopes, which drop away to a lively, tumbling stream, and with every break in the enclosing walls the earth has fallen away farther beneath you. From the traffic and commercial bedlam of the last urban conglomeration—Charlottesville's environs, in this case—you are elevated not physically alone. *The mountains that rise above the jangling turmoil of the civilized lowlands are like headlands imperturbable above raging seas.* Thus speaks Zarathustra into the tape recorder, which is losing some of its power to abash. *Every blatant commercial appeal derogates from one's self-respect by the low regard in which it holds one, leaving one diminished.* And I do think the picture we have of ourselves tends to conform to the estimate others entertain of us, especially if they din it into us. *No tyrant steeped in cynicism ever had a more contemptuous opinion of human character than the advertising agencies. . . . One is a mirror of one's surroundings far more than is generally recognized.* But the recorder is not supposed to be for the registering of Thoughts.

At three thousand feet or thereabouts you come out into the open and, in the clean, cool air faintly spiced by the woods, find yourself in the domain of an assembly of great hills under pelts of forest and with rounded peaks lost in ruminations attuned to infinities of time. It is true, I am thinking: when one's surroundings are discordant, one is disintegrated within oneself. And just so, the patience, steadfastness and endurance of trees and hills tend to reknit one together.

These reflections come naturally with the Blue Ridge Parkway. If you are like me, to turn into this enchanted road is to feel unburdened of your cares in a release, as it were, of pent-up breath. If you have the prospect of following it to its end, you look back over the recent past to see by what deprivations and miseries you have purchased this lovely dispensation, which, unpaid for, might be snatched from you by an attack of appendicitis or motor breakdown.

With its northern segment, the Skyline Drive, the unassuming, two-lane road begins within 25 miles of Virginia's northern border and for 575 miles, to the Great Smoky Mountains National Park, follows the Blue Ridge—affectionately, one would say. It clings sinuously to the curve of mountain and gap. It slips circumspectly past mountain meadow and the massed, lichen-covered trunks of the high woods, past spring flowers in their delicate, eager beauty and through the robust Indian-festival colors of autumn. It takes you on turn-offs to look across the broad lowlands fading away to the eastern horizon and to the tumbled sea of mountains, receding westward, tier on tier. If we have to have motorcars and highways, this is one to be thankful for. A National Park Service officer associated with it at the time it was being laid out, in the 1930's, S. Herbert Evison, observes that it "shows the highest regard for the works of nature at the same time that it reveals a unique region and a unique way of life," then declares simply, "The Blue Ridge Parkway is a work of art."

It might be called one. In a nation where almost every great artifact has been constructed for doing business, moving people faster or otherwise scoring gains in the subjugation of Nature, this road, which throughout its length is virgin of billboards, trucks, commercial development, traffic lights, and grade crossings, has no purpose but to embark the motorist on a kind of ocean voyage by land, removed from the clutter and stridency of the world we have elsewhere built for ourselves, among scenes that evoke the noble features of an untamed America and a frontier life that lingered in these resistant hills through the first third of the century—and still lingers in some remote recesses. (As a seventeen-year-old on a walking trip from Nantahala to Highlands in western North Carolina, I startled a middle-aged couple working in a vegetable patch who, it developed, had never been as far from their mountain cabin as the nearest town, Franklin, fifteen miles away.) There is traffic on the road, to be sure, but few of the tourists come with any ulterior motive or in any hurry, so that a peace prevails of the kind that is said to reign among ordinarily competitive animals at a waterhole in time of drought. One further fact: the Skyline-Blue-Ridge Parkway is incomparably scenic —among eastern roads—not only by virtue of the mountains through which it passes but because its surroundings along most of the route are protected in national parks and forests.

The Blue Ridge Mountains themselves, rising in Maryland as a single ridge and fanning out southward, are older and quite different from the mountains to their west—though they have a chain of counterparts to their north in the hills extending across northwestern New Jersey to the highlands of the Hudson, in the Berkshire and Green Mountains and in the Long Range of the horn of

Newfoundland. The differences go back to the origins of the range.

Like other, great, long mountain ranges the Appalachians derive from deposits that accumulated and solidified into sedimentary rock many miles in thickness, over tens of millions of years, in a sagging trough of the ocean's bottom. With the Appalachians, this was at a time when North America was still joined to Eurafrica, and the trough, and the range which subsequently arose from it—I was electrified to learn—extended from west Texas and Colorado (there were two prongs) through the present Eastern States and Maritime Provinces across the southern British Isles and northern France into Saxony. (The Glass Mountains of Texas, the Ouachitas of Arkansas, the Appalachians proper, the Kerry Mountains of Ireland, the mountains of Brittany and the Ardennes and of the Frankenwald in Germany would seem all to be one range in origin.) A cross-section of the portion of the trough from which the Appalachians derived would evidently have shown that the trough sagged much more deeply, under a much greater depth of deposits, on what is now the eastern side, the side toward the coast. This meant that the bottom thousands of feet of sedimentary rocks on that side came under the fierce pressures and temperatures by which they would be metamorphosed into the harder schists and gneisses or melted altogether and reconstituted as granite, harder than steel. So as the Appalachians arose—floated up might be the way it was—they did so with a core of resistant rocks that gradually emerged as the miles-deep covering of newer and weaker sedimentary strata was stripped away by erosion. Of this core the Blue Ridge and its northern counterparts are composed.

On the inland side of this chain—the forged-rock Appalachians— the strata of sedimentary rock remained substantially unaltered; they were sandstones, shales (originally of mud) and limestones (formed of the compacted and cemented shells of marine organisms, accumulated on the sea-floor to a depth often of thousands of feet). However, as the forged-rock Appalachians arose, these strata were gradually pushed back and raised in great folds. The results are to be seen in the sedimentary-rock Appalachians of today—long, level ridges separated by correspondingly long, level valleys, forming a corrugated topography. The Long Ridge Mountains, as I call them, they having been given no other collective name, took shape as the limestone strata and shale wore away, leaving the tougher sandstone strata to stand as ridge-crests. Where an east–west highway like U. S. 50 cuts through them you can see that they are formed of wafered rocks, the even, parallel—and varicolored—layers at an angle and in some places absolutely vertical; such was the terrible force of the thrust.

Between the two systems is the Great Valley of the Appalachians, which runs from Kingston, on the Hudson River, to Birmingham, Alabama, and includes as its most famous part the Shenandoah Valley of Virginia. This came about because here the up-tilted lime-stone strata were particularly thick and when dissolved by eons of rains left a broad gap.

It all sounds school-bookish. Yet it is different when, having been steeped in it, you are alone with the rocks themselves as they have arisen from the seas of time with which your mind has become half drugged, as it can be from the vistas of ocean from a ship's deck. . . . Upon this rock I will build my church, you think, if you were going to build a church. Basalt and granite would be the foundations of mine, as they are of the oceans and continents. There are both in the Blue Ridge. Along the Parkway in Virginia you pass miles of greenstone, so called, a dull, gray-green or gray-blue-green rock, dense, heavy, and smooth. There is even a Green-stone Overlook; it is an authentic sight. And greenstone is basalt, lava that flowed out of fissures in the earth in time to be thrust or dragged down into the inferno with the rocks that would form the Blue Ridge and later be elevated with them.

But you cannot tell what the character of the rocks is except in the recent road-cuts, which reveal the fresh face of the green-stone, the pepper-and-salt, sparkling gray granite or the schist, like gray loaf sugar marbled with quartz. In the older cuts the rocks are indiscriminately discolored and where naturally exposed have a drab weathered surface like an epidermis and have been colo-nized by flaky tripes, mosses, and ferns. They break through the soil as great warts or blisters, or lie like huge beasts half exposed. They seem to warrant infinite respect, these mighty progeny of fearful birth and veterans of eons beyond reckoning. You would like to render them their due with appropriate obeisances and professions of deference, and mentally do so.

In early May, the higher elevations are still only touched by spring. But the pink-flowered trillium and the Pink azalea are in bloom and everywhere there are beds of pink-lavender Wild

geranium and tufts of blue-lavender Field violets, all at their loveliest and most delicate against the dour gray of rock and treetrunk
—life at its most elfin sprightliness and trustfulness. Imagine in this
grim world putting out these fragile petals that tremble to the
lightest stir of air, these blooms, so open, that hold forth only
beauty to make their case for survival! Yet, "Brute force and overbearing may make a terrific effect. But in the end, that which lives
lives by delicate sensitiveness," as D. H. Lawrence wrote. "Brute
force crushes many plants. Yet the plants rise again. The Pyramids
will not last a moment compared with the daisy." *

The trees as well are in bloom. The flowers of the Serviceberry
are white powder-puffs set in caramel-colored new leaves, each
cluster a sundae. Those of the Cucumber magnolia stud the forest
like lemon-sherbet stars four inches across. Everywhere, all along
the way, are the dogwoods, trees fully leaved in white, and a soft,
rich white of such purity you would think they came from a spirit-
realm untouched by sorrow or mortality, from Olympus, where always shines the sun and there is neither wind nor snow.

To make the heart leap there is Flame azalea, of flowers ranging
in color from buttery yellow and pale salmon to near-vermilion—
the torch of the woods. When you first see it you can scarcely believe it. How could these constellations of ember-bright blossoms
have been kindled from the drab branchlets in leaden winter
woods? How could the processes of life, mechanical as science reveals them, taking place in a molelike obscurity of microscopic
cells, burst forth with this—this annunciation of gladness? How,
for that matter, could they produce the whole wealth of patterned
and symmetrical brilliance of color and beauty of flowers, birds,
and butterflies, of jewel-fishes of tropical reefs? To which question
our betters—and scientists are assuredly mine—would reply that
symmetry is to be expected in a mathematically derived universe
while the notion of beauty is a purely subjective one, an attribute

* The question of whether to capitalize the names of animals and plants has
always given trouble. To write "I saw a Crow and a Duck" seems silly. Yet a
wild turkey may not be a Wild Turkey and a truly black duck would not be a
Black Duck but a scoter. A pink azalea may be a Dwarf Azalea or Early
Azalea rather than a Pink Azalea, which may in fact be white, while a Pink
Azalea is more apt to be an early azalea than an Early Azalea. I am going to try
capitalizing the specific names but not the generic. Thus, crow and duck but
Common crow, or Fish crow, and Black duck, or Shoveler (duck); cottonwood,
but Plains cottonwood; phlox, but Sky-pilot (a kind of phlox). It may, however,
be difficult in some cases to decide whether a name is specific or generic.

that inheres in our way of seeing, not in the objects seen. But if this be so, it merely removes the problem to the other side of the page and takes us back to the enigma of man. How could blind mechanical processes assemble from those atoms in the lifeless rocks and empty seas of Archaean times an animal species capable of being moved to rapture by the efflorescence of mechanics represented by a Flame azalea or a Hermit thrush's song?

2

THE SOUTHERN APPALACHIANS

I have long thought mid-June to be the perfect time in the southern Appalachians. By then the Catawba rhododendron is in full bloom, its flowers in orchid-pink clusters the size of grapefruit; it and the later-blooming Rosebay rhododendron are of all plants those that give these ranges their special character, forming extensive and virtually impassable thickets that oddly, because of the formal appearance of their evergreen foliage, give the scene the air of an estate. They begin to be common after you have made the ascent from the Parkway's lowest point, nine hundred feet at the crossing of the James River, to its highest in Virginia, at the four-thousand-foot summit of Apple Orchard Mountain—so called because of the fancied resemblance of the stunted oaks standing on it to fruit-trees. From there on southward you are in the realm of the Catawbas, and in mid-June the Mountain laurel is also bearing its big, pinkish-snowball heads of blossoms while the Flame azalea is still in bloom; and all are together where the woods are thin or lacking at the mile-high elevations of the Craggy and Balsam Mountains, in a floral transfiguration of heights so recently savaged by ice storms. But in early May there is the first touch of gentleness and the still incredulous wonder of the reprieve from the death-dealing cold. And there are the flowering trees—by which I mean not only those literally in flower. To the eye, all trees in spring with leaflets opening are in flower. Newly minted green-gold, and old gold, bright bronze and carnelian, and over whole mountainsides the form of every tree is picked out as in ethereal little lights.

At Whetstone Ridge Restaurant, where I stop for gas, I take time for a brief chat with a young National Park Ranger, one of the few chances in three weeks to talk with anyone other than fuel-pump operators or grocery-store check-out clerks. It turns out that he has taught geology and—I have forgotten how the subject came up—has been as struck as I by the predilection of past generations for naming the more arresting or intractable terrain features after the Devil. The Ranger had once asked his students on a test to name all they could—and I have been keeping a list of them: Devil's Pulpit, Devil's Garden, Devil's Thumb, Devil's Golf Course, Devil's Courthouse, Devil's Postpile, Devil's Playground, Devil's Cornfield, Devil's Hole, Devil's Orchard, Devil's Elbow, Devil's Lake, Devil's Punchbowl, Devil's Den, Devil's River, Devil's Slide, and Devil. What feebleness of cramped imagination it exhibits! And what a revelation one must suppose it of the narrow, slanted view of the universe their religion taught our forebears, by which any unruly expression of the earth forces was, almost automatically, conceded or attributed to the Evil One! Doubtless it is true that in Christian iconography the Devil stands for Pan or Faunus, or the two together—the woods gods who conveyed fertility, danced with nymphs, and loved the pipes. And much that tells us of Christianity!

Christianity laid a heavy hand on the people who took over these hills from the Indians, and they in turn laid a heavy hand on the hills. But one thinks of them now not so much for the fear of damnation that beset them or the desperate emotionalism of their anxious creed, or yet for the toll they took of the wildlife and the slopes they denuded of forest and exposed to the pelting rains. It is rather for their closeness to their beautiful but refractory uplands. The Park Service has preserved the vestiges of their culture along the Parkway, an occasional forlorn little log-cabin, a farm with its small, weathered outbuildings and, in North Carolina, a restored and now functioning grist-mill. They bring home to you how largely the Southern Highlanders had to look for their necessities to their ability to fashion them from what the hills provided. The siding and shingles of their dwellings and sheds, their tables, chairs and beds, the railings for their bear-proof pigpens. gates, hasps, the oak-stave bucket and windlass for drawing it up from the well, ax-hafts and plow handles all must be hewn from the standing tree, chimneys pieced together of raw field-stone, homespun taken from the sheep's backs, cures and dyes gleaned from the woods. And in the process they entered into the warp and woof of the land, and the hills into theirs. Their obsessive, withdrawn individualism, their fatalism and occasional violence, their intense personal loyalties, their stoic, inarticulate pride, their gaunt stature, all seem consistent with the high, mountain-shadowed valleys in which they stubbornly lived and begat too many children.

Why did they cling to their slab-sided cabins, corn patches, and thin, lonely pastures? Shyness of the busy, outside world? The grip of a religion that discounted material success? Love of their hills? Whatever the reason, they have, in a way, been recompensed. Departed, they still haunt their hills, still are present in the moss-grown split-rail fences, in a whiff of hickory smoke, perhaps imagined; still have a home among the overgrown pastures, by the crumbling springhouse, on the old lumber road, and where the sun-warmed rocks ripen the blackberries, while we eight million who yearly drive the Blue Ridge Parkway vanish into limbo when we have gone.

On into North Carolina, the weather is tumultuous. The wind in the gaps almost sweeps the little bus away with it. We keep running into one deluge after another. *I'll see if I can pick it up,* I say into the microphone. But the tape, replayed, emits only a roaring that might be static. There are no downpours on earth, in my experience, like those that assail the southern Appalachians. The heavy-laden rain-clouds dragging up from the Gulf of Mexico liquefy on striking the cool air above the mountains. To be beneath is to be beaten under lashing, veering cataracts. The raindrops are pellets discharged as from a shotgun. The silver sheets obliterate everything from view and striking a car or house set up a drum-fire. No one who has been through one of these summer torrents ever forgets it. Owing to them, an oval area in the northeast corner of Georgia has the highest rainfall on the continent outside the Pacific Northwest, where precipitation is spread more evenly over the year. Hurricane Camille, following the cloud-path up from the Gulf in August 1969, dumped as much as thirty-two inches of rain in the hills just east of the northern part of the Blue Ridge Parkway in less than five hours, more than had been known to fall in so short a time anywhere in the world, ever; farms and villages were destroyed and 152 persons killed in the floods and landslides.

During a downpour in the rugged, more grandly sculptured mountains of Doughton State Park and below, where the road twines along at about 3,400 feet, the sun is shining brightly; as we were told as children, "the Devil is beating his wife." It had to be the Devil, of course; and highly complimented he is, being credited with the spectacle of the earth hung with swaying curtains of silver strands flashing with the molten fire of the sun. When I pull into a scenic turn-off for supper, the sky overhead is almost as black as the dripping rocks, and so are the nearer mountains. But those off toward the Piedmont are catching the sun. The whole ridge is alight and is like a mountain sun-flooded in the Western desert. Irradiated myself, if inwardly, by the knowledge of being where I am, I write two cards over a small cup of sherry to bring home to myself the felicity of my circumstances.

May third, and a brilliant and sunny morning; I am working out my relationship with the tape recorder. I have waked with the first light between walls of Rosebay rhododendron after a night in the black and silent campgrounds located in the woods beside a lake in Julian Price Park, on the outskirts of Blowing Rock. Brilliant and sunny, and, with the bunk having been reconstituted into seats and a table, the sleeping-bag rolled up and stowed away, shaving with the plug-in electric razor got over with, face washed, one set of attire shiveringly exchanged for another, and breakfast set out, entirely mine, waiting to be lived.

The only link remaining to be completed in the Parkway after more than thirty years of piecemeal construction comprises a dozen miles south of Blowing Rock. Here the State road to which one transfers passes under the most dramatic mountain in the East. Grandfather is not quite six thousand feet high and thus is more than seven hundred lower than Mitchell, but it towers, without neighboring rivals, above the hills falling away to the Piedmont, a monolith of sheer granite cliffs broadside to the rising sun. A stinging northwester is pouring down from it when I stop alongside to gaze up at the smooth walls of the billion-year-old forged rock, antedating all but the simplest forms of life, but a gray cloud clings to the summit, concealing it. The mountain is a scene for a saga of gods and heroes. And, in truth, the action of heroic legend could be imagined in progress, for, crowding the lower slopes, the pointed hemlocks have the air of a besieging army. While the main body throngs the base, seeming to press forward, those in the van have scaled the slopes above as far as footholds offer. The ranks thin out with altitude, until high up in the clefts of the precipices only a scattering of individual champions clings to the walls. Each dark spire stands exultant, if emaciated as Don Quixote, a figure a contemporary sculptor in metals might conceive and execute, proud warrior and tattered banner all in one. . . . I can hardly stand in the wind howling down from the somber aeries. But it is time to press on—as always. A Ruffed grouse steps out into the road, attenuated but by no means crestfallen—crest-erect, actually—then roars off with a display of rufous, fan-shaped tail.

Is there any satisfaction quite like that of traveling south in winter and having the first mild air touch your cheek where the broad-leafed evergreen vegetation begins, a satisfaction making you glad to be alive in quite the same way? Yes, and it is ascending the mountains in sultry summer and breathing the first eddy of air cool as peppermint and seeing the first firs and spruces, pickets of the North Woods. In early May, of course, while it may be, and is, full summer on the Yadkin and French Broad Rivers, in the mountains three thousand feet above them the deciduous forests are still leafless and on the far slopes resemble a fuzzy, gray-brown carpet. But it is still an excitement suddenly to find the first lance-straight northern conifers beside the road. You are really getting up there! And you know that these are the outposts of a forest of dark and fragrant trees that, descending the mountains as you go northward, reaches the sea in central Maine and, with kindred species of firs and spruce, girdles the globe below the Arctic. This is a forest that gives the Green Mountains of Vermont their name and the Black Mountains, north of Asheville, theirs. The higher mountains of North Carolina are mantled by it. The first detached stands you come to on the exposed slopes make you think of encampments of Indians, of nearly black tepees in a hunting ground above and beyond the world of mortals to which the vanished tribes have come. And what mountains they darken, these Southern Balsam firs and Red spruce—the Blacks and Craggies, and, beyond Asheville, the Balsams and Plott Balsams, finally the Great Smokies! They seem to shoulder their way to the sky, ranges steep as fins, their gaps over a mile high. Climbing the circuitous roads edging the slopes that slide away for thousands of feet, looking up to the narrow crowns of the buttressed monsters, you feel you are being borne to an awful seat of unappealable judgment.

Though time is lacking, I cannot pass Mount Mitchell by and so turn into the side road that winds to near its summit. My excuse is that I must know what kind of rocks stand higher than any others in the eastern three-fifths of the continent. (Garnet schist and quartz-feldspar gneiss are the names that William Melson of the Smithsonian Institution is to give the samples I bring back.) An unexpected sight meets the gaze as we near the crest of the huge ridge over which Mount Mitchell presides. On the higher western slopes and on the summits, the Black Mountains are white. The woods are rimed. Evidently this is the condensation of clouds the trees have combed. The needles and twigs are densely spined with half-inch ice prisms.

Sky and mountains—an immense and radiant sky to which one is no nearer for all one's elevation above the plains, and wild, humped mountains in processions as far as one can see. Nothing could make it seem vaster than the tiny Winter wren at the top of a Red spruce, ejaculating its tripping, twittering, intricate song, fairy-like and poignant against the colossal bulk of the mountain, over the abyss in which its notes are lost. So might you hear it from such a tree in southern Alaska or Newfoundland, or, for that matter, in Scotland, Finland or Kamchatka. And in any of those places it would have for companions other birds of the high Appalachians—the Red crossbill, Golden-crowned kinglet and Brown creeper, although one or two of these would belong to a slightly different species. . . . Though late enough in the morning for other tourists to be at the tower surmounting the summit, the temperature is still only thirty-two degrees.

Also at the summit is, of all things, a grave, a human grave, enclosed in an iron picket fence. To employ the highest of all eastern mountains as a pedestal for a puny mortal's finalizing! A certain Elisha Mitchell is buried there, a botanist killed in the mountains he explored and doubtless a worthy man who deserved better than to be made a mockery of in this fashion. For who, given a choice, would have his trivial "hope of redemption"—which the gravestone assures us was the subject's—forced on the notice of

visitors to such a spot? And who, for that matter, not a megalo-
maniac, would not be dismayed at having a mountain, and such a
mountain as this, required to bear his trivial name? The *Bandar-
log* have been busy. Perched atop the exalted ridge not very far
distant is a big white building with a mast antenna, conspicuous
for twenty miles, erected lest anyone forget what place the gainful
distribution of cosmetics, breakfast foods, tooth paste, motorcars
and detergents and the purveying of entertainment for a mass
audience occupies in American society. (*Now we are acting just like
men!*) There is only one way to deal with such structures. I call
up in my mind a future when our obligations to the continent we
have made ours will come to be understood, and, before my eyes,
outraged crowds from that enlightened time tear down the television station and smash its remains into rubble. They serve in a
like manner the suspension bridge—a footbridge only, to be sure,
but widely conspicuous—erected over a high ravine on Grandfather
Mountain by the proprietors to bring the top within easy reach
of the sedentary; for this noble landmark, if you please—as, indeed, are not a few others—is in the hands of private owners, to
do with as they wish.

About forty miles from its terminus the Parkway climbs steeply
to the shoulder of Richland Balsam. Here at the loftiest point of
the Parkway, 6,053 feet above sea-level, in a grassy expanse bordered by the spired woods, I have lunch, more than ever light-
headed at being abroad in such a world. The dome of the mountain is 350 feet nearer the smudge of cloud against the blue. . . .
Twenty-five miles farther on and 3,000 feet below, the Parkway
enters the Cherokee Indian Reservation for its last ten miles.
There are scattered farms, anything but prosperous-looking. One
hardly knows what to think of the swarthy cottagers. Real Indians?
In the *East?* One thinks back, unwillingly, fifteen years to a trip
through the nearby town of Cherokee, where tourists are, or
were, catered to with soft drinks, camera film, fake Indian gew-
gaws, and the spectacle of a miserable black bear in a coop and
braves in Sioux warbonnets marking them for the paleface as
bona fide Indians. I am also taken back to my recollection of an
account by William Bartram, naturalist son of the pioneer botanist
John Bartram of Pennsylvania, of his travels in the Cherokee country of southwestern North Carolina in the 1770's.

"I ascended a green hill to the house, where I was cheerfully welcomed at the door and led in by the chief, giving the care of my horse to two handsome youths, his sons," Bartram wrote. "I experienced the most perfect and agreeable hospitality. . . . My venerable host gracefully and with an air of respect led me into an airy, cool apartment; where, being seated on cabins, his women brought a refreshing repast, consisting of sodden venison, hot corn cakes, etc., with a pleasant cooling liquor made of hominy well boiled, mixed afterward with milk. After partaking of this simple but healthy and liberal collation, and the dishes cleared off, tobacco and pipes were brought. The chief, filling one of them, whose stem, about four feet long, was sheathed in a beautiful speckled snake skin and adorned with feathers and strings of wampum, lit it, smoked a few whiffs, puffing the smoke first toward the sun, then to the four cardinal points, and lastly over my breast, and handed it toward me, which I cheerfully received from him and smoked. . . . He was tall and perfectly formed; his countenance cheerful and lofty, and at the same time truly characteristic of the red men, that is, the brow ferocious, and the eye active, piercing or fiery as an eagle. He appeared to be about sixty years of age, yet upright and muscular and his limbs active as youth." The party moved to "a building about 30 feet high" and "capable of holding several hundred people" when presently, to the accompaniment of music "both vocal and instrumental . . . a company of girls, hand in hand, dressed in clean white robes and ornamented with beads, bracelets and a profusion of gay ribands, entering the door, immediately began to sing their responses in a gentle, low, and sweet voice." Soon "we were surprised by a sudden and very loud and shrill whoop, uttered at once by a company of young fellows who came in briskly one after another, with rackets or hurls in one hand. These champions likewise were well dressed, painted and ornamented with silver bracelets, gorgets, and wampum . . . with high waving plumes in their diadems. They immediately formed themselves in a semicircular rank also, in front of the girls." After describing their evolutions, Bartram adds from his experience with the Cherokees, "All their dances and musical entertainments seem to be theatrical exhibitions or plays, varied with comic and sometimes lascivious interludes. The women, however, conduct themselves with a very becoming grace and decency, insomuch that, in amorous interludes, when their responses and gestures seem consenting to natural liberties, they veil themselves, just discovering a glance of their sparkling eyes and blushing faces, expressive of sensibility."

By the time of Bartram's visit to the Cherokees, the barrier of the Appalachians to the westward movement of settlers had been breached. For a century and a half the rugged mountains, range on range, backed by vigilant human foes—Indian and French— had held back the perpetually land-hungry Americans. But by 1763 the French had been eliminated and the Indians demoralized and the mountains threaded, across the grain, by military roads. In a Royal Proclamation of that year, the trans-Appalachian West had been reserved to the Indians until a land policy should have been decided on. "We do strictly forbid," the Crown ordered, "on pain of our displeasure, all our loving subjects from making any purchases or settlements whatever in that region." But the Americans, wrote Lord Dunmore, Royal Governor of Virginia, "do not conceive that Government has any right to forbid their taking possession of a vast tract of Country, either uninhabited, or which Serves only as a Shelter to a few Scattered Tribes of Indians. Nor can they be easily brought to entertain any belief of the permanent obligation of Treaties made with those People, whom they consider, as but little removed from the brute Creation."

The tide was not to be held back. As Ray Allen Billington puts it, "Land was the magic lodestone to wealth, the panacea for all misfortune, the one word invariably capitalized in all correspondence of the day. In England and in America humble commoners, merchant princes, and cabinet ministers scrambled to share the riches to be made; the people of all the empire, wrote George Grohgan after a visit to London, were 'land crazy.'" The pioneers pressed through to the upper tributaries of the Ohio in western Pennsylvania. Soon thereafter they were on the upper tributaries of the Tennessee. Then came the blue-grass region of Kentucky and central Tennessee. "The most striking features of this migration were its spontaneity and the intense individualism of its members," Samuel Eliot Morison and Henry Steele Commager observe in *The Growth of the American Republic*. "No government provided his [the pioneer's] means of transport, or protected him at his destination. No church or benevolent society provided him with priest or minister, school or poor relief. But—and this exception is as American as the rule—he generally had to secure a land title from speculators." The speculator was always in there and generally in there first—for the most. And the speculators are still with us, more than ever, clustering around the expanding cities, enriching themselves on the labor of others and with the acquiescence of legislators.

The grasping of land, and more and more land, and the pursuit of the profits of land: you would think that a people with the opportunity to indulge such a mania on such a scale would have been corrupted to the core. And for all the courage and resourcefulness that went with it, you come to see the Indians as not necessarily fiends after all for having in disgust said, "There's your land for you!" in the gruesome way they did, by cramming with dirt the mouths of the settlers they managed to kill. But the Indians had no chance. Done out of their hunting grounds by generally unscrupulous treaties and later out of even those rights they had been left with, they were pushed westward with the object of clearing them out of the whole territory east of the Mississippi.

In the South, most of the tribes yielded to the threat of military force and by 1837 had been moved to the Indian Territory. The Cherokees, however, in the hills of north Georgia, to which they had fallen back years before, proved resistant. The excuse for ejecting the Indians from their lands had always been that they were unable to adopt the ways of civilization, but the Cherokees had settled on the land in solid houses as farmers and herdsmen, had built roads, welcomed Christian missionaries, and published books in the alphabet invented by the son of a Cherokee girl and a white father, Sequoiah. It availed them nothing. The citizens of my native state were determined on their expulsion, and President Andrew Jackson backed them with the Army. The Cherokees, their lands seized by the Georgians, were forced out—all but several hundred who hid in the North Carolina mountains. Between 1836 and 1838, they straggled westward to Oklahoma on the "Trail of Tears," on which a quarter of them died of disease, hunger, and hardship.

Our crime against the Cherokees and the curse of slavery that we invited! It could be said at least that Georgia paid. The form of payment was most vividly and succinctly expressed in the course of the motion picture of *Gone with the Wind* by the apparition of a black horseman against a background of roiling, blood-red flames that consume the screen, and the legend . . . *SHERMAN!*

But the past is never wholly expunged, as if it had never happened. "We create our buildings, and then our buildings create us," Winston Churchill declared—and it is a perception to shudder at as we behold the glass-walled hexahedrons a hundred or a thousand feet high with which our cities are growing up. And it seems to me that also we create pictures of ourselves, roles for ourselves, which then create us. If we act heroically and magnanimously, heroic and magnanimous action will tend to come naturally to us. If, our weakness tempted, we resort to brutality and treachery, the face we see in the mirror of our minds will be the face of a brute and betrayer, and as brute and betrayer we shall be more apt to act again, shall be subtly influenced to act so that we may establish such conduct as normal and ordinary and thus spare ourselves the pangs of conscience.

But the cruelty to the Cherokees was duplicated and exceeded on a score of battlefields in the grinding reduction of the Indians to impotence, though never at the expense of a tribe that so commended itself to our sufferance. Five years before the expulsion of the Cherokees another example had been made of a tribe that wished to continue to farm its ancestral lands in amity with the whites. Black Hawk and his Sauks, having been driven across the Mississippi by the State of Illinois in the fall, and nearly starving, returned to raise corn in the territory of their friends the Winnebagos in Wisconsin and were immediately set upon by the Illinois militia—in which, incidentally, young Abe Lincoln was a captain. With Black Hawk's offers of peace ignored, as Allan Nevins and Henry Steele Commager recall to us in their *Pocket History of the United States,* "his despairing followers were driven through southern Wisconsin to the Mississippi again, where men, women and children were mercilessly cut to pieces as they tried to cross." (It is pleasant, at least for one of Southern extraction with the Cherokees on his conscience, to read in *The Growth of the American Republic* that "the only redeeming feature was the chivalrous consideration shown Black Hawk by Lt. Jefferson Davis of the regular army.") If the United States was, as time went on, to exhibit a surprising capacity for dispassionate, methodical ruthlessness in war—by no means negligibly exhibited in the total destruction of Georgia between Atlanta and the sea—the proclivity has not been without background, surprising though it may be on the part of a people ostensibly so committed to humanitarianism.

Well, thank God for what lies at the Parkway's end and for what it reveals of another side of American character. There are those among us who not only decry our depredations upon the continent and its offspring but who exert themselves with passion and persistence to halt them. Of such number were those whom we may thank, and can never thank enough, for there being a Great Smoky Mountains National Park. Among them, it was Willis F. Davis of Knoxville and other private citizens who took the lead in the 1920's. Within a few years, a majority in Congress and in the legislatures of North Carolina and Tennessee had acted to make the park possible. Sufficient public funds were allocated and private donations made—with John D. Rockefeller, Jr. matching the State contributions—to enable the two jurisdictions to purchase and in 1930 present to the Secretary of the Interior the nearly twenty-five hundred square miles the park contains.

Within the park's boundaries are the finest mountain wilderness and virgin hardwood forest in eastern North America, as they have been called. With sixteen summits over six thousand feet in height and some hundred species of trees, including individuals supreme of their kind, among thirteen hundred flowering plants, they are easily that. In my view, they are the outstandingly irreplaceable public treasure within fifteen hundred miles of the Atlantic Ocean. There is only one paved road through the park, as distinct from spur roads into it, and for that, too, we may thank embattled conservationists. U. S. 441, which crosses its middle, is heavily traveled and often disagreeable. (At this particular time there is a traffic jam on it, occasioned, as it develops, by a small black bear almost upside-down in a trash-barrel, to the enchantment of a crowd, whose day has been made.) You have the sense, however, that within a few feet of the highway's shoulder the wilderness begins.

The Smokies, which take their name, some say, from the blue haze of their distant vistas, others from the mists that so often clothe their summits, have a somewhat different character from the Blue Ridge, or so it seems to me—and I use the term Blue Ridge not only in the conventional sense, for the easternmost escarpment of the southern Appalachians, but in the geological, to include all the ranges of similar morphology, which extend westward to and even into the Smokies. The Smokies appear steeper, with slopes often like walls, more crowded together and more heavily forested, with fewer rock faces showing. If this be so, it perhaps reflects their different composition. They are of sedimentary rock, though of pre-Paleozoic sedimentary rock, six hundred million years old or more, so old as to be fossil-less. On the crest of the range at Newfound Gap the structure of the ridge is laid bare in a highway cut through the steeply tilted strata. Power-shovels are at work when I drive up, digging away more of the banks to facilitate the movement of motor traffic or extend the already acres-wide parking grounds. I get out to climb to the top of the cut for a photograph of the rocks.

There is, as always, no time to linger, and perhaps it is mistaken even to linger in memory of this spot. For I have been here before, when along the route of U. S. 441 there was only a wagon track through the woods up from the little village of Smokemont—where the big campgrounds now are and, I must add, the wonderful museum of mountain culture. By means of a rope attached to the front axle, we managed to haul the Model A Ford pickup truck up the parts too steep for it to climb unaided—half a dozen of us, boys and two girls. And so, before having to get out and hike with our blankets, frying-pan, tin cups, and provisions, we managed to get most of the way up to Newfound Gap. (I think it was a point of pride with our young leader to extract the last foot of which the car was capable.) From there we had six or seven miles to go on the trail, now the Appalachian Trail, that followed the crest of the ridge to the south through fog-shrouded forest to the top of Clingman's Dome, second only to Mitchell in height and only by forty feet at that. It was cold in the dark woods on the heights of that immense wild mountain, but I was with companions I still hold in my heart, and we were moved and excited to be re-enacting, symbolically or ritually, anyhow, the kind of trial that was the price of existence for our early forebears—a procedure that seems to answer a need or longing on youth's part.

It would be difficult to make my children understand how remote the fastnesses of the southern Appalachians were in those days. To find mountains equally so today you would have to seek out those repelling human approach by their harshness or rising in distant and alien lands. The lost reaches of the Smokies, Nantahalas, and Balsams were clement and verdant and were part of North Carolina and Tennessee. At summer's end, I could see the ranges, blue and aloof on the horizon, as the Southern Railroad train bore me northward. They were as close to the everyday world as that. They were home. I might even be seeing one of the balds I had climbed and, in the stillness of the sun-warmed thickets from which a towhee dashed with flirting tail, had felt as I scanned the herds of mountains fading away into the infinite that I stood on the threshold of immortality. Watching the ranges to the last, I suffered an anguish, not so much because I was leaving as because, millions of years hence though it might be, they were destined to be worn away. On the former score, I had my life before me and was confident I should be returning, though I never guessed that the next time I saw Clingman's Dome it would be from a macadam road leading to the spot where we had spent the night shivering in the thin air of that high summit but content in the knowledge that we had around us only the wild mountains and over our heads nothing but the black limbs of the trees and the sky alight with stars.

3

THE MIDLANDS

When the Appalachian Mountains were thrust up, the crustal rocks to the west were also elevated, but here the overlying strata were not folded as in the mountains but lifted horizontally. The plateau region on the inland side of the Long Ridge Mountains, called the Allegheny Plateau from Pennsylvania into West Virginia and the Cumberland Plateau from West Virginia into Tennessee, would be level but for the action of millions of years of rains. The runnels, streams, and rivers, frantically nosing out the easiest paths to sea-level, like fleeing snakes, have cut the Plateau into steep hills of haphazard pattern divided by narrow, twisting valleys. It is a topography that impedes the establishment of avenues of communication through it; and of all the Appalachian valleys, some of those of the backwoods of the Cumberlands remain the most isolated.

One other fact is of importance about the Cumberland Plateau. During the early chapters of their imperceptible rise, the Long Ridge Mountains created a basin on their inland side, from which the Plateau was later to be raised. Repeatedly over many millions of years great forests of primitive trees related to our club-mosses and horsetails grew up in the warm, humid basin and as repeatedly were inundated by the advancing sea and their rotting remains buried under mud or sand. Hence the coalfields of today—the strata of carbonized plant remains alternating with strata of shale or sandstone. Rich in timber, rich in coal, the Cumberlands have been the site of an encounter between the human qualities that we are taught have made America great and those that actually have done so—or that have made it powerful. Uncompromising independence, simple integrity, and religious faith have in every engagement been defeated by organization, mechanical genius, and the fierce energy called forth in the pursuit of profit furthered by corporate unscrupulousness. The Cumberlands have been stripped of billions of dollars' worth of resources and a comely and worthy people left impoverished and demoralized in junk-filled valleys.

But it was another trip that took me into the Cumberlands. The route west from Gatlinburg, where you pick up Interstate 40, passes south of the mountainous part of the Plateau. It is the beginning, for me, of an unknown America and one of the many that I am to wonder why I have not heard more celebrated. There are, to begin with, lovely green woods and rich-looking meadows, much like the Virginia Piedmont but more fertile-looking and more choppy in configuration than the Piedmont with its graceful undulations. But sundown is imminent, raising the question of where I am to put up for the night.

This is usually an open question. Though bothersome, it does add interest and adventure to the trip. Paid lodgings are a last choice except every fourth or fifth day when a shower can no longer be put off, even by a solitary traveler. The budget will not accommodate them more often, and neither will the rules of the game, which make it a sporting proposition. Simply pulling off to the side of a road is out. A small bus in such a spot with curtains drawn across the windows and windshield will be adjudged by the police irregular, hence subversive of order, hence impermissible. And the further you remove yourself from the likelihood of apprehension by the police the more you expose yourself to possible intrusion by less benign intruders, who would have the advantage of surprise. Once, with darkness falling, I asked a policeman if he thought I should be safe pulling up for the night off one of the roads in the Jefferson National Forest. I added that I was unarmed. (This was at Bluefield, just inside West Virginia, where on the west the highway cuts reveal the horizontal strata of the Cumberland Plateau, those on the east the up-ended strata of the Long Ridge Mountains.) "Mister," he said, "even if I *was* armed, you wouldn't catch me spending the night up there!"

At dusk, a sign beside the highway points to Cumberland State

Park, which I had not detected on the road-map. And, oh joy, it turns out to include a campground that is all it should be, in a woods with tidy campsites, almost all empty; and, while I am all for roughing it when I am prepared and not rushed, I am delighted as things are to find showers with hot water in a clean lavatory. In minutes, one exchanges the harassments and uncertainties of the highway, dive-bombed by oncoming cars, for the hush and im-mobility of darkening woods and the prospect of a leisurely and acceptable supper requiring little more than the emptying of a can into a saucepan over a gas burner. What a luxury! My soul within me lolls like a reclining Roman banqueter.

At 5:00 A.M.—4:00 by the new Central Time—I wake up to a gray light and the singing of a Wood thrush. In the upshot it is even better than the morning before. Having shaved with a real razor at a basin and had that shower, I go for a jog, covering about a mile on a pleasant country road, with a few short stretches of walk-ing, and so sit down to breakfast and coffee in a glow of cleanliness, activated circulation, virtue, and anticipation. I even have a philo-sophical observation for the occasion, albeit one that bears hard upon me, who fall into routine as naturally as a dormouse into sleep: we are alive only insofar as we do not know what the day ahead may bring.

The oaks are in half leaf, the Black locusts hung with clusters of blossoms like those of white wisteria, and I cannot get over the charm of the country on the way to Nashville. The topography picturesque in its irregularity, the deep and beautiful courses cut by the waterways, the pastureland and woodland laid out with unstinting copiousness, all as lushly green as you would have it, make up a kind of boundless and untrammeled park. And the rocks! Why are these highway cuts not famous? They are walled by the edges of severed rock strata as by courses of stone blocks. The blocks are irregular in every dimension but thickness, in which all those of the same course are perfectly even. As between courses, the thickness varies from less than an inch to several feet, and the strata come in a range of colors, from a pale sandy shade to rusty brown and near-purple and from pale gray, almost white, to nearly black. Each was in its turn the floor of the sea during the Paleozoic era, when for hundreds of millions of years the sea was alternately advancing over the continent—up to the Canadian Shield at its farthest—and receding; and they are formed by residues washed into that sea from nameless highlands of lost eternities, or of the inexhaustible multitudes of dying protozoans whose limy shells filtered to the bottom in an everlasting snow. The limestones—source of the land's fertility—are the gray strata; and some contain fossils, especially clam-like brachiopods, as you will find if you unobserve the rule against stopping on the shoulder of an Interstate and poke about among them.

I do stop. For miles on end the highway passes again and again between these extraordinary walls, some of which rise like the sides of Toltec pyramids to heights of fifty or maybe even eighty feet, and I must pull over, clamber up to a vantage point and photograph them. (*Two hours gone, and only seventy-six miles!* I am unburdening myself more and more to the tape recorder, self-accusingly and otherwise.) It is an overcast morning, drizzling occasionally, and the photographs will be a woeful disappointment. Experience gives me every reason to anticipate that. (Can that gray smudge be the heroic mountain wall at which I aimed the camera?) I tell myself it is for the record, but the truth is I feel one must *make* something of the things that arouse one, not passively relinquish them to the oblivion of the past, into which life ungrasped is fated to dissolve. So it is up the hill again with camera and exposure meter, surely not to fail this time, *surely* to capture the quintessence of that ancient wall of rough-hewn blocks. (*At this rate I'll never get out West!*) Starlings nest in niches in the shale, Bank swallows where burrows can be excavated between crumbling sandstone blocks. The walls are picturesque indeed where the strata have been cleft, and cleft deeply, not for the highway but by a river, like the Caney Fork. There, moldy with the years, overtopped and overhung by wild vegetation, they make you think of the sides of abandoned moats or of ruined temples in the jungles of India. Romance almost writes itself at the sight of them.

In England, you reflect, a country as distinctive as that on the eastern approach to Nashville would have a special name—the Grens, or the Midland Fells—and have given rise to a special local culture and ways of speech and have a distinctive place in literature. But not here. No one has given himself sufficiently to this part of the world to have worked it into a human composition. For all the claims we make on the land—and they can be ruinous—we do not recognize that it has any on us, such as would hold us to it through thick and thin. We do not stay with the land because it is ours.

There are farms all along through here, but most are conspicuously in decline; the barns, of vertical siding, are unpainted—adding, it must be admitted, to the landscape's picturesqueness—and the roofs of many are rusty and sagging. Ours is a nation of the Main Chance, and the Main Chance has evidently been drawing population away from the Midland Fells—the reason, no doubt, why so much is in woods. Human habitation takes the form mostly of stark, ugly houses of brick-patterned, asphalt siding, cells of concrete-block construction and one-story dwellings of ugly, dark-red brick that look as if they had been bought from a mail-order house and set down where they are by a delivery truck.

The drabness of most of the United States takes you aback. Where does all the vaunted income go? Presumably to the well-to-do in suburbs and for the rest into motorcars, travel, television sets, transistor radios, appliances, alcohol, tobacco, hunting gear, and cosmetics. At any rate, it seems to go more into comforts, diversions, and evasions than into making the most of the settings in which we live. These are likely to receive short shrift. The owners of sub-urban homes tend the lawns and put in shrubs to improve a tem-porary tenancy, but generally no lasting commitment is made—or invited by the mass-built units. Our cities are machines for the transaction of business, and for the most part monstrous ugly ones, in which living quarters are largely cells in honeycombs. So when you do come upon a dwelling that owed its existence to begin with to a human being and not a company and bespeaks a solicitous stewardship over the years, you rejoice. If such places are in a small minority, even in the parts of Virginia I am most drawn to, long-settled localities are usually favored by at least a few—houses to which men and women have given of themselves and which, framed by maples or oaks, box or lugustrum, iris and roses, seem to offer security against the nothingness into which it is so easy for exist-ence to ravel out.

In the course of these recurrent reflections—I tend to become preoccupied with houses—a flatbed truck overtakes us and I gaze admiringly after its burden, a 1929 Ford roadster, maroon with yellow wire wheels, which looks as if it had just rolled, new, out of the showroom. I realize that what I am thinking about is partly care for what things are in themselves, rather than for what they may be as mere utilities, the kind of care the owner feels for that forty-year-old Model A. "Men who have given their lives to labors of love," says Antoine de Saint Exupéry, "go straight to my heart." As to mine.

In *A Municipal Report*, O. Henry addresses himself to Frank Norris's contention that "there are just three big cities in the United States that are 'story cities'—New York, of course, New Orleans, and, best of the lot, San Francisco." In a tale of Nashville ("Fancy a novel about Chicago or Buffalo, let us say, or Nashville, Tennessee!" Norris had scoffed) he successfully refutes the assertion. But the truth is that, regardless of what may go on in them, there are few American cities in which, if you were set down in one, you would have the least idea where you were, whether in Portland—Maine or Oregon—Birmingham, Spokane, Kansas City, or any of a hundred others in the absence of some natural feature to give you a clue. For all O. Henry's skill, I should not have known that I am in Nashville—as I am not, admittedly, except to pass through. Or, later, in Memphis.

Between the two, there is business to think of. There always is, of course, but here there is a notable geological sequence to be aware of. It is plainly apparent on a map I have with me prepared by the U. S. Geological Survey on which the age and type of the surface rocks over the entire continent are indicated by color—and which, because the colors are soft but vivid, is quite beautiful. One of those crustal domings up that raised the Black Hills and Ozarks took place in central Tennessee, and while it was not extreme enough to raise the basement rocks on high, as in those two places, it was sufficient to bring the strata formed between 360 and 440 million years ago to the surface, where they now stand exposed as a result of the stripping away of the superincumbent strata. From fifty miles east of Nashville to Nashville itself (which thus has a distinction O. Henry concealed from us), the rocks cut by the highway were sea bottom when the earliest vertebrates—the armored ancestors of the fishes—first appeared. From Nashville on, as you descend gradually to the Mississippi, you pass over ever younger formations, as if you were leafing through the pages of a book from back to front. At the Mississippi, in crossing from the bluffs of Memphis to the flat lands of Arkansas, you are leaping from an early chapter of the current Cenozoic (or "Recent-Life") era, forty to fifty million years ago, when the orders of modern mammals arose and the flowering plants emerged triumphant, to deposits no older than mankind.

Alas, none of this is apparent. In the Nashville Dome, the courses of sandstone and limestone blocks do, if you give your imagination a chance, bring back the shores of those early seas; for split, eerie instants you stand there, hearing the waves smash on the strand which no living thing, no plant, even, has yet crossed. Westward, however, rocks are not much in evidence, and crossing the Tennessee River to formations the map says are of the last chapter of the Mesozoic (or "Middle-Life") era, you are disabused if you have felt against all reason that somehow the ghosts of Tyrannosaurus and Brontosaurus should be abroad, staring two or three stories high over the lower trees, and the air rustle to the twenty-foot, leathery wings of Pteranodon or the pinions of the tern-loon Ichthyornis. It is contemporary country.

Yet the link with the Mesozoic is not entirely lacking. In the last millions of years of that Age of Reptiles, a forest including oaks, willows, poplars, sassafras, sycamores, and magnolias stretched across North America and indeed, it would appear, across the Bering land-bridge and on to Southeast Asia. And here the forest still is—far more of it than I expected. *Woods, woods, woods,* I marvel to the tape recorder. From the Atlantic westward to the conifer bogs and maple-basswood forests of western Minnesota, the oak groves intermingled with the prairies of southern Iowa, the eastern parts of Nebraska, Kansas and Oklahoma and northeastern Texas (even with long salients of oak-hickory woods deep into southern Texas) the East is inherently a forest province. Basically, its heartland is in hardwoods—deciduous forest—of which the leading types are oak, hickory, maple, beech, birch, tuliptree, basswood, and buckeye; some predominate in one section, others in another. To the east and south of the heartland, across the Piedmont and the coastal plain, the hardwoods are heavily mixed with pines and with Bald cypress on the floodplains, to the north of the heartland with pines and hemlocks, then spruce and fir; conifers tend to replace deciduous trees where conditions are unfavorable because of long, hard winters, poor soil, and desiccating sunlight or, in the case of the cypress, where the soil is under water. (The more primitive forms, they must make do with second choice.) To the west of the heartland, the hardwoods become more and more widely invaded by grasslands. As classified for the American Geographical Society by A. W. Küchler, there are twenty-four types of Eastern forest and nine more of mixed Eastern forest and grasslands. For the forty-eight states as a whole, 116 types of "potential natural vegetation" are recognized, and the extent of each is indicated on a map put out by the Society—one three feet by five that with its marbling of lovely colors is a repast for the eyes, a match for the Geological Survey map.

With Memphis 112 miles away, the country is largely flat with a gentle rise and dip, the woods going on and on, as beautiful as could be wished. Once it must have been farmland. You realize how quickly the forest would reclaim the land if given the chance, though to reattain the fecundity and awesome stature it once possessed would take centuries, if not millennia; for topsoil accumulates at a rate of only an inch in five hundred years, and we have managed to get rid of most of the continent's store. By contrast with their forebears, today's descendants of the forest of the past are a scrubby lot, on the whole. (Those of spreading domes of foliage sanctioned by man to provide homestead and churchyard with shade and dignity are exceptions.) Their prospects, moreover, are poor; they will be felled long before they achieve the dimensions that are their birthright. Yet to travel the route I am taking across the East is to be astonished at how much land the trees have reoccupied. Part of your astonishment is owing to the Interstate Highways, which go across country, spurning towns and villages between the cities they connect, and being of limited access do not immediately result in the spawning of real-estate developments alongside. So far they present a faithful cross-section of the countryside, and in the East it is a countryside with trees almost everywhere forming the background, near or far, trees all reaching for the sun, spreading their myriad leaves before its grace, holding them up to its munificence. Having it brought home to you how much this is a land of trees, your mind goes back to the time when the forest was sovereign in fact as well as by right.

"What they looked down on was a dark, illimitable expanse of wilderness. It was a sea of solid treetops broken only by some gash where deep beneath the foliage an unknown stream made its way. As far as the eye could reach, this lonely forest rolled on and on till its faint blue billows broke against an incredibly distant horizon." Such was the sight from a ridge on the far side of the Appalachians that met the pioneer family whose lives are unfolded in a novel you read as you would the testimony of those who were there: Conrad Richter's *The Trees.* For days beneath "that ocean of leaves" into which they had descended, they kept "watching dully ahead for some sign that they might be coming out under a bit of sky. Down in Pennsylvania you could tell by the light. When a faint white drifted through the dark forest wall ahead, you knew you were getting to the top of a hill or an open place. You might come out in a meadow or clearing, perhaps even in an open field with the corn making tassels and smelling sweet in the sun. But away back here across the Ohio, it had no fields. You tramped day long and when you looked ahead, the woods were dark as an hour or a day ago. . . . Around the night fire . . . under the big butts they looked like little people. The black arches were mighty far overhead. Even when you threw bark on the fire, its light was swallowed up before it went a dozen poles down these dark forest aisles that ran on and on only God knew how many miles to the English Seas"—the Great Lakes—"and the New Orleans river."

The forest, where "the great butts stood thick one against the other so that in places a yoke of oxen would have had a hard time getting through," the forest that was the lair of Delaware and Shawnee, wolf and puma, was an enemy, the pre-emptor of the rich soil it had created, and it had to be dispossessed. All summer and autumn they cut and burned and "all winter the air around the cabin was dyed a fine color with hardwood smoke, . . . and still the ground lay thick with the giant carcasses. Most of them had been straight as a handspike, some thirty feet without a knot and so almighty thick you could hardly look over them at the butt. Black walnut, white ash, three kinds of oak and plenty more, all worthless, good for nothing, cluttering up the black land."

So it went, the cutting and burning for a corn field, multiplied hundreds-of-thousands-fold. Still, vast tracts were left. But the settlers were only the beginning. The lumber companies followed. If the lumbermen could help it, nothing would be spared. Year after year for a hundred years the axes rang, the steel blades spinning in the sawmills screamed. The gangs moved through the New England hinterland, through the Middle West, through the North Woods of the Great Lakes, through the pineries of the South, through the Appalachians. A parvenu offshoot of a parvenu species was on the make, with the parvenu's insatiable appetite for gain. At the end, of that once stupendous virgin forest, product of a process of self-improvement and diversification reaching far back into Cretaceous times, a hundred million years in the perfecting, there remained only some scattered islands which for one reason or another had escaped: chiefly a few thousand acres in the Allegheny National Forest of Pennsylvania, a few thousand in Linville Gorge in the Pisgah National Forest and a few thousand in the Nantahala National Forest, both in North Carolina—and fifteen hundred square miles in the least accessible reaches of the Great Smokies, saved at the eleventh hour.

The forest did not go the way of the Passenger pigeon, whose swift hosts, flowing, sinuous and majestic as rivers, across the sky from horizon to horizon, were its unique expression. For one thing, enough of the nation recoiled in shock from the devastation to give protection of sorts to the nearly three hundred thousand square miles of forest lands now in the National Forests—mostly in the West. The lumber companies, moreover, became converted to the principle, if not altogether to the practice, of sustained yields. For another, the forest could not be wholly eliminated unless its historic domain were to be rendered lifeless—which is not to say that it may not yet be. (I remember being flown home from Karachi in World War II and finding that from the airplane's take-off nearly until it reached the Atlantic at Casablanca, 4,600 miles distant, the land beneath the wing was almost entirely desert, and desert in large part of man's own making—and making with but feeble weapons of destruction.) Let the fields and roadsides and the suburbanite's lawn but go unmowed for a season, and up come the tree seedlings, as they come up wherever the soil beyond the pavement's edge is undisturbed. All along the horizon over most of the East the banners of the trees are raised. You cannot help reflecting that should we manage to curb our zeal for expanding our works and numbers and pull in our horns, the climax forest of the past would return to any parts of its old domain we might leave alone. Return in its grandeur, bringing its denizens with it, hawk and owl, raccoon and fox, mink and otter, bobcat and puma, Black bear and, yes, in places even wolf, all the creatures that in grace of bearing and proportion, in artistry of form and variety, do such credit to our common origination. The thought also asserts itself that if our compounded follies should prove our undoing, the forest (unless we have meanwhile rendered the continent sterile and unlivable) will return on its own terms, with its wolves—especially with its wolves.

Having been backed up on itself by damming, the Tennessee River with its side channels separated by bars and islands crowded with trees is a mile wide where Interstate 40 crosses it, and three times as wide downstream, to the north. Because with its blue waters and wooded banks bursting with green it is as beautiful as it is wide, the Tennessee builds you up for a disappointment in the Mississippi at Memphis.

This the Father of Waters? The great Mississippi, longest river in the world? It strikes you as rather narrow and certainly discolored.

At Natchez it is different, at least to me. That is because I know it there from the waterside, not merely from the heights of a bridge. For a time during World War II I was stationed close enough by to spend a few week-ends in Natchez, where it is natural to report first thing to the river. I would descend a steep road past little moldering brick buildings directly to its edge, where the water lapped a ramp and stirred the weeds that grew out into it. You have a different feeling about it if you sit there beside it, dreaming on the giant old serpent gliding past you with its arcane knowledge of the land.

It bears dreaming on. It is a serpent with a thousand tails. From five-eighths of the states into which we have divided the land it gathers itself, from the Great Smokies and Mount Mitchell, the Alleghenies of western New York, the glacial ponds of Wisconsin and northern Minnesota, the prairies and the Great Plains, Lake Yellowstone and the Absarokas of Wyoming's farthest corner and the melting snows of Colorado's and New Mexico's highest peaks. It carries a third of the water that falls on the forty-eight states and drains two-fifths of their area, and the sediments it carries to the Gulf of Mexico—a cubic mile every fifteen years—have extended its sinking delta several hundred miles across the continental shelf and beyond. Oil rigs drilling to four miles down have not come to the bottom of its deposits, and if an expert of the Geological Survey— Philip B. King—is right and those deposits, accumulated during and since the Mesozoic era, go down to twice that depth or more, they have reached the thickness of those that formed the Appalachians, raising the possibility that the Father of Waters may prove in the course of time to be part father of a range of alpine mountains.

It is a writhing serpent, too; for by an odd circumstance the wave motion, so common vertically in nature, is one that rivers on flat plains describe horizontally. As if alive, the Mississippi will execute its snake-like motions whatever man's desires and designs, even leaving detached bends of itself behind—the noted oxbow lakes. It is the river's restlessness in its bed that in part made it traditionally the hazardous water-road to the interior that it has been, requiring a special breed of man to take a steamboat up it. "Your true pilot," the ultimate authority on old times on the Mississippi tells us, "cares nothing about anything on earth but the river, and his pride in his occupation surpasses the pride of kings." A labor of love! Only that could have accounted for it:

"This sun means we are going to have wind tomorrow; that floating log means that the river is rising, small thanks to it; that slanting mark on the water refers to a bluff reef which is going to kill somebody's steamboat one of these nights, if it keeps on stretching out like that; those tumbling 'boils' show a dissolving bar and a changing channel there; the lines and circles in the slick water over yonder are a warning that that troublesome place is shoaling up dangerous; that silver streak in the shadow of the forest is the 'break' from a new snag. . . ." So the young apprentice pilot admonished himself.

Shipping continues on the Mississippi, may for all I know move more tonnage than ever before on strings of barges, but doubtless with a full suit of modern navigational aids. One would wager that no longer is heard the leadman's cry: "M-a-r-k three! M-a-r-k three! Quarter-less-three! Half twain! Quarter twain! M-a-r-k twain!" Certainly no such scene as that offered us by the young man who took his name from that call need be looked for again:

". . . A Negro drayman, famous for his quick eye and prodigious voice, lifts up the cry, 'S-t-e-a-m-boat a comin'!' and the scene changes! The town drunkard stirs, the clerks wake up, a furious clatter of drays follows, every house and store pours out a human contribution, and all in a twinkling the dead town is alive and hurrying from many quarters to a common center, the wharf. Assembled there, the people fasten their eyes upon the coming boat as upon a wonder they are seeing for the first time. And the boat *is* rather a handsome sight, too. She is long and sharp and trim and pretty; she has two tall, fancy-topped chimneys, with a gilded device of some kind swung between them; a fanciful pilot-house, all glass and 'gingerbread,' perched on top of the 'texas' deck behind them; the paddle-boxes are gorgeous with a picture or with gilded rays above the boat's name; the boiler-deck, the hurricane-deck and the texas deck are fenced and ornamented with clean white railings;

there is a flag gallantly flying from the jackstaff; the furnace doors
are open and the fires glaring bravely; the upper decks are black
with passengers; the captain stands by the big bell, calm, imposing,
the envy of all. . . ."

We hardly need have it recalled to us, so much a part of the
national consciousness it is. But it belongs to the past. The intimate,
deep, even passionate involvement of our people in our great river
is a thing of a century ago, and you cannot pass it by without that
knowledge affecting you; the name "Mississippi River" says too
much. The river serves us still, oh yes. It is a utility, a transporta-
tion utility, a recreational utility, even, and an indispensable sewer.
(Where else but in the Mississippi, it has been asked, would St.
Louis put its two hundred thousand daily gallons of urine?) But
the motor traffic races unretarded across it, and thirty thousand
feet above it the passengers in the giant flying cylinder are not
even aware that it lies below.

One wonders what that early modern American, whose name,
rather ironically, is inseparably intertwined with the river's past,
would have thought. Would he have found anything to be dis-
turbed about in this parting of the ways between the nation's vital
processes and the waterway that had been a central theme in the
lives of so many, as it is a central theme of the continent's? Presumably not; the railroad had already doomed the river traffic he
knew and the river ports were already in their long decline when
he wrote *Life on the Mississippi* in 1883—cheerfully enough. Acidic
anti-sentimentalist and anti-romantic, disdainer of the past and of
society for its social forms and distinctions, pragmatist and realist,
Samuel Langhorne Clemens *was* an iconoclastic, even essentially
anarchistic, modern American—and an illustration of the rule that
precursors of new ways are apt to be their most engaging and admirable exemplars, coming as they do when they are most needed.
Moreover, he was successful, very much so, and success brings an
ambience of its own—the successful man is at home anywhere—and
its own reason for being. It remains for the rest of us to find self-
justification and a place for ourselves when technological progress
renders our labors of love meaningless and destroys the continuum
of man and earth in which we are part of a whole and share in the
justification of all that is.

But the Mississippi must be presumed unfazed by the bridges and
roar of airplanes. This is a very old serpent, which has seen much

come and go. Four times during the Pleistocene, when the ice sheet had pushed south out of Canada and in its eventual retreat was still blocking the valley of the St. Lawrence and the drainage to Hudson Bay, the Father of Waters bore seaward for centuries on end the floods pouring from the melting glacier. And it was ancient long before that. It remembers when the plains were lush with verdure, before the Western Cordillera rose to intercept the rain-clouds from the Pacific. It saw the heyday of the dinosaurs and carried the remains of the last of them to the Gulf. It will carry much else to the Gulf, too, in times to come, being surely beyond man's capacity to destroy—and how inconceivable it would have been when the first steamboat was launched in the river in 1823 that we should ever be content to recognize a limit to man's power!

The alluvial plain on the far side of the Mississippi differs greatly from the higher land on the east, being all in cultivation. The doubtlessly rich soil has just been plowed and is the color of wet coffee grounds. After twenty-five miles and a crossing of the St. Francis River there is a special feature to take note of: *We are now rising. I suppose this must be the levees of the river. I don't know. The embankment of the road is stepped, four or five steps on each side. They are going up very sharply. They must be the levees.* But is that where floods stop, twenty-five miles from the river? *We now go down from them, as I have heard is the case.* Curiously enough, the Mississippi builds up levees of its own. The geologists say this is because at the crest of its floods it deposits part of its load of sediment along its margins. That I can grasp, but what defeats me is that the land should slope *down* on the far side of the levee. While I nod sagely over the explanation as I read it, I find that I cannot repeat it later, though the geologists sound as if the phenomenon is just what they would have expected.

Looking back on my times, my grandchildren will envy me the opportunity I had to venture through a still unconfined and romantic America, as it will seem to them, as we look back with envy on Audubon's travels a century and a half ago: that is what I tell myself at times of depression on the trip (without dwelling on the kind of America I am postulating for my heirs). Actually, until I get back to the Atlantic seaboard, there are few such times, there being so much to offset the reasons for depression. But the few hours after crossing the Mississippi are one. I am no sooner on the other side than my spirits begin to sink. *There are a number of waterways in through here, all terribly muddy, dirty-looking. Everything looks poor and cheap and commonplace. The shanties of the Negroes, who are evidently only tenant farmers on the rich plantation lands, are in a shocking state. Even if they have outhouses, the outhouses are falling into ruin.* The reasons, I suppose, are various and reflect small credit on the ruling class, but at bottom, I have little doubt, is the fact that mere human labor no longer commands much price on the market. The Communists may romanticize labor all they please with their monumental representations of squared-off, muscular, half-nude workers and peasants brandishing their sledgehammers and scythes, but the club-footed Joseph Paul Goebbels was closer to the mark of actual truth when he said that to be human is in itself nothing. Machinery has seen to that. Who today wants the man who has only his native equipment to offer? And who tomorrow will want the man whose work the computer can do better? In Mississippi you can look across the flat, alluvial plantation lands and see not a sign of human life but a little tractor combing the soil.

Only parts of Interstate 40 are open through eastern Arkansas. Across the breaks you have to take the pre-existing transcontinental highway, U. S. 70, which spares you none of the grubby details. (All the old National Highways numbered in a multiple of 10 go across the country on an east–west course.) The Interstates conspire with other new departures in American life to preserve the well-to-do from exposure to the nation's more sordid failures. But I weakly yield: *Back on Interstate 40, thank heavens, which goes right through the countryside and reflects the national prosperity rather than the local poverty. Again there are lots of woods and a good deal of pastureland. But:*

Well, 40 didn't last long. We're back on U. S. 70—that bloody road. Here we go. We'll be back on 40 I suppose in another fifty miles or so, if we can survive all that time. Heading right into the afternoon sun, too. The road stretches out straight as far as the eye can reach. . . . Except that there are no pines here, none at all, it is very like a rural part of the Deep South coastal plain with tumbled-down, unpainted Negro cabins. Listen to that truck pass. . . . Even the better houses are disspiriting, put up by lumber companies. And there are more, lots of them, of that fake asphalt-brick siding, also weather-stained little billboards. This is a narrow road with lots of interstate traffic on it. The trucks come tooling along. Let's pick this one up now. They make a racket. They almost pull the little bus in behind them. Here the words on the tape are drowned out by the roar and clatter of the juggernaut.

It was not many years ago that the prevalence of draft animals was a mark of the South, as it is always a mark of a place where there is work for strong hands—from which all of us had our beginnings, even if these were generations back: draft animals, the dropping of the "r" before consonants, the poorer look of things, the more and darker Negroes, the distance between towns, the more relaxed attitude toward life. But the Americanization of the South has proceeded, and I am surprised to find even a few horses and mules on the road to Little Rock.

Hog-tusk Creek, and the start of the rice fields: these take me by surprise. The young shoots are fairly up, imparting an intense yellow-green bloom to the fields, across which wind little earthen retaining walls, calling to mind all the photographic travelogues of Southeast Asia one has ever seen. Even more surprising than the rice fields, astonishing, in fact, is a building on the horizon resembling a castle, with two mighty towers. "Riceland Rice," I read on it when we come abreast and am staggered by the quantities of rice connoted. A billboard advertises "Ban 34. Kills grasses, kills weeds. For more rice"; another, "Stim-Su-Soy. Get more beans to the acre." The Orient in Arkansas; and, near another of those incredible castles, on the outskirts of Brinkley, there is a deodar, a conifer of India of graceful branching habit and misty foliage. Run-down little cafés, run-down grocery stores, a little movie-house, old merchandise shops barely surviving. . . . I am immediately caught up in a terrible fantasy that is apt to afflict me in places of this kind. A high authority about whose nature I am a little hazy has me brought before him and tells me that I am being sent to Brinkley to live. "What you're to do is get the town stirred up intellectually and artistically. I want to see young men there giving up everything to paint and write poetry, living in garrets. I want to see them in the cafés in the evening with their girls debating theories of aesthetics. I want to hear arguments about, er—well, about Macaulay and Taine's criticism, and, and . . . the Pre-Raphaelites, say: that kind of thing. I want the place in a ferment —fists flying. Take a couple of years to see what you can do and report back to me." . . .

Typically, there is a thriving agricultural-machinery dealer in

Brinkley. Someone must be making money here, but someone who lives and spends it elsewhere. Or such would be my guess. But there is a neater part of town on the way out, with huge oaks ballooning over it. Massive oaks—willow-leaved Willow oaks and Spanish and Water oaks, both also with rather slight leaves for their size—lend an opulence to many an otherwise shabby old Southern street. And in charge at the gas station is a courteous, most considerate gray-haired gentleman who replenishes the fluid in the master brake-cylinder under the floorboards as if nothing could be worthier of his attention. He must wonder at the impression I surely give of being about to embrace him.

But on into the setting sun, and past stagnant waterways through the woods: Bayou de View, Relief Cash River, other "Relief" Bayous, which presumably take flood waters when the Arkansas or the great Mississippi rises. "Rex's Restaurant. Catfish. Hushpuppies. Country Fried Chicken." And three stands selling cypress knees—the stalagmite-shaped protuberances that Bald cypresses put up through the water to bring air to their roots. Numbers of little houseboats are on the White River, which is mud-colored. But that was how Audubon found it in 1820—"a dull red clay color." Audubon's party, having pulled a skiff up the river with a rope of grapevines, struck out across country and encountered hard going. "We walked through a *Narrow Path* often so thickly beset with green Briars that We Would be forced to give back and go round— this followed through *Cypress Swamps* and round *Pounds* and Cane Breaks." These "Breaks," dense stands of southern cane—a species of bamboo growing up to thirty feet tall and with stems up to three inches in diameter—once rendered vast areas of the forests of Kentucky and those to the south all but impassable and contributed to the impression formed by early visitors of a North America in which Nature expressed itself in superlatives, on a scale of heroic prodigality. Which it did. . . . Until recent times, geologically, a bay of the sea reached up the present Mississippi Valley all the way to the juncture with the Ohio; everything below the juncture is recent "fill." The flat rice lands go all the way to a promontory above the Arkansas River christened Le Petit Roche; one is apt to forget that the French were the first in here. (Le Grand Roche, in its obscurity, is a mile upstream.) Rock is, indeed, what is arresting about the place. The terrain suddenly rises and you are back among the formidable courses of Paleozoic strata.

It is night in Little Rock and I stop only for the tonic of a telephone call home—a luxury permitted once every other evening; I am unable to rise as superior to the bonds of affection as could Audubon, who wrote, "After Breakfast We Left the Post of Arkansas with a Wish to see the Country above, and so *Strong* is My Anthusiasm to Enlarge the Ornithological Knowledge of My Country that I felt as if I wish Myself *Rich again* and thereby able to Leave My family for a Couple of Years." The nearest discoverable campground is in the Ouachita National Forest, thirty-five miles west. Finding the entrance to the National Forest is not difficult and neither is finding a sign to Lake Sylvia Recreational Area, but finding the area itself is another matter. Back and forth I drive on rough dirt roads, up and down among the dark wooded hills with, I fear, increasing peevishness. Fifteen hours on the highway is too much for one day. Finally, back in the nowhere, I ease the bus off the road into what is designated a campground. There *is* a water faucet, in addition to some small clearings in the woods, and that is always to be welcomed. How would it be if I found myself in so unlikely a spot at such an hour for no special reason, in the ordinary course of events? The mere thought sends a sort of panicky tremor through me. But there is the work. I am carrying out a mission. I am *supposed* to be here. So it is All Right. But while My Anthusiasm to Enlarge my Physiographical Knowledge of My Country is *Strong,* I think what incredible confidence Audubon must have had in what he was doing to consider cutting himself off from his ties for a Couple of Years with nothing to steady him but his faith in an unproved, unprecedented and fantastic enterprise. . . . It is after eleven o'clock when I turn in—and seven-thirty before I am under way again in the morning.

The Geological Survey map shows a series of black lines curving through the Ouachitas parallel with one another and with the east–west warp of the range. These designate faults—lines along which the rock strata in being accordioned in the process of mountain-making could no longer absorb the tension and snapped, the upper part of a fold overriding the lower part in front of it, a little as an ocean comber breaks on the train of its predecessor. There are the same lines in the Long Ridge Mountains of the Appalachians. That the two ranges were cast in the same mold is evident. Long, parallel ridges rising above the fog that lies in the valleys: such are the Ouachitas this morning from State Highway 10. The Ozark Frontier Trail, as it is called, skirts the main body of the range on the north, following Petit Jean Creek—and there is no question but that French names add sauce to the mundane Perrys, Danvilles, and New Blaines.

All of a sudden there is an abundance of pine. We have entered, or re-entered, the oak-hickory-pine forest that, virtually without a break except for the Mississippi floodplain (oak-tupelo-cypress), extends eastward between the Appalachians and the Deep South coastal plain to meet the Atlantic from Delaware through the Carolinas—the largest forest of a single type in the country.* . . . A Pileated woodpecker, dazzling the cloudy morning with his banner display of scarlet, black, and white, flies walloping across the road, filled with the wild, exuberant vitality of his species. It was shortly after leaving the Arkansas on his way back south that Audubon ran into the Pileated's even more spectacular cousin, which we have since almost if not quite exterminated. ("Saw here 5 Ivory Bill Wood Peckers feeding on the Berries of Some Creeper they were gentle—Keeping a Constant Cry of *Pet Pet Pet.*") And I recall that it was while on the Arkansas that Audubon entered in his journal a casual observation that for me was one of those that bring into focus and illuminate a world of things about which one has collected a confusion of thoughts and impressions. He had encountered some Indians, and his reflection upon their nature struck me as no less revealing of Audubon than of the redmen— and I suspect that the reaction of all white men to the red tells us as much about the newcomer as about the aborigine. Was it as suggestive in its actual wording as I remember? At the first opportunity I look it up and am not disappointed. "Whenever I meet *Indians* I feel the greatness of our Creator in all its Splendor, for there I see the Man Naked from his Hand and yet free from Acquired Sorrow."

The Indians have gone from here long since, however, and with

* From the coward's sanctuary of a footnote, I might point out that the designations of the forest types are merely shorthand. The oak-hickory-pine forest, as A. W. Küchler explains in the manual accompanying the map, has as its dominants one of several species of hickory, Shortleaf pine, Loblolly pine, White oak, and Post oak and as its other components Bitternut hickory, Pignut hickory, Shagbark hickory, Mockernut hickory, Flowering dogwood, Persimmon, Sweetgum, Tulip-poplar, Black tupelo, Sourwood, Sassafras, Virginia pine, Scarlet oak, Southern Red oak (Spanish oak), Blackjack oak, Chestnut oak, Northern Red oak, Shumard oak, and Black oak—and what better than that unadorned catalogue could evoke a Southern woods?

many Acquired Sorrows, and their successors would appear to be following them. Fair-haired children, alert and promising-looking, are waiting for a school bus, but the stamp of poverty is on the country. The houses are small and ill-kept and fewer have flowers by them than have a car body with weeds growing up through it as through a skull. There are no cultivated lands to speak of, only woods and fields, with cattle—beef cattle, Herefords, which call for little human investment in the soil. Adona has a population of 194 and two little fly-blown shops with façades almost scaled over by metal advertisements many years old. Olla has a two-story hotel, but where the name used to be, nothing is legible and the ground floor has been given over to a café and some despairing shops. How, then, explain Andro, which has a new Piggly-Wiggly, a new Western Auto, a camping-trailer sales agency, even a new library? One way or another, I warrant it signifies the intrusion of Big-Time America, a plant near by or large-scale cattle operations. For the rest: *The little towns*—I unload on the tape recorder my continuing consternation at the thought of being trapped in one—*are indescribably ugly, bleak—impossible.*

But I am beyond being more than briefly touched by the awfulness. Part of it is the relief and guilty delight of escape. The plain fact is that today unless one gets away from time to time, even at the cost of uprooting oneself from one's family, life becomes a punishment. And by *away* I mean away from the newspapers and magazines and the terrible afflictions of the world that they bring one and the endless appeals in the mail to do something about them. All that we gain from material and scientific progress, all the comforts and excitements and relief from illness, it sometimes seems to me, are counterbalanced by the zealous capacity of modern communications for keeping us up to the minute on all the ills of the world, the whole world—the hungry peoples, the monstrous wars, the cynicism and venality in high places, the brutal crimes, the piling up of ultimate weapons, the pillaging of the planet to provide for the pathologically multiplying human race and to set the new rich up in vulgar luxury. One's head is turned into an echo-chamber of the world's evils. I could spend all my evenings reading reports of the threatened annihilation of riversides, sea-shores, woodlands, marshes, animal species, even the essential abode of life as a whole. Send money, I am urged. Write my Senators and Congressman. Attend meetings. I do these things, but not enough, nowhere near enough. So to my knowledge of all the wrongs being done is added endless self-reproach. But on the open road there is simply nothing I can do, and hence I need not accuse myself of doing just that. In our day, if every possibility of being anguished usefully is closed to you, it is permitted to be joyous.

And this morning it is not hard. The sun has come out and the landscape is alight with green, is singing with green. I cannot get over the beauty of the countryside wherever it has succeeded in reasserting itself, I exclaim into the microphone, meaning the countryside everywhere I have been. In its repair of man's ravages and winter's there is an air of triumph in Nature, and in this one feels oneself sharing. A triumph of Nature's, too, seems to be signalized in the green, forested wall rising less than a mile north of the road. It is *Le Mont Magasin,* mid-America's highest and, with its head in the clouds, looking much more imposing than its 2,823 feet; Mount Magazine, it is rendered.

The continual change in the natural landscape as you travel across the country—change in landform, change in vegetation—is engrossing. Hour by hour it is far more pronounced than I had anticipated and seems to be especially radical between one state and another. But of all the transitions, few affect you more than that in leaving Arkansas. Past Fort Smith, on the border, Oklahoma opens out before you between the widening gap of Ozarks and Ouachitas; you have seen the Ouachitas curving off away from you, far to the south, carrying the oak-hickory-pine forest into southeastern Oklahoma for the last hundred miles of its 1,350-mile arc from Delaware Bay. In half an hour, broad, nearly flat cattle-ranges stretch before you into the distance. The trees, interlopers now in an alien realm, huddle together for mutual support—or do to my somewhat infatuated gaze. You have entered "the celebrated Cross Timbers"—so called in early government reports—of Little-Bluestem prairie and scattered groves of Post and Blackjack oaks from which westbound wagoneers had a last chance to replace broken tongues, spokes, and axles. The Cardinals, Mockingbirds, and Blue grosbeaks of the morning are gone with the East and in their place—behold!—pale as the dry grass and sand of the plains to come, settling light as a leaf on a fencepost, the first Scissor-tailed flycatcher! And, an hour after the last, thin, pretty little Appalachian mountaineer girl-child holding a mule by its halter, here in a road-repair gang, a dark, heavy-set, fleshy-faced Indian!

4

INTO THE WEST

At the state border you are entitled to expect a dramatic marker boldly proclaiming the beginning of the West. If what you get is a sign saying "Oklahoma: Home of Miss America," you should be able to take the discrepancy in stride; otherwise you have no business making pilgrimages in the American Republic. Whatever a century of commercial bustle and growth may have done to it, this after all is Fort Smith.

It was from here that the coaches of the first regular transport service to the Pacific Coast took off across the wilderness of grass on the 2,800-mile road to El Paso, Tucson, Los Angeles and San Francisco—the famous Overland Mail, organized by John Butterfield and Associates in 1857. Moreover, this broad, murky river half-encircling the town is the great, far-journeying Arkansas, one of the only four rivers north of the Rio Grande and its tributary the Pecos to cross the Great Plains after taking their initial draughts from the freshets and cataracts of the Rockies—and of the four, one, the Canadian, is a tributary of the Arkansas. The 2,000-mile-long Arkansas has its source in the heart of the Colorado Rockies, but one valley removed from the headwaters of the Colorado and no farther from those of the Rio Grande. This was discovered when Lieutenant Zebulon Pike in the winter of 1805–06 led a party up the river into the snow-bound ranges and, after an unsuccessful attempt to climb the peak later named for him and the most dreadful sufferings on the part of all, descended the upper Rio

Grande to Santa Fe. And subsequently, with Santa Fe as its terminus, the first and for decades only road to the Southwest followed the Arkansas for part of the way from St. Louis. That was
the famous Santa Fe Trail, over which, beginning with Mexico's
independence in 1821, lumbered wagon trains in increasing numbers to exchange American textiles, cutlery and tools for the products of Mexican mines and ranches. Fifteen miles a day was average
for the big prairie schooners outbound on the Santa Fe Trail.
Weighing two or three tons each, they were drawn by four or five
teams of mules or horses or six yokes of oxen across a country
parched with heat and drought and cut by streambeds that after
rains were deep in mire, where behind every rise was the chance
of a raiding Indian band.

North of the Arkansas are the Platte and the Missouri, the former
branching off from the latter in Nebraska. Named by the French
for its flatness, the Platte provided the avenue for the first wave
of American migration to the Far West. That was in the 1840's,
and the route of march was the Oregon-California Trail, which
followed the Platte and the North Platte to the neighborhood of
South Pass, across the Continental Divide. The Pass had come to be
known in 1824 thanks to pioneers of the fur trade, specifically the
Thomas Ashley party, which included the Sublette brothers,
Jedediah Smith, Jim Bridger, and others later among the most
famous of the "Mountain Men." Shortly after reaching the
westward-flowing Snake, the trail divided. One branch proceeded
northwest up the Snake, then over the Blue Mountains to the
Columbia River and Oregon. The other turned southwest to trav-
erse Nevada via the Humboldt River (which disappears in the
Humboldt Sink) across or around the Sierra Nevada to San
Francisco. In either case, it was a trek of months. Those columns
of swaying Conestoga wagons raising the dust of the plains; the
sturdy pioneer women holding the reins; the scouts out ahead;
the feathered Indians peering from behind rock outcroppings; the
formation of the defensive circle at night; the war whoops and
bison stampedes; all that the screen has made part of our growing
up—that was the Oregon-California Trail along the Platte across
Nebraska and Wyoming.

Last—and first—there is the Missouri, the only river navigable
across the plains and the one chosen as the route to the Rockies in
the first American crossing of the continent. In the predominantly

unsatisfying annals of history, in which, generally, purposes are confused and the admirable and the sorry intermixed, the expedition to the Pacific led by Meriwether Lewis and William Clark, which departed from St. Louis in May 1804 and returned two years and four months later, is one of the human performances that, to me, stand apart as exemplary, very nearly the perfect exploit of its kind. Few land-borne expeditions can have been longer out of touch with any base; have brought more territory of more stunning character into the world's ken; have more narrowly escaped disaster as comprehensive as that which faced this one in its crossing of the Lemhi Pass into Montana's Bitterroot Valley; have witnessed a more touching scene, or one more crucial to the expedition's survival, than that when, in the hour of its sorest need, the young Shoshone wife of the expedition's translator, recognized "with every mark of the most extravagant joy" a band of Indians as her own people, from whom she had earlier been taken by force; have known a more dramatic moment than that when the fog lying over the mouth of the Columbia lifted to reveal "the delightful prospect of the ocean, the object of all our labors, the reward of all our anxieties"; have come more safely through more hardships and dangers, with only two men out of forty lost.

The expedition's achievement and the enormous contribution it made to the nation's knowledge of the continent were owing most directly, of course, to the workmanlike character of the two leaders, which was in no way more strikingly revealed than in their extraordinary ability to share command as equals, for which purpose Lieutenant Clark was given the complimentary rank of Captain, which was Lewis's official rank. Behind the two Virginians, however, was a third, the American embodiment of eighteenth-century enlightenment, President Thomas Jefferson, whose offspring the expedition was. Jefferson was determined that the undertaking be a "literary" one, in the sense that it would be concerned with the orderly acquisition of knowledge, and his instructions to that end were detailed. Moreover, he had arranged for Lewis to receive intensive training from the scientists of the American Philosophical Society in Philadelphia. Lewis was an apt pupil, as Clark proved to be too. They brought back with them a wealth of information on the topography, soils, minerals, flora, fauna, climate and character and customs of the Indians of the country they traversed that was probably unprecedented in the history of exploration and certainly did the thirty-year-old Republic extraordinary credit. The expedition not only provided the nation with invaluable advantages in its pursuit of the Western dream; it also established a tradition of scientific seeking in the opening up of the continent. The tradition was to bear precious fruit in the explorations of John C. Frémont, the great geological surveys of Ferdinand Hayden, Clarence King, Grove Karl Gilbert, and Major John Wesley Powell, first navigator of the Colorado, champion of the redman and of the land itself. It was a tradition of observation exemplified by painters like George Catlin, William H. Holmes, and Charles Russell, and by John Muir, whose evocation of the splendors of the Sierra Nevada was a powerful plea for the succor of all wild America. These were among the many who "went in search under the Western star" (in the memorable phrase of Coronado's annalist, Pedro de Cantenada de Najera) not for booty but for knowledge, if sometimes in part for self-knowledge, who came as apprentices and in one way or another to celebrate the continent and glory in it.

That is one tradition. There is another I associate with Andrew Jackson. As Jefferson, with his respect for the nature of things, his versatile and creative mind, his rational and inquisitive intelligence to which no field of knowledge was indifferent, exemplified much that seems to me best in American character, so Jackson exemplified traits I find among the most antagonistic. Old Hickory, he was called, and tough is what he was, the belligerent, aggressive frontiersman and killer. As the Southern historian Thomas D. Clark observes in *Frontier America,* "Jackson's attitude toward Indians was precisely that of the border warriors who had returned from raids with grisly strips of brown skin to use for razor strops." More than anyone was he responsible for the expulsion of the Indians from their homelands in the East to the trans-Mississippian West and must be answerable for the terrible sufferings that befell them, of which those of the Cherokees on the "Trail of Tears" were simply the worst. He stands, in my mind at least, for that national type to whom life makes one clear call, "Come and get it," and who goes and gets it, to whom the cultivated arts except as they bear on that main purpose are effeminate fripperies and empathy an unmanly weakness—the spoilsman. And there were to be spoilsmen aplenty to tackle the territory the United States acquired in the Louisiana Purchase and what lay beyond; this territory, which included within its natural boundaries the drainage areas of all the rivers flowing into the Mississippi from the west, Lewis and Clark had been sent out to make part of the nation in fact as well as in title.

The first were soon following in the trailblazers' footsteps. These were the Mountain Men, frontiersmen such as had come over the Appalachians into Kentucky and Tennessee, whose object was furs, particularly beaver. They traded with the Indians for pelts and trapped on their own. Nothing stopped them, the vast distances, the loneliness of the high ranges, the dangers of Indians, sickness, broken limbs, fatal exposure. And they died liberally—but not nearly so liberally as they killed. What men they were!—expecting no quarter of the wilderness they penetrated to its remotest valleys, gazing daily on grandeurs of forest, gorge, mountain height, or rushing river no white man had ever beheld before, living for months on end on what they could carry or capture, hearing no voice at the campfire but the cry of wolf, owl or cougar, untouched by any gentleness other than the caresses an Indian girl taken to wife might bestow at the foray's end. What men!—and what trails of blood and stripped carcasses they left, destroying their own kind's means of survival, leaving a mountain wilderness sacked of half its living treasure. The winning of the West was on.

Well, the past is past. At its worst, as at its best, it afforded a display of courage and hardihood that today we might well find almost incredible, accustomed as we are to facing life's physical challenges behind phalanxes of technological myrmidons. Spoilsmen and explorers, adventurers, homesteaders, and questers, all were alike in their quality of nerve and stamina. But as you stand at the threshold of the West, having the procession of its yesterdays come before you, it is not so much the courage and hardihood required of its invaders that is in your mind. It is what called them forth. What that was, the sixteenth-century Spanish explorer Cabeza de Vaca put as simply and eloquently as words could perhaps express it: "We ever held it certain that going toward the sunset we should find what we desired."

Infinite promise! That was the West: all but interminable plains black sometimes with bison as far as the eye could reach; at their end, fading north and south into mystery, ranges of Olympian peaks sheltering high valleys timbered and grassy; and beyond these, on the Pacific slope, a temperate, well-watered country of incomparable forests inviting the kind of settlement the East had nurtured. It was a land of which the parts as they became known, piling one extravagance of nature on another, incited the imagination to outdo itself in filling in those unknown, which for many years remained much the larger. It was, moreover, a land of an immensity far beyond the comprehension of us today who have pawned the illimitable magnitude and majesty of the earth as it was for the satisfactions of scooting hundreds and thousands of miles a day across its face. And to the newcomer today the country that looms before him is still the country that slowly unrolled its plains and raised its buttes and peaks before the first explorers.

Of the prairies the early settlers knew, little remains, of course. Almost nothing: a few scattered patches and the memory of a time when a horseman could travel for days across the sea of Big Bluestem, through Iowa into Nebraska or from Oklahoma into Saskatchewan, and seldom see much above the bird's-foot seed-heads of the reed-like grass. "I do not know anything that struck me more forcibly than the sensation of solitude I experienced in crossing this, and some of the other large Prairies," wrote a traveler, William Newnham Blaine, in 1824. "I was perfectly alone, and could see nothing in any direction but sky and grass. Leaving the wood appeared like embarking alone upon the ocean; and, upon again approaching the wood, I felt as if returning to land. Sometimes again, when I perceived a small stunted tree that had been planted by some fortuitous circumstances, I could hardly help supposing it to be the mast of a vessel. No doubt the stillness added much to this strange illusion. Not a living thing could I see or hear, except the occasional rising of some prairie fowl, or perhaps a large hawk or eagle wheeling about over my head." And this was written of the circumscribed prairieland of southern Illinois.

To drag a plow through the virgin sod of the prairie took five yoke of oxen, and often the plow broke instead of the sod; but the issue was hardly in doubt from the start. The Big Bluestem and its associates have given place to a Mexican grass, *Zea mays;* and those who have seen the maize standing twelve to fifteen feet high in Iowa should have a good idea of the fertility of soil the tall prairie-grasses built up—the most fertile in the nation. Of the mid-height grasses of the prairie farther west—those that once spread over the Dakotas, Nebraska, Kansas, western Oklahoma (minus the Panhandle) and in wedges deep into Texas—wheat is the principal successor. Like the Little Bluestem and Western Wheat-grass it has supplanted, wheat can get along on between twenty and thirty inches of annual rainfall where the tall grasses require between thirty and forty.

On the road to Oklahoma City, what you mostly see is cattle range—and also, rather disconcertingly to me, a recrudescence of the woodland to which I had bade farewell. This should not be surprising. What has always been difficult to account for is why the moister prairie, on which trees planted by man generally grow handsomely, should have been so largely in grass instead of in forest. None of the various explanations offered has satisfied everyone. It seems very likely, however, that fires played some part in it, incinerating seedling trees while leaving the grass roots unaffected. In the dry season these ravaged the prairie, often having been started by Indians to clear areas to which the bison would repair for the new growth in the spring. A terrifying spectacle a prairie fire must have been, too, though "sublime" was how William N. Blaine described it. He wrote: "I have seen the old Atlantic in his fury, a thunder storm in the Alps, and the cataracts of Niagara; but nothing could be compared to what I saw at this moment. The line of flame rushed through the long grass with tremendous violence, and a noise like thunder. With such vehemence did the wind drive along the flames, that large masses of them appeared actually to leap forward and dart into the grass several yards in advance of the line. It passed me like a whirlwind, and with a fury I shall never forget."

Back on Interstate 40 for the first time since Little Rock—"40 WEST," the little shield-markers say, stirringly enough—at twelve thirty, with Oklahoma City 114 miles away. There have been Western flowers on the roadside—low-growing, lavender asters, multitudes of Yellow clover, a yellow-orange coreopsis, and the massed violet spires of a wild larkspur. The highway is virtually deserted. Low, wooded hills retreat into the distance, some ahead with lightning flashing over them. And imperturbably in the great sky, you feel, reigns the god of spaces.

Here comes the downpour.

It rains, deafeningly, during lunch (in a beautiful rest area on high ground) and is raining when the first oil wells put in an appearance—or so I take them to be. There is no tower of scaffolding, only a pump, usually off by itself. This rather resembles a large,

steel-work bird rhythmically and deliberately pecking at the ground
while pedaling a bicycle. It is sparsely settled country.

At four o'clock comes Oklahoma City, and with it the dull conviction that I have lost the West—a come-down, to say the least.

*Very gray, but it's not raining anymore. For over an hour we've
had torrents and cars with their lights on sending sheets of water
up from the highway. Oklahoma City is the big American city all
over again: red-and-white checked water-tanks; long, low industrial
buildings; shopping-centers; traffic-lights; cars by the tens of thousands; a subdivision in the distance; a restaurant; more shopping-
centers; offices, billboards, motels. Maybe Interstate 40 will go all
the way through and we'll be in luck. Burger Family Drive-in. More
gas stations. A clump of thirty-story office-buildings up in front.
Downtown Oklahoma City. . . .*

*Well, Interstate 40 gave out and now we're being shunted through
a dismal scene of urban outskirts on a rough asphalt road to U. S.
66, which goes west to Amarillo. It's drizzling and gray and gloomy.
. . . Going along now beside a railroad train. . . .*

On the farther outskirts of the still dismal city, I pull over to
cheer myself with some tea, while the trucks thunder by a few
feet away, and . . . *I got it all made, then turned the whole thing
over, all over the seat, all over the bus.* It is the nadir of the whole
trip—as I wish I could have known at the time.

Except that the nadir is not quite over. Back on 40, I have hardly
had time to expatiate on the beauty the country would possess if
the sun were out on the new wheat covering the gentle slopes that
roll off ino the distance when the little bus develops an uneven
beat. . . . Into each life some rain must fall, and in each life some
tires must be changed while it is falling. But this is one of four I
have just had recapped for the trip and it is blistered and ruined—
just what is to happen to two more within the fortnight. A replacement at a gasoline station in the next town costs twenty-two dollars
and is installed while I have dinner in the bus, unhappily aware
that I have been only about four hundred miles so far today—not
enough, not enough.

Now and again I think we are driving out of the storm. There
come hints of a pale blue behind the clouds and a silver light
bathes part of the landscape, which recalls all one has read of the
prairie's oceanic character: there is a low, in places hardly perceptible, swell in the configuration of the land, with wheat on the

upland parts and clumps of trees in the troughs. But the rain is relentless and at Elk City I give in and put up at a motel.

It is still raining in the morning, drizzling beneath a low overcast, but it is what lies only an hour ahead that counts. That is the 100th meridian, which forms the border between Oklahoma and the Texas Panhandle, and the frontier of the realm of the sun. It is at this line of longitude, along which, more or less, from Mexico to Canada the annual rainfall declines to about twenty inches, that the *real* West is said, only somewhat arbitrarily, to begin. From here on, except for the Pacific slope above mid-California, water is a perennial concern and drought the rule below the high elevations of the mountains. About nine-tenths of the western half of the forty-eight states is arid or outright desert, too dry to sustain a continuous plant-cover, and most of it in consequence of lying in the "rain-shadow" of mountains. That mountains should be able to extract so much of the content of the clouds is an extraordinary thing. At least I have found it so since seeing a cross-section, prepared by my friend William Melson, of the Eastern seaboard in the latitude of Maryland extending through the Appalachians and out across the continental shelf. "Why didn't you show the mountains?" I asked. As their idolater, I was shocked at his reply: "On this scale"—and the section was a good three feet in length—"they wouldn't be much higher than the thickness of the pen line representing the surface of the earth." In comparison with even a small section of the continent, mountains of three thousand feet hardly exist. The higher Western ranges would make a better showing, of course, but not much. If the state of Washington were a yard across, the Cascades would run less than a quarter of an inch in height. Yet they can so deplete the clouds that plains a thousand miles away go thirsty. How thin is the biosphere! And that, for us who wield such powers of destruction, is the lesson to be drawn: how paper-thin and vulnerable the earth's veneer of soil, water, oxygen, and clemency is, in which alone life can survive.

It is in the neighborhood of the 100th meridian that, by nature, the mid-height grasses of the prairie give way to the short grasses of the Great Plains, especially the buffalo-grass, which somewhat resembles depressed sea-oats, and Blue grama, which puts out toothbrush seed-heads at right angles to the wiry stalks. Also along about here the land achieves an elevation of 2,000 feet—for imperceptibly, from a few hundred feet in the east, the plains rise to a mile high at the foot of the Rocky Mountains. The rise of the Rockies was accompanied by a general uplift, which gave the land a downward slope to their east. This was accentuated by the dissolution of the sedimentary rocks which came up ahead of the forged-rock cores of the ranges and the spread of their sediments across the plains in the course of millions of years. Deepest at the foot of the ranges, these sediments, mostly re-formed into rock, thin out progressively to the east. On Interstate 40, you reach their leading edge just about at the Oklahoma-Texas border.

It is, in short, an important frontier, and having been deprived of the annunciation you felt you had a right to expect on entering Oklahoma, you watch for the border to see what will be made of the great 100th meridian. You notice a sign warning "Last Chance. Next Beer 106 Miles," and—oops!—that was it.

But however disregarded, signal changes are unmistakably afoot. Plains cottonwoods are already common in the hollows: they told the pathfinders of the arid grasslands where water was to be found, even if it had to be dug for, and they have made an obligatory appearance in every Western romance ever since. They are handsomely sculptured trees with lustrous, heart-shaped leaves. There are also mysterious small trees with coarse little leaves like an elm's on pendant branchlets. At Shamrock, I learn by inquiring of a man on the street that these are Chinese elms. "Some years ago they had the idea that this was the only kind of tree that would grow around here where it's unprotected and they planted a number of them, but now they're trying other kinds too." The small trees make a difference to Shamrock's array of gasoline stations and cafés—how much difference you are all the more aware when you get to McLean. There the backdrop of gasoline stations, grocery stores, second-class tourist courts, and various squat buildings with home-made billboards is unredeemed by any greenery at all. I get out to buy some cottage cheese, bologna, and other comestibles, and among the scattering of citizens of set, unexcitable expression and deliberate movements, on whose temperaments perhaps rests the weight of their enormous, vacant sky, I feel like a volatile exotic, as if I had just stepped out of *La Bohème*.

"West Wind Motel. Howdy Y'All." Seventy-two miles to Amarillo, where you can get a free dinner if you will eat a seventy-two-ounce steak in an hour.

Drabber grows the rangeland, a gray-olive under the furrowed clouds, and the knots of trees seem positively to cower in the hollows; the wind is almost too much for the bus. But canyons have begun to appear. They are only a few feet deep at first, but within an hour have been cut down by water-courses as much as forty feet —a presage of things to come. . . . You never know what to expect as you drive along. The sunlight, at last beginning to break through, falls in patches on dark, lonely green fields with beautiful wheat crops. These must be irrigated, though in one place the water is so deep a pair of Shoveler ducks has put down on it. Visible from miles away, there are lofty, compound towers of white concrete built, you would think, to enable a moorland earl to withstand siege on a wild frontier rather than for storing grain. . . . Onto the tape there goes, with apologies to Kipling implied:

> When here and there the land's been won,
> For irrigated crops;
> When the earth is flat and it's mostly dun,
> And there's nothing else but sky and sun,
> And the wind that never stops;
> When refracted light forms a phantom lake,
> And you're challenged to eat a four-pound steak;
> And your spirits are not at their very best,
> Why, then you'll know (if you haven't guessed),
> You're in Texas, Pard, on 40 West!

Actually, a four-and-a-half-pound steak. But it is factually accurate about the lake. Repeatedly you would swear that is what you are seeing on the horizon, with grass and a few patches of trees growing out of the water.

Amarillo: try not to look, try not to think. The approach via U. S. 66 is a commercialized strip of brain-bruising garishness, the city, or what you see of it, a rabble of motels and service stations.

"Welcome to Vega, Crossroads of the Nation." Of the *nation!*

But rewards are coming. Twenty miles short of the border, before your eyes, are the first mesas! With them, New Mexico could be said, in effect, to begin. The one nearest the highway, it is true, turns out to have a few hundred car bodies at the foot of it, apparently pushed off the top, but my enchantment is beyond being dispelled by that. (Native peoples always have native ways.) Mesas —"tables"—are of course the steep-sided tops of plains left standing high above their surroundings when the latter have been cut down by erosion. The nature of things can be plainly seen when unexpectedly the highway comes to the end of the terrain it has been crossing which, when it has descended steeply to other flatlands below, looks just like the bluff of a mesa. The geological map shows that it has dropped from a surface laid down only 12 or 14 million years ago, when the landscape was much as it is today and home to aquatic rhinoceroses and shovel-tusked mastodons, to the valley of the Canadian River, where everything has been washed away down to a formation dating from the first chapter of the Age of Reptiles, 160 and more million years ago. It does not seem right that it should be in the desert, where rainfall is minimal, that the effects of erosion should of all places be the most arresting. But where water is insufficient to provide for an unbroken covering of vegetation, the land lies exposed to any downpour that may assail it. Downpours, moreover, are what do assail it, for such rain as falls in the desert comes mostly in cloudbursts that flay the naked slopes and can fill a dry arroyo in minutes with a rampaging flood capable of tossing motorcars ahead of it.

And this is where the desert begins, and with it the dramatic West. There are plains of sparse, sandy-colored grass waiting for summer rains to revive it and low, green shrubs that turn out to be mesquite, and in the south, the mesas, the ruined front and outliers of the Great Plains. As you can see later where there are others close to the highway, the mesas have withstood the assault of time because of their capping of resistant sandstone. The thick, blocky layer of rock protrudes over the declivity at their edge, giving the formations frowning and commanding profiles, such as to intimidate upstart man, you would think.

With the sight of the first of the monstrous survivals you are back with the earth's antiquity, a fledgling of the present among brooding ancestral shapes. There is paradox in this effect of the West as there is in the prevalence of the rain's marks in the desert. In the geologically ancient East there is little to make you aware of remote epochs; the earth-shaping processes have largely done their work; age has mellowed the landscape. Time rests on the pastoral East as lightly as a leaf on the surface of a pond. Except where land meets sea in a shifting frontier, time in the East means mostly the round of the seasons. In the much younger West the processes that take scores of millions of years for fulfillment are still in mid-course and the formations laid largely bare to view ex-

hibit the variety of their handiwork, from the monumental remnants of vanished plains to still-seething volcanoes. Thus to the
physical grandeur and immensity of the West is added the grandeur
and immensity of geological time, of which its sculpturing makes
you unremittingly conscious.

An hour before we reach it, a butte rises on the horizon. A
towering eminence it becomes, too, as we shorten our distance
from it; it overlooks the subject lowlands with the lordly and inscrutable mien of a Sphinx. (A butte, which is any solitary, steep-
sided mountain, is what a mesa is eventually reduced to.) The West
is coming in gratifyingly on cue: a windmill water-pump in the
emptiness with Hereford cattle standing around it, another little
herd of Herefords with some Indian cowhands, and the mesquite,
which is a charming, bright green shrub with rows of small leaves
on either side of the stems, like a honey-locust's. Ahead, the town
of Tucumcari looks leafy. . . . The butte, now that we are even
with it, turns out to be crowned by four television broadcasting
towers—and what did one expect? Working the pumps at a service
station in Tucumcari (where again I have to put out twenty-odd
dollars for a new tire) is a young Indian with whom I feel as
unnatural and artificial as a passenger ashore from a cruise ship
and apologetic for everything that has happened since Columbus.
But maybe he is just like anyone else? Maybe he prefers television
programs to corn dances?

Fantastic to see the four-lane highway, and the sun glinting
on eight or ten cars speeding along it, as if it had been peeled off
the urbanized East and laid out in total incongruity across a
country that, except for the occasional lonely cluster of ranch-
houses, might never before have seen a human being. I get away
from the anomaly by turning off beyond Santa Rosa on the road
north to Santa Fe. This is a national highway but almost without
traffic. You can tell how few cars have recently been along it by
the number of pipits—our nearest thing to the skylark—that we
flush from the roadside; they fly briskly off, unbothered by a wind
that threatens to blow the roof off the bus and the bus off the road.
There is the Pecos River, which you could wade across, and there
are the fifteen or twenty low adobe structures of Dilia, preceded by
cottonwoods with trunks two feet through, along a ditch. And finally . . . finally and fully, and in a way to sweep through the
imagination like the wind through the silvery-tawny grass of the

rangeland all around, there is the West. It is on this road that I understand how, if once you give in to it, nothing less will ever be big enough to contain you, for this is the first time—stepping out of the bus into its imperturbable silence—I have ever been alone with it and felt its tremendous extent and fathomless solitude. The plains, sprinkled with dwarf Western junipers, dark but vivid green, and silvery-green cholla of fuzzy, segmented branches roll away to long, low, flat ridges with stepped ends and doughty little junipers clinging to their seamed and obdurate flanks. Somber and redoubtable as fortresses are these formations, and they call to mind a picture of a young knight cantering across plains like these to prove his steel in a legendary and menacing Land of the Giants.

Now deepening in color as sunset nears, the undulating ranges float away to a pearly, translucent shadow on the horizon ahead, graceful as a train of smoke—the southernmost range of the rising Rocky Mountains. The wind has fallen, but a gust bends the silken grass, and just as by that movement of air do you feel yourself touched in passing by the proud, free-roving, ceremonious spirit of the Indian, which seemed so expressive of the land from which it will never be altogether banished, in which the drums still sound for the listening ear. . . . To leave behind the convoluted civilization that requires of you the subtleties and equivocations of the proverbial Philadelphia lawyer and to make a home in the saddle under the open sky in the world of inexhaustible space and heroic forms in which your antagonists, the elements, fortify as they test you and life's demands, however harsh, are straightforward, addressed to you as a man—in short, to live the legend of the West: that is what you think of.

And is the legend altogether a myth?—the West that has given rise to an endless cycle of romances and to which we repair generation after generation as our ancestors did to another West in which an immortal cycle of romances sprang from King Arthur and his knights. If not an objective, it must have a subjective reality. Whatever the legend of the West may or may not tell us of the nature of the West, it surely throws a light on the needs of our own natures. And it strikes me as curious, as I think about it, and as perhaps indicative of how deep-seated those needs are, that the popular romances of the West should have so much in common with those of the Arthurian cycle. In both, the theme is chivalry—

a word that, not without significance, I should imagine, is derived from *chevalier,* horseman. In Western as in medieval romance, the basic story is of an essentially unworldly young man of uncomplicated moral code who pursues on horseback a calling or quest beyond the purlieus of ordinary men in a large, romantic, untamed world of lurking perils in which, ultimately alone and overmatched, he must meet the forces of evil in a life-and-death contest in defense of the pure and helpless—a youthful school-marm or damsel in distress whom he approaches only with a reverential idealism. Life, to be sure, is not as simple as that, and anyone who behaved as if it were would come a fearful cropper. Still, if man requires parables illustrative of the moral meaning of life, I must say I prefer the mythic tale of chivalry to others that have been laid down for our guidance.

I am too old to see myself now as a cowboy matching my horsemanship and coolness of nerve against the badman's but not beyond using words like "thrilling" to the tape recorder for the sensation of driving along through the spacious, golden afternoon with the junipers and bunchy little pines casting long shadows, and other shadows separating the rocks forming the parapet of a giant, conifer-clad mesa beneath which the highway passes. . . . The dwarf pines, with needles that look as short as a Balsam's, are the first Pinyons. They have suddenly put in an appearance, indicating, it seems, that the plains have gained a few hundred feet in elevation. Ahead, the rising ramparts of the Rocky Mountains have acquired solidarity.

The highway has joined Interstate 25 and is headed for Glorieta Pass at the southernmost end of the Rockies, by which I am already prepared to be moved—so much so as to be able to blot from sight all incompatible structures. Wagon-trains on the Santa Fe Trail traversed the pass on the last twenty-odd miles of their long journey. So, in 1862, did a force of Texans carrying the Confederate flag to its farthest west. But as much by its name as by its other distinctions am I won to it. As Roman Catholic troops in the religious wars cried *Ave Maria,* so mine, when I have some, will cry *Glorieta!* And it is a dramatic enough place. *A huge butte or mesa on the left, darkening against the setting sun, like a battleship.* But in a few minutes: *The battleship butte turns out to be the end of a long escarpment around which we are going, jutting out in headland after headland.* However they may look in the

daytime, these jagged ends of the plains above the Pecos are terrific in the failing light, like the overlapping prows of colossal,
flat-topped warships cheek by jowl, overawing and ominous. And
on the other side, mounting in waves like the Blue Ridge, is the
Oku Range of the Southern Rockies. It was called Sangre de Cristo
by the Spanish, who, it is said, managed to be reminded of the
blood shed at the Crucifixion by the red glow of the setting sun
on the snowy heights. Being unable to imagine any circumstances
that would reconcile me to so unnatural and revolting an epithet,
I set about to ascertain what the local Indian designation was (this
is some time later) and am rewarded at length by the Indian
Museum at Santa Fe, where it is on tap. "The Turtle," as it is
called, presumably with reference to the dominant hump of the
massif above Santa Fe, may not be the most expressive name for
mountains rising to over fourteen thousand feet—in Colorado—but
I am glad to settle for it. The Okus, to me, they shall be.

At Glorieta you come to the beginning not only of the Rockies
and of the mountainous West but also of the Western forest. At
the level of the pass and below are only the junipers and Pinyon
pines, which are compact, endearing little trees, perfect miniatures
usually between six and ten feet tall. These two form widely open
orchards where (I learn) the rainfall is between twelve and twenty
inches, which is apt to be between 3,500 and 7,000 feet. Above
Glorieta there is the first true forest. Of conifers, it clothes mesas
and mountains indiscriminately in a uniform dusky green, in Eastern eyes a sober monochrome. And it is up into the forest for
the night for me, to a little red arrow on the road-map denoting a
campground in the National Forest above Santa Fe.

5

CROSSING THE DESERT—I

In the East, an hour's walk through the countryside is likely to offer a continuously changing scene, particularly in the variety of plants along the way. In many parts of the West you could walk for twenty miles with little sense of having left your starting place. But in others in the space of a few miles you might well find more change than you would between Quebec and Georgia. Compared with the East, the West is almost impossibly complicated in physiography. The geological map is so closely mottled, as if in specks and blobs of oil colors in intermingling flows, that very little pattern emerges. The map of potential vegetation, which shows two-thirds of all the country's types located in its western half, is almost as confusing. However, the West has a basic structure, to be grasped with the aid of the right kind of map, and I think those who travel in the West or read much about it will find the effort of grasping it worthwhile. At any rate I am tempted to set forth the way in which I have learned to visualize it for the sake of anyone who may care to follow me on the accompanying map or a larger one in color showing land forms.*

The central feature of the American West is an expanse of arid

* One of the best is the widely distributed Natural Color Relief Map published by Jeppesen and Company of Denver, Colorado, of which the accompanying map is a small-scale photograph. It shows the nature of vegetative cover as well as topography with a remarkable effect of realism. For a more discriminating but nonpictorial, schematic representation, there is Classes of Land-Surface Form prepared by Edwin H. Hammond for the Association of American Geographers and for sale by the U. S. Geological Survey, Washington, D. C. 20242.

plains and tablelands having on the map the shape of a mitten, thumb protruding to the right to the western edge of Wyoming, cuff (the Mojave Desert) occupying inland southern California and fingers extending up through inland Oregon and Washington to within fifty miles of the Canadian border. While the terrain of the Central Desert, as we may call it, is prevailingly more or less level, steep hills or mountains rise abruptly from it at intervals. In its southern half, embracing all Nevada and western Utah, these consist mostly of parallel, north–south ridges, many of great height. This is the Basin-and-Range Province, as it is called, and it accounts not only for the southern half of the Central Desert but extends on far below (like a sleeve to which the mitten is pinned) southeast across southern Arizona down into western Mexico (the Sonoran Desert, this extension of the Province is called) and across southwestern New Mexico and thence down through central Mexico (the Chihuahuan Desert). North of the Basin-and-Range Province, making up the fingers and thumb of the mitten, is the Columbia-Snake Plateau, a tableland of lava drained (insofar as it is drained at all) by the Columbia River and its major branch, the Snake, which joins it after flowing the length of the thumb through southern Idaho.

High, forested ranges rim the parched Central Desert except in the south. Even there, however, such a range extends halfway across the bottom of the mitten from the coast; called the Transverse Range, it comprises the San Gabriel and San Bernardino Mountains, which run east and west above Los Angeles. On the west, the Central Desert is bounded by the Sierra Nevada (alongside the palm) and the Cascades (alongside the fingers). For its full length, the Sierra-Cascades belt is paralleled on the west by the considerably lower Coast Ranges, rising out of the Pacific.

Forming the entire northern boundary of the Central Desert (along the upper edge of the fingers and thumb), from which they rise abruptly, the Northern Rockies run northwestward through western Canada, forming the fjord-riven northern Pacific Coast. In Alaska, they divide into the Brooks Range, in the north, overlooking the Barren Lands that fade away into the Arctic Ocean, and the Alaskan Range in the south, which rises to the continent's highest peak before running out the Aleutian Archipelago and maybe into Asia. The Northern Rockies are a western analogue of the Appalachians, having had the same kind of genesis, albeit at a much

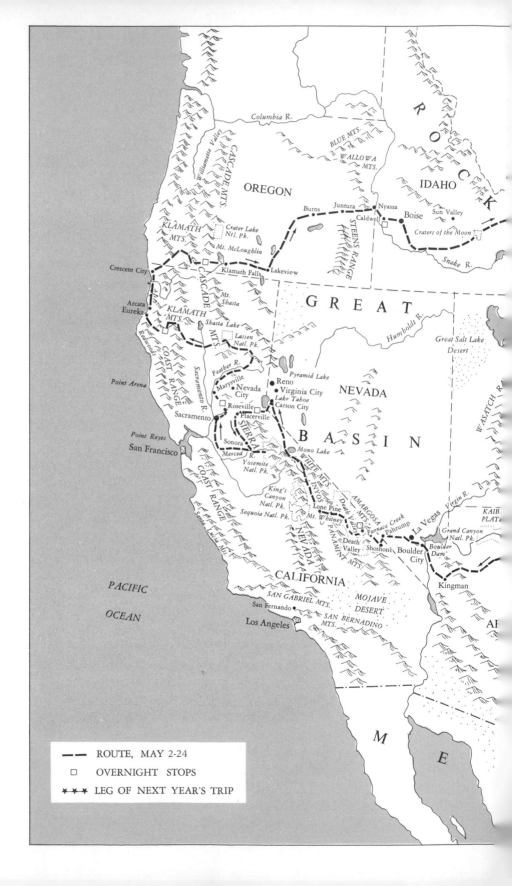

ROUTE, MAY 2-24
□ OVERNIGHT STOPS
★★★ LEG OF NEXT YEAR'S TRIP

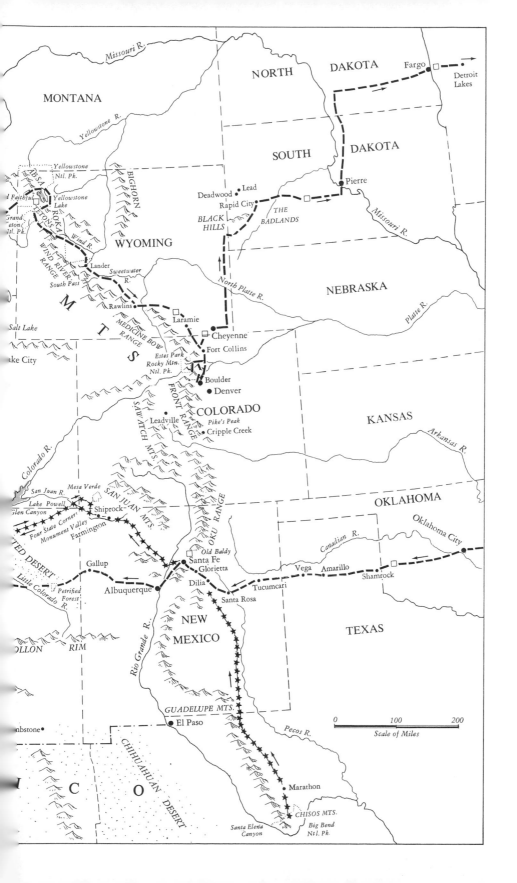

later date, and having a comparable structure, though in a much more youthful phase. Probably they once extended down through the United States and Mexico but disappeared in this section in the course of catastrophic crustal disturbances—catastrophic to the Rockies, that is.

Bordering the Central Desert on the right below the thumb, looking westward over Great Salt Lake and Great Salt Desert, the Wasatch Range bisects Utah from north to south, almost reaching the Kaibab Plateau of Arizona, which the Grand Canyon transects, before bending southwest to form the wrist of the mitten.

The Central and Southern Rockies are geographically unrelated to the Northern. Both on a land-form map have somewhat the outline of an eastward-facing animal's head. The Central, a cluster of ranges occupying northwestern Wyoming and an adjacent part of Montana, bear a resemblance to an elephant's, with the thumb of the mitten as the neck. Forming the cranium, the Absaroka Mountains descend into Yellowstone Park, which would be just about covered by the ear. Below the ear, near the root of the two downward-pointing tusks, are the Tetons. The Bighorn Range is the elephant's trunk, curled up nearly to touch the forehead.

With their main mass taking up half of Colorado, the Southern Rockies and their neighboring ranges on the west are comparable to a goat's head, but one with a long muzzle like a mule's. At the brow is Pike's Peak. North of it is the great Front Range, from which stem two of the three extensions of the system that run up into Wyoming and suggest horns. Shaping the back of the goat's cranium is the Sawatch Range, topped by Colorado's highest peak. To the south of this, the Oku (or S. de C.) Mountains descend to Santa Fe, forming the animal's long nose-bone. Making up the massive jawblade and occupying much of southwestern Colorado are the great but strangely little renowned San Juan Mountains, largely formed of lava.

Between the Wasatch Range and the Colorado mountains, accounting for most of southeastern Utah and the adjacent corner of Colorado, is the upper part of the Colorado Plateau. Widening to the south, the Plateau embraces northwestern New Mexico and most of northern Arizona and ends in the Mogollon Rim, a band of north-south-running mountain ranges resembling a pleating of the earth. The Colorado Plateau is a block of the earth's crust raised in the several stages of uplift that brought the Central and Southern Rockies into being.

Where the goat's upper lip would be, in the cluster of Okus above Santa Fe, part way up the road to Old Baldy, I awaken on May seventh to a clear, cold dawn and to my first near view of the Western forest, in which the wind is sounding with a restless spirit. As day comes, I can see that the trunks of the conifers around me are as straight as masts and the trees themselves almost as narrow as folded umbrellas. And *tall*. Douglas firs and Ponderosa pines, they should be, by the books, and the former are especially attractive with their long needles, entirely encircling the twigs, of a silvery cast. The Douglas fir grows taller than any other tree on the continent but the two sequoias, up to the height of a twenty-five-story building, and the lumber industry would be lost without it. . . . All is strange to me, the ground almost bare beneath the conifers, and a vivacious, seemingly imaginary bird, extraordinarily beautiful, with a black, highly crested head and black upper back and with wings and tail of a blue deep and luminous as the desert sky—a Steller's jay. And there is the alarming experience of finding myself winded, lungs laboring, after only a brief run. What can the matter be? . . . The matter is that I am almost nine thousand feet above sea-level.

From farther along up the road can be seen mountainsides of aspen forest, leafless and gray now but destined in autumn to transform the slopes into shimmering expanses of golden sequins. Pale-skinned of trunk—rather pea-soup colored—and growing as slim as the conifers, the Quaking aspen, though no very big tree, warrants respectful attention. Of all the trees in North America, it is the most widely distributed, at home on the East Coast between Virginia and Labrador and westward in a broad swath across the northern Middle West, Canada, and Alaska and thence down through the mountainous West into the Sierra Madre Occidental of Mexico—and, if you lump it and the very similar Old World form together, across Europe and Asia. It must be the most successful tree in the world. How is it that one species will thrive among its competitors over a large part of the world, as if it had an innate vigor and aggressiveness, while another, so sensitive in its requirements, so shrinking, as it were, will hold its own over a few hundred square miles only, like several species of Western pines?

All plants, of course, are successful only within certain latitudes of temperature and moisture. Temperature everywhere varies with altitude, and in the West, moisture does too, markedly. That is one reason why travel in the West, where altitudes themselves vary so greatly, is so fascinating. In general, away from the northern Pacific slope, which is rain-drenched from top to bottom, the greater the altitude the greater the precipitation, the cool air over mountains having the effect of condensing clouds. You can count on a new vegetation and a different bird-life with every two thousand feet of up or down, on the average; that tends to be the vertical breadth of a life-zone. Beginning with the Upper Austral of junipers and Pinyon pines, you can see five such zones from vantage points at Santa Fe, six from the Sierra Nevada, which are all there are in North America above the tropics.

There is a special satisfaction and comfort in seeing the changes take place as they should, just as there is in watching a drama of which the playwright is in sure control; to have a sense of order in what we are involved in is one of the most deep-seated and underestimated human needs, I think. On the gravel road up which the bus is taking me, you leave the Ponderosa pine and the Transition Zone (twenty to twenty-five inches of annual precipitation) at about 9,000 feet and the Douglas fir and the Canadian Zone (twenty-five to thirty inches) at about 10,500. There you enter the Hudsonian Zone (thirty to thirty-five inches) and a forest of Engelmann spruce and Subalpine fir, which also have a silvery cast of foliage. Through most of the Rocky Mountains these two species, standing like ramrods, ascend the slopes as far as trees can stand at all. Above timberline there are only rocks, low grasses, and sedges, prostrate flowering plants and lichens—the Arctic Zone. Into this is thrust the summit of Old Baldy, which from two miles away resembles one of the Smokies, though it is over 12,600 feet high and in early May still partly snow-covered. The Arctic meadow that Mr. Küchler's map shows on its crest is the southernmost in the United States, the last before the giant volcanoes below Mexico City, of which the tallest is a full 6,000 feet higher than Old Baldy—and what would one not give for a chance to start in the hot lowlands inland of Vera Cruz and work one's way up to the snow fields on Mount Orizaba! The nearer the Equator, the higher the levels at which the life-zones occur, of course, and the nearer the Poles the lower. Timberline, which is about 12,000 feet at the latitude of Santa Fe, reaches sea-level at Hudson Bay and on the Yukon River.

The descent to Santa Fe is steep, past gnarled crags of reddish and salmon-colored granite outcropping in the forest—the rocks of the pre-Paleozoic basement and perhaps of the Appalachians; for, incredibly enough, the Southern Rockies are composed in part of the rock of one of the two extreme western spurs of that most elongate eastern range. Santa Fe itself appears to have a quality of an outcropping of what is indigenous and old. After numberless American cities that occupy the land by right of conquest, this, one feels, is what one has been looking for. Santa Fe gives an impression of having, at least in part, grown out of it and out of man's experience of its setting. No dwellings, even the log cabins introduced by the Swedes or the sod houses of the prairie-settlers, could be more an outgrowth of the land than adobe structures, which are integral with the soil; and the mission style of architecture which developed from them is the style of Santa Fe. Pink-brown, like adobe, with rounded edges and slightly sloping sides and with the ends of the roof beams often protruding, the houses and other buildings seem to rise naturally from the ground. Perhaps there could be more variation in hue without departure from the tradition; but the combination of earth color and the intense and lively green of trees, shrubbery, and vines in the plazas and narrow streets, where the plants grow or pour over garden walls, is like an anointment of the spirit, a benediction after the discords built into most other cities. Harmony of structure and setting: without it can there ever be ease of mind?

That business buildings should conform to the mission style of architecture, as do the Bank of Santa Fe, Sears, Roebuck, Montgomery Ward, Safeway, and others, may seem a bit ridiculous. It is a little like a soap tycoon and his overweight wife donning court dress to be received at Buckingham Palace by the heir of Alfred, Harold, and the Plantagenets. Yet it is still good, I am persuaded. It is right in both cases for merchantdom to do obeisance to an idea of man that is not wholly subservient to the vagaries of time and the marketplace, even in a society supported by merchantdom. After Saint Augustine, Santa Fe is the oldest town in the United States; it claims that a small adobe house it possesses, much like an above-ground cave, is the oldest continuously inhabited building in the country; its cathedral incorporates part of a church believed to have been erected in 1627. Undeniably, though, the Santa Fe that so fits its setting is largely an artifice. It is not a spontaneous expression like the Zia Pueblo's adobe dwellings which cluster as naturally on a hill above a marshy river not far from the city as the semicylindrical nests of Mud-dauber wasps on a rock face. Yet one may argue that naturalness, once we have broken out of the matrix of Nature, is to be achieved only at the end of sophistication, like the naturalness we lose with childhood and regain only with maturity, a maturity to be attained only after long travail, and not by everyone. At any rate, gazing up past a sheer adobe wall through the budding branches of a tree into the heavenly deep blue of the desert sky, the sun warm on one cheek, the air cool on the other, I can only envy those to whom this is steady fare.

They themselves add to the attraction of the town—even though, from living so much in the bus, I feel like a tramp in their eyes. Among the faces one sees there is intelligence, sensitivity, and cultivation. In expressing such a view, one is uncomfortable; in our society, no one is better than anyone else—if as good as. And it is true that those of whom I am speaking belong to a privileged minority. But I cannot conceal from myself that, regardless, I greatly prefer persons of quality and, if one could be sure that the privileged were those who deserved to be, should be very glad to see more privilege rather than less. The problem, of course, is with criteria. The ability to make money, either through individual talent and drive or through ganging up with one's fellow operatives to extort more from the public than one's contribution would bring of itself, is not one to be regarded with enthusiasm. Still, it is remarkable how many estimable persons have gone to the top in our country, where this criterion largely prevails, along with the boors and thugs. Indeed, it is amazing when you take account of how inhuman the machinery is for getting ahead and making money in an industrial society—grim or tawdry and mercilessly competitive. This machinery, which the elect of Santa Fe have come here to get away from, reigns nevertheless, to be truthful, over the main approaches to the town, which are like those of any other in suggesting a world's fair of the harlotry of commercialism.

In Santa Fe's little park there are persons of other kinds at odds with the civilization those approaches stand for. One of them is a long-haired, elderly Indian under a high-crowned hat with small, black eyes set close to a thin, blade-like nose—the whole figure is bladelike: a flint knife. And he is totally unseeing, it would appear. Such creatures as I do not impinge on his consciousness. He seems oblivious even of the woman beside him, presumably his wife. She, however, being a woman and one apparently nourished on fat as her husband on lean, is necessarily an habituée of the practical world in which children are reared, meals prepared, and refrigerators latched onto if obtainable, and hence is well aware of her surroundings; apprehending and cataloguing me is the work of a glance. But the man: what goes on in his mind? As well ask what the thoughts are of a pinioned hawk: they could not be expressed in terms comprehensible to me, and the nearer they were brought to it the more they would become my thoughts and cease to be the hawk's.

The thoughts of four or five outsiders of a different sort nearby would be more comprehensible, I imagine, but not wholly so. These are young drop-outs of mixed sexes, shaggy of hair and of costume. Sitting around a monument in the park, they are inert, slow and vacuous as reptiles sunning themselves. Perhaps they are a bit drugged. It has become impossible to contemplate the drop-outs of our society, with their rejection of material acquisition and the supremacy of reason and their predilection for oriental mysticism and the occult without thinking also of the drop-outs of imperial Rome, among whom were the Christians. These had their own narcotic, a whole-souled belief in the imminence of the Second Coming and their own advent into eternal paradise. Arnold J. Toynbee says that "if you had asked a citizen of the Christian Roman Empire whether the anchorites and stylites were performing any valuable function by withdrawing from society, he would have replied that by withdrawing from it they were saving it." The same claim has been made for those of our youth who are taking to the hills, joining in rural communes, or in other ways creating what Theodore Rosak, the California professor, calls a counter-culture. The thought does obtrude itself, however, that those who held that the Christians were saving Roman society were revealed as poor prophets. While Christianity itself proved to be the wave of the future (though a wave that Christ himself might not have acknowledegd or even recognized), the Christian Roman Empire collapsed utterly—some say with Christianity itself implicated in the disaster—and was succeeded by four centuries of cruel barbarism and darkness. One may doubt that the rebellious young or very many others accustomed to the security, comforts, and luxuries we have been brought up on would care for the kind of existence to be expected in the aftermath of a similar debacle befalling our own civilization—an existence only a minority would have any hope of clinging to at that.

Yet I am persuaded that the more one can free oneself of dependence on Technocracia the better off, on the whole, one will be; and more, that the greater the number who go this way, the better the prospects will be for mankind. It would be a way of holding the juggernaut within bounds. Why then not flee Technocracia and strike out anew under a simple regimen far from the city and close to the soil? Is it a matter of inability to forego those conveniences and material rewards Technocracia heaps on its favorites? Not altogether, I should say, or even of one's bonds with one's fellow beings; these might be closer away from the distractions and pressures one would be putting behind.

Against a return to Nature, in the sense of cutting oneself off from civilization, Nature itself speaks up. It is Nature's imperative, urged by the genetic impulses of millions of years of the survival of the fittest, to meet the challenge of the environment and prevail against it, not shrink from it. *Succeed* is Nature's one injunction, which to the male animal means also: *Make your presence felt.* And though there may be little in one to suggest the stag waking the echoes of the hills with his trumpeting, of the bighorn ram meeting his adversary head-on in a clap of thunder, still less of the thrush at evening constraining the world to hold its breath to listen to its mellifluous cadenzas, yet one is obedient to the inner compulsion to count for something—a compulsion that does not necessarily by any means spare the female of our species either. And if the likelihood of coming to feel that one does count grows more diminished in a civilization ever more massive, complex, and indifferent, one goes on trying. Even for Henry David Thoreau, contentment was not Walden alone. It was Walden plus making the world listen to it.

One goes on grappling with the juggernaut, moreover—so my friend John George, a graduate of the East Africa bush, would tell me—because one is the tribal hunter schooled by countless millennia of wilderness to safeguard his young from the cave-bear and equip them to cope with the cave-bear when their time comes. One's children may turn their backs on the fields that provide the abundant life in order to avoid the embrace of today's cave-bear— a civilization of industrial conglomerates, mass-media, predatory pressure groups, and the cult of the public image. They may feel that the benefits the system affords are not worth the price it exacts. But one wishes the choice to be theirs, not to have it made for them.

Lastly, one stays around to raise a protesting voice, however feeble, at outrages against Nature and to give such support as one can to the valiant defenders of what remains.

In driving westward, I have come to a part of the country where the federal government has long been waging a merciless campaign against the original inhabitants of the land. Coyotes, prairie-dogs, squirrels, and gophers are poisoned wholesale, with badgers, bears, foxes, raccoons, ferrets, skunks, hawks, eagles, and vultures as incidental victims of the massacre. (Apart from the backing the operation has among ranchers and farmers, the jobs of many scores of hacks in the "Wildlife Services Division"—yes, that is its name, the *Wildlife Services Division*—of the Department of the Interior are at stake in it.) It is a part of the country where mountainsides are sprayed with herbicides to eliminate plants that divert rainfall from the shower-baths and swimming-pools of the spreading subdivisions. . . . There is always something to keep one reminded of what is in store, everywhere, as man's appetite for ever more material goods on top of his proliferating numbers diminishes his tolerance of other forms of life that draw on resources he means to commandeer.

It makes me think how much our ancestors were spared, not to have to worry about man's growing too powerful at Nature's expense and laying waste the earth. They should, of course, have worried more than they did—those who left the deserts stretching from Rajputana to Mauretania and scalped the hills of Greece and Italy. Presumably, however, the degradation proceeded too slowly for them to be aware of it. Living under Nature's rule was harsh, but at least man could then live naturally—which is to say aggressively, taking all he could gather into his hands without troubling himself about the consequences. Nature limited his powers to work mischief and his own undoing. It was an enemy able to give as good as it received and one, moreover, that augmented the stature of him able to contend with it. You strove with weapon, ax, or plow to the limit of your capacities and bred children as you listed and your only concern was that your capacities might not be sufficient. Frontiersman and husbandman, villager and townsman alike could rejoice in each new victory over Nature, confident that each enhanced his prospects or his people's.

Such simpler times lasted in the American West until less than a century ago; and we may well look back on them with nostalgia, beset and harassed as we are by warring considerations. The age-old battle for existence has been transferred from without to within us. The task has been forced on us of reconciling the claims of our instincts of self-aggrandizement with the claims of the earth we inhabit, which those instincts are driving us to destroy piecemeal, with consequences that very plainly are catching up with us. The passions and appetites with which Nature endowed us for survival in the natural order drive us as hard as ever but without Nature's controls now that we have gone so far in freeing ourselves from the natural order and making ourselves superior to it. Indeed, with imagination to incite them, they drive us far harder.

Like many another twelve-year-old who is captivated by birds and wild creatures in general, and by the idea of the wild, I was on their side against man, and I remained so for some years. And I still am—more accurately, against *men*. But this is not because I prefer Nature to man, as I once supposed I did. My concern with Nature is with what it must mean to man—man the paragon of Nature. The understanding of physical creation man has gained moves one to inexpressible admiration, the warmth of his magnanimous personality floods the heart with emotion, and his works of art put one in transports. And it is because man in the fullness of his self-realization is so great that human beings in their debasement—the brutes, the criminals, the vandals, the slobs, the vulgarians—rouse one to such wrath: traitors, all of them, to those who have exalted our kind. And it is because one is concerned with man that one is on Nature's side—as two centuries and more ago it would hardly have occurred to one to be.

Man, it seems to me, has grandeur only as his background has grandeur. He is inseparable from what he is part of. In a setting of natural moment, he gains moment, as an actor from the greatness of the drama in which he is cast. Whether you are exhilarated or discomforted by the spectacle of wild mountains, cavernous forests and storm-lashed shores, it can hardly be that you do not feel that the figure of man against such a landscape has a stature and consequence it lacks amid the boundless warrens of the metropolis. In a world still vast, still largely untamed and unexplored, the human experience had a savor and a quality of heroic adventure which I think must be lost—whatever else we may gain—as Nature is subdued to model cities, mechanized farms and the "recreational facilities" of crowded billions on continents traversable between meals.

There are, to be sure, the lunar and interplanetary voyages. But the astronauts, zippered up and almost immovable in their space gear, like children in snowsuits, contained in all-providing capsules, the near-puppets of ten thousand technicians and acres of electronic machinery, seem to me unbelievably courageous but not heroic figures as the early navigators of the dread Atlantic were heroic figures as they fought the seas alone with bare hands swollen by the brine-soaked ropes, in barks of timbers hand-hewn and mortised by men with only their muscles to drive their tools. Perhaps, too, because in the primitive recesses of my heart I see the forest-girt and craggy hills as the abode of gods I am far from cast down by instances of the earth's refractoriness to technocracy's designs; let it act up and make trouble! Lest I be thought a monster, I shall not particularize beyond confessing that when the press acclaimed the conquest at last of Chomo-lungma (Mount Everest, it called the mountain) I deeply regretted the event. If I had my way, the would-be conquerors of great mountains would find the obstacles insurmountable and turn back, or, if they persisted in the assault, which after all nobody asked them to undertake, perish in the attempt. If civilization were forced back from a goodly portion of the earth by a resurgent Nature, I should not be inconsolable in my grief over the loss to mankind. If fatal maladies were found to afflict those who design airplanes and missiles, I could bear it.

Traveling westward from Santa Fe, and especially beyond the Colorado Plateau, a day's journey ahead of me, you see mountains, and not a few of them, standing stark as the day the white man first beheld them and looking still unbroken to man's whims. They rise behind sere and barren flatlands, those with juniper-freckled flanks likely to resemble newspaper crumpled vertically. And you know that if you were set down in them it would mean death. Dehydrated by the wind—the one that fans you when you leave the car—you would die terribly of thirst. You wonder how those waterless, lethal wastes ever got explored.

Leaving Santa Fe, you see from one spot mountains of more different origins than you would in the entire eastern three-fifths of the continent. At the goat's chin on the right are the domed and gently peaked summits of the extinct super-volcano of the Jemez formation, topped by 11,250-foot Redondo. On the left, to the south, looking as if accumulated of sand trickling from a perforated box, are the Ortiz, an erosional remnant of a plain, but with igneous bodies in them. (A small, obscure range, the Ortiz in the 1820's provided a hint about the continent of the greatest importance to the inhabitants, but nobody grasped it.) Then, coming around broadside after a terrific descent to the Rio Grande past great blocks of red and golden sandstone, the Sandias rise on the left, a recrudescence of the Southern Rockies, *very austere and grand, of incised cones and hatchet-blade cliffs,* I exclaim to the recorder. Road-maps—the oil companies' sterling philanthropy—tell you what mountains you are seeing, and they are the only maps I know that will. Albuquerque surrounds a long oasis—the wooded banks of the Rio Grande. The fresh, succulent green of the leafy trees after the desert is as refreshing as watercress, though traffic on Interstate 40 sweeps you along too fast for you to enjoy it much. From thirty-nine degrees in the Okus, the temperature has risen to ninety-two.

Like a virgin violated on her wedding night. This purple thought, which I trust I should never have consciously conceived, may be recorded as part of the sociology of the trip since it comes to me, literally, while I am asleep at night as descriptive of the experience of a debutant to the West on U. S. 66 beyond Albuquerque. *Billboards, billboards on either side. And an Indian reservation. "Buy now. Real Indian Hogan. Be prepared. Desert ahead. Ice. Gas up. Thermojugs. Desert ahead." Real desert now, the dead grass only half concealing the dry, gravelly sand. Not a green thing in sight except the backs of the billboards on the other side of the highway. God, how dreary. "Deckhouse. Squaw books. Mexican serapes. Cactus hankies, 6 for $1.00. Last chance water-bags, post cards, stamps. See free diamond-backed rattler." . . . "This is it. Navajo trading post. Ice-cold pop. Gas. Free shade. Ice jugs iced. . . ."*

But it never stays the same for long. We have been climbing grades the bus can hardly make in high, and there are mesas to be exclaimed over; 125 miles this side of Arizona, we have, I judge, gained the Colorado Plateau. *We can see huge mesas all around before us. . . . There's one off to the north topped by a great red-sandstone wall. The whole face of a mesa we are passing quite close to now on the south is a mass of big blocks of mauve sandstone that have tumbled down from the capping. The mauve blocks capping one mesa look a hundred feet from top to bottom.*

Lunch is always an especially agreeable occasion. Little housekeeping is to be done then. I am still not tired and have lots of day on both sides of me. Midday is more timeless than morning or evening. Time then is flat, not deep, echoing and mysterious as at the halfway stages between day and night. Pleasantly winded from a jog, relieved of the demands of driving and with a good appetite to be indulged, I feel as relaxed and expansive as if I had been poured out of a bottle. From the windows of my traveling den, in which I am as thoroughly at home as a nautilus in its shell and a lot better provided for, I gaze out upon a wholly new and exotic landscape. I feel as free inwardly as the balls of tumbleweed that go rolling and bouncing across the highway in the gayest, most delightful fashion, and as well served by life as one could legitimately hope to be.

The landscape at lunch today is of lava fields. These, say a sign at the rest area that has been laid out here to exhibit them, extend for forty miles and are between one and two thousand years old— no more than that. While some is solid rock, a great deal of the lava near by and for miles on the road to Gallup resembles aerated asphalt, with the lines of flow preserved in it, and some looks like clinkers, straight out of the furnace. One of the surprises the West has in store is the evidence of how widely it has been under volcanic assault, if that is the word. In the past 70 million years, according to the Geological Survey, large parts of the Rocky Mountain states and Texas and nearly all of the states westward of them have been covered by volcanic rock. The geologic map shows that this rock still forms the surface of much of the region's higher parts.

Lava—molten rock—behaves in ways as wildly different as the forms it hardens in, which include the densest and heaviest rock that ordinarily reaches the surface of the earth, rock that is sponge-like in texture, rock so frothy it floats, and natural glass, such as obsidian. In places it simply wells up out of the earth, as it did to form the Columbia-Snake Plateau and the broad, shield-type volcanoes of the Hawaiian Islands; lava of this kind is basaltic. In others, having steam in it, it erupts violently in lumps and blobs to form tall, conical volcanoes like those of the Cascades and Aleutian Islands; this sort tends to be intermediate in composition between basalt and granite and is called andesite. (Basalt is of iron-manganese compounds and feldspar, granite largely of feldspar and a lesser proportion of quartz, and andesite mostly of feldspar alone.) Basalt is usually very dark gray or greenish-gray to nearly black, andesite a lighter gray. A third kind of volcanic eruption sends up vast outpourings of incandescent grit which fuses solidly on settling. Thousands of square miles of the West's highlands were created in this fashion, of lava which in composition is all the way over on the granite side and is called rhyolite. (Granite is called granite only when the molten minerals of which it is composed have cooled deep underground and so slowly that they have had a chance to sort themselves out and form large, homogeneous crystals.) The dull brown rhyolite predominates in large parts of the San Juans, the Yellowstone Mountains, the lava mountains of the Basin-and-Range Province, the Jemez and the Chisos Mountains. These last rise far to the south in western Texas where the Rio Grande dips deep into Mexico—the Big Bend area.

Before I set off on my trip I tried to lay out a course that would take in as much as possible of the country's physiography within the mileage I thought I could cover. With two small extensions, I doubt if it could be greatly improved on within a limit of ten thousand miles. But what if a respectable allotment of time were available? I often think what a pleasantly challenging task it would be to design a trip to do as full justice to the country's varied character as could be contrived for a traveler with a month or six weeks to spare. One place I have to forego that I should certainly try to include in the ideal excursion is Big Bend National Park. I say this on the strength of visiting it the next summer on a month's camping trip with my wife and daughters.

Ogres among mountains: that, if you are like me, is the thought that comes to you on the road to Big Bend as you near the cluster of the Chisos, jagged and weird in silhouette across the desert. Lava mountains, in my experience, are always somber; you feel they have brought the quality of the underworld up with them. But that is their strength too. In shades of brown earth-color, the Chisos rise in sheer cliffs from the conical slopes of their detritus like fangs thrust up out of gums. And to what splendid heights, what commanding domes, crowns, and pinnacles, 4,000 feet above the desert floor, the scored rock rises! In the mile-high "Basin," where the campground is, you are up among these relics, the cores of volcanoes that have survived the wearing-down of the softer rock around them. Five of the peaks rise to between 7,000 and 7,800 feet in a semicircle before you. If it is true that the name given them comes from the Spanish *hechizos,* meaning "enchantment," you can understand up here how it came about. Hour by hour the deeply chiseled and precipitous

tors around you are transfigured as the shadows, advancing or re-
treating with the sun's movement, bring out new shapes among the
flange-like buttresses and grotesque towers and steeples. In the morning, when the giants seem purposefully to breast the sun, the varying shades of the weather-stained, granite-born lava, the light browns
and pale reddish browns, stand out most clearly. By noon the color
has nearly faded out and the massive forms seem less substantial,
seem withdrawn in a dreamy, blue-misty somnolence. With the lowering of the sun they come to life again and the rites of evening see
the rock faces illumined orange against the dark shadows, then
stained crimson while the farther ranges stand out in a depthless,
dusty purple.

The great volcanic structures are only some of the monuments to
the upheavals dramatized here. On the way south to Big Bend Park
from Marathon, you pass what could be a super Great Wall of China
undulating along the sides of a chain of mountains—the up-ended
strata forming their skeletons. On the southern borders of the park
are the famous gorges of the Rio Grande. These came about as a
consequence of the uprearing of blocks of limestone miles long
above the surrounding plains from what, in late Mesozoic times,
had been the bottom of a sea extending inland to western Texas.
This uptilting of monstrous blocks of the earth's crust is what makes
the Basin-and-Range Province what it is, and at Big Bend you are
on the Province's southeastern edge—the edge of the sleeve sus-
pended from the mitten.

The uptilting evidently took place with a deliberateness that
made nothing of time, slowly enough for the Rio Grande to wear
down its bed as fast as the rock rose beneath it. Santa Elena Canyon
is the name given to the ten-mile-long defile it has cut, and for depth
and narrowness there can hardly be anything on the continent surpassing it. A trail goes up into it from its mouth, skirting the little
beaches along the river and the blocks of pale gray limestone, some
house-sized, that have toppled down from the heights. You can follow it upstream with little effort though not entirely without a
sensation that the irregular, layered walls, holding close communion
with each other hundreds of feet overhead, are going to close in on
you. Downstream of the defile, the highlands, beside which the river
flows after making a right-angle bend on breaking through to the
sunlight, rise in the background more than 10,000 feet above sea-
level—such has been the uplift of the old limestone sea-bottom.

The tableland thus raised is Mexico, of course, but in staring up at it, at the long precipice in which it breaks off, standing 8,000 feet above you, all so immense, you feel it to be outside the human scheme of things altogether. As for the Rio Bravo del Norte itself, as the Mexicans call it, when not in flood it is not much of a river. Thirty feet wide and easily wadable, it meanders between broad banks of sand and cobbles lined with little Seep willows, ten-foot-high stands of tasseled reeds (*Phragmites*) and the small trees with a stringy version of juniper foliage called tamarisks. Yet to how many victims of the desert in the course of time this ribbon of water between its living, green embankments has meant the sudden, unreserved gift of life, of heaven itself!

You are not long in the desert before you find water always on your mind—less than an hour: water as the life-blood of the living. As you drive, your eyes are constantly seeking out evidence of moisture—the creases in the sterile mountainside with dark threadings of juniper and Pinyon pine, the dark bandings at the foot of cliffs, bottomlands where the sparse vegetation of the desert takes on a livelier green or there is a higher mound of it, meaning trees. The arroyos, dry as they appear, are crowded with the plants that on the flats are widely sprinkled out. Since here in western Texas this is the Chihuahuan Desert—Chihuahua itself is only across the border —these are the many-stemmed Creosote bush with very small, olive-drab leaves and fuzzy, white fruit, and acacias, a legume like mesquite with its rows of leaflets pale and tiny and bearing yellow or white balls of flowers. These two go on for endless miles, sometimes with Ocotillas putting up their whip-like branches resembling the attenuated tentacles of some sea creature, stinging-cells and all, or with a few man-high yuccas which, with heads of bristling blades on trunks around which the blades hang lifeless, make you think of gaunt human figures, armless and shaggily cloaked. If this were the Sonoran Desert, on the other side of the Sierra Madre Occidental and in southern Arizona, there would be Giant saguaros and, along the stream washes, that other great desert legume, yellow-flowering palo verde with its green branches.

At the higher elevations there is Sotol, a sphere of radiating, sharp-toothed leaves like a yucca's from which rises a veritable war-club of a flower-stalk, its head a cylinder of creamy blossoms. There is Lechuguilla, forming beds of even more dangerous, needle-pointed leaves and producing a similar flower-stalk, but one with the blooming portion like the glowing embers of a torch. Most spectacularly of all, and in the Chisos Mountains alone, there is the maguey, *Agave scabra,* most splendid of the "century-plants" and a close relative of the mescal, source of the fermented beverages tequila and pulque. The flower-stalk of the maguey, as big at the base as a man's ankle, rises fifteen feet or more with horizontal members bearing cushions of flowers at their ends, like curry-brushes bristle-side up, those at the top of the stalk orange, the others yellow. The stalk, when its season comes, grows at a rate approaching a foot a day and is so taxing to produce that the plants require from ten to thirty years to amass sufficient reserves and never survive the effort. But what a consummation, this raising of a standard in which one so far surpasses oneself, a spear-shaft of a dozen arms each holding a handful of living gold to the sky!

What is it one looks for in the natural world that keeps bringing one back, to take note of what one sees? What one looks for anywhere, I should think, is but one thing: how better to bear one's lot in life. Is not that the question to which we ceaselessly seek answers? Nature can hardly supply one that will fully meet our needs. Only a revealed religion promising an after-life can do that, and only for one who can take it on faith, and only at a cost of separating the believer from much of the richness of his earthly abode. His needs are satisfied by a packaged and complete truth, and he hardly knows the hunger that drives the hunter on and focuses his senses. No one who has pursued the quest in Nature has ever discovered a truth so satisfying as to persuade him he need look no farther. His discoveries may even leave him worse off than he was before. It could happen that the spectacle of unending carnage that Nature presents would put him off Nature altogether and bring him to look on life itself with horror. Most of us are probably acquainted with that revulsion. Little more is required to excite it than, for example, the hairy tarantula creeping across the desert road like some long- and eight-fingered, detached monkey's paw. It is not pleasant to think of the spider crushing a beetle of awkwardly waving legs in its jaws, still less to think of its own helplessness before the wasp known as the tarantula-hawk, which will paralyze it with the venom of its stinger to preserve it for the nurture of its young. Then when we multiply the individual victims by the dimensions of life on land and in the oceans, we may well see the planet as a place of unspeakable nightmare. (Those, however, to whom Nature is characteristically "red in tooth and claw" and to be recoiled from do not generally reject steaks cut from pole-axed cows, the breasts of chickens bled to death through severed jugulars or the skins of furbearers held in the vise of steel jaws pending the trapper's leisure.) But if we try to take a sum of global sufferings, do we arrive at a conception with any meaning? Can the dimensions of suffering be greater than the capacity of a single sufferer? Nature, for all its seeming callousness, has made a most merciful provision for those under its dominion. Wild creatures, living in the present moment with little memory or anticipation of suffering, must endure only such suffering as the present moment may encompass. The herd of zebras, once the lion has made its kill, graze placidly, agonizing neither over what has been nor over what must be. Wild animals, uncaged wild animals, taking things as they come, do not generally give an impression of sorrowing. Only man does that. It is for man and man alone to endure interminable vistas of anguish. That is the fearful price he pays for the mind that has made him autonomous.

But if a return to Nature in the sense of re-entering the natural order is not really a choice open to us, and if Nature cannot relieve us of the pain of living as religion may the trustful, recourse to its province may yet moderate that pain. Under the sky, responding to physical demands on us—miles to be hiked, the elements to be met with hardihood, soil to be turned—we come more under the beneficence accorded animals and to live in the present with less of us left over for cares behind or ahead. There is that in Nature, moreover, which provides something of what we look for in religion but without sacrifice of open-mindedness. Sir Kenneth Clark, the justly renowned historian of art, speaks in *Civilisation* of "that belief in nature which expressed itself in the landscape painting of the nineteenth century and has remained the most productive source of popular art to this day." Actually, as he observes elsewhere, the feeling for nature inspiring that belief appears as early as the fifteenth century in "the first evolved landscape in European painting, the background of van Eyck's *Adoration of the Lamb*," in which "our eyes, passing over the dense greenery of laurel and ilex, float into a gleaming distance." Ever since then Nature has been progressively supplanting religion as an inspiration of art. The "belief in nature," Clark goes on to say, is one that "cannot be justified by reason alone and seems to lift the life of the senses onto a higher plane."

The belief has no doubt a number of sources, even apart from all we ourselves owe Nature—all our sensory satisfactions and life itself. Chief among the others is perhaps the radiance and splendor of Nature, that "gleaming distance" to which the eye is led in the van Eyck landscape. Then there is that marvelous order of Nature inherent in the character of matter and process and, in the realm of the living, a matter of checks and balances requiring only that each living being strive to realize itself. The universe may serve no humanly recognizable purpose, but it is not chaotic. The beauties of Nature testify to its symmetry, balance and internal harmonies: that, I think, is why they *are* beautiful. It is a universe of laws, and where there are laws there is an Authority; however, in this case, it is to be conceived. Whatever else one may be riven by doubts about, there is the security of knowing that the cosmos of which one is part is an ordered whole. And there is the vitality of Nature, in the rampaging of the storm and the raising of mountains and in the quiet of a plant.

To see a plant, self-created in its green foliage out of the inert soil, outstretched and unfolded in an acclamation of the sun, and so beautifully organized withal, and bursting with flowers that cry, "Here I am, I am!"—to see this, really to see in the plant what it says of life, one must be far gone in despair indeed not to feel a little more like living oneself. And the profession that plants make, those of the desert make with special force. I think the thrall the desert casts on many may be partly explained by its combining a vision of what is vast and raw, monumental and elemental in the cosmos, aloof and unappeasable, with the intimate appeal of small things awake with life and undaunted in their vulnerability by the harsh immensity. Employing every stratagem, every eccentricity of form to wrest a livelihood from the barren sand and gravel and cast a crop of seed where they will germinate, the plants are adventurers, explorers, all of them. To make do with the meager moisture they stand apart from one another and claim your attention as individuals, and stout ones too. As any impressionable person in the desert, where the structure of the earth stands so stark, becomes a geologist, so also he becomes knowledgeable about plants, each of which is a personality, even a celebrity.

Arid plains with a sparse growth of Creosote bush the color of World War II Army woolens. On the nearer, worn, gravelly hills the yuccas stand about like souls in purgatory watching the mortals pass. There is a hot, dry wind and a spent silence. Off in the west are mountains topped by deeply gouged cliffs, a whole procession of them, their very shadows hot. After such landscapes—this one between Big Bend and New Mexico—it is a joy that the Prophet might have promised to climb to an elevation at which more rain is extracted from the clouds and the stringencies for plants are less cruel. On the trail out from the Basin at Big Bend, in addition to the Sotol, Lechuguilla, and man-high clumps of Prickly-pear, assembled of sections resembling splayed feet fringed with big toes, there is positively shadowy vegetation in the moister draws. The little White oaks called Gambel's oaks shelter there together with Pinyon pines, junipers, including Alligator junipers of plated trunks and lovely, gray-green foliage, and shiny-leaved sumac. The trees are depressed and dwarfed and in this conform to the feeling one has of being in one of childhood's private sanctuaries. The air is cool and aromatic with the breath of the pines, among which a free-booting band of blue-and-gray Mexican jays is disporting clamorously. It is purely delicious. The scent of Pinyons is of newly cut branchlets of hickory or pecan.

Another reason for including Big Bend in a model itinerary is the chance it gives, in driving on to New Mexico, to skirt the pediments of the Guadalupes. Forming a southward-pointing V, fifty miles on a leg, the Guadalupe Range, like the Mesa de Anguila, through which the Santa Elena Canyon has been cut, is an uplifted block of limestone, but limestone of a far more ancient sea. The whole right-hand leg of the V, including the point, is a section of a monster reef, many hundreds of feet in height, which almost encircled that sea. It is in this part that underground streams, when the block was below the water-table, leached out the miles of corridors and caves known as Carlsbad Caverns, the greatest limestone caverns in the world. (Not even yet fully explored, they include one room with "a floor as extensive as 14 football fields," the National Park Service notes, "and a ceiling as high as a 22-story building.") The approach from the south is across those desiccated plains. For miles the range is no more than a misty shape ahead. Gradually it looms before you until you are gazing up at a fluted block of limestone at the apex of the range that towers on its broad, pyramidal pedestal to 4,000 feet above you. Behind El Capitan and separated from it, Guadalupe Peak rises an additional 550 feet, to 8,750 feet above sea-level, the range's highest and also Texas's. One marvels to think of that giant reef, of which El Capitan is only a fragment, built up over 200 million years ago by minute sea-creatures. But there is a picture in your mind almost as wonderful as that, when you have come to the range from across the Salt Basin. It is almost as wonderful, even, as that vertical mass of stone ascendant against the blue sky like a vision of a tower of Notre Dame de Paris in vestal white, on a scale of fifty to one. The picture, as you drive along beside the mesa-like range, looking up at the crest clad in dark pine forest, is of the canyons back in there that collect the rainfall the Guadalupes conjure from the temperamental heavens. Of these, one even has a permanent stream which, as Weldon Heald, a conservation writer of the Southwest, reports it, "musically cascades down its rock bed between borders of arching trees." One must feel one has come upon a secret Eden. Mule deer and elk are numerous in the range and, as Mr. Heald writes, a few mountain lions and Black bears still linger in the upper canyons, while a small band of Bighorn sheep also survives on the cliffs. It is a world apart.

There is no chance on the family trip to go up into the Guadalupes, but there is an opportunity to make up for it at Mesa Verde, just inside Colorado at the edge of the Colorado Plateau, and to be astonished all over again at the difference two thousand feet can make. Climbing up above the buff sandstone cliffs walling the precipitous drops, you enter mountainous uplands, forested and with inviting grassy valleys. In addition to the usual somber conifers— and beside them, it strikes me, like a salad after a diet of starches —there are slopes brightly verdant with leafy vegetation, Gambel's oaks and bush oaks of glossy foliage and the dense shrub called Mountain mahogany. And the flowers! Your eye travels from the orange of Indian paintbrush and of Shooting star, with blossoms like Trumpet honeysuckle's, to lupine with its sensational spires of blue to Yellow melilot and Carmine thistle—and to the Mariposa lilies, or Butterfly tulips. These last, with their disks of three petals, creamy to yellow to a near flame-color, of a waxy purity and delicacy, are so lovely, turning up their faces to you, that they appear, as noted beauties among women habitually do, to be posing for their pictures. . . . No, it is more than what I have said about flowers. Almost, they have the power to dispel one's better judgment and make one fall in love with life.

Greenwood islands of fragrant shadows above an ocean of drought: such are the mountain heights in the desert. Partly because of a notion I have that Nature, like the Oracle at Delphi, answers with parables, if at all, the questions that gnaw at us, I cling to the knowledge I have acquired from reading that always above the most parched and seemingly interminable flatlands, two miles in elevation in the rugged and intractable-looking ranges, there are glades where the murmur of flowing water is heard, where deer graze on sweet meadow grass and snatches of birdsong pierce the quiet of the pines.

6

CROSSING THE
DESERT—II

Mesa overlapping mesa, terminating in red-sandstone cliffs hundreds of feet high on the way to Gallup, some nearly detached, like towers, the road rising to a crest at the Continental Divide and a raven coasting by, looking like a flying cross of an emblematic kind. Then, on the other side of the Arizona line, a procession of magnificent yellow headlands of weathered sandstone walls sloping back to the crenellated brows of the mesas, all powerfully sculptured in rounded forms that stand out from the cliff faces. The Colorado Plateau is the place of the megalithic structures superbly contoured that stand commandingly against the desert sky in all the hues and flowing smoothness of water-shaped sandstones. Confusingly named, since only a wedge of its northeastern side is in the state of Colorado, the Plateau was raised in the two crustal uplifts, each lasting millions of years, that also raised the Central and Southern Rockies. One reached its climax at the dawn of the present, Cenozoic era, 60 million years ago, the other perhaps 30 million years ago, though this is debatable. Altogether, the Plateau must have been elevated more than two miles. Since the beginning of the process, superincumbent sedimentary rocks to a depth of more than a mile have been eroded away, exposing strata laid down in Mesozoic times and even in later Paleozoic where the uplift was greatest, especially in the Kaibab Plateau of northwestern Arizona—a plateau above a plateau—through which the Colorado River has cut the Grand Canyon. The erosion was uneven, however, and left remnants of younger rocks standing above the older of every form—even buttresses that have been undercut by streams to create natural bridges. So today, in traversing the broad Plateau, almost the size of Texas, you feel that man has here ventured into the remains of a colosseum of a dimly human race of super-giants that has eluded history. You feel as the discoverers of Easter Island must have felt on beholding the stone heads gazing inscrutably off to sea, except that you look up not thirty or forty feet but hundreds or a thousand to the even more enigmatic petroglyphs of Time.

Extravagant is the architecture of the desert Plateau and extravagant the only words I can find for it. *Great cliffs topped by breastworks, entablatures of statuary displaying all the virtuosity and grandeur of Nature, a ruined Parthenon, a ruined Hagia Sophia.* This, actually, is from the family camping trip of the next summer, and from a route northwest from Santa Fe. State Highway 44, to be honest, passes some deadly plains. But after the irrigated green cropland and orchards of Farmington, stretching for miles along the San Juan and Las Animas Rivers, themselves bordered by willows and tamarisks, you soon find, rising ahead of you as you near the northwestern corner of the state, the extraordinary apparition of Shiprock. And not to be overlooked on the way to it—the highway passes by its feet—is a formation of sandstone blocks reminiscent of the giant figures of Rameses II and his queen cut in the living rock of Abu-Simbel. A cluster of volcanic cones, like the peaks of the Chisos, and like them also of brown rhyolite, Shiprock resembles a vastly greater Mont-Saint-Michel, a fasces of spired towers rising one above another to a height of fifteen hundred feet above the desert floor.

A dazzling succession of mesas in this area, step upon step in the distance. There is no disguising that I am helplessly subject to the impact of these frowning colossi of the ancient past. *What is particularly moving about these escarpments are the giant friezes of unformed figures composing their capping cliffs. These have a vitality of line and power of latency that many a contemporary sculptor has sought to capture. It is as if they descended from a time when the universal mind was itself only groping its way to self-consciousness. . . . Across northeastern Arizona the country becomes increasingly spectacular.*

It is the country of the illustrious Navajo red sandstone—or if it is not illustrious, it ought to be. "Take me to see your Navajo sandstones," should be the wish of every official visitor from abroad. In contrast to ordinary sandstones derived from deposits laid down on the bottom of the sea in level layers, the Navajo sandstones originated as enormous dunes on which the sand—and sand of a fine, pure kind—had been deposited by the wind in layers conforming to the dunes' shape. That was in the middle chapter of the Mesozoic era. Later, the desert in which these dunes arose was inundated by the sea and remained so for millions of years while the buried dunes were percolated and cemented by mineral-bearing waters. Probably these were rich in iron, accounting for the color of the sandstone thus created. It is not actually red, of course, but a pinkish-rosy tan, or tannish-rose. Where marine sandstones cut through by erosion or by man present a picture of straight, even courses, the strata of the happily termed aeolian sandstones are curved, as if the rock had hardened from a thick liquid poured, layer after layer, over a convex surface. The sweeping swirls are full of grace and where junipers and pines stand dark green and sagebrush a greenish gray against the soft brick-color of the flowing sandstone you have a picture to frame in the mind. The Navajo monoliths reach their most spectacular in the buttes, pinnacles, and spires of Monument Valley— unless it be in the thirty-story-high arch of Rainbow Bridge or the two-thousand-foot walls of the Virgin River (or Zion) canyons. On the otherwise empty plain of the valley you would think yourself among the widely scattered remains of an Attic city of temples and statuary of surpassingly heroic mold. But marvelous as these are, they do not exhaust the interest of that theatrical place. Among the statuesque and reposeful pantheons of the sandstone rise veritable geysers of rock, manifestations of Gaea, the earth-goddess, which, like Shiprock, are in fact the feeder tubes of otherwise obliterated volcanoes and are of soft shades of rhyolitic brown. While smaller than Shiprock, the largest of these, Agathlan, rises from lesser peaks to a soaring block of superb proportions.

Monument Valley extends from northeastern Arizona up into Utah, and as we follow its direction I am again, it appears, "dazzled" by the wealth and boldness of sculpturing in the lofty rock strata and by the shades of coloring. Yet my joy in them is compromised, I regret to say, because I cannot somehow possess them. Possessiveness withers the spirit, as we are told, and I have only too good reason to know; but I am what I am, alas, and: *one's collector's instinct is aroused to a fever pitch, but hopelessly, hopelessly.* It certainly rises to one before the blocky, sandstone cliffs for which the town of Bluff, Utah, is named. An old mining town and formerly a place of substance, or so several multi-storied stone houses of a Western style, two standing empty, would signify, Bluff might not be the most stimulating place in which to live. If a girl keeping a dingy shop there is any indication, it is not; she is a pathetic young creature, blonde, pregnant, and, one would say, quite defeated, with no wares to offer but some soft drinks, postcards, rocks, a basket of Indian shards, and second-hand furniture. But I am carried away by the sandstone bluffs themselves, which are of a soft, sandy color on top staining into pale chocolate below. They must be, I tell myself, among the most beautiful rock-structures in the world. I recognize that what I need is to be dumped somewhere out on the Colorado Plateau with no water and no knowledge of where to find any, to make me see that country with the eye of realism.

There are those who live far out in it, in the Navajo sandstone country and beyond. These are the Navajos themselves—and they cannot find their lot easy. You see their shacks or squat, cylindrical hogans—if that is what they are called—miles apart on the infertile lowlands below the great mesas, one or two small dwellings with an old car, lost in the limitless expanse. Occasionally there are a few cattle or a herd of sheep with some goats tended by a couple of children, and these children, when close enough to be seen well, are comely little fellows.

The Navajos are a striking-looking people. Of an even brown coloring, they are broad of face, suggesting Japanese with a large Mediterranean admixture, but of full stature and handsome. The women in colored-velvet jackets and plentiful skirts to their ankles remind one of gypsies. In the trading posts—genuine ones, here— both sexes appear utterly distant, unresponsive, inaccessible—and irreconcilable. Perhaps those whites who more nearly share their lives find them quite different, knowing them as individuals and hence not being afflicted by the diffidence I feel in their presence; for these I do *not* think are converts to television or the tourist trade. Indeed, they seem an alien people, of another world. If Technocracia in North America were knocked out, as by nuclear-armed missiles from abroad, I suspect the drums the settlers heard would not be long in sounding once more and, judging by the Navajos I see, the Western Indians would be riding again in short order with no less élan than a century ago. At least, in a world of increasing uniformity, I like to think so. But if the twentieth century proceeds as it has, how long will any special Indianness remain?

From U. S. 164 between Four-State Corners and the neighborhood of Grand Canyon, called the Navajo Trail, may be seen schooling centers set up under the Department of the Interior consisting of a dozen or two new, low buildings in tight ranks. Here, Uncle Sam is trying to make it up to his charges. What this means, I see written somewhere, is providing technical training with emphasis on fitting the trainees to develop the resources of their reservation, especially mineral resources. All that the recipients of our patronage have had to give up in exchange for a possibly remunerative place in industrial civilization is their pride, birthright, and manhood. True, there are those missions, Baptist and Seventh-Day Adventist, to which signs point down minor roads, and in giving the Indians a religious going-over on top of everything else, it seems to me we are rather rubbing it in. But what better deal avails than the one the government offers? With developed mineral resources there is no gainsaying that one can cut quite a swath. And who would fix on another people a poverty he would never willingly accept for himself? Only . . . gazing upon the lone Navajo on his horse, shepherding his flock on the sparsely scrub-grown plains over which the long shadow of the barbaric mesa is creeping, I cannot help feeling that with the disappearance of that figure something irretrievable will be lost from our country that technology can never make up for.

As for one's own people living in the landscapes one has been traversing—what can it be like for them? I should like to wander about the West, not so fully committed to the natural scene as I am this time and as unhurriedly as I am afraid only youth is permitted to be, and see what human lives are being lived back at the ends of the unpaved roads. What does the loneliness of this remote country do to one? Very likely one would find that nothing in the United States is any longer remote and that those farthest separated from their fellows are not very different from them. Still, I should like to find out. I am even tempted to drive up to one of the isolated ranches of a few buildings shaded by cottonwoods one sees from the highway and ask whomever I meet what it is like to be he. Does one —this is the question I should most like to have light thrown on without being entirely clear what I have in mind—face up to one's fate as a man in confronting these spacious solitudes and calling on one's individual resources to see one through or in wrestling with the spirit of one's age in the city and struggling not to be buried beneath its multitudes?

Perhaps that is not the issue at all. The Mexicans and Mexican-Americans I see would make me think not. They make us Anglos, as I gather the rest of us are called, seem constrained and hidebound —yes, as if our skins were too tight for us. The men and women of Mexican origin you see on the streets of Santa Fe and the Mexican border guards (as I suppose they are) relaxing in the general store in the hamlet of Castolon at Big Bend, not very closely shaved or cleanly uniformed, strike one as having roots in a more fertile human compost than ours. There is an easy, slumbrous warmth about them and a comfort-loving cat-like containment. They are redolent of rich cooking richly enjoyed and of emotions spontaneously indulged, calling up scenes, strip-lighted through blinds, of limbs conjoined in darkened afternoon chambers. Beside them we appear straitened and unnatural: manikins in a department-store window. We look blanched; and we are—blanched from an aseptic upbringing, blanched from emotions denied and satisfactions postponed, blanched from electronic living, blanched by the glare of world events. It occurs to me that there is no getting away from Churchill's iron ring: we create our technology and then our technology creates us.

But in drawing comparisons unfavorable to us Anglos, I must say I am thinking especially of the tourists the traveler is thrown with, even if he is not one himself; and people of all nationalities show at their worst, I think, as tourists. Tourists are by nature separated from their reasons for being—their work, their ties, their habitat. What is more dismal, more connotative of human futility, than a holiday crowd as afternoon wears on?

Work: once you are committed to the fully conscious life, it is, I am persuaded, the only salvation. To the extent that you cannot be at one with, and merged in, the great universality as an animal is, or as a *paisano* is more likely to be than the rest of us, or a lover in the arms of the beloved, or an outdoorsman in the intoxication of an early morning in spring, or a sailor betwixt wind and seas—which is to say by being contained in the totality of the present, in the world that *is*—you must achieve that at-oneness by work. You can be part of the universality only by making yourself, in however modest a way, a co-creator of the Creator's. That is the price of admission, without which all enjoyments pall and you find yourself in time demoralized in a barren land. It may be true, as Antoine de Saint-Exupéry, for one, has observed, that happiness is to be known only in the warmth of human relationships, but work is the price of qualifying for them.

"So you think God is love!" exclaims W. G., writer and ex-editor with *Fortune* and a friend of mine given to mocking flights of acid realism. "You'd like me to believe that God is love. Well, that's peachy. It's dandy. God is love. It takes care of it all. There's just one little way in which it doesn't quite ring true, don't you think? One teeny weeny thing wrong with it? Suppose someone told you God is not love. God is work. Do you think he might have something there? Eh? Do you think maybe all this time we've been kidding ourselves, telling ourselves that God is beaming at us from behind that great big loving heart when the fact is that God is that figure with crossed arms standing over the workbench?"

"Nature," says Turgenev's young, self-styled nihilist, Bazárov, "is not a temple but a workshop."

The most enviable man I see on my travels, unless it be I, for whom these travels count as work, is a young archaeologist at Lipon Point above the Grand Canyon. He has just been brought up by helicopter from the banks of the Colorado where for seven weeks he has been excavating a Pueblo site of around three thousand years ago. He has a flaming suntan, and around him, as if he were indeed a flame, the tourists cluster like moths. He is brimming over with information about what he has been doing and with enthusiasm for it and unquestioning of its value. To the mere vacationers he is irresistible, as I have learned that a cow in labor is irresistible and exciting to her fellows, whose common cowhood is elevated and enhanced in meaning by the creativity of their sister.

In speaking as if I were the first ever to have recognized the importance of work—and in getting away from my chronicle, as I have been almost entirely since being diverted to Big Bend—I have been thinking that this importance grows as, with mechanical progress, we are separated further and further from the natural world and the absorption in present living that is of its essence. Thrown back on ourselves with the acute awareness of self that comes with liberation from the environment, we have more reason than ever to seek self-justification in work. But what if our work seems futile? The jobs provided for the majority by technology grow more limited, dull and debased, while among the elite with responsibility and decision I suspect there is going to be less and less satisfaction in work designed to further the kind of progress civilization has been making.

In taking up again where I left off on my solo journey—and I had barely crossed into Arizona after lunch in the lava field—I should be very glad to pass over the Petrified Forest, which could well be taken as illustrative of the futility of work and everything else; but it lies athwart the highway from Gallup to Flagstaff and the Grand Canyon, at the start of the Painted Desert, and cannot in honesty be evaded. Beginning about forty miles inside Arizona, the Painted Desert curves with the Little Colorado River some two hundred miles up to the eastern end of the Grand Canyon and on to Utah. However it may be after a rain or lighted from a colorful sunrise or sunset, it is not very striking in its hues—gray through mauve to brick—on a dry, late afternoon. It is a kind of badlands predominantly of clay which began as volcanic grit. It is utterly desolate and as an exhibit of wastage by erosion equaling any even of man's doing. Capping rock strata give some protection to the low buttes and mesas into which the terrain has been cut, but as these are further scoured and reduced by rains, the slopes grooved as finely as wrinkled visages, the blocks are undermined and come tumbling down. *The heroic forms of these great blocks of sandstone and shale and their slow, inevitable decomposition remind me of, or link up in one's mind with, the disappearance of the monolithic Indians through the erosion worked by white civilization.* (The tape recorder encourages a pronunciamento style of address.)

It is the eroding away of the clays in which they were embedded that has brought the petrified logs to light. These brown fossils are seen perched along the rim of Blue Mesa (actually gray), typically on pedestals of clay which they protect for a time before they too are undermined and roll down the slope. The logs lie all about the floor of the canyon, which recalls a battlefield. They resemble drums, some as much as three feet in diameter. They are sections of the trunks of coniferous trees that in early Mesozoic times, more than 150 million years ago, grew on uplands from which they were washed down to be buried in the floodplains under the silt and volcanic grit carried by the streams. Here their tissue was gradually replaced by the silica in the waters and reproduced in some of the numerous forms that wonderful chemical takes—agate, jasper, and quartz. And now here they are, laid bare in these stricken barrens by the fortuitous elevating of the Colorado Plateau. They are all that remains of a country like the Everglades (so the National Park Service tells us) inhabited by amphibians and precursors of the dinosaurs which endured for twenty million years, ten times as long as beings describable as human have been on earth.

"Two vast and trunkless legs of stone/ Stand in the desert. . . . Nothing beside remains./ Round the decay of that colossal wreck, boundless and bare,/ The lone and level sands stretch far away." At Blue Mesa, Nature might be addressing us from that desert in the words of Ozymandias, whose legs of stone those were: "Look on my works, ye Mighty, and despair." Only the works that Nature has swept away were not the mere vanities of a human tyrant but those, infinitely greater, of its own creation. A purposed cruelty could almost be read in the scene. Nature has not merely resurrected the pathetic corpses in witness of the mortality of all things, of whole worlds, but has travestied them by refashioning them ironically in faithful detail in gems. ("Those are pearls that were his eyes.") Well may the Mighty and the Humble too look on these works and despair—all who obey the primal human hunger and build for permanence, for immortality. There is no permanence in Nature, except in its laws, which govern the ceaseless, all-consuming, ever-renewing change.

Yet men must build. The doubts I have of it vanish when I see human genius take chisel to inert marble—of all things, the compacted remains of sea life metamorphosed in the earth's demonic grip—and extract from them Michelangelo's *David* and Bernini's: images of man god-like in figure and stamped with defiance of the Goliath forces that would make nothing of him. Who could doubt in the face of such an assertion that man is a worthy offspring of the Creator, standing up to his Maker in pride and independence as a manly son should and, like a dutiful one, carrying on the Creator's work as a collaborator? Who could doubt it or doubt that the work is worthwhile? Yes, the noblest works of man's execution will be extinguished by time. The extinction of all things is inevitable. One must accept an order in which death is an integral part of life—how could it be otherwise?—the two making up inseparable parts of a single fulfillment. I do not say I am a great hand at this, or that I am able to accept it at all where those I love are concerned, but the difficulties I have with it only make me more aware of the necessity. It helps to recognize that Nature is a closed system in which, while oblivion awaits all, nothing ever ends. Everything is transmuted as Nature proceeds through its cycles toward inscrutable goals. And one may reflect that our conception of time, on which change and mortality are predicated, may be so limited as to be entirely untrustworthy and deceptive.

But the world hath few more imperfect philosophers than I, and as I drive away from the Petrified Forest, the recording has little in common with the foregoing. *Five miles of the road unpaved, as is not shown on the map. It's been unsurfaced for repairs. Bus is filling with dust so you choke on it. These side excursions are very costly in time. Damned road and the dust. The bus is going to be thick with dust and it's being shaken to pieces. Empty country all around, just range land. Lousy unpaved road goes on and on and on and CLOUDS of dust behind. I'll be two hours from Flagstaff when I get to the end of this and then I have the problem of finding a park. Bloody road goes on and on and on. . . . Thank God, the end at last! The Little Colorado River—we just crossed it: you could jump over it.* But I still cannot shake off the Petrified Forest. *Disturbing, at least with the sun going down, to think of desert now where once there were those vast swamps teeming with life, and the great Aurocarias, I suppose as big as any but the biggest trees today—all gone.*

At nine o'clock, half an hour from Flagstaff, there is still some light in the sky—*blue light a little tinged with red around to the north behind some mountains toward which we have been driving. They seem to be quite small mountains but we never seem to get any nearer to them. The desert is like the ocean at night, completely black except where you see a single light that might be a ship, then a string of lights that actually is a town but might be an island. The desert is darker than the sky. Now there are no cars coming or going and there is not a light to be seen except for one ocean liner off to the north.*

The campground shown on the other side of Flagstaff in the State Development Board pamphlet turns out to be boarded up, so I backtrack and put up for the night in a rest area I had passed. This is not only alongside the main highway but also on the Atchison, Topeka and Santa Fe, so that the intermittent thunder of passing trucks is occasionally drowned out by the truly mighty roar of a train. Still, between tracks and highway is a pine woods traversed by a lane on which I have a pleasant jog in the morning, finishing to the sweet flutings of a bird I have no time to run down.

And then, on the north side of the quite ordinary city, very abruptly from the high plain, rise the peaks of Novatukia Ovi; so they are known to the Hopis and to me, who see little connection between the cluster of summits, which met the gaze of the first people of the continent ten or twenty thousand years ago, and a thirteenth-century Umbrian saint, even a most appealing and praiseworthy one. The San Francisco Peaks, as they are more widely called, are the small, receding mountains of the evening before, actually the tallest in the state, the highest standing more than 12,600 feet above sea-level. The Place of Snow on the Very Top, as they are to the Hopis; and the peaks to which the slopes sweep up so splendidly have in fact a crusting and edging of snow which sparkles in the triumphant morning sunlight above the shadow-filled hollows. Novatukia Ovi, before erosion removed its top several thousand feet, must have resembled Fujiyama. U. S. 180 to the Grand Canyon rounds its shoulders, passing through miles of a Ponderosa pine forest, the sun lighting the heavy, dark, yellow-green tufts of needles and pouring into the aisles of columnar trunks darkly fissured between massive plates cream-colored to a light cinnamon. Olive-green pines and pale green or platinum grass below them, and a Wild turkey hen dancing across the road upstretched with anxiety. And volcanic boulders, magenta-colored in some stretches, in others dark gray with a nearly white side (from calcium carbonate in the soil, according to my Smithsonian friend).

Descending from the sylvan serenities of the Coconino National Forest, U. S. 180 delivers you—and I can hardly believe what I am seeing—to realtordom. *"Buy Arizona. Grow rich in good living. Grand Canyon Subdivision,"* says a sign. Is this a satire on America? The broad plain is tenanted only by junipers and Pinyons, and by few of these. But it has even been laid out in imaginary streets, with street signs. U. S. 180—it cannot be, but it is: *"Linger Lane South."* Billboard after billboard is waiting for you. *"Only $5 down, $10 a month, for plots of over an acre."* . . . *"You can become a landowner in five minutes."* Unfazed by the reality, a sign blandly proclaims: *"Commercial zoned."* Over much of the "subdivision" not even juniper and Pinyon will grow. *"Immediate possession,"* you read. The gall takes your breath away. You would like to laugh, but there is little amusement in the thought of what these transparent real-estate come-ons presage for the future of the Southwest, into which people are pouring; Arizona's population is growing faster, in percentage rate of increase, than any other state's but Nevada's.

You cannot forget that for a generation it appeared doubtful that the Grand Canyon itself could be saved—and that was in the past century. During that time all efforts to protect it were thwarted by interests bent on turning it into profits. As Thoreau declared, there are those who would bear our Lord himself to market if there were prospects of a sale.

Probably it is natural to see your own people as one over whom the forces of good and evil contend for possession with peculiar intensity. It certainly seems to me that in the American people the crassest materialism is pitted against an altruistic and noble idealism. A nation as ruthless in war as any in history and capable of as great magnanimity as any to a defeated foe, ours is also one that has dealt with the lands it holds with a destructive rapacity unmatched by any other and has set a model for all others in the veneration it has shown them in the individual acts of countless lovers of the land and in the peerless system of national parks it has created. Legislation to add the Grand Canyon to the system, first introduced in 1887 by Benjamin Harrison as a Senator from Indiana, was not passed by Congress until 1908. In that year it was signed into law by President Theodore Roosevelt, who had enjoined his fellow countrymen when he had first seen the canyon, "Do nothing to mar its grandeur. . . . Keep it for your children, your children's children, and all who come after you, as the one great sight which every American should see."

Grand Canyon National Park incorporates some two hundred miles of the Colorado River, but that represents only about a fifth of the magnificent gorges through which the river flows. In the 1960's, the fate of three of its outstanding canyons was brought to issue and bitterly fought over. The battle to save Glen Canyon, well upstream of the Grand Canyon and mostly in Utah, was lost early in the decade and the canyon is now flooded behind a hydroelectric dam under a lake 130 miles long. Eliot Porter, the master photographer who depicted the canyon's glories in *The Place No One Knew,* also pronounced the valedictory: "The waters impounded by this plug of artificial stone spread back through Glen Canyon . . . inundating the sparkling river, swallowing its luminous cliffs and tapestried walls, and extinguishing far into the long, dim, distant future everything that gave it life. As the waters creep into the side canyons, enveloping one by one their mirroring pools, drowning their bright flowers, backing up their clear, sweet springs with stale flood water, a fine opaque silt settles over all, covering rocks and trees alike with a gray slimy ooze. Darkness pervades the canyons. Death and the thickening, umbrageous gloom take over where life and shimmering light were the glory of the river."

Sickened and outraged by the needless sacrifice of Glen Canyon, the protectionists threw everything into the next fray—and succeeded in preventing the construction of hydroelectric dams in Marble Canyon, just above the Grand Canyon, and in Hualapai Canyon, just below. In the words of the *Congressional Quarterly,* they "took on—and defeated—a powerful coalition of interests which included the Interior Department's Bureau of Reclamation, the Colorado River Association and like-minded lobbies in the Southwest, the American Public Power Association as well as several large private power companies," while "also opposing the united position of the seven Basin states, with their 51 seats in the House and 14 seats in the Senate." It can be done. But the epochal victory was not without cost. Moved by vindictiveness to act with a speed unprecedented in such cases, the government revoked the right of the Sierra Club, which had led the fight, to receive tax-deductible donations.

In approaching the Grand Canyon from the south there is evidence of gradually increasing altitude—the Ponderosa pines reappear —but until the last few paces none whatever, of course, of what lies ahead. No one, accordingly, can fail to wonder what it would be like to come upon that unbelievable chasm with no foreknowledge of it, as López de Cárdenas and his small party did in 1540—the first white men to see it. In being deprived of the impressions of the Conquistador we perhaps need not be inconsolable, however. Cárdenas it was who, east of Albuquerque, introduced the Indians of the region to Christendom by offering clemency to those who would capitulate, then when the chiefs accepted his terms, burning at the stake thirty of those who surrendered and slaughtering sixty who struggled to escape.

Given that you know what to expect, the first impact of the Grand Canyon is likely to be visual only, as that of a picture would be. And however grand its subject, we do not gasp at a picture. There it is, very much as represented, and none the less extraordinary, to be sure, for having been represented so frequently. There it is, banded in all its colors, from the palest gray and ivory to meat reds and purple, an abyss of walls stepped back one above and behind another, each rising from a sloping shelf and deeply and intricately gouged from top to bottom, with matching walls and shelves encircling the buttes and pinnacles rising to various altitudes from the depths of the Canyon. The reality of the twisting chasm's dimensions do not immediately strike home. It comes to you only as you adjust your sense of scale to what you know of the Canyon's dimensions: that the little pale-green pane of water discernible at the bottom— a fragment of the Colorado River, relieved of most of its burden of sediment in Lake Powell, behind Glen Canyon Dam—is 300 feet in breadth, the narrow gorge through which it flows 1,500 in depth; that the height of the layers forming the steps of the Canyon's walls runs to that of buildings of between ten and sixty stories; that the chasm itself is a mile deep and between four and ten miles across at the top. "And now the real magnitudes begin to unfold themselves, and as the attention is held firmly the mind grows restive under the increasing burden. Every time the eye ranges up or down its face it seems more distant and more vast. At length we recoil, overburdened with the perceptions already attained and yet half vexed at the inadequacy of our faculties to comprehend more." So wrote the geologist Clarence E. Dutton, whose major work on the Grand Canyon, published in 1882, exhibits the perceptiveness that is often given to the early comer, the discoverer. And he declared: "There are in the world valleys which are longer and a few which are deeper. There are valleys flanked by summits loftier than the palisades of the Kaibab. Still the Grand Canyon is the sublimest thing on earth."

I make the mistake of arriving in the late morning, when foregatherings of tourists at the initial vantage points are assured. Hence my first impression is of a need, which at that moment I am prepared to fill at my own expense—I know it is small of me, but I cannot help it—for a large sign commanding SHUT UP. It really does not matter, but such a quacking of nasal voices there is, the onlookers all ostensibly persuaded of the world's hunger for their thoughts before the great prodigy of nature—a score of little Napoleons beside Cheops, all quacking away. "Well," says a motherly harridan looking around for our approbation, "I'll tell you it's good to see something made in U.S.A. and not in Japan." It may be self-consciousness, but I think only partly. As a nation, we seem to be uneasy in the presence of silence. Our automatic response is to fill it with sound. Silence is menacing; it gives the stage to the contents of our minds, which resonate in the void, and raises the question of what we are.

Certainly the Grand Canyon does. Even with all the tourists, you readily find yourself alone with it, if you are at all given to walking; its size and the irregularity of its perimeter soon bring that about. And when you are alone, it is as if you had come to the very source of silence, the inexhaustible font of silence, the well into which all the world's din could be absorbed and stilled. And on the shores of this ocean of silence and because you feel you are closer than you have ever been to the origin of all things on earth, you are very much faced with the question of what you are, in yourself and as part of a human species mysteriously inserted in a mere sliver of a stretch of time far beyond human capacity to make real.

At the brink of a promontory above the chasm is a superior little museum—the Yavapai Museum—with samples of rock from each stratum exposed in the canyon and fossils from as many as contain them. And here in an admirable explanatory talk by a Park Ranger the claim is made that from the edge of the Grand Canyon, alone of all places on the planet, is it possible to see from one spot exposures of rock representing all major eras into which geologists divide the earth's history. The bottom, inner gorge of the Canyon is gouged deep out of the dark gray schists, cut by dikes of white and pink granite, of the continent's early pre-Paleozoic basement, at least 1,350 million years old and probably much older. In places above this, layers of vermilion shale, dark limestone, and purple quartzite of the late pre-Paleozoic are exposed. The upper four thousand feet of the Canyon, more or less, are of the varicolored shale, limestone, and sandstone strata of the Paleozoic era. These strata, by the way, are those that, thickening westward, filled the trough from which the Rocky Mountains proper arose. The top stratum, on which rest the museum, the big old El Tovar Hotel, the lodges, railroad station, and other tourists' and campers' accommodations, the pine groves and everything else within miles is of sandy Kaibab limestone, three hundred feet thick, of the last chapter of the Paleozoic—the Permian—like the limestone of the Guadalupe Mountains. The later, Mesozoic strata, of which the heroic sculpture of other parts of the Colorado Plateau is composed, have been stripped off the Kaibab Plateau—but not entirely; there are remnants in two buttes visible from the Grand Canyon—

Cedar Mountain and Red Butte, the latter a sombrero-shaped eminence you see above the plain en route to the Canyon from the south. The current, Cenozoic period is represented on the horizon by the truncated cone of Novatukia Ovi. What it means is that you are in the presence of more time than anywhere else on earth. And you feel it.

The Grand Canyon is not beyond rational accounting for. Successive uplifts of the earth's crust raised the Kaibab Plateau so high that even after having been planed down by thousands of feet it stands seven thousand feet above sea-level at the south rim of the Canyon and between one and two thousand feet higher at the north. And evidently the Colorado River, flowing down from the western side of the Plateau, in the course of eons ate its way back into and through the Plateau to "capture" the waters of what is now the upper Colorado, which presumably until then had flowed along the eastern side, via the Little Colorado, into the Rio Grande. It is reasonable enough, assuming that a reason for crustal uplifts will eventually be found (possibly in the mechanism that moves the continents), and if you can picture the Colorado as adequate to the task of excavation (though of course it was assisted by the heavy rains of the Ice Ages).

But the imagination is hardly contented with so pedestrian an explanation. The Grand Canyon is too deeply disturbing. Its architecture, of storied edifices oriental in splendor of ornateness and of color, beside which our greatest artifacts would shrink to playthings —temples, towers, rotundas rising in a void hazy with distance as in a dream—is too far beyond relating to anything you have ever seen. "Everything is superlative," as Dutton wrote, "transcending the power of the intelligence to comprehend it." Before it you understand as perhaps never before the necessity for primitive man to invoke deities to account for forces before which his powers were as dried leaves before the wind. You do not actually believe in a Creator who would have commanded the embodiments of the successive ages of the past to stand forth from the limbo—from the hundreds of miles of Stygian blackness beneath the crushing weight of the overlying rock whence the strata emerge—and reveal themselves. But it is as if you did believe this when you gaze at the stone visages jutting from the walls lining the abyss, all the more momentous-seeming for their indecipherability. Even the geologist Dutton had trouble. "The dominant idea ever before the mind is the architecture displayed in the profiles. It is hard to realize that this is the work of the blind forces of nature."

Have I not heard of a people whose belief it is that a knowledge of the Creator's true name would be deadly dangerous to the possessor since to speak it even in inadvertence would blast him into eternity? I rather take to that idea, of which I am reminded while walking the rim trail west of the mule corral. There, at the brink, busybodies have erected a green wooden cross. I can see them dusting off their hands with satisfaction as they march off. God, one may be sure, has been liberally and facilely called upon. The Canyon has been put in its place, themselves protected from what it has to say. (And were they actually suffered to go in peace? To be sure: "The heavens," as Joseph Conrad observes in a rather similar context, "do not fall for such a trifle.")

And what has the Canyon to say? Great mountain ranges carry one's spirit sweeping upward with them, exhilarated. But the Canyon has more the effect of plunging one into a profound, meditative receptivity. All that would come to one in it if one remained I shall hope someday to find out. Of all the places I visit, Grand Canyon is hardest to leave. Indeed, pressed for time though I am, I cannot bring myself to push on until the next morning. The tape gives inklings of what I feel. *If I were going to kill myself by jumping from a high place, this is the one I should choose. The exalted frame of reference would relieve it of at least some of its terrors. . . . Probably everyone who comes here feels that the Canyon has some special meaning for him that he would like to explore as deeply as he could.* To reconnoiter the full length of the Canyon by boat on the Colorado, as others have done—that would have to come early. But I should begin by walking to the bottom and back, as my wife did when a girl in 1940, though the Park Service warns against it. ("Unless you are very certain of your stamina, do not hike to the river.")

As it is, I can make time only to descend past the Kaibab limestone, the Toroweap Formation of red sandstone and gray limestone and the pale Coconino sandstone of windblown sand from sea-beaches and into the red Hermit shale of river mud—these formations all between 225 and 350 feet in depth. This is not far, but with only cotton socks and thin soles between me and the steep, rocky trail, enough to raise blisters—and increase my estimation of three young men with packs and a look of keyed-up exhaustion who have been all the way and are returning. But there are more lasting effects than the blisters. Walking back through the history of life where its antecedents are laid bare, as they are here—all the way back to the one-celled algae that laid down the dark limestone of the late pre-Paleozoic rocks—brings home to you how compact the family of living things is, how close we are to the salamander-like beings that left their tracks in the Hermit shale, how fully we are the offspring of the maternal earth, and the unweaned offspring at that—if we can be said to have sprung off at all. Contemplating the Coconino sandstone, I am bemused by the realization that the particular layer of rock one sees was deposited at a specific moment—one that felt exactly like the present, one that was the present!—200-odd million years ago. To the maker of the lizard-like footprints in the sandstone, that moment contained all life. The world of dunes around him was fully and finally the way things were meant to be, as ours is to us. These thoughts are like a drug to me. I am enervated and oppressed by the extent of time and puzzled to know how to come to terms with it.

There is that about the Canyon, but there is something else as well. Even as you half-lose yourself in the vistas of ancient millennia brought back by the works of time made overpowering in it, a quite different feeling is stirred in you by those same works. They make you see the actual, living moment in which you are having your being as a dispensation miraculous in its uniqueness, to be regarded with amazed appreciation that, against infinitely great odds, you are alive in it, alive in this rare, special, luminous, living now. And if you are not a perverse and irredeemable ingrate, surely all your pores will be open to it, to drink it all in! The train is bearing the girl away: learn while there is time that you love her.

Perhaps the birds of the Canyon enter into this. More than any other organisms, birds seem to me vibrant upon the very point of the present. Expressing and symbolizing life in the sharpness of the moment, they have an uncommon power of recalling me to it. A Rock wren with breast like a cottonball gives full voice to a series of ecstatic trills, ponders the effect, then is off in flight across the cliff, entirely at home though no more than a mote against the rocks—unaccountably tiny; whatever reminds you of the scale of things disconcerts you. Violet-green swallows of snowy underparts sweep out over the bottomless depths to conduct their aerial gambols as over summer meadows giving you a touch of vertigo where you stand on the rim. And a raven rises wonderfully on an updraft directly before you or a Turkey vulture coasts by with a *whooh* of pinions, and being up there with them above the void, you share, perilously, the sense of tacking, weightless, on the sea of air, nothing beneath you, sustained by exhilaration.

In the morning I am back on the east-rim drive for a last look. It is the hour when all things seem attentive to a single mind—the Pinyons and Ponderosas, the Gambel's oaks and Utah junipers, even the herbs like the Cliffrose and its relatives, Fernbush and Rock spirea. The sun has not yet emerged from behind a low cloud and the great hollow is filled with shadow. More than ever the Canyon seems not only an abyss in the earth but an abyss in time. Maybe it is as I told myself in the ruined landscape of the Painted Desert with day's end coming on, that the nature of time is beyond our grasp. As the tape is my witness: *You feel here that all time is present at once.* The totemic countenances standing out from the broken strata remain expressionless. The incarnations of ages going back probably two billion years, they could hardly regard the ephemeral living as equal to a communication. One has a sense of them as of actors summoned to present themselves to the audience at an intermission in the drama—awful and unbending actors to be sure, but actors no less extant for having fulfilled their parts.

7

GREAT BASIN AND VEINS OF TREASURE

Ordinarily I make no attempt at the start of the day to fix on a place for the night, but this time there is no choice. It is the campgrounds at Death Valley or nothing.

The morning brings a long, long series of descents. You come down from the Colorado Plateau by one step after another, with the prow of the escarpment showing in the north, like that of a ship you have left. The landscape grows drabber. You wonder what on earth there is to feed the cattle for which the pens beside the Santa Fe Railroad are waiting. Yet along one stretch so much tumbleweed has fetched up against a fence that the highway department has a grader pushing the plants into windrows, which are being burned. It is a slaughter of the innocents. I love the tumbleweed and the irresponsible spirit that sends it across the road and fields in bounding cartwheels. Later that day there are tumbleweed's partners in insouciant delinquency—dust-devils. These miniature whirlwinds go pirouetting frolicsomely across the plains, like playful djinns, sometimes rising clear of the ground only to settle lightly on it again a few yards farther on. Some day when it is too late I shall realize how much better it would have been to be more like tumbleweed and dust-devils instead of glooming over ponderosities and multiplying possessions with the obsessiveness of the tiresome ant in the fable, which, in contrast with the improvident grasshopper, never sang a note in its life. (*Some day* when it is too late?)

Down from the Colorado Plateau and into the periphery of Kingman: the outskirts occupy miles of U. S. 66. For sheer unrelieved drabness they surpass anything I have ever seen and almost belief itself—trailers, and cabins that look like trailers, widely scattered over the dreariest of plains. You see them from afar, colonies of them. WILD WILLY'S TRAILER SALES, a sign announces. There's a man to inspire your confidence! $695 FOR A CITY LOT WITH WATER. A commercial strip has an atmosphere hardly approximated by the most sordid, treeless seaside community at home. What depraved, spiritual runts have created this? Quite ordinary people, with regulation sons and prettyish daughters, as you see on the streets of Kingman, and the business district is like any other, with a lot of motels, very spruce. There is even a Santa Fe steam locomotive enshrined in a little park; someone actually cares!

U. S. Highway 93 northwest to Boulder Dam and Las Vegas brings a relief from the traffic hell-bent for Los Angeles and a landscape wearing a faint green bloom. In some stretches grass comes in the form of grizzly-bear-colored hedgehogs, armies of them; in some are flowers that you feel (with little warrant, I fear) must make anyone happy just to hear about them: sagebrush-like plants with little yellow-centered, pale-orange poppy-flowers, large daisies of the most brilliant possible gold, and pads of charming, minutely leaved ground-cover flecked with flowers an eighth-inch across like white Sweet williams with purple centers. In a pasture where I have a run before lunch, a kind of prickly pear called Beavertail is in bloom. As with other cactuses, the flowers are like lights of pure color. They almost persuade you that ethereal spirit can escape the gross, earthbound body—though I should prefer mine to triumph in another shade than the cerise of Beavertail.

But there is a warning of what is to come in the sudden appearance of tree-yuccas, or Joshua trees. Resembling crudely improvised scarecrows, they bespeak conditions as grim as they look. What we are coming to is the Central Desert, which, up into southern Idaho, comprises the largest area of the country of minimum rainfall. It comprises also the Great Basin. Out of this sink, which has the mountains of southern California at its lower rim and the mountains of central Oregon and those east of Great Salt Lake at its northern, no river flows. Such rain as falls on it and does not evaporate sinks ultimately into the ground. Corresponding roughly with the Great Basin is that part of the forty-eight states in which you could walk farthest while meeting fewest people.

The thing about the West—and how often that phrase comes to mind!—is that over so much of it you feel you are in a vast stockroom in which raw earth forms of every description are spread out, waiting to be finished against the Management's need of furnishings for another conventional country. Basaltic lava in hills south of the Grand Canyon; ridges of tumbled granite east of Kingman, the Aquarius Mountains to the south resembling the mountains that come with toy electric trains, and the savage, scraggy Grand Wash Cliffs to the north; then . . . but I babble away into the tape recorder with no thread of continuity, like a schoolgirl trying to describe an eventful day to a companion trying to do the same. Nearing Boulder (or Hoover) Dam, the highway cuts through a most extraordinary succession of rounded, parallel ridges, perhaps thirty of them, and what is more amazing, they seem to be of gravel to begin with, then lava and finally, I would swear, limestone. What can they be? In the East they would be famous.

Up ahead by now is a wilderness of jagged mountains of purplebrown rock, and soon we are in it, the rock rising in hundred-foot, weather-gnawed cliffs. These turn out to frame the gate to the deep, narrow gorge cut through the hepatic mountains by the Colorado and—presto!—to Boulder Dam, which seals it off and over which the highway runs. The dam, over seventy stories tall and the highest in the world when built—still the highest in our hemisphere—curves into the water it impounds. At an exhibition hall for the tourists a guard hands out on request a slip of paper explaining that the rock is andesitic breccia (*breccia* meaning a rock containing angular fragments of other rock), though most of the formation looks like rhyolite. Where it has long been exposed, it appears fireblackened, and the effect of the whole scene is of Hades cooled off.

The circuitous road up from the dam on the Nevada side offers a wide view of the lake; about the last thing you would expect in the charred and almost barren landscape, it is said to stretch back 115 miles, halfway to the Grand Canyon. Another anomaly crowns some ashen hills above the canyon. It is as if some super-Orpheus had come up from the underworld below bringing with him Euridice Hills, a Planned Community of Gracious Living at the Heart of Famed 2,000,000-Acre Lake Mead National Recreation Area. It is Boulder City and to me incredible, a garden town of small, neat, new houses, many low and snug, of one story, and many with red, barrel-tiled roofs, all set about with the brightest green Chinese elms, palmettos, arborvitae, oleanders, and emerald lawns. As I learn in the haberdashery when I buy some trousers, everyone living here is here because of the dam. "Before the dam, there was no Boulder City. They tell me there was nothing here but the canyon and those cottonwoods you may have noticed coming up." The inhabitants are visibly of a superior order, the youngsters pouring out of the modern school building good-looking, cheerful, gregarious, and seemingly confident of the world, the breviskirted girls in the mode.

Preserved as it is, Boulder City would doubtless give the future an idea of what America today was about to which in fairness we could hardly take exception. The kind of life the Boulderites would seem to be living is probably about the kind most of us have in mind for ourselves. And it is rather striking that so representative a community should be a graft on such an unrelated stock, a town owing nothing to its surroundings but its water supply and probably even less to their historical past. That there is little native to Nevada in it would certainly, I feel sure, be the opinion of the miners, teamsters, general-merchandisers, hotel- and saloon-keepers, machinists, gamblers, and female entertainers who brought Nevada's first towns into being. To the founders of Virginia City, Gold Hill and Austin, Boulder City would probably have appeared the spiritual heir of an Eastern Sunday School. They would, however, very likely have come rather soon to feel at home in Reno or Las Vegas. Yet those rakish towns themselves have little about them that is indigenous. They are the outgrowth of what pertained elsewhere: the restrictive laws of the other states respecting divorce and gambling. And for that matter, the mushroom towns of a century ago— the Virginia Cities and Gold Hills—were just that: mushrooms that sprang up on readily extractable nourishment and withered when they had used it up.

In all the Great Basin the one sizable human community that sank roots and prospered to a large extent on its own resources was that established by the Mormons in 1847 when they crossed the Wasatch Mountains over the trail blazed the year before by the Donner party on the way to its terrible fate in the Sierra Nevada. Brigham Young, their extraordinary leader, had also preceded them by a year, and they had come to occupy the green valley of Great Salt Lake which he had determined to be the "gathering place for Israel" he was seeking. That was the beginning of a remarkable success story. "Never in the history of human migration," the English historian John A. Hawgood writes in his discerning and highly readable *America's Western Frontiers*, "have a dedicated people more decisively made the desert bloom like a rose"; the Mormons were the first in the United States to carry on large-scale irrigation.

The achievements of the Mormons would seem to demonstrate that as far as concrete results go, it matters little what human beings believe so long as their belief calls for work, self-denial, and organization and they have the advantage, initial at least, of able and indomitable leadership. Bearing in mind that the Church of Jesus Christ of Latter-Day Saints is vigorous and thriving and claims a million members, it is discouraging for those who put their faith in human reason to read of the origins of the Church in the claims of Joseph Smith: that, acting on the instructions of the angel Moroni, who had thrice appeared before him, he had on September 22, 1827, on a hill near his home in Manchester, New York, dug up a book six inches thick of thin gold plates eight inches by seven bound together by three gold rings, which book, although inscribed in the "caractors" of the "reformed Egyptian tongue," he was able to translate by reading them through a pair of spectacles combining two magic crystals (Urim and Thummim by name) which he had found with the book. (That the golden volume would have been too heavy for him to carry—215 pounds, more or less, exclusive of the rings, if my calculations are correct—seems not to have occurred to him or to have troubled his followers.) And it is not very reassuring to learn that the book, when Smith had dictated his translation (from behind a curtain) to secretaries handier than he at reading and writing, proved to be a history of pre-Columbian settlers in the New World, one influx from the Tower of Babel, a second from Jerusalem, and to contain the information that the book was destined to be unearthed by God's chosen prophet—Joseph Smith, as it developed—to whom all power was to be given and all obedience rendered. (Divine sanction of polygamy, regularizing a proclivity of Smith's which but for Brigham Young, an early convert, might have seen the infant church dissolved in scandal, was not received until a revelation of July 12, 1843—for revelations had continued to be vouchsafed to Smith.)

It makes unhappy reading, too, for those who believe that myths play an important and influential role in civilization. And I must say I have come to be one who feels that a body of myth in which a society can find its aspirations and conception of a higher order symbolized and elevated, and which it can celebrate in its painting, music, dance and poetry, may be essential to its stability and inspiration. In that view, the nature and quality of myths are highly significant, both in what they reveal of a society (as our daydreams disclose us to ourselves) and in the effect they are likely to have on its course. It is difficult—again, in this view—to feel very sanguine about a nation in which a myth originating in claims of unearthly visitations and hidden golden plates chronicling the doings of peoples unknown to history, which to a rationalist has the character of a crude and far-fetched confidence game, has found such fertile soil. The response to Joseph Smith's revelations has of course been comparatively very limited in point of numbers involved. Yet it seems to take one—and perhaps I am being unfair—to a vein of poverty in the American soul that shows itself in strident religious revivalism, the narrow tradition of "the Bible on the table and the flag upon the wall," a hostility to distinction and an anti-aestheticism and prevailing artistic sterility. To this I should add, if it did not seem fanciful, the bitter lines around the mouths of so many of us in middle age—the tightness of skin that sets us Anglos off from our Spanish-descended fellows. Sometimes I think we Americans as a whole are starved for what we do not allow ourselves or have lost the capacity for. We remind me of those ladies of my grandmother's generation who would never have quaffed an ounce of wine with Bacchus but resorted to patent medicines twice as strong in alcoholic content.

But the creed of the Latter-Day Saints, like Americanism itself, has been shown to work, even to work wonders. As Hawgood declares, the Mormons were the first to prove that the Great Basin "could be settled and could support a large, self-sufficient and growing population." It need not detract from their achievement to point out that it could probably have been brought off nowhere else in the Great Basin but in the valley Brigham Young found just inside its eastern rim. The Basin is the most inhospitable part of the continent south of the Arctic. The character of its mountains one tends to associate with the dreadful events that brought them into being and produced the topography of the Basin-and-Range Province (which includes all the Great Basin but the Great Sandy Desert of Oregon).

These began some 10 million years ago. For reasons no one is

sure of, but perhaps because it was stretched out by the spread of
the plastic rock beneath it, the earth's crust in this region was split
at intervals, the rents running chiefly more or less north and south
—faults, geologists call them. Some force, and maybe the same one,
then caused the long blocks into which the crust had been divided
to tilt. The eastern sides, for the most part, were the sides that
came up, the vertical shift amounting to miles. A fearful spectacle
of havoc it would have been, one seeming to presage the end of
the world, had it not taken place with consummate slowness. Probably the softer rock topping the blocks would have eroded away
about as fast as the blocks were tipped. At any rate, sediments accumulated deep in the troughs between the blocks. Today, long,
parallel, widely separated mountain ridges of harder rock rise like
islands from an ocean of plains. They are islands with beaches, even,
for the residues washed down by the fitful cloudbursts form "alluvial fans" that spread out at the foot of the ravines with which their
fronts are scored. Only what the beaches characteristically slope
down to are dead-white, lifeless salt flats.

As you see at the start, the ranges of the Great Basin are grim.
But there is more in them than meets the eye. There is more in
the fault-block ranges as a class, including the Sierra Nevada, and
there is also more in the Rocky Mountains, Northern and Southern
especially, more in the Wallowa Mountains of Oregon and Klamaths of Oregon and California (which are detached parts of the
original Rocky Mountain chain) and more in the northern Cascades. And this little, imperceptible bit more had an immense effect on American history, bringing rivers of men westward beside
which the trek of the Mormons with their two-wheeled hand-carts
was a mere trickle.

The minute, added component came down from a time long
before the present Western ranges were raised, when the rock of
which they are formed was liberally fractured by movements of
the earth's crust. Into these fractures hot water from greater depths,
rich in dissolved minerals, was forced. In them, as temperatures
and pressures dropped, the minerals were deposited. Thus when the
mountains rose they brought with them, in the fissures of their
rocks, irregular sheets, varying in thickness, of the crystallized minerals. Among these was one that evidently plays a negligible part
in Nature's economy but a very substantial one in man's. While
some had been mined in the Ortiz and neighboring San Pedro

Mountains of New Mexico, which you see in the south driving west out of Santa Fe, its occurrence elsewhere in the West, let alone its wide distribution, was unknown until January 24, 1848. In the early morning of that day, James W. Marshall went out to have a look at the trailrace of a sawmill he was building on the south fork of the American River, a tributary of the Sacramento, some thirty miles northeast of the present city of Sacramento, for John A. Sutter, the Swiss-born proprietor of a huge tract he called "The Kingdom of New Helvetia." Returning from his inspection of the trailrace with some bits of yellow metal he had found in it, Marshall sought out a companion. "I have found it," he said, holding out his trove. "What is it?" the other asked. "Gold." The West would never be the same again. Neither would the nation.

What Sutter's contractor had detected was placer gold—a Spanish term introduced into the language that year. Were it not for gold occurring in placers—banks or shoals of sand or gravel in streambeds—the history of man's pursuit of the metal would be very different and the stampedes called gold rushes hardly have been occasioned. Flakes and nuggets of gold accumulate in placers as the gold-bearing rock is decomposed and the detritus washed down the mountainsides. Other ingredients of the rock are mostly so reduced by abrasion that they are carried away by the flowing stream or are dissolved outright, but gold is highly resistant to both processes and, being heavy, tends to be deposited along with other heavy minerals in "black sands," whenever the current is slowed down, as at bends.

Skepticism greeted Marshall's discovery. That was not surprising. Gold-mining by Americans had hardly been known outside the southern Appalachians, where deposits were of limited extent (though some in Georgia were very rich). But by the end of May, a San Francisco newspaper was reporting that "The whole country, from San Francisco to Los Angeles, and from the sea shore to the base of the Sierra Nevadas, resounds with the sordid cry of '*gold*, GOLD, *GOLD!*' while the field is left half planted, the house half built, and everything neglected but the manufacture of shovels and pickaxes."

The like of it had never been seen in the world before and scarcely can be again. Up and down the coast from San Francisco as the news spread, then in Oregon and British Columbia, before long in Mexico, Peru and Chile, men dropped their tools and made for the streams flowing down from the Sierras. Troops stationed in California and the crews of ships in California ports took off without ceremony, gripped by the fever. In the harbor of San Francisco, John C. Frémont's wife reported, "deserted ships of all sorts were swinging with the tide." There they rotted and sank. Within a year, between four thousand and five thousand men had made their way to California, and by the end of 1849 their number had increased tenfold. "In wagons they toiled along the Oregon Trail to the Rockies, thence across the arid lands of Utah and Nevada to the final barrier of the Sierra Nevada," Rodman W. Paul writes in *Mining Frontiers of the Far West.* "In sailing ships they fought heavy weather off Cape Horn, pumped endless hours to keep their leaky ships from sinking, and lived on poor food and rationed drinking water. The lucky few who found passage on steamers via the Isthmus of Panama traveled more quickly than the rest, but had to endure tropical diseases in Panama and severely overcrowded conditions afloat. . . . English, Irish, Germans, French, Spanish Americans, Kanakas [from Hawaii], Australians, Chinese, Malayans —men from virtually every part of the civilized world—responded with like fervor."

For every migrant drawn to the colonies of agriculture at Great Salt Lake and in the Willamette Valley, ten or fifteen flocked to the Mother Lode, as it was called in the mistaken belief that all the gold in the streams that coursed down from the central Sierras had a common source. (By "lode" in mining parlance is meant a vein above a certain magnitude or a compact system of veins.) By the end of 1852, the population of California, which had stood at 14,000 exclusive of Indians three years earlier, had reached 250,000; by 1860, 380,000. All in all, $1.3 billion in gold was to be mined in California by the turn of the century. With such an output, it is not surprising that a number of men struck it rich. Huntington Hartford, Leland Stanford, and George Hearst, father of William Randolph, built their fortunes on their profits from the gold rush and, in the palaces, the railroads, the university, the great library, the collections of art masterpieces, the newspaper empire, and the Spanish monastery moved to San Simeon that their money paid for, gave the nation reason to remember them.

A great many more fared a great deal less well, however; and as shallow placer gold was exhausted, the independent miner with his pan or rocker (both of which took advantage of gold's propensity to sink in moving water that carries off clay and sand) found his opportunities shrinking. To supplant him came the company capitalized to extract less accessible deposits. First came hydraulic mining, a fiendish precursor of today's strip-mining in which whole hillsides were washed away for the gold they contained and fertile lower valleys buried in the rubble. Then the mining companies went after the veins in which the pristine gold occurred, generally embedded in quartz; after excavating the rock, they pulverized it with power-driven stamps.

But the money that was made and the money that was lost had this in common, that most of it went to the entrepôt of San Francisco. Between 1848 and 1850, Yerba Buena, as it was called, had grown from 800 to 25,000 in population. By the 1870's, with its superlative natural harbor and spectacular vistas, its absence of winter (as of summer), its exotic connections and full-blooded living, the wealth of the moguls of mining and railroads who built in character on Nob Hill, and that something in the air that is California, San Francisco was on its way to becoming the city in which more Americans say they would rather live than any other.

Though nothing else was to match the Mother Lode, California was not the whole story, by any manner of means. In the corner of Nevada abutting the Sierras and Lake Tahoe, some placers had been producing for ten years when, in 1859, a settler took it into his head to have assayed some blue-gray sand and quartz from a decomposed vein then being dumped aside as "black stuff" from the Ophir mine. It was found to be silver ore with a value four times as great as that of the gold in the ore the Ophir was working. Word got out and the rush was on. The lode, named after Henry H. P. Comstock, a Canadian who by sheer effrontery had maneuvered himself into the original claim, eventually proved to extend for two and a half miles along the eastern face of Sun Peak (renamed Mount Davidson). Reaching maximum production in 1877, the Comstock Lode by the end of the century had yielded gold to the value of almost $150 million and silver to the value of $200 million. It gave George Hearst his first fortune and made the four once-penniless Irish immigrants who owned the Consolidated Virginia and California, the "Big Bonanza,"—John W. Mackay, James G. Fair, James C. Flood, and William S. O'Brien—among the richest men in the world while also, as has been said, "creating a score of mere millionaires." As Rodman W. Paul observes, "Flood's lavishly ornate houses on Nob Hill and in suburban Menlo Park, Mrs. Mackay's European extravagances, and Fair's purchase of a seat in the United States Senate (by outbidding that other Comstock millionaire, William Sharon) became international symbols of Comstock prodigality."

Another symbol was Virginia City. The "livest town" in the country, as it was called by Mark Twain, who got his start in journalism there, it was a dwarf cosmopolis clinging to a mountainside with streets crowded with men and mule wagons, a place of hard work in the hot depths of the mines and of a heady atmosphere of fast business, speculation, and vice. Of mining towns in general, a Colorado geologist quoted by Professor Paul wrote that, upon the discovery of gold, "a boom follows. The off-scourings of the country pour in with the saloon, dance hall, and gambling hell element. A murder or two follows. Lynch law takes a hand. Then a horde of real estate men come in, and lots are sold at fabulous prices, and the town is inflated with a population and everything else usually far above the capacity of the mines to support. A collapse follows, and a steady retreat of hollow-eyed, disappointed adventurers. In time the town and camp assume their lawful proportions and business settles down to its lawful regime."

Ten years after Marshall's find, gold was discovered in the Pike's Peak region of Colorado's Southern Rockies by a party organized by a Georgian miner. Thereupon a hundred thousand fortune-seekers set out from the East under the slogan "Pike's Peak or bust!" Half of them made it, the rest settling for the alternative, turned back by a returning stream of their predecessors, who had found the pickings slim. Already, however, two other prospectors—another Georgian and a Californian—had struck it rich in the mountains east of Denver and a second influx followed: the rush of the Fifty-niners. But Colorado did not really begin to pay off until the 1870's, when Leadville came in—to eclipse Virginia City by the end of the decade. "The silver princes of Leadville's heyday surpassed in picturesqueness, if not in out-and-out wealth, the big four of the Big Bonanza," John A. Hawgood writes. "H. A. W. Tabor, a semi-illiterate miner, who bought himself an actress ('Baby Doe' eventually became his second wife and survived in reduced circumstances until 1935), an opera house for her to perform in, and a seat in the U. S. Senate for his own performances, was the most fabulous of these, but the Dexters and the Healys ran the Tabors close." In 1890 came one of the great gold finds of the West on the southwestern slope of Pike's Peak. "Cripple Creek," says Professor Paul, "became El Dorado, a miniature California with modern conveniences . . . electric lights, telegraph and telephone lines, daily newspapers, and connections with two railroads."

The 1860's saw the Boise Basin and the rugged Northern Rockies draw the harder-bitten types from farther west and gave Idaho and Montana a mining-frontier past complete with desperadoes like Plummer and Slade and vigilante groups to deal with them. In Alder Gulch, it also gave Montana a Nevada City and a Virginia City—mementoes of the hopes and nostalgia of those who built them. The next decade brought the Black Hills to the fore—even while the Sioux were still strong enough to finish off Custer and the 7th Cavalry. The most prosperous of the South Dakota camps were Lead (still productive) and Deadwood, where Wild Bill Hickok met his fate and Calamity Jane made her reputation (as what, I have never been quite sure). Claims made for the Black Hills as the "last frontier" of Western mining might well be contested. And that would be without counting the renowned little river that flows into the Yukon shortly before the latter crosses from Canada to Alaska halfway up their north–south border, the Klondike, on which more than twenty thousand converged in 1897-8, many after enduring the worst hardships of any gold rush on the passes of the mountain trails. In 1878, when Deadwood offered at least as much security for life and property as the nation's capital today along with "all the conveniences and even luxuries," we are told, a thirty-year-old veteran of indifferent luck in various gold fields ignored Army warnings of the Apaches and wandered into the southeastern corner of Arizona. As he is described, already looking middle-aged from hardships, he calls up the indelible figure of the prospector with his long, unkempt hair and beard, his patched and ragged clothing, and slouch hat mended with rabbit skin. And it was the prospector's dream that Schieffelin realized—a silver strike that enabled him to sell his claim, the Lucky Cuss Mine, in two years and give himself up to the good life in Los Angeles. Tombstone, which he laid out and named, quickly became a national byword for silver mines "in bonanza" (in fair weather) and for lawlessness. Handsomely as its mines paid off, more money was to be made in the long run from the exploitation of its outlawry. The mind reels to think how many versions and derivatives of the feud between the Earp brothers and the Clantons and the gunfight at the O. K. Corral Hollywood and the television industry have contrived, and for what profits.

Land-hunger had taken the American people from the Atlantic littoral across the Appalachians to the Mississippi and into Texas. Government explorers and fur-traders had blazed trails to the Pacific. Farmer-colonists had followed them to the Willamette Valley, Great Salt Lake, and the Central Valley of California. But it was the prospectors and miners who opened up the Far West and were to see the frontier relegated to history. The mining camps of the Northern Rockies witnessed the cruel retreat and subjugation of the Sahaptin (or Nez Percés) under Chief Joseph, Deadwood the murders of Crazy Horse and Sitting Bull and extinction of Sioux independence, Tombstone the surrender of Geronimo and "pacification" of his Apaches.

The gold-rush chapter of American history may seem to outsiders to epitomize what is most characteristic of the whole, and perhaps not without some justification.. There was the pursuit of riches in their starkest form that made nothing of distance, wilderness and hardship; the mass excitement; the heterogeneity of the crowds that poured into each new El Dorado (or El Argento); the attraction exerted by the freedom of the frontier; the violence both of the transgressors and of the community's avengers; the immense vitality that was unleashed; the democracy that prevailed; the wealth that was won for the nation; the technology that was developed; the overnight creation of millionaires, dynamic, crude, daring, grasping, and capable of great acts of public service. There was the essential American restlessness and preference for a chance at the big killing to steady, humdrum work. "Our countrymen are the most discontented of mortals," a New England woman wrote of the Feather River mines in 1851–2. "They are always longing for 'big strikes.' If a 'claim' is paying them a steady income, by which, if they pleased, they could lay up more in a month, than they could accumulate in a year at home, still, they are dissatisfied, and, in most cases, will wander off in search of better 'diggings.' "

There was finally the human appeal—and the fate—of the men who made the raw, remote, and isolated mountain camps their home. On this, we may accept Mark Twain's deposition, with some allowance made for the hyperbole of youth and journalism. They were, wrote the author of *Roughing It,* "erect, bright-eyed, quick-moving, strong-handed young giants—the strangest population, the finest population, the most gallant host that ever trooped down the startled solitudes of an unpeopled land." What he adds may be more strictly factual. "And where are they now? Scattered to the ends of the earth—or prematurely aged and decrepit—or shot and stabbed in street affrays—or dead of disappointed hopes and broken hearts—all gone, or nearly all." That, too, says something about America, where a peculiar emptiness and hopelessness lie in wait for failure and where failure, by the standards we set, is very common—is perhaps more characteristic of our country than the success we read in our history and see in our material greatness.

I am to spend nearly a week traversing the country of the gold and silver strikes, from just about one end of it to the other. The part where I enter it would give anyone a respectful opinion of the grit required of its first invaders. *A barren, wild, rocky country. The plain is strewn with basaltic boulders, like cannonballs. . . . A Joshua tree: if there ever was a defensive-looking plant in a hostile land, this is it.* Massive fault-block ranges lie ahead on the road that leads westward from Hendersonville toward Pahrump, passing south of Las Vegas. Real brutes, they seem to me, with snow in the higher crevices. In the first can be seen the strata that formed the earth's crust before the huge block was wrenched loose and uptilted like a rearing horse. The second is enormously high, of pale rock riven down the face—*about the color of meat fat with some of the meat still in it. God, they're tough-looking mountains, of hard, resistant-looking rock. Ahead of us is a range that goes up summit on summit to what must be a tremendous height.* It is indeed; the Spring Mountains rise to almost twelve thousand feet. *You can hear the bus laboring to get up a road that looks perfectly level. The wind blowing, and it's getting very gray. We keep on climbing. Ruined walls tower over us here, walls forming part of the face of the mountains. The architecture of rock reminds one of an Angkor Wat that was built without a plan, that just grew by fantastic excrescences. . . .* Across such thankless, rock-strewn plains only nominally redeemed by Creosote bush, and into such blasted mountains, undeterred by the excellent chance of his losing his scalp to the Indians or perishing through some other misadventure, trudged, a century ago, the solitary figure of the prospector with his gear-hung, heavy-headed burro. A self-exiled, unstable, foredoomed misfit, he must have been in most cases. He was certainly no element on which to build a society. Yet, like the fur-trader of a generation or two earlier, he went to the heart of the matter, where there was no one and nothing but himself and the primitive Earth; and I think he proved the human spirit in a way that has left us in his debt more than for the precious metals he put in circulation when his luck was in.

The road goes perfectly straight for twenty miles between ridges obscured in rain-clouds before we break out through a window in the overcast. Pahrump, preceded by an unexpected expanse of plowed fields, lies in the sun, a few houses, a gas station, a stand of cottonwoods, and, to let you know you are still in the *bona fide* United States, a promise: "Coming soon! Golden Valley Shopping Center." And then, farther along on the road to Shoshone, following a farm and a ramshackle house or two, a bigger sign for something or other "in the heart of the fertile Pahrump Valley." The fertile Pahrump Valley! And nothing meets the eye but desert. No small part of the fraud practiced in America could well be the product of a half-genuine belief that advertising makes it so. It is a faith in faith itself. It sends a hundred thousand of us streaming westward at a breath of gold in Colorado. . . . *Still the infernal wind. Terrible country this is. "Welcome to California," says a sign. "Charles Brown Highway." There is nothing else. . . . Listen to that wind!*

On and on the highway goes, up the long, wide valley, which slopes gently and evenly down to the middle from the ranges on either side—rawboned mountains, precipitous and peaked, unsoftened by vegetation. They look as if a climb up into them of an hour or two would take you to reaches where you could remain ten years and never glimpse another soul. Lonelier country I have never seen. No other car is on the road, no living creature in sight but a kestrel maneuvering skittishly on the wind and a raven rising on downsweeping wings, perhaps to report me to the shadowy, cloudwrapped hulks. Stopping for gasoline at a fork in the road called Death Valley Junction, I ask the boy filling the tank if it is always as windy as this. He says no, it's like this for about three months of the year and they really get sick of it. He is about nineteen with red hair and sideburns and could be plucked from this region of utmost desolation and set down anywhere else in the United States and appear perfectly natural; he would be astonished and offended that anyone could suppose otherwise. What is it like living here? He says it's great, he wouldn't change it for life in any city. Wasn't it pretty dry? "There's plenty of water. All you have to do is dig down four feet for it." But I suspect it would be a long four feet.

You look at the pitiless country before you—pitiless because itself the victim of pitilessness, you would think—and imagine how it must have appeared to the first whites who set out to cross it. Forty-niners making up a wagon-train, who had been following the trail from Salt Lake to the frontier town of Los Angeles, they had attempted a shortcut. They were already worn out and hungry when they crossed the Amargosa Mountains (as I am doing, heading into the last glow of day between the black masses of the range, with not a light in sight anywhere) and saw before them the alkali flats of the worst desert of all and, behind it, rising to a greater height above their base than any other mountains in the then United States, the Panamints: "the stoutest heart sank then," one reported.

The unmarried men, abandoning most of their equipment, continued on their own. To strike a swashbuckling pose and make it easier to face what they were doing, I suppose, they called themselves the Jayhawkers slang for irregular soldiery. After painful struggles, nearly all of them made it across the valley, the mountains, and the Mojave Desert to the settlements. Those left behind, some too exhausted to go on, comprised fifteen men and women and seven children. At length two of the men volunteered to try to find a way out and bring help. The rest remained camped by a spring until, twenty-six days later, the two forerunners returned with pack animals, having reached San Fernando in the course of fearful hardships. After falling upon the necks and at the knees of their deliverers, the party, less one who had died, set forth anew. On the farther heights there was a pause for a last look at the place that few, probably, had kept alive much hope of leaving, and a young member, a girl, gave it the name it was to bear thenceforth: "Good-bye, Death Valley."

It is an intimidating name, and descending to the notorious sink you have odd feelings. Or you do at night, with the forms of the dark cumulus clouds hardly separable from those of the mountains and only one other car between Death Valley Junction and your destination, twenty-nine miles away. "Elevation 3,000 feet," says a sign in the headlights at 8:11 P.M. . . . At 8:15: "Death Valley National Monument." . . . At 8:18: "Elevation 2,000 feet." . . . At 8:25: "Elevation 1,000 feet." . . . At 8:37: "Sea Level." There is still considerable down hill to go, but there are also some lights. I had not been fully convinced by promises of a campground, but here one is, lavatory building and all, with half a dozen other equipages in a grove of tamarisks, though the wind is blowing up so much dust that not much can be seen.

But at dawn the air is still, the temperature a lovely seventy-eight degrees; for one of the few times on the trip, getting up does not mean extruding myself shiveringly from the sleeping-bag. And what an oasis I walk out into! I am taken aback by it—the grove of date-palms, the golf course, green tamarisks, and mesquite. Furnace Creek, this is, and it affords (which I am sure I could not) two elegant ranches, now closed, for winter vacationers, with horses, pasture, and cottages under tamarisks with trunks up to a foot and a half in diameter. I had forgotten, if I had known, that this is a winter resort, with mild daytime temperatures for six months of the year. A long, low hotel, of yellow plaster with a red, barrel-tiled roof luxuriates in ornamental shrubbery and palmettos. I am continually being struck by how much is done to make things inviting and pleasant for the well-to-do—albeit to no avail, we are to understand; happiness cannot be had for money.

The green anomaly of Furnace Creek is at the center of the 140-mile-long basin. This was created when a block of the earth's crust sank to abysmal depths in the dislocations that raised the fault-block ranges, and it must be matchless on earth for the appearance it presents of a land doing penance for some unimaginable provocation of the divine wrath. Death Valley's maximum recorded temperature of 134.6 degrees in the shade (a temperature at which water is unbearable to a finger dipped in it) has been slightly exceeded by a temperature reported from Libya. Nowhere else, however, has such heat been recorded with such drought. The basin's yearly average rainfall is only an inch and a half. More here than anywhere else you are struck by the paradox that where precipitation is least, the effects of the rare cloudbursts are most devastating. What poor, wasted ranges hem in the valley! They rise on either side above the aprons formed of their sediments, bare, fissured, gullied, breached by canyons; there is no part of their surface that is not the flank of a crevice or ravine, great or small. Erosion has hewn their lower slopes to the configuration of huge gaunt claws, like gryphons' talons, extended out on the flats. The Panamints, sharply peaked and ridged, topped by Telescope Peak, snow-crested at eleven thousand feet above you, seem to—and must at their altitude—support a dark vegetation on their higher parts, but below are naked, as if skinned. Laceration by water and cauterization by

fire you would think have been the fate of the mountains of Tomesha, "Ground Afire," as it was to the Shoshones. Only heat fierce
enough to scorch clay and rock could, you feel, account for their
colors, which range from white to black through all shades of brown
—fawn and gold.

During exceptional springs, after rains normally spread over several years have fallen in one winter, it is said that the drab alluvial
fans, washes, and canyon floors are transformed for a few days by
outbursts of bloom, by the flowering of white and golden primroses,
desert sunflowers, purple phacelias, blue lupine, and white Gravel-
ghosts. For from five to ten years the seeds will have abided their
time, awaiting their chance. Life never misses an opening; given
time, it will, in its unconscious ingenuity, find a way even against
apparently insuperable odds. But, knowing this, one must all the
same rub one's eyes with disbelief at the sight of those grim flats
radiant with colorful, living cheer.

From the mouth of Desolation Canyon, which is as far as I can
go, the basin appears utterly lifeless but for a herb beside me and
an inch-long moth on the windshield. The center part of the long,
gravelly plain, leading south to Badwater, 280 feet below sea-level,
and beyond is white as snow with salts deposited by the evaporating
run-off of the hills. Depressingly, indescribably bleak, it would be
even more formidable to cross than I imagine, the map showing it
to be ten miles wide as against my estimate of two. Yet I find it
hard to turn back—to give up Death Valley. Few natural landscapes
are so characterless—which no one would call Tomesha—that they
do not seem to have something to communicate, something of bearing on the central mystery, if one will but steep onself in them.
And those in which men have strived, as man's way is, and been
ultimately defeated or discouraged or for some reason given up and
left their ghosts behind have, one feels, more to tell than others.

Death Valley is one of those. Its heyday came with the exploitation of the borax deposits in the alkali flats, beginning in 1882.
These were refined at the Harmony Works above Furnace Creek.
At the borax museum at Furnace Creek is displayed one of the rigs
in which the product was transported 160 miles southwest to the
town of Mojave. It is made up of a lead wagon and a cargo trailer
on enormous wheels with a capacity of twenty tons, that of a mam-
moth truck of today. In addition there was a water-wagon with a
1,200-gallon tank. It is no wonder that between twelve and twenty

mule-teams were needed to haul the assembly. Even the hardest-bitten mule-skinners who helped take that string of animals and lumbering rig—the check line was 125 feet long—down the basin, over Wingate Pass near its southern end and across one hundred miles of the Mojave Desert must have felt they were hewing out the stuff of saga, of national legend. But in our nation nothing lasts. The museum also exhibits the steam tractor that supplanted the mules in 1894 and the steam locomotive that supplanted the tractor when a branch railway reached the valley in 1907—only to be abandoned when richer borax deposits were found in the Mojave Desert.

So long as the scenes of history survive, so do the shades of those associated with them. Such scenes, however, generally receive short shrift among us; our dead are customarily condemned to a second, conclusive death. Yet the route of the twenty mule-teams through the basin has been little altered. The ruins of mills and mining communities are scattered in and around Death Valley, and so are the graves of more than a few of the valley's invaders. These go back to the victims—several at least; no one knows quite how many —of the first crossing in '49. Many wayfarers since then, prospectors among them, have left their bones here after losing their bearings or their burros, miscalculating the distance to the next spring or succumbing to the heat—and Tomesha is still taking its toll. One was Jim Dayton, a caretaker of Furnace Creek Ranch, where the mules used to be pastured. Starting out alone on an August day in 1898 for Daggett, 110 miles due south, he gave out before he had gone twenty miles and was buried where he was found. Many years later, another old-timer of the valley died and at his own request was buried at the same spot. His epitaph is one he wrote himself. Taking you unaware halfway through, it leaves you deeply touched. It reads:

HERE LIES SHORTY HARRIS
A SINGLE-BLANKET JACKASS PROSPECTOR.
BURY ME BESIDE JIM DAYTON
IN THE VALLEY
WE BOTH LOVED.

Shorty Harris, I learn, was one of two partners who discovered the rich Bullfrog gold lode across the Amargosas, which gave rise to the boom town, now ghost town, of Rhyolite. He must have made a pile, but his take slipped through his fingers. One suspects that unconsciously, anyhow, he did not wish to be spared the need to pursue never-ending trails with his burro through and around the valley he and the caretaker of Furnace Creek both loved—Death Valley!

What was it they loved? Separation from the harassing human crowd? The depths of the valley's silence? The serenity of its distances and stoic mountains? The companionable brushes with creatures that shared its solitudes and meager pickings—Kit fox, coyote, wildcat, ground-squirrel, Kangaroo rat? The delight in elementary pleasures hard-gained—spring water, green shadows in shimmering desert heat, aroma of wood smoke, warmth and dancing light of a fire at a winter camp? The sense of containment and peace in a great simplicity? The comradeship, beyond words, of man and man in a land hard and spare but without smallness? All these things? Others as well? The answer, I imagine, would define the secret of the West!

State Highway 190 climbs the Panamints up the wash the Jayhawkers followed in their escape from the valley. On the way it looks down on the sand dunes trapped in the valley, moved this way, then that by the winds, their ridge lines forming the most graceful curves—a small Sahara. Jagged rocks and basaltic boulders form the mountain you are ascending. At five thousand feet you reach Townes Pass and have Panamint Valley below you. The descent is beyond any of my acquaintance, four thousand feet in a few miles with the bus roaring down grade in second speed at forty miles an hour with my foot on the brakes. *Steep mountainsides that are masses of lava rocks. Going over a bridge above a chasm that looks like the entrance to Hell.*

Panamint Valley appears to be Death Valley all over again, walled on the west by another stark fault-block range. This is the Inyos, and it is every color that earth could be. Leaving behind the small group of little white houses among tamarisks that is Panamint Springs and climbing into the range, I really do not know what to think. One has never learned what to think of such an uplift of granitic and volcanic rock. It has never been part of the reading for the course. These might be the internal organs of the earth heaped up here by some Satanic surgeon. The viscera, the basaltic rocks, looking heat-brazed, are black and reddish brown verging on purple. In a road-cut the rock is white and granulated—volcanic tuff, compacted of spicules of volcanic glass. Glass also coats many of the black boulders, which look greased. . . . *The bank is steep up on the left, steep down on the right—and lava, lava. This is no place for a nervous driver.* I am having my introduction to secondary roads in the mountainous West and to recurrent spasms of fear when I think how easy it would be to drive off the side in an instant of preoccupation with the geology while holding the microphone to my lips with one hand and steering with the other. . . . Ahead is an almost flat plateau cupped by mountains and occupied by a congregation of Joshua trees. Poor damned souls, signaling with handfuls of radiating blades, of which their heads are also formed! I cannot help feeling a twinge of guilt at leaving them to their perdition.

"Good-bye, *Death Valley!*" I'll wager the girl who put the bitterness of the long ordeal in that dismissal found as the party plodded westward that dismissal was not the same as exorcism. Even I take with me those gaunt mountains across the lethal flats banded and blotched with buffs, russets, and purple browns which Shorty Harris preferred to wealth in easeful surroundings.

Him I cannot forget. I think I shall remain haunted for good by his last message to the world.

BURY ME BESIDE JIM DAYTON

IN THE VALLEY

WE BOTH LOVED.

It comes to me how I am drawn as irresistibly to mankind by that simple statement of love of a friend and love of Nature as I am put off it by the revelations of self-intoxicated prophets, strangers to either kind of love, whose visions through supernatural lenses, touching the raw nerves of human masses, set them by their ears.

8

THE SIERRA NEVADA

From the high saddle of the Inyos where the tree-yuccas have assembled comes the sight of a world you feel your eyes might be the first ever to have alighted on, a world yet to be set down on the earth. Floating in midair, it seems, is a procession of white peaks across the sky, fading away to north and south.

The Sierra Nevadas! And looking enormous—snow-etched and enormous. That sort of peaked dome you see there could well be Mount Whitney itself! (It is said that from the summit of the Black Mountains, rimming Death Valley on the east, you can look down into Badwater, the continent's lowest point, and across the Panamints to Whitney, the highest in the United States proper.)

Nine thirty-two, and the Sierras are really coming into view over the crest of the Inyos. My God, what a range! Snowy crests with fingers of snow pointing down the slopes, they seem to hang all by themselves in the sky, the mountainsides below them being the same misty blue as the sky above. What an incredible mountain wall! The first man who stumbled over a pass, unprepared, to find this before him must have suffered almost as unnerving a shock as the first to behold the Grand Canyon. The whole rim is irregularly saw-toothed—that being, of course, what *sierra* means: serrate. And it is *nevada:* besnowed. The snowpack descends the gray front of the range, formed of overlapping semi-cones, as I can see now, in long pencilings. The apparition looks every bit of what it is, the continent's single most formidable mountain barrier, four hundred miles long, and probably the world's greatest fault-block range. It is a mass of granite torn from the depths of the earth's crust and upthrust so high on its eastern side that it still stands two and a half miles above sea-level after having lost probably thousands of feet of overlying rock.

Eleven-thirty, as down we begin to go. Another of these into the jaws of death, into the jaws of hell, into the valley of death; on a descent like this even a quotation rehearsed *ad nauseam* cannot make a proper entrance. Owens Lake, at the foot of the range, is eight miles long on the map but hardly to be noticed within the surrounding salt flats. When the ice-sheet stood along the Canadian border fifteen thousand years ago, it covered 150 miles of the valley. (At that time all the salt flats in the Great Basin were lakes and all the lakes vastly larger than now. Death Valley stood under six hundred feet of water. Why the glacial ages should have been times of such heavy snow and rain, or, indeed, why there should have been glacial ages, is still a matter of speculation. But without the underground catchments of Pleistocene precipitation, which we are rapidly draining, we should be even worse off for pure water than we are.) The Sierras rise up from the desert flats almost as abruptly as the Grand Canyon falls away from them, but with the effect of incongruity intensified by the perfectly ordinary foreground encumbered with telephone wires, with some kind of industrial works—salt mines, maybe—trucks plying the highway, roadside businesses: the usual. Even later, where there is pastureland with horses and cattle grazing, your eye travels from the splayed fundaments of the mountain wall up over the steep succession of pyramidal forms into which the front of the granite has been hewn, to the peaks that pierce the white mantle, eight thousand feet or more above you, with snow blowing about them, and you could believe you are seeing things. That the jagged, continuous block of the massif bears little resemblance to conventional mountains adds to the sense of illusion. If one could imagine, beside a scene of everyday mortals going about their business, repairing the highway, selling gasoline, painting a storefront, a woman talking to a friend from a car window, the figure of the Omnipotent gazing over them from a height just below the clouds, one would have an idea of the effect. The highest peaks in the Sierras, up to 14,500 feet, are only between ten and twelve miles, horizontally, from the highway.

"Can you tell me, please, which Mount McKinley is?" I ask at a gasoline station in Lone Pine.

"Mount McKinley?" The operator is puzzled! He has never heard of Mount McKinley, and it is right up there somewhere, one of the peaks as plain as if you could touch them!

"Oh—I mean Mount Whitman . . . Mount Whitney."

He points it out without hesitation. So there is local cognizance of the apparition filling the western sky.

What is more immediately relevant is that I shall find every road into the range blocked by snow all the way up to U. S. 50 from Carson City; the operator is sure of it. That includes all the roads into Sequoia, King's Canyon, and Yosemite National Parks from the east. If I am to see Yosemite, as I must, it means that while passing within five miles of the park I shall have to drive 110 miles north of it, 90 miles west, then all the way back southeast, at a cost of at least a day.

There is nothing for it but to press on northward on U. S. 395, up the valley of the unseen Owens River. The Inyos continue on the right, parched in the cloud-shadow of the mighty Sierras. . . . But what is this? Within an hour the Inyos give place to a giant range that rises superior to the thralldom of the Sierras and exults in a snow mantle of its own. The White Mountains are what I am seeing, according to the road-map, and the tallest is only 250 feet lower than Whitney itself. Why do I not know about them? But I must, for the map shows that they encompass the Ancient Bristlecone Pines Area, a special reservation in the Inyo National Forest. The longevity of these gaunt, twisted patriarchs of the dry, gravelly heights westward of the Southern Rockies, which cling obstinately to life when nine-tenths or more of their trunk and limbs have been killed and stripped bare by the whiplash of the winds, was discovered only in 1956. In that year, by means of core-sampling, a specialist from Arizona (Edmund Schulman) found several Bristlecone pines in the White Mountains to be over 4,000 years old—trees already venerable when the Achaean Greeks built lion-gated Mycenae to greatness nearly a thousand years before Homer. And since then, one 4,600 years old has been found. How admirable they are, refusing to surrender, putting out their new growth year after year, century after century, when the citadel appears as good as lost! Recently, still-standing dead Bristlecones high up in the Ruby Mountains of northeastern Nevada have been discovered to have been young trees 7,000 years ago!

The long ranges rising on either side of the highway to serene, snow-capped summits seem to assure the possibility of ascending to some higher realm of being and of singleness of soul: so, at least, I intimate to the tape. To find something to be worthy of, then devote oneself to being worthy of it: it comes to me, in the upsweep of those mountains crowned in white, that this must be the secret of life.

But before long I am finding it difficult even to live up to what little is required of me, which is merely to take in what I see. I have been growing wakeful too early in the mornings. The highway has been following the Owens River up into the highlands now bordering the Sierras and with this exciting prospect I am actually finding it hard to stay awake. Shameful and incredible, but true. Is there such a thing as impression-fatigue? Is the absorption of sights, like the absorption of alcohol, eventually soporific even while stimulating? I doubt it. I am simply brutish. . . . When the highway reaches the level of the lowest snow in the creases of the mountains I get out for a run. Fortunately, the icy keen air is bracing, even medicinal, for we are among groves of Ponderosa pines, and with the warmth of the brilliant sunlight, rehabilitating. I am brought back to life—but only for a spell. In less than an hour it is worse than ever. Not for a long time do I realize that the source of my trouble is the thinness of that bracing air; that, on top of lack of sleep.

At Dead Man Summit (meaning pass) we are over eight thousand feet up. Near by are the headwaters of the Owens River, around which for the second half of the past century, acting on the babbled recital of a crazed German, prospectors combed the hills for a vein of "cement" containing "lumps of gold set like raisins in a pudding." The German was one of three brothers who came on the deposits in the 1850's while attempting to cross the mountains, only to be driven off by an onslaught of winter in which two of the brothers lost their lives and the third his senses. I cannot help reflecting that the Almighty has it within his power to lead me unerringly to the "lost cement mine"—whatever the "cement" may have been—and that if I gave the thing a chance it is just possible, in view of my special deserts and of my being I and hence unique. . . . With reluctance I keep on going.

The peaks and domes of the Sierras are crowded above us in the west, their crags too steep for snow to cling to them, their flanks hung with clouds so that they appear to be steaming. It is all one would have expected. The high plains we cross are still wintry and dead. *(These are wonderful mountains, but I don't think anywhere in the East would you find a natural scene as dreary as this high flatland.)* They are, moreover, swept by a terrible, rasping wind that roars down from the range. One of my most consistent impressions of the West is fighting inexhaustible, gusty blows to hold that little windjammer of a bus on the road. . . . The blue-green waters of a peculiar lake, a dozen miles long, are being churned to froth by the gale. This is Mono Lake, and I learn that the froth is a soapy foam generated by the alkaline salts so concentrated in the lake that nothing animal will live in it but brine shrimp and the larvae of a fly—which puts it in Great Salt Lake's class. The black island rising in it is the dome of a small extinct volcano, while the white island and the weird, upright forms along the shore resembling the ruins of a Burubadur are apparently of tuff. A very strange lake indeed. Here on the eastern side of the central Sierras is the beginning of one of North America's two great volcanic creations, the Cascades-Columbia-Snake highlands.

Facing it, and roughly along the line of U. S. 395, is the granite of the Sierra batholith—the three-hundred-or-more-mile-long granite block hatched deep in the earth 100 million years ago or thereabouts and raised long after to form the body of the Sierras. Where it is exposed, it is riven vertically by weathering, especially by frosts, and this adds to the air granite has of upward impulse. It is a rock that in its sparkle and the general light value of its colors seems destined for loftiness. Among the ridges, barren as the Inyos, rising to Conway Summit, it is upthrust like broken bones through flesh. Granite yields to time, as everything must, but with a defiance that sees everything against which its dissolution might be measured gone before it. Everything, that is, but the sea. The sea endures because it gives, granite because it does not; it will wear steel files smooth. The most enduring human monuments are of granite, and to granite itself the Sierra Nevada is a monument. Where the road maneuvers into the range, the granite bastions tower overhead in giant Gothic formations—Gothic in intricate architecture and ascending lines and Gothic in mood of romantic, super-earthly power and hint of ruin in the rubble of boulders beneath them.

But grogginess has been overcoming me again. *The problem is that with this drowsiness, the sense of reality slips away from you. You have to fight it every instant.* The erlking's daughters could spirit you away from the hard practicalities of the highway to dreamy and enchanted groves without your suspecting what had happened until you crashed. I have sense enough just in time to give up the struggle and pull over to the side of the road. Though no daytime sleeper, I am actually blotted out for five minutes. . . . Circulation: everything, I tell myself, is circulation! It takes some doing to get myself out for a run. But running followed by a big cup of hot, strong tea followed by another run brings me pantingly back to life. The setting helps, too, I think—the unexpected natural garden of a marshy, mountain meadow over which Cliff swallows are fluidly coursing and a magpie takes off, flying in a leisurely way, hardly more than opening and closing its wings. It is a fine, consequential bird, the magpie, streaming its long, graduated tail and unabashed at being the most conspicuous object in the landscape in its sartorial bravura of whitest white and greenest black. Why the East is denied a bird common over the Far West and Europe is hard to understand.

Halls of mountain kings! Only the Norse gods could feel equal to the overpowering granite structures rising from the shadows of approaching evening.

By the time I reach U. S. 50, only twenty miles south of Gold Hill and Virginia City, day is nearly over. I am lucky to find even this highway open. Eight inches of new snow were plowed off it only hours ago. Just before nightfall I have a view of Lake Tahoe which I am not likely to forget. An inland sea, it appears, and a wild, gray one, its waves running high before a wintry wind and forested, snow-capped mountains all around, some rising to over 10,000 feet. And in fact, though over 6,200 feet in altitude, it is almost 200 square miles in extent. The highway lies back from the wooded shores. Where these are settled, there are summer cottages which look as if they take means to own. Lake Tahoe—and we are indebted to an official of the Department of the Interior for the preservation of its Indian name in disregard of the laws of California, under which it is Lake Bigler, in honor of some governor—has a possibly fatal malady. Half the basin is in National Forest, but the shores are nearly all privately owned, and development is now the order of the day. Giant draglines are excavating for "Tahoe Keys . . . lagoon living." Back from the highway is the longest string of fancy motels I have ever seen; and in the town of Stateline, just inside Nevada (which encompasses the eastern side of the lake), are gambling palaces in which vulgar ostentation achieves a regal splendor: the blinding sheets of lights, one of scarlet lights covering the whole side of a considerable building, would inflame the fantasies of a parvenu maharajah. Signs advertise craps, poker, and slot-machines, 250 of the last in one establishment. And through the windows are to be seen the devotees rapt at the devices. Unbelievable.

Lake Tahoe is the creation of a natural dam. The glaciers that scoured out its bed piled the rubble they carried with them in a moraine that blocked the southern end of the valley. U. S. 50 passes among its hills on the way westward. I have no desire to follow it farther that night but cannot find a campground. I drive for miles—thirty-five, all told—over a 7,400-foot pass, then down through the dark, with deep snow alongside and snow flurries in the air. These make me nervous, for the bus is not equipped to deal with snow-storms and is bad on ice—and I am constantly expecting the water on the road to be frozen, the temperature having been only thirty-one at the lake. Safely below the snowline, I trust, and the danger of a frozen radiator, I violate my rule about camping and, taking a chance on the police, pull a mere fifty feet off the highway for the night, into a turn-out.

Inevitably I have been thinking of the Donner party, which endured its ordeal just northwest of Lake Tahoe. Like the first to cross Death Valley three years later, the emigrants led by the Donner brothers had attempted a shortcut. Following an arduous passage of the Wasatch Range they had been exhausted by days and nights of travail without water in the desert west of Great Salt Lake and stopped for a few days of recuperation beside a river at the present site of Reno. That was fatal. At the crest of the Sierras the travelers were caught and immobilized by an early blizzard. Soon the snow around their camp was twenty feet deep. Their cattle lost and provisions exhausted, they ate mice, bark, and, as they died, one another. Fifteen of them, in a desperate effort to get through, had gone on. Of this party, seven survivors after a month of unspeakable miseries, in which they had also been reduced to cannibalism, reached an Indian village. All five women members but only two of the ten men had come through, interestingly enough. By February 19, the first of several rescue expeditions reached the encampment of the main body. Of the original eighty-one, only forty-five finally came out alive.

People are still living today who could easily have talked with survivors of the Donner party, and doubtless some are who have. The event was thus not so long ago. Yet there, a few miles from where the pitiable emigrants discovered their helplessness in the wintry grip of the North American wilderness, is lagoon-living at Tahoe Keys and Stateline's citadels of magic lights—the casinos where hundreds squander the gift of life which the emigrants stopped at nothing to hold onto and must have seen as precious beyond all the tears that could be wept for it. The scene has changed indeed. It is a question whether or how long the waters of Lake Tahoe, which Mark Twain pronounced so clear that even where eighty feet deep "every little pebble was distinct, every speckled trout," will remain unclouded by the defilement of the emigrants' descendants. In other heartlands of the wild Sierras, Yosemite Valley on a week-end is clogged with smog from campfires and motorcar exhausts, and a Walt Disney fantasia of an Alpine village with twenty-two ski-lifts, skating rinks, heated swimming-pools, etc., is planned for King's Canyon. I could add that from the south end of the lake discovered in 1844 by John C. Frémont, whose crossing of the Sierras two years before the Donner party's was so grueling his Indian guides abandoned hope, I am able, thirty seconds after I pick up the telephone, to hear my wife's voice in Virginia as plainly as if it came from the proverbial next room. ("I'm calling from Arlington Boulevard," I exclaim brightly, that being the name under which U. S. 50 passes within seven miles of our house.) So far have we come in so short a time (Frémont's life over-lapped by five weeks with my mother's, which is still in high gear), and such is the direction in which we move into the future at an ever-quickening tempo. It is remarkable that we Americans are not more unsettled and confused as to reality than we increasingly appear to have become.

There are three eggs left out of the original dozen, so this must be the tenth day.

I have awakened among broadswords of trees, Douglas firs, between two torrents pouring down an almost vertical mountainside into a green river tumbling through a rocky ravine. The river, unbeknownst to me at the time, is the historic South Fork of the American River. Placerville, twenty-five miles down the highway, which leaves the river just below my campsite, is only seven miles from the site of Sutter's mill.

I should pay more attention to Placerville than I do. Known for years as Hangtown for the number of outlaws strung up on one of its oaks, it was one of California's most important towns when the Butterfield Overland Mail first came through it in 1858, the Pony Express in 1860, and the telegraph in 1861. But about all I notice is how cramped it is, constricted longitudinally by the mountains, and the number of its businesses named for the Mother Lode. Driving under a low overcast and still worried about snow, I am more impressed by the two palm trees at Diamond Springs a few miles farther on.

Is there anywhere in the West what we think of as *country* in the East? I have never been sure. But from State Highway 49 wending a southeasterly way along the western foothills of the Sierras, I should certainly think there was. Hilly green meadows bordered by trees just coming into foliage roll off away from you. The road passes by willow-lined streams and Live oaks that are miniatures in spread and leaf of the giants of the Southeast.

The sunlight is coming out on this beautiful steep countryside, and across the stream beside which we are driving the hillside meadows are half lavender with some lily-like flower, incredibly beautiful.

But the flowers, not lily-like at all, adorn a plant that grows larger with the miles, becoming almost a shrub. And it is that glory of the West, lupine, with pale blue-lavender pea-blossoms in tall spires. I read with incredulity in John Muir that "by the end of May the soil, plants and sky" of this benign landscape will "seem to have been baked in an oven. Most of the plants crumble to dust beneath the foot, and the ground is full of cracks; while the thirsty traveler gazes with eager longing through the burning glare to the snowy summits looming like hazy clouds in the distance."

With so effervescent a past, it is not surprising to find Californians conscious of it. Amador, a gold-rush town beside a creek, has preserved itself as it was, and a fetching place it is with quaint little houses each exending over the sidewalk a kind of porte-cochere supported on pillars at the curb. It is not only preserved but tidied up, the little buildings freshly painted white and beautifully planted. Altaville, in Calaveras County, is celebrating Jumping Frog Fair—reaching pretty far for a distinction, to be sure—with clothes-lines strung high across the street and Victorian garments of every description hung from them—skirts, dresses, trousers, underwear. There must be twenty of these lines: an astonishing sight. Where did such quantities of antique apparel come from? And the fair is to last four days. Sonora's streets are festooned with the bear-flag of the State of California (the only place where the California Grizzly survives) and notices of the Mother Lode Roundup. Here, too, period houses extend out over the sidewalk. I remember the same kind in a little North Carolina mountain town in which I spent a night on the walking trip I took in my seventeenth year.

If the things in which the past survives have a peculiar appeal today, as I believe they have, it is not hard to understand why. With pleasure domes of unbridled lavishness springing up where yesterday body and soul could only by struggling be kept together; with news broadcasts of a possibly imminent Armageddon juxtaposed to dramatic announcements of a new ingredient in a detergent; with the remote moon brought into our houses by waggish astronauts; with museums of art displaying the cullings of junkyards and paintings of which nothing can be made; with a village people on the other side of the world made enemies of and butchered because they resist; with new freedoms asserted with old obscenities and primitive ferocity; and all in all with our poor minds threatened with utter disorientation, there is a comfort and sense of safety to be known in the company of the bygone. The past for all its shortcomings is comprehensible, for all its perils was survivable—which is more than we can say with confidence of the present and the future.

So for those worthies in towns and cities all across the country who have been banding together to preserve historic houses, blocks of buildings and other moorings of the community—here's to them! Here's to them especially on behalf of the middle-aged. That old locomotive in Kingman, the twenty-mule-team borax-wagon, the innocent, century-old dwellings of Amador and Sonora all keep alive a past possessed in our eyes of the freshness and charm of early morning. They mean to us a time when, like the day at dawn, potential and unrealized, our lives were still unlived and infinite in possibilities, as we knew them in childhood!

On the steep grade down to the Mokelumne River, the vacuum bottle of coffee pitches off the motor hood to spill its contents on the floor. Though not the stark tragedy it would have been had I not finished my doughnut, it is bad enough. It demonstrates that free-standing bottles are incompatible with Western topography. From here on I resort to a practice I unhesitatingly recommend to other hurried travelers—suspending the container from a string around the neck with the straw just below the chin. In order not to exercise the peasantry, however, they may wish to remember to remove it while in slow traffic or when stopping at a service station. All the streams Highway 49 crosses were worked over in the scramble of the gold-rush. And not to be too far beguiled by the winsomeness of the period's legacies in the houses of Amador, it is worth recalling that in the town of Mokelumne Hill, one four-month period is said to have witnessed a killing every week-end and four during a single week.

The road grows steeper and more twisting. The descents to and climbs up from the Stanislaus River and the Tuolumne, at which I turn east toward Yosemite, beat anything I have yet seen. They take you back up into the boulder-formed mountains, granite outcroppings, precipitous slopes, and forest. The snow, from small patches, spreads and deepens to form drifts higher than the bus; the trees grow larger.

"The coniferous forests of the Sierra are the grandest and most beautiful in the world," John Muir declares. But I have to confess that coniferous forests, generally composed over large tracts of but a few species, and these similar in color and in their simple, mast-like trunks, are not my favorites. Neither are they the favorites of wild animal life and other plants. No Western forest I have yet beheld can compare in atractiveness or interest with the forests of the southern Appalachians, in which clouds of foliage of every shade of leaf-green soar upon the spreading limbs of a score of differently formed, intermingled species—a score to an acre—above the liveliest profusion of intermediate growth, flowering plants, ferns, mosses, and fungus. But having said that . . . *My God, they're enormous,* I exclaim, trying to see the tops of the trees above the aisle down which the road runs, a narrow canyon of green above the snow. And the Incense-cedars are in fact beautiful in their bright-green, bird's-foot foliage—they are relatives of our Eastern White cedars—and dark-brown, deeply furrowed, and fibrous bark. Of course, I do not know the forests of the Sierra as Muir did.

With altitude, up in the Canadian Zone, the Ponderosas yield to even bigger pines, with shorter, closely tufted needles. These are Sugar pines, the largest in the world, with cones a foot and a half in length. ("Kings and high priests," Muir called them at his famous meeting with Ralph Waldo Emerson, seeking to rally the failing sage's enthusiasm for a night in the woods, "the most eloquent and commanding preachers of all the mountain forests, stretching forth their century-old arms in benediction over the worshiping congregations crowded around them.") With the Sugar pines come the Red firs—Silver firs, as they were to Muir by virtue of their frosted foliage. Some of these are three or four feet through at the butt and taper only very gently to their pinnacles. All along the highway, and in places growing no more than four or five feet apart, are trees standing a hundred feet high or even more, by my estimate, and they seem immense, and are, if you think of their tops as being even with eleventh-floor windows. But before the lumberman came, some of the Ponderosa and Sugar pines and Red firs stood twice that height or even more, the Sugar pines having butts up to ten or even twelve feet in diameter and the others not being far behind. And of course the Giant sequoia, or Mountain redwood, customarily dispenses with branches for the first hundred of its 275 to 325 feet and is not uncommonly 25 feet through the trunk 4 feet from the ground. ("These trees," said Emerson, with a gentle smile for his ardent guide, "have a monstrous talent for being tall.") As they are pictured—and I am not to see any—their crowns have the shape of the bulging columns of smoke blasted from a steam locomotive's stack. They are at home only in the Sierra Nevada, in groves beginning spottily near Lake Tahoe and expanding southward for some 250 miles.

Having descended to 5,000 feet from the high pass over which the road enters the National Park, I have lunch at a scenic overlook on the rim of the canyon cut by the Merced River and the glaciers of the Pleistocene. The canyon, Yosemite Valley, is so deep that from here the river cannot be seen, but the granite giants of Yosemite stand up fearsomely—Elephant Rocks in front of you and on the left, Half Dome and Rock Chief, as it was to the Indians (El Capitan to the whites). What a marshaling of megaliths!

The valley, when you descend to it, partly through a long tunnel bored through solid rock, turns out to be quite flat; it was once a lake formed behind a moraine, like Tahoe, but the lake was gradually silted in by the Merced, which now flows between level banks, aquamarine in its shallows, a marbled green in the depths. Flat and narrow; you are walled in at close quarters by the conifers and behind them by the nearly vertical walls of the incredible, towering

masses of granite. You feel yourself at the heart of the Sierra batholith, in a sanctum and on sufferance.

I had expected to find few other visitors, the caking of the snow
beside the higher parts of the road indicating that the plow had
only just been through. However, I had not reckoned on the lower,
more southerly entrance. Campers are in occupation and the lodge
seems to be full. At the edge of Yosemite Village, the assortment of
gasoline stations, shops, and other tourists' attractions and conces-
sions, including Yosemite Lodge, for which the valley is notorious,
I am solicited for a ride, and not in vain, by a personable miss on
foot. Newly arrived from a college in Michigan, she explains, she
is working at the Lodge. She is not entirely content, it appears, and
speaks of the cold after sundown, for which she hasn't the right
clothes, but hints indicate that the real trouble is that she is being
left too much to her own devices after hours. However, she seems
to expect, reasonably in view of the influx of her contemporaries it
will bring, that summer will remedy her state. She is a curious sight
to me, in the bus, a dainty and exotic seabird put down upon a
stodgy, coastwise tramp. If I am as much attentive to her as to the
road, however, it is not for the reason she might imagine if she
noticed. It is because she is at that fascinating age when, having so
far had the world at second hand through the intermediacy of parents, a youngster comes into direct relationship with it. Here she is,
two thousand miles from home, looking somewhat uncertainly
around, alone with a world that in the past few days has become *her*
world. Does she realize how remarkable it is that she should have
made it here? Take it for adventure, I should like to tell her. Don't
pursue the ordinary. You don't have to. It will pursue you.

Briefly as she is with me, my passenger's youth and its reminder
of the unfilled agenda of my own adds to my unsettlement. One has
heard how animals engage in "substitute activities." Some male
birds may peck at the ground instead of fighting or, in the stress
of some other emotion, pick up and put down pebbles. "A cat," says
Munro Fox, "may be stalking a bird and the bird flies off; then the
cat will sometimes sit down and wash." And so with me. I have been
pouring didactic observations into the tape recorder. *It is apparently a buff-colored to gray granite which is stained dark by weathering. . . . The granite seems to be a large-grained, light-gray variety
which weathers buff and then I think turns dark gray. I have a piece*

here which has a finer-grained, dark-gray inclusion. I take the tape recorder up to Cascade Falls. *(The next voice heard will be that of the falls. . . . That's how it sounds.)* What disturbs me is Half Dome, Rock Chief, Glacier Point, Sentinel Dome, and Cathedral Rock—the whole setting and what goes with it in my mind.

"Every rock seems to glow with light," John Muir wrote of the "park valleys of the Yosemite kind"—and it would take presumption to describe anything in these ranges that found expression in Muir's writing. "Some lean back in majestic repose; others, absolutely sheer, or nearly so, for thousands of feet, advance their brows in thoughtful attitudes beyond their companions, giving welcome to storms and calms alike, seemingly conscious yet heedless of everything going on about them"—yes, that is how it is!—"awful in stern majesty, types of permanence, yet associated with beauty of the frailest and most fleeting forms; their feet set in pine-groves and gay emerald meadows, their brows in the sky; bathed in light, bathed in floods of singing water, while snow-clouds, avalanches, and the winds shine and surge and wreathe them about as the years go by. . . ." If Muir wrote long sentences, it was because he was carried away.

No one who knows anything of the intense, auburn-haired, blue-eyed, Scots-born champion of the wilderness can be in Yosemite without his being present too. This was where he was quartered during most of the six consecutive years he spent exploring the Sierra Nevada; "The Range of Light" he called "this most divinely beautiful of all the mountain chains I have ever seen." Through his cabin, opposite Yosemite Falls, he had deflected a rivulet of Yosemite Creek so he could hear it "sing and warble in low, sweet tones" from his bed of Incense-cedar boughs.

I can hardly read Muir's accounts of his adventures without a sense of how much I have neglected of the gift of life, of which he made so much. In these scenes that recall their flavor I can feel in myself the stirrings he obeyed wholeheartedly, whether incited by the seductive airs of spring or by the challenging roar and blast of a mountain gale, "the wild gala-day of the north wind [that] seemed surpassingly glorious." Here is where Muir urged the aging Emerson to accompany him on "an immeasurable camping trip"—and in that unexpected, amusing adjective is to be glimpsed the veritable Muir in his individual, uncontainable enthusiasm, which was forever taxing the resources of the language. (He himself was constrained to admit, wryly, to an over-resort to "glorious.") He thought nothing of setting forth alone into the deep wilderness of the forest, into the stark wilderness of granite peaks and glaciers, with no provender but a package of tea and some stale bread. Of such an episode he writes:

"I made my bed in a pine-thicket, where the branches were pressed and crinkled overhead like a roof, and bent down around the sides. . . . The night wind began to blow soon after dark; at first only a gentle breathing, but increasing toward midnight to a rough gale that fell upon my leafy roof in ragged surges like a cascade, bearing wild sounds from the crags overhead. The waterfall sang in chorus, filling the old ice-fountain with its solemn roar, and seeming to increase in power as the night advanced—fit voice for such a landscape. I had to creep out many times to the fire during the night, for it was biting cold and I had no blankets. Gladly I welcomed the morning star. . . . Breakfast of tea and bread was soon made. I fastened a hard, durable crust to my belt by way of provision in case I should be compelled to pass a night on the mountain-top; then . . . set forth free and hopeful.

"How glorious a greeting the sun gives the mountains! . . ."

This particular excursion was aimed at an ascent of Mount Ritter, a peak over 13,150 feet high above the Mono volcanic basin and Owens Valley. "King of the middle portion of the High Sierra," Muir called it. It had never been climbed, and almost was not this time. Muir had as close an escape as he probably ever had in his life.

Summoning Emerson to the high woods, Muir cried, "The mountains are calling; run away, and let plans and parties and dragging lowland duties all 'gang tapsalteerie.' " I am younger than Emerson was but a lot older than the Michigan miss, with several life-lines in my keeping and a deadline to meet and no way of recovering the years I let slip by. So my response is as Emerson's was on the urging of his cautious friends. Under a weight of regrets, I turn to follow the Merced back to the lowlands, in the direction of dragging duties, but little rallied by the sarcastic realism of a disrespectful inner voice I am sometimes troubled by. ("Oh, how put out we are that we didn't pitch headlong to our doom at age thirty, as would have been our fate in the wild Scotsman's place, you may be sure! What a joy of living fully and dangerously would have filled our heart as our brains were bashed out on the rocks!") I shall have to make do (for the present, I tell myself) with seeing the Sierras through Muir's eyes.

There was no one like John Muir. If he stands as an enduring and uncomfortable reproach to the weak in spirit, he is also the answer to the doubts that may infect us who make much of Nature in our scheme of things, who see in Nature the expression of a creative presence on which we draw for our vital energies and which we may legitimately revere. Would a thoroughgoing exposure to the natural world disenchant us? Should we see it ultimately as a horror? Muir exposed himself to Nature all but unreservedly—and no one ever bore more passionate witness to its beauty, its grandeur, the grace it bestows. No one ever found it more "glorious"—whether in the mountains of the West, the glaciers of Alaska, or the forests of the Himalayas and of the Amazon. At times I have felt that in the joy he attributes to mountains and divine music he finds in streams he over-does it; but he had a right to speak as he might choose. He earned the right high on Mount Shasta in a blizzard which no one below thought a man could survive. (He was "lying like a squirrel in a warm, fluffy nest, busied about my own affairs.") He earned it in a December gale before which trees were crashing all through the forest when, "to obtain a wider outlook and get my ear close to the Aeolian music of its topmost needles," he climbed to the summit of one of a stand of hundred-foot-tall Douglas firs and "clung with muscles firm braced, like a bobolink on a reed," while "the slender tops fairly flapped and swished in the passionate torrent, bending and swirling backward and forward, round and round."

"To enjoy keenly the mixed texture of human experience, rather leads a man to disregard precautions, and risk his neck against a straw. For surely the love of living is stronger in an Alpine climber roping over a peril, or a hunter riding merrily at a stiff fence, than in a creature who lives upon a diet and walks a measured distance in the interest of his constitution." So wrote Robert Louis Stevenson at a time, as nearly as I can tell, not long after he and John Muir had both married, both in San Francisco (in 1880, about two years after each had got his start as a writer) and at about the same time that Muir, in Alaska, was suiting the deed to the word. "The most memorable of all my wild days," he called it. Accompanied by a mongrel dog, he had recklessly ventured far out on a glacier and in trying to return had found his way barred by a seventy-foot crevasse crossable only by a deeply dipping "sliver-bridge" of ice. "At worst we can only slip," he reported having assured the frightened dog, calming himself, "and then how grand a grave we will have, and by and by our nice bones will do good in the terminal moraine." And we need have no doubt it was just what he said.

Probably one has no business making a divinity of Nature, or of looking life in the face at all, unless one is capable of such a view. The narrowness of Muir's escape (and the dog's) on this occasion almost matched that of the other, on Mount Ritter's precipice. What he wrote of the latter, together with the uncanny prescience he exhibited at times, almost persuades one that his outgoing devotion to Nature had a kind of counterpart in a return flow from Nature to him. Clinging to the cliff as he was, with arms outspread, unable to move up or down, his doom, as he thought, "appeared fixed. I *must* fall." Becoming "nerve-shaken," his mind "seemed to fill with a stifling smoke. But this terrible eclipse lasted only a moment, when life blazed forth again with a preternatural clearness. I seemed suddenly to become possessed of a new sense. The other self, bygone experiences, Instinct, or Guardian Angel,—call it what you will,—came forward and assumed control. Then my trembling muscles became firm again, every rift and flaw in the rock was seen as through a microscope, and my limbs moved with a positiveness and precision with which I seemed to have nothing at all to do. Had I been borne aloft upon wings, my deliverance could not have been more complete."

But I must keep my feet on the ground. Let it be noted that Muir was a responsible naturalist. If not a scientist, he was the equal of any in acuteness of observation. The discoverer of the Sierra's glaciers, he was also the first to grasp the role of their giant Pleistocene forebears in the excavation of the "Merced Yosemite" as of its kindred "Yosemites"—and this he announced at a time when learned geologists were ascribing the valley positively to the subsidence of a crustal block. Writing in the decades when the assault on the continent's natural endowments, especially its forests and wildlife, had reached a pitch of frenzy such as is said to possess sharks incited by an abundance of easy game, his eloquence was the scourge of "the money-changers . . . in the temple," as he called them, and the inspiration of all whom he awakened to the treasure of which the nation was being plundered. Yosemite was one of the six great National Parks that Muir was vitally instrumental in bringing into being.

It was not the first of the National Parks. It had, however, become their precursor when, in 1864, Congress passed and President Lincoln signed a bill deeding "Yo-Semite Valley" to California in perpetuity "for public use, resort, and recreation." This, it may thus be said, is where the National Parks began. And by the signs one hears of—the hordes that crowd the valley in the summer, the motorcars, trailers, truck-mounted campers and "motor homes" that jam its roads and campgrounds, the pack trains in the high country "like huge cavalry troops"—this is where their end is beginning, unless they are to be protected from their popularity with an ever-growing population with ever more money and time for travel. . . . When I think of the over 300 million Americans there are due to be at the present rate of increase by the time my children are my age and of the mobility and wealth that will enable them (if all continues as at present) to subordinate and put their stamp on ten or twenty times the amount of country the 130 million of my own youth were able to, I wonder what we can possibly bequeath our heirs to make up for what they will be deprived of.

The road that follows the Merced out of the park finds the valley too narrow to accommodate it, finally, and must zigzag its way over an enormous ridge. The sun is declining when we descend to a zone of low, rounded hills very shapely against their shadows and very tranquil, with scattered herds of cattle grazing on them. . . . What a state it is, California, in which, two hours after leaving a far north of granite tors and boreal forest deep in snow, you are sailing through lush summer pastureland with a palm and a palmetto rising forty feet from someone's yard as from a Javanese kampong! The Sierras are still to be seen, low in the east, but by the city of Merced, farther on, past miles of peach orchards, with the first shaggy eucalyptus trees, they have disappeared, and far off in the west is the shadow of the Coast Range.

9

SIERRAS TO PACIFIC

California! ". . . The land of our happy future," Robert Louis Stevenson exclaims of his arrival. "At every turn the cocks were tossing their clear notes into the golden air and crowing for the new day and the new country."

Well, it is nothing exceptional from State Highway 99, the artery of the great Central Valley. Nondescript towns and wearisome commercialism predominate. The rich effulgence of the sunset is like a dream following the sun to sea from a land which has other things to think about. And the evening is of the kind I am always apprehensive of running into. After scooting through night-lighted Sacramento on a freeway and turning north at Roseville, I search in vain for a sleeping-place. Needing a bath, I am reconciled to a motel, but one I come on is too expensive and the only other full. What is worse, it is after ten o'clock, the service stations are closed, and I am running out of gasoline. But fortune relents. At Sheridan is a station where the proprietor has opened up again to accommodate a friend and not only fills my tank but authorizes my parking across the street by his house. Highway 99E is a busy thoroughfare with a railroad beside it, but I am done in and hear nothing until five-thirty.

And the morning is something else. It is the new country of Stevenson's, sunny and mild, without a cloud in the sky, and beautiful in the green pastures and orchards it unfolds before me. I could crow in the golden air. Marysville, where I make an early stop, the bus being due for lubrication and a change of oil, is beaming in the infant day. Jogging along the residential streets I am amazed at the variety of plants around the houses and in the park—palms, palmettos, young redwoods, orange-trees, and with them, Sycamores, American elms, apples, cedars, and pink-flowering hawthorns, all flourishing. So might plants of all kinds thrive together in paradise. . . .

No, that is a bit strong. But it is true that the air is light and luminous and quickens the spirit. There is something different in the atmosphere, something I take to be California. I had remarked it even on the other side of the Sierras. *(These highway towns in California like Bishop have the same commercial strip as elsewhere, yet somehow they're not as depressing. Maybe because there's a little more money and things are better maintained, because the air is better, or because of the background of the mountains, the people look more alert, seem to have more spark. There's a difference.)* To be sure, you would expect running to be less strenuous near sea-level than some thousands of feet above, but—I can hardly stop! When I do and drop in at a café for coffee and a doughnut, my fellow diners appear to me unoppressed by cares in the usual sense, as if life's burdens had less weight here. Yes, it is as if, along with the force of gravitation, there were a force of levitation in California.

The operator of the service station tells me that he came here from Kansas at the worst of the Depression, in 1937, with two bits in his pockets when he arrived. Things started looking up for him from the first day and have been looking better ever since. I can believe it, and since it was in 1937, as it happens, that I drove to California once before, I have the sensation Ponce de León would have known on learning thirty years too late that waters he had come on could very well have been the Fountain of Youth. Or is it too late? Even while wincing at the banality of the impulse, I actually conceive for a time of sounding out my wife on the possibility of dropping everything and moving out here—joining the tide of immigrants that (this time by impulsion rather than expulsion) is bringing about the second loss of Eden. Is it possible that California, like sex, speaks a universal language which there is no gainsaying?

Well prepared for the panorama as I should be, having seen it pictured more times than I can remember, I am further subverted as I drive north by the sight of the snow-capped Sierras on one side and the snow-capped pinnacles of the Coast Range on the other over orchards of lustrous-leaved orange-trees in the virginal ripeness of their seductively scented ivory blossoms. (This is the way Bi-Coloured-Python-Rock-Snakes always talk, Best Beloved, at least in a California morn.) It is late in the day, in the foothills of the Klamath Mountains, when I am all alone with it, that the potency of this land rolls fully in upon me, like a breaker of the sea—unless, then, it is the earth itself and not California alone.

Meanwhile, in the reasonable view that a geology-quester ought to see the country's most recently active volcano (excluding those of the Aleutians) but neglecting a reasonable estimate of the chances of getting to it at this season, I set off up the Feather River Canyon for Snow Butte (or Mount Lassen). It proves to be a canyon indeed, a tremendously deep cleft cut by the Feather River in the Sierra batholith, as Yosemite by the Merced. An initial climb is so long and steep that when the gradient lessens you would take an oath that it has been reversed and become a decline. I have seen other streams beside a road seeming to flow uphill in such topography, but none so convincingly as the Feather River here. There it is, gushing and bounding energetically up the rise you are sure you have come over. And when the bus, in neutral, coasts backward in the same direction, I have every sensation of its rolling magically uphill.

On the steep slopes, some magnificent in lupine, are thickets of a shrub I remember arousing my enthusiasm all those years ago when I first saw it, Manzanita. It is a heath, like rhododendron, Mountain-laurel and blueberry and, strangely enough, while it grows to twelve feet high, a close relative of the prostrate Bearberry that carpets so much of the sands of Cape Cod and Long Island. Its attractive, evergreen oval leaves are carried on branches as smooth and subtly muscled, and as warmly reddish-brown, as the supple limbs of Indian girls (virginally ripe ones). I dare say it was when my youthful head was still hospitable to Polynesian fantasies that it made its indelible impression on me. Botanists, less concerned with the invitation of its branches to caressing fingertips, tell us that Manzanita is a leading component of chaparral, a community of evergreen shrubs forming a low jungle (in the original sense of a dry, tangled, wooded wasteland) on the seaward slopes of the mountains of California, especially the southern Coast Range where rainfall is too scant to support forest.

Every now and then I realize I am looking too much at the rocks and am likely to drive right off the precipice. The variety of these is confusing. Among them is the slatey kind I saw yesterday all along the western foothills of the Sierras—the small outcroppings compared by Muir to ancient tombstones—evidently the remains of the mid-Mesozoic rock that covered the area before the earth gave birth to the Rocky Mountains proper, from the ruins of which in their southern part the fault-block of the Sierras was to arise. But the exciting rock is a kind exposed in some of the deep highway cuts. Here, owing to the convex cleavage-planes in which it splits and its waxy surface, it glistens like the scales of a dragon, or of some splendid armor. Its colors are the intermingled greens and subdued green-blues of the ocean seen from a height on an overcast day. *Verde antique,* often mistaken for a marble, is a variety of it. It is serpentine, and its presence might well be signaled by the powerful, brooding strains to which, in Tchaikovsky's *Swan Lake* ballet, the Prince of the Underworld appears, for that is what it is. Peridotite from beneath the earth's crust, altered by hot aqueous liquids on its way up—such is serpentine, its green colors derived from olivine which, in its transparent varieties, is known to jewelers as peridot and chrysolite. How pleasant it will be if peridotite turns out to constitute the material of the earth's mantle, as some evidence indicates it does, so that we may picture the plates of the earth's crust resting on a bed of gem stone! Serpentine's somber resplendence fits its role. And the block of it I take back with me from the Feather River Canyon, shaped like a bishop's miter, will, I imagine, remain with me for life.

But up near five thousand feet, where the river has been dammed for a large reservoir in a glacial valley, snow fields begin, ominously for me. The road becomes the narrowest of defiles through the great Sierra forest of White fir, Sugar-pine, Ponderosa pine, Incense-cedar, and Douglas fir (Küchler listing 5), about which I retract any reservations I had. The foliage of the firs and Sugar-pines is furry and as if formed as is hoar frost. It is lovely, and in its simplicity and constancy there is a kind of purity. The forest rises absolutely sheer from the sides of the road, and the erectness—the alertness, I am tempted to say—of the slender, immensely tall trees

literally causes one's spirit to stand straighter, I do believe. With
the admonitory bite in the air, it is as if one were being recalled to
a higher purpose. . . . For the time being, there are no more grim
lumberyards of smoking kilns, thank God—only an occasional motel
or lodge.

At lunch, I am able to fill the ice-chest from a snowbank; there
is always that about snow. A few more miles bring Snow Butte into
view, a volcano of five or six summits, as white as if overspread with
marshmallow sauce. The highest is nearly 10,500 feet. . . . "Morgan Summit. Elevation 5,700 feet." . . . "Lassen National Park, 4
miles." *Is it open? By gosh, I believe it is. . . . I believe it is! The
snow is over the height of the bus, but I think it's open. . . .*
"Closed 6 miles ahead." So that is that.

I go as far as I can, however, passing a plow which is shooting
snow off the road in an arc thirty feet high. A young highway
worker stripped to the waist says that a foot and a half of new
snow fell a few days ago, and that yesterday a storm had blinded
them and forced them to quit work. Ordinarily the road through
the park is opened by Memorial Day, but this year he doubted that
they will be able to get through before July Fourth; the snow is
twenty-four feet deep in places. All I can do is go a mile farther and
record the bubbling and hissing roar of some hot sulphur springs—
asphyxiating if you get in the way—and photograph one of the un-
approachable white-clad peaks against a burning blue sky, conifers
like a crowd of dignified courtiers on the saddle below it and the
bus in the foreground with the snow alongside standing twice its
height.

Snow Butte is the last of the chain of volcanoes, extinct or dor-
mant, that crown the Cascade Mountains southward from just below
the Canadian border. (The Cascades and Sierras, while totally different in origin, form a single, continuous range, as far as I can
tell.) It and the adjacent summits were formed of pasty lava ex-
truded from the sides of a larger volcano which subsequently collapsed into the void left by the evacuations. Plug-type, or lava-
dome, volcanoes are dangerous. The fearful eruption of Mont
Pelée, on the island of Martinique, in 1903, in which an avalanche
of fiery gases and incandescent grit racing down the slopes extinguished thirty thousand lives, followed the shattering of a plug-
dome. It was in turn followed by an appalling and eerie extrusion;
for in the wake of the holocaust, up from the crater, there arose

mysteriously in the course of several months a gigantic spine of lava which towered like an Excalibur in inscrutable pronunciation, then rapidly disintegrated. It sends a chill through me to think of it.

Snow Butte's late eruptions, which took place in 1914 and 1915, were modest. A crater was, however, blasted out of the volcano. Up-welling lava poured through a rent in it and, melting the deep snow on the northeastern flank, sent a mudflow eighteen miles long down the creek-beds, twenty-ton boulders with it. Later a cloud of hot gases and dust, blowing out the plug that had closed the vent, poured down the slope to destroy a belt of forest four miles long.

The question is, are these quiescent volcanoes of the Cascades, some exhaling a bit of vapor, dead and dying or only slumbering and capable once more of belching forth yellow-hot torrents of lava and devastating clouds of explosive gases? Who knows? The Pacific Coast States are geologically active. The Coast Ranges have long been rising and presumably still are. In and around them, and all through southern California, sections of the earth's crust have been in slow motion with respect to adjoining sections along cleavages called faults. Along the San Andreas Fault, the northward slippage of the crust on the west has in the course of perhaps 100 million years evidently carried slices of granite from the area where the batholiths of the Sierra, Transverse, and Baja California ranges come together all the way to Point Reyes and Point Arena north of San Francisco—an uneasy neighbor and erstwhile victim of the fault's. The more violent of the earthquakes accompanying the slippages seem to come about when movement has been arrested for a time and strains have been built up as in a tightened spring. One of these shook Yosemite while John Muir was living there, sending showers of slabs down from the granite monoliths. And what might we suppose Muir's response to have been? What *would* it have been? "A noble earthquake!" that incredible man cried, sustained in his fright by the confirmation he was witnessing of his theory of the origin of the talus slopes below the peaks.

I have a theory, too, or an idea. Could the youthful geological vitality of the land have something to do with California's charged atmosphere? A virtue of this notion is its unsubjectability to test.

Late that afternoon it is in my mind that tomorrow I shall see the Coastal redwoods and the Pacific. I am crossing the Central Valley near its northern end, having taken State Highway 36 from

Red Bluff—a road I shall never forget for more than one reason. *Going under Live oaks that meet in the middle, as if this were the coast of Georgia. Rich bottomland pasture of fervent green, the road curving gracefully beside it, with Live oaks all along it, the landscape, completely unpopulated, as beautiful as anything could be. . . . Here's a ranch, the Hi-Lo Ranch, with broad, low buildings, a few of them, but you don't see many inhabitants. Hard to account for so much meadowland. . . . We are driving along in rather high country now, with small Live oaks as if in an orchard and Manzanitas the size of small trees, off on one side the thick white dome of Snow Butte, on the other the higher peaks of the Coast Range. There's nobody up here at all, not another car, no houses.*

In no other place I have ever seen could a countryside so pastoral, so enticing, be found so untenanted. A pair of California quail scuttle across the road, plump wooden toys on a blur of legs, the male with frontal plume erected like an apostrophe curving forward from his forehead. Several times, Acorn woodpeckers, redcapped, flowingly patterned in black and white, fly up from the roadside, lapidary offspring of Nature's unaccountable, zestful artistry. And a large pigeon—a Band-tailed pigeon—waits on the shoulder until we are almost on it before springing into the air. As in some great houses suites of rooms are kept in readiness for special guests, this is a country that might have been fashioned for settlers worthy of Nature's favor who have yet to appear. In twenty miles I count only three human habitations. Up and down, left and right, the little road goes, through a landscape illumined by the late afternoon light as through a golden mist.

The hills, as they grow higher and steeper, are less fertile. After passing a sharp ridge with other ridges running down from it, the vegetation on them rather like a bear's fur when it is shedding, I stop for a run and some tea. The valley is as green as ever. Beside the bus is a little stream bordered as far as I can see by a matted plant with white flowers. It is only six inches wide, but it is hurrying along, chortling, as if to an appointment. In the sweet, cool quiet a bird is singing, and from afar a cow lows once. There is that feeling the West communicates of something lost elsewhere, a feeling that the land is still the freehold of an ancient serenity as unruffled by time as the sea's depths by the storms that agitate its surface. Serenity and distance! It is as if there were lingering on the air the inaudible reverberations of a bell's toll that had sounded the infinite reaches of space.

How express the tranquillity and confidence imparted to me as I linger in that spot? I have a sense of return over many difficult and confusing miles to that to which I belong. This is what I am part of, and to which nothing of me can hence be alien; and if it were possible to offer up my soul to Nature by the little stream, as a subject his duty to his rightful liege-lord, I should do it in perfect trust.

When you journey alone you are possessed more fully by whatever mood circumstances conduce to. Knowing from experience the heart-sickness that may overtake the solitary traveler in the early darkness of chill, gray winter days, I vow I shall remember how sure I was that the emotion born of a lovely valley in the warm glow of a late afternoon in May more faithfully represents the truth of things.

My plan had been to see what the Coast Ranges were like, but as the road climbs, bringing the sight of coagulated metamorphic and igneous rocks, I am moved to consult Philip B. King's *Evolution of North America*. This shows that the mountains I am actually preparing to cross are a detached remnant of the western Rocky Mountains that divide the much younger northern and southern Coast Ranges. That is to say, they are the Klamaths.

A climbing, twisting road: when I am not pulling the steering-wheel hard over one way I am usually bearing down on it in the other. Up among the big pines and White firs of the Trinity National Forest, where the Manzanita is bearing clusters of little bell-flowers, the chill of altitude and chill of evening are coming on. *It's a wonder anything in the bus is still in place. . . . Now it is even worse because we are on a detour. The road through Peanut is closed, presumably snowbound. A really dusty dirt road. . . . Man with a house beside the road and a rather screwed-up face says it's sixteen miles to Hayfork where we rejoin 36. The dust in the bus will be an inch deep on everything by then. . . .*

Abandoned mines and piles and piles of spoil . . . a huge saw-mill and fleet of logging trucks . . . the slightly grubby town of Hayfork, with an altitude and population of about 2,300 each. Then back in the National Forest.

A sign at the head of a steeply descending gravel side-road says Philpot Campground. *Should I try it? Be nice to stop before day-*

light. Here goes. I mean before dark. Down in low. I suppose we'll get back. Holy smoke, this is just a mass of stones, and . . . oops! [A big boulder.] *A lumber road. See a bridge of logs. Ouch! Passed Philpot Creek, but I don't see any campground. . . . By gosh, here it is. Little outhouses. Nobody else, of course. . . . Oh, it's a lovely spot with White firs and pines all around, and a grassy place across the creek there!* What a joy at the end of a day, and what a contrast with the highway at Sheridan—a campground all to oneself far from the road in a dell of the silent, lofty forest and enough daylight to last through a glass of sherry and a dinner produced by a few twists of a can-opener, a match to the gas burner!

It is seven-fifteen in the morning when we claw our way back up to the State road, old 36, and ten o'clock by the time we have gone a mere fifty miles and across the main part of the range. Such a drive I have never had. Over much of it, the road is only one lane wide. Fortunately, I am almost alone on it. Steep up and awesomely down it goes, twisting and bending back on itself as it hugs the convoluted mountainside. Past the giant boles of the trees we creep —deeply furrowed trunk of Incense-cedar, massively plated trunk of pine. The top of one giant, fully a hundred feet in front of us, cannot be seen through the windshield, crane as I will. As we gain a ridge, the trees disappear above us in the cloud. . . . *Early morning, and blue sky overhead, and the sun picking the great conifers out of the mist: could anything more beautiful be imagined?* Pea-green lichen resembling our Usnea—Old-man's-beard—but a foot long drapes the boughs. In the gorges, fissured and seamed with antiquity, the old metamorphic rock ranges in color from almost-red to almost-green. Three deer with black noses go dashing off, black tails depressed—so supple and alive! They are shorter-faced and stockier than our White-tailed deer, and grayer: Columbian Black-tailed deer, they must be.

Climb, climb, and the ridge across the way comes up high above the low-lying cloud, the sun full on it. Getting up among patches of snow now. . . . Piles of snow, and these enormous firs, and clouds lying in the valley below—what a world this is! . . . Here it is: South Fork Mountain Summit. Oh, God, look at that sight over there! Suddenly you can see all the snow-crested ridge to the south! Three more deer, just standing there looking at me, identical statues with heads slightly on one side, and wonderful black eyes and noses.

Among the broad-leafed evergreens on the western slopes is a fantastic tree, laurel-leaved and with outer branches absolutely orange; orange and as smooth as a Manzanita's. It is a Madrone, I find, and a relative of Manzanita's. You might expect monkeys hanging from it. . . . *Down and down and down. A huge valley here between mostly bare or grassy flanks. Using your brakes and in second speed you twist and turn, twist and turn. Steepest road I've ever been on.*

"I've bent my bus on your road," I complain at the Bridgeville post office, where I have stopped for some stamps. The nice-looking postmistress and a companion, a stocky, white-haired, pink-cheeked man, both laugh. They are greatly entertained to learn that I picked Highway 36 for a crossing of the mountains simply because I saw it on the map and are, I think, tickled at its making so pronounced an impression on a stranger. Rather to my gratification, I learn that it has very much of a reputation. The man recalls having once while driving on it come face to face with a logging truck which he was unable to pass, then, before he could back up to a wider place, having a truck with a trailer van pulling a wagon (as they do in the West) come up behind him. That had done it. No one could move. Obviously the tandem rig could not back up, and neither, it appeared, could the other truck, which was loaded with logs of the maximum length permitted on the highway. For an hour and a half they had debated what to do. The logging driver could have jettisoned his cargo but was reluctant to do so and see it roll off down the mountain. Finally in another car a man appeared who said he thought, being an old hand at the game, that he could back the logger down the mountain to a passing place. And, backing and filling around the serpentine bends, he had actually succeeded in doing so.

The conversation I have interrupted had to do with the collecting of bottles. This I learn on questioning the postmistress about an assortment of conspicuously old ones she has on display. Both, it appears, are collectors, rummaging for their finds in old dumps. This pursuit has its devotees all across the country, as has the collecting of rocks and minerals; so I have discovered from the houses at which the objects of one quest or the other are advertised for sale. (Is it another case of people seeking a stability they cannot find in contemporaneity but can in the past and in Nature?) As I can imagine happily applying myself to either pursuit, I listen with interest to what they can tell me about bottle-hunting and its prizes. Impressed by that characteristic of the United States that makes it possible to chat as naturally with strangers on one side of the continent as with one's neighbors on the other, I am also loath to give up the unaccustomed pleasure of so agreeable a conversation. But go I must and do, taking with me the gift of a ballpoint pen stamped with the postmistress's name and an admonition not to miss the cliffs above the Van Duzen River leaving town. To do this, it transpires, would take a feat of overlooking, for the moss-grown precipices rise nearly straight up to a height of several hundred feet, one would guess.

I also take with me the information that the road I have traversed is to be replaced by a modern, graded highway. This is not surprising. Roads have priority in the national pursuit of smooth efficiency—of the totally bland existence. They are the symbols of the rationalization of life we seek, we disciples of technology—the rationalization of transport, of education, of personnel-placement and career-management, of diet and the daily physical regimen, of marriage, and of sex in and out of it. . . . But really, why do I carry on so? Would the irrationalization of life make me happier? With no roads? It is a question I am much given to fretting over, as who must not be? What shall we aim for? An irrational world in which, deaf to all that science can teach us of cause and effect and the determination of truth through experiment, we condemn ourselves to short lives filled with hardship and surrender to superstitions that set us at one another's throats? Or a rational one from which all spontaneity, all excitement, all poetry, all passion, all ecstasy, the sense of life itself will have disappeared?

If it is a matter of which side of oneself is to predominate, the critical-intellectual or the ardent-instinctual—mind-knowledge or blood-knowledge—it is evident to me which I am obedient to this morning. Certainly it becomes so when, shortly after Bridgeville, I enter that strip of the Pacific Coast extending from just inside Oregon southward to the Santa Lucia Mountains, nearly halfway between San Francisco and Los Angeles, where winter temperatures are mild and summer fogs roll in from the sea. This is the belt of the Coastal redwoods.

Where these begin, they are scarcely larger than the greatest of the firs. They can be told, however, by their short-needled, hemlock-like foliage and also, I notice, by their very dark trunks and the veritable pinpoints to which they narrow at the top. The branches tend to curve down and out from the trunk, like the roofs of a pagoda. At Grizzly Creek State Park I get out and have my first sight of a virgin grove of the full-sized trees.

There are sensations you are prepared for on your introduction to redwoods and others you are not. Those expected are no less powerful on that account. The quiet of the colonnades is a hush imposed by the presence of something very great, very venerable, very awesome. You can understand how the architects of the great cathedrals, seeking to build an abode for the spirit of the Deity, found their model in the aboriginal Gothic forest. But this grove of redwoods is more commensurate with their purpose, more august, than any forest our ancestors could have known.

The trunks, separated in many cases by a distance much less than their diameter, are of a warm, dark brown and taper upward from their solidly planted bases in the most graceful lines. The delicate, bright new foliage seems a thing apart from them, attuned to the hours and seasons, responsive to a breath of breeze and a sunbeam glinting through the lofty skeins of foliage, where the massive columns have their being in the tempo of centuries. As under the dominance of mountains, you feel yourself in a different scale of time altogether. As you wander among the boles, through the ferns in a shadowy cool delightfully aromatic with a sharp, spicy incense, you could be a Robinson Crusoe admitted to a realm of time beyond man's province.

For all their girth and almost indeterminate height, the trees do not seem overbearing. This is part of what I had not expected. They are not monstrous but refined. *Delicacy* is the word that keeps recurring to me. They are delicate in taper, fluting, and shades of coloring of trunk, delicate in the almost floating foliage. One's sympathy goes out to them too strongly for one to feel overwhelmed by them, as one's sympathy does go out to enduring patience. As if there were something endearing about them, one has a warmth of emotion for them; and this, I have no doubt, is because they are so great, so beautiful, so noble—and so helpless with the gimlet-eyed *Bandar-log* investing the land with their clever power-saws. When I get back to the bus I remind myself that *it's as if you meet them somehow, have contact with them in a sublime realm which the human spirit doesn't often touch, or reach*—the same realm that between the snowy heights of the White Mountains and the Sierras you feel to be possible of attainment. A conviction I come to, absolutely, is that any church not regarding these groves as close to the divinity would be essentially irreligious. It may be that Nature is a workshop and not a temple. Yet since I can remember, there has been, for me, a Presence in Nature. I am conscious of it in all woodlands, but in no other have I been so aware of it as here. It is almost believable that these trees, so great in years, so lofty in stature, have attained an attunement to the eternal denied us by our commitment to the fleeting moment but which we dimly apprehend in their company. I know better what I am talking about when I recall faces I have seen pictured of men and women of great years and natural dignity who have lived in close community with the earth and the elements; I am thinking especially of certain Indian chiefs.

As I am leaving, two Pileated woodpeckers go careening through the forest in pursuit one of another. There is an engaging awkwardness and energetic ungainliness about these big birds that, with their size, seem to belong to a past age when Creation was more extravagant in mood. They appear admirably fitting protégés of the heroic trees, immemorial scions of a race that in more salubrious times millions of years ago reigned across the northern hemisphere.

Not many miles farther on, Route 36 ends in U. S. 101, the great artery of the Pacific slope, here called the Redwood Highway. In another few miles the river beside the highway widens into an estuary. At twelve-ten blue water appears ahead. It is a lagoon behind a barrier beach. Then, past the commercial welter of Eureka, past Arcata, ten miles north of it, the continent ends and there, blue and green to the curve of the earth, is the Pacific.

Thalassa. The Infinite, the ocean that is without bounds, that there is no going beyond—in this world, at least. Sea and sky, the great emptiness, and that all-conquering light!

But I cannot stop long where I am. Farther on, the highway dips close to the water, where the sinuous waves, gem-like in color and luster, explode and are pulverized in dazzling white surf. And just beyond there is Clam Beach Park, with a place for parking the bus and access to the ocean.

What few others there are on the beach are mostly youngsters, absorbed in games or in one another. A broad strand of grayish sand runs down to the enameled sea, fringed with the beautiful, white glassy foam. Partly buried in the sand, along with much other driftwood, are tree stumps with enormous roots.

Automatically, first thing, one goes down as close to the ocean's

edge as one can and stares off across its plain, lost to all that preceded the moment. As well one might. The sea holds all the lands
of the earth in its embrace and within its power to grant, and if
one has been long away from it, they loom before one: the frigid,
rocky shores where glaciers calve their icebergs and seabirds swing
on the wind, and those siren paradises that start to work the voyager's undoing from afar with the waft of lemon trees, cinnamon,
or frangipani. The possibility of all is contained in that expanse
of shimmering water. And is it not possibility that brings us alive—
the infinite possibilities of youth, the day at dawn, the awakening
of love, mystery, and the sea? So at last it is with a sigh that we
reclaim our mesmerized attention from the endless play of waves
and our hearing from the sound of the breakers that crash with the
same dull thunder on all those other shores. One cannot have everything, can one?

Leaving my shoes behind, I run along the beach where the sand
is packed until I am thoroughly winded.

Perhaps for the unfortunate young who have grown up under
the dominion of the airplane it is not as it is for their elders. Can
they know how the windows of the spirit are thrown open by the
sight of the oceanic horizon for those of us not yet entirely beyond
the spell of a time of life and an age that have gone or are going,
when the world was before us and still enchanted with the names
of ports only to be gained by many days or weeks at sea, and by the
adventurous alone? The distant lands are all passing, like the wilderness. They yearly grow more commonplace. The problems of
Yosemite will soon be the problems of Bali, Madeira, and Tahiti—
if they are not already—and then of the Moluccas, Tongareva, Iqui-
tos, and Antarctica. That is what is in store for tomorrow: a world
no part of which is farther from any other than Kansas City from
New York today, in which, wherever you go, you can count on finding what you left behind. But the day after tomorrow?

That is not so clear. And it is a matter about which one is privileged to have one's own ideas.

Behind the dunes the ground is covered by a tall plant with
cones of yellow blossoms. A young woman seems glad to be able
to tell me it is yellow lupine. Of course: even one unaware of there
being such a thing should have been able to guess that. The blue
has been cropping up everywhere beside the road and is here too,
farther back from the dunes—and with a *white* lupine!

Above the highway going north are shrubs of remarkable pow-der-blue, privet-like flowers. They are Blueblossom, or California lilac. It is a stunning coast. At intervals, from the highlands that form it, ridges run out into the ocean, ending in stern headlands, one in boulders sixty feet high, some in stacks, as they are called—headlands cut off by the action of the waves. As a young coast that breasts with rocky cliffs the waves that have a fetch (the oceanographers term it) the width of the Pacific, it is one of active confrontation by the two primordial antagonists, land and sea.

In this unceasing contest, the assailant, the sea, has to me a cat-like quality. It pours caressingly over the rocks. It draws back and pounces playfully on them, or swirls around them insinuatingly. Then it will deliver a harder smack—still all in sport. Its voice, in this mood, is soothing even while it growls—for it cannot entirely dissimulate the menace in its tones; and if the sound like a loud intake of breath that accompanies its withdrawal from beach or shingle suggests the honorific hiss of correct Japanese deportment, one is not to be disarmed by that oriental guile. The land is not deceived. It stands in disregard. Aloof, gazing horizonward, it does not acknowledge the existence of its restless and hungry foe. And this (in my fantasy) at length enrages the sea. The tiger in it aroused, it rampages over the low-lying coasts or hurls itself upon the stoic ramparts, leaping high in savage transports. The coast of the Northwest is notorious for the size and power of the waves that come hurtling in on storms from out of the Pacific's vast sweep. Breaking and rebounding in the shallows below the coastal cliffs, these have been known to send sheets of water two hundred feet high.

Even small waves move sand along the shore, ultimately to repositories beneath the surface; larger ones breaking on pebbles roll and abrade them. The still larger loosen rocks from the continent's bulwarks and use them to batter and help dislodge others while wearing both down. In the ceaseless friction with the sea, the land, on balance, can only lose. But constantly as it is worn away, it is continually replenished by lava brought up from below the crust and by the imperceptible raising of new mountain chains which rise like phoenixes from the residues of their predecessors claimed by the sea.

That the Coast Ranges have been growing is shown by the shelves cut into them by the ocean that have been lifted above its reach to form high terraces complete with any stacks the sea had left stand-

ing. Where New England's coast—our other rock-bound littoral—
is deeply indented, being a sunken one, its river valleys invaded by
the sea, the rising West Coast is bluff. But it reminds you of the
coast of Maine. Both are dramatic as only shores can be where
ledges of rock throw back the seas and an advance guard of a coniferous forest stands above them just back from the spray's reach.
Here on the northern coast of California the conifers are Douglas
firs, Grand firs—and redwoods. (To the north in Oregon and Washington they are predominantly Sitka spruce, Western Red cedars
and Western hemlocks: Küchler listing 1.) They stand unyieldingly
straight in great dignity, a convocation of dark-mantled chieftains,
the true North Americans, gazing seaward and awaiting with steady
resolve what the sea may bring. Magnificent columnar redwoods on
rock-girt redoubts above the greatest of oceans: what a coast this is!

It is all redwood country. Out of sight of the water, the highway
takes you through what a sign calls seven miles of memorial groves.
You thread a narrow aisle through the enormous, sunlit forest in
helpless wonder. Coastal redwoods (*Sequoia sempervirens*) are known
to have lived 2,000 years, but they do apparently die eventually in
the ordinary course. (Mountain redwoods—*Sequoia gigantea*—which
are larger in girth though none has been known to rival the 365-
foot height attained by a Coastal redwood, have achieved 3,400
years, or even 4,000 if a ring-count by John Muir was accurate.)
From the highway are to be seen several stumps remaining of fallen
majesties. About thirty feet high and jagged at the top, one of them
at least wider than the bus is long, they resemble lighthouses.

It is or *was* redwood country. Since leaving Virginia I have seen
no sight as horrifying as the knolls and hillsides where the redwoods
have been logged. Saturation bombardment by artillery might do
as thorough a job. Not only is the forest gone, its grandeur, the
sensitivity of its living forms, the elevated quiet of its deep, sun-
flecked, shadowy glades mocked in a litter of branches, stumps, and
pieces of trunk above which a few half-stripped, half-dead trees remain standing in a baking glare of sunshine, but from top to bottom the slopes have been gouged out by the tractors—demolished.
You would suppose that a malevolent and savage vindictiveness
had here been given free rein. When you think what a struggle it
has been to safeguard any substantial tracts from this fate the gall
rises in your throat. It took years of soliciting private contributions
from all over the country for the purchase of groves, years of effort

PACIFIC

OCEAN

COAST RANGES

CASCADE MTS.

SIERRA

NEVADA MTS.

COLUMBIA-SNAKE

PLATEAU

GREAT

BASIN

BASIN-AND-RANGE PROVINCE

NORTHERN ROCKY MTS.

CENTRAL ROCKY MTS.

WASATCH MTS.

COLORADO

PLATEAU

SOUTHERN ROCKY MTS.

SIERRA MADRE OCCIDENTAL

GREAT

PLAINS

TOPOGRAPHICAL MAP

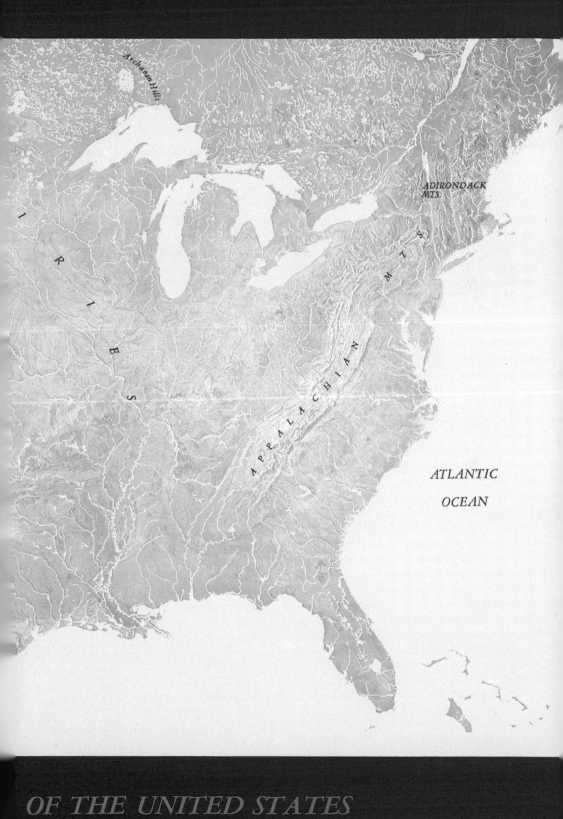

ATLANTIC

OCEAN

OF THE UNITED STATES

to win legislative approval of the creation of State redwood parks. It took that fierce battle to prevent the robots of the California Highway Deparment from ramming an autobahn through the very groves that private contributions and legislative action had supposedly saved. It took that protracted campaign to move Congress to provide for a Redwoods National Park—an only partly successful campaign; the park is little more than half the size the defenders of the redwoods had striven for, Congress having proved in the end unwilling to increase its appropriation by an amount it authorizes for expenditure every few hours for slaughter and destruction in Vietnam.

And one remembers how, while Congress was moving at its glacial pace, the lumber interests accelerated their cutting to ruin the forests designated for protection and thus defeat the aims of the park. One remembers, too, how the argument was pressed that the park must be forestalled and the destruction of the redwoods continued in order to provide jobs. *To provide jobs!*

And where was that institution that represents itself as the Creator's agency on earth? The Church was where it has been in every battle to save something of the Creator's handiwork from human appetites. It was remote from the scene and indifferent. It was wholly occupied with the internal affairs of the human race and mankind's expectations of another world in which all the grievous faults it finds with this one will be made good. God's self-denominated vicars could meet the object of their worship face to face and not recognize him. Indeed, they do meet him face to face whenever they go out beneath the sky and evidently not recognize him. "To a Christian, a tree can be no more than a physical fact," Lynn White, Jr., professor of history at the University of California at Los Angeles, observes. "The whole concept of a sacred grove is alien to Christianity and to the ethos of the West. For nearly two millennia Christian missionaries have been chopping down sacred groves, which are idolatrous because they assume spirit in nature."

"Render therefore unto Caesar the things which are Caesar's; and unto God the things that are God's," said Christ; but from the burden of his teachings it seems evident that he was concerned with the distinction between Caesar's claims and humanity's, comprising our fellow men's and our own. That we have an obligation to both the State and the human beings it incorporates is excellent counsel now as then; and originally, when Caesar was omnipotent and humanity largely helpless between his rule and an obdurate and powerful natural order, the force of the Christian message was to redress a cruel imbalance. It gave human beings as such an inherent value and the lowliest a claim on God's attention equal to the mightiest's. In so doing it released revolutionary forces which are still far from spent. But of celebration of God, there seems to me little to be found in it, less than in the sacred dances of primitive tribes. God is invoked often enough, but as a patron of mankind—our Man in Heaven, as it were. His will be done and His kingdom come, yes, but with us as the beneficiaries, if we behave humanely. No doubt many impecunious nephews have been devoted to uncles from whom, if they restrained their grosser impulses, they stood to gain a fortune; and what is at stake here is nothing less than eternal paradise. But one is bound to reflect in such cases how easily devotion must come.

In the Christian message there is no expression of wonder at the splendor of God's Creation, no value placed on any part of it or any living thing but man. It is of no account except to serve man's wants. (The nephew does not share the uncle's interests except as they advance his own.) Of gratitude for all the joys the earth affords —God's gift to us—there is nothing in the Gospels. This world is spurned, and all the ways in which Nature—surely inseparable from God—speaks through man are disregarded if not condemned: our earthly ardors, our pride, our creative drives, our sense of kinship with the living world, our delight in play, our incentive to excel, our exhilaration when the sense of life is strong in us. (The nephew disesteems the provisions so far made for him and disapproves of the uncle's gusto.)

"Especially in its Western form, Christianity is the most anthropocentric religion that the world has seen," Professor White goes on to say. And further: "Man shares, in great measure, God's transcendence of nature. Christianity, in absolute contrast to ancient paganism and Asia's religions (except perhaps Zoroastrianism), not only established a dualism of man and nature but also insisted that it is God's will that man exploit nature for his proper ends.

". . . In Antiquity every tree, every spring, every stream, every hill had its own *genius loci,* its guardian spirit. These spirits were accessible to man, but were very unlike man: centaurs, fauns, and mermaids show their ambivalence. Before one cut a tree, mined a mountain or dammed a brook, it was important to placate the spirit in charge of that particular situation, and to keep it placated. By destroying pagan animism, Christianity made it possible to exploit nature in a mood of indifference to the feelings of natural objects."

What Christianity permits and encourages, the business ethic and economic policy (a steady rate of growth in things produced) promote and demand. So does the popular appetite for ever more and fancier material goods. To these must be added patriotism, which in our country has always comprised national expansion into wild and otherwise profitless areas and chamber-of-commerce boosterism. The American people could scarcely be more powerfully conditioned in favor of the progressive despoliation of the continent in their hands. Those who would save it have a task before them dwarfing that which had to be accomplished in its conquest.

At the celadon-green Klamath River—the largest since the Colorado—is a bronze sculpture of a bear on either side of the road, and most engaging it is. After ten thousand billboards, a tribute has been erected to something in Nature. But lest you be encouraged there is another kind of statue a little farther on. It is at the parking grounds for "Trees of Mystery," a much-advertised and presumably privately owned redwood grove, and it is a crude representation, fully thirty feet high, of Paul Bunyan. Thus are trees of mystery celebrated for the public—by an overbearing, vulgar likeness of Super-Axman, the greatest tree-slayer of them all! And with him, proportionately even wider, is that everlasting damned blue ox.

At Crescent City I make an inexcusable mistake. I should continue on up the coast of Oregon (even if Washington and the Olympics are out of the question) and see the northern Coast Range, which sends spectacular spurs to the ocean and in Fairview Mountain, only four miles inland, stands 2,300 feet above it. But my mind is aswirl with all I have seen and, rather demoralized by the urban confusion I have run into, I yield to a passing weakness. *Enough is enough,* I mutter lamely to the recorder and make the decision to call this the farthest point from home. I turn east and soon find myself climbing a gorge above the opaque, sea-green waters of the Smith River, beside banks of serpentine and Madrones clustered with racemes of small white flowers, on my way back across the rugged Klamath Mountains.

10

THE REALM
OF VULCAN

Seven o'clock and we're on Interstate 5. It is evening, and Oregon, with the flat valley of Grant's Pass behind us. *We've still got these abrupt little mountains around us that look as if the material of them is at the angle of rest. Somehow, I have got to see the Cascades.*

My stars, you suddenly come around a corner and there is this enormous volcano standing up higher in the sky than anything I've seen on the trip. There are no mountains at all, and now suddenly there are the Cascades, and there is one of those volcanoes with an almost perfect cone, and pure white on top. It seems to be in the general direction of Crater Lake.

Of all the world's mountains, the great conical volcanoes are surely the queens: Tacoma, Orizaba, and Chimborazo, Etna, Kilimanjaro, Fuji, and Semeru. Great peaks of other kinds are parts of lofty ranges and generally but little overtop their neighbors. The volcanoes, however, stand alone, as by the divine right of majesty, and to heights so far above the generality as to seem outside the natural order. But which volcano is the regal beauty I am seeing? Her form is of a monarch in coronation robes sweeping upward from the ground, dark velvet of forest yielding to ermine. You could suppose her an unearthly visitor which, if you looked away, you might find vanished on looking back. A dozen volcanoes crown the six-hundred-mile-long chain of the Cascades, but this one corresponds in location to none of the major ones. By the map, it can only be Mount McLoughlin, of 9,500 feet elevation. I should have thought it half again as high—and if that is the drab name they have given it, I should prefer not to know. Perhaps it is really a spectral manifestation.

Up among the Cascades, where the snowfields are taking color from the last of the sunshine, the range appears higher than at a distance. *Very dark down in the V-shaped ravine below us. And very far down, too. Little Hereford cattle look tiny. Big trailer van, Red Ball, has the hind legs of the trailer off the road in a hole and the driver asleep in the cab. We're climbing just about as fast as the sun is sinking. And beautiful it is. The pasturelands almost like lawns going up the mountainsides are turning gold in the sun; and so are the oaks, which diminish in size as they climb them—oaks with mistletoe and little gold clusters of budding leaves. A drop of about a million feet right off the side of the road.* [This is State Highway 66 to Klamath Falls.] *Those jagged rocks on the mountain in front of us like citadels and castles—tremendously picturesque. The rock in the road-cuts is dark and volcanic, probably rhyolite. It's the color of dried coffee-grounds, or milk chocolate. We're under a frowning bluff of it now, and it looks like Indian totem poles crowded together. Dark and somber rock, believe me, like something the Mayas might have built. The chill of evening is coming on, as it always does, very quickly. I must say it seems kind of lonely out here. However, it always seems better in the morning. . . .*

As indeed it will again. Tubbs Springs Wayside, on which I had my sights set, turns out to be nothing more than a siding off the highway, but with the deep boreal forest all around it looks good and I take a chance on it for the night. So long a day has it been, beginning in the deep forest dell off California 36, that I sleep without hearing a car until dawn. At thirty-seven degrees, my hands turn numb even in gloves from the cold of the rocks I carry on my run before breakfast, but the sun is just lighting the mountaintops, the morning wonderfully clear, the air invigorating as spring water, the virgin world all mine. There is a mountain spring, too, from which I fill the water jug. The egg is the last; this is the thirteenth day.

From Parker Mountain Pass, my ghost volcano of yesterday evening is visible in the north. And in the south, from the other side of Klamath Falls, far, far in the distance, is another conical volcano of perfect symmetry, white far down its sides. Though Shasta is sixty miles away, Shasta it must be, over fourteen thousand feet in height and second only to Tacoma of the volcanoes north of Mexico, a solitaire of the skies. . . . Klamath Falls, despite its name, is a conventional industrial town, which is to say a blot, but brighter and more open than most with nice little houses up on the low hills. And it cherishes another of the old locomotives in a little park. One is surprised by how many towns do. The nostalgia is evidently widespread. And why should it not be? Everyone who knew them recognized that with the end of the hot-blooded, iron thunderers running wild across the plains or panting with stentorian blasts up to the mountain pass, sending that lonely, warning, yearning wail across the nighttime distances of our continent, something integral with the country's soul was extinguished. But efficiency-wise and profits-wise the steam locomotive had become obsolete. So there could be but one verdict: the hell with it.

On the grassy plains along the Klamath River (and how in the world does it get across the mountains to the Pacific?) Western meadowlarks sing, as they do all through the West where the country is open yet not barren. Their song is as clear and far-carrying as the knife-sharp, striving whistles of the Eastern bird, but more warbling. In a marsh bordering the Klamath, a little flock of redheads paddles off, large heads erect, and from the flat pastureland a snipe puts up on quivering wings, then, long beak pointed downward, slowly descends—a dainty creature tremulous with life. From here, a hundred miles on to Lakeview, is the place to drink your fill of greenery, for beyond is the Great Sandy Desert. There are rich bottomlands and sloughs on the way, but the depressed mountains—actually, it is the valleys that have been filled to a high elevation—grow drier. The juniper reappears, and with it a silvery brushy plant just coming into leaf. We have reached the enormous empire of the sage, which reaches northward more than halfway through Washington, eastward two-thirds of the way across Wyoming, southward to southern Nevada, and in islands across northern Arizona and New Mexico. Sage is in its element in the northern and eastern portions of the mitten-shaped Central Desert as Creosote bush is to the southwest and south. Lakeview, where I turn northward for the Snake River and Yellowstone, has that bare, sunsmitten look of the heartland West.

If the major kinds of country the world contains could be displayed for inspection, I venture to believe our original forty-eight states would be found to embrace much the larger part of them, perhaps all but Equatorial rain-forest and Arctic coasts. Traveling over it day after day at fifty-five to sixty miles an hour, by telescoping the country's physiography, brings out its variety. But there could be nothing like walking its breadth to give one an appreciation of the extent of the differences and of the continent's magnitude, as a lone sailor circumnavigating the globe will understand the ocean's truth as no conventional traveler can; and were I to fall into the power of an unsparing autocrat who ordered me to take such a walk I should not be too dismayed. At least I can see myself setting out not unwillingly if I were given the power to convey to others what I was able to take in.

These thoughts come to me, by no means for the first time, in the valley—and it is rather like a trough formed by a worn, mottled-green carpet bunched up alongside—through which U. S. 395 (my avenue up the Owens Valley) is taking us, and at the arresting sight of a huge mesa rimmed by a cliff perhaps 150 feet high. Other similar formations may be seen ahead of us. These, I surmise, struck by the theatrical suddenness of the apparition, as by the entrance in formidable guise of a leading character of the *dramatis personae,* can only mark the frontier of the Columbia-Snake Plateau. Farther along, where the highway passes between the sloping base of the mightiest of these escarpments and an enormous desert lake, blue as a jewel, the supposition is confirmed. A handsome sign with letters routed out of dark wooden planks between heavy posts stands at the foot of the slope with this notice:

OREGON GEOLOGY
ABERT RIM

Discovered by Captain John C. Frémont December 20, 1843, and named in honor of Colonel J. J. Abert.

Abert Rim, some 2,500 feet above the valley floor, is one of the highest fault scarps in the United States. This basalt formation, a basic lava covering much of eastern Oregon, issued from great fissures during the Miocene period of geologic history many millions of years ago. After this extensive lava flooding, the earth's crust was fractured at many points and great blocks were tilted. Abert Rim is the western edge of one of these tilted blocks while Abert Lake lies on top of another.

At long intervals one comes upon a sign of this kind, always with gratitude—gratitude for the information, gratitude for such a show of respect for a country placarded from end to end with the manifestos of hucksters.

For almost twenty miles the highway skirts the lake and the face of the liver-colored fault-block, which looks as if it had been cut back by the sea, with not a single tree to be seen and almost no other sign of human intrusion than the highway. To the north, among other escarpments displaying the layers of the different lava flows, there is not a bush, even at a cattle-watering station where several hundred Herefords are resignedly gathered. After a settlement of a dozen houses and trailers and a few trees comes mile on mile with no sign of human life other than a rare other car. Where I stop for lunch on a dirt road to Dry Valley—a plausible destination, I must say—I have a closer look at the sagebrush and conceive a great fondness for it. Much of it is gnarled and twisted, with trunks several inches thick. It makes you think of dwarfed Live oaks with soft, pale gray-green foliage and should be perfect for bonzai. (But two specimens I clumsily dig up succumb.) A plant that grows where little else will is almost bound to win one over, and sage, an *Artemisia* and close relative of the Wormwood or Dusty Miller of the barren beach sands, is a doughty member of a doughty genus.

The largest town in the southeastern quarter of Oregon is Burns, with a population of all of 3,500, or thereabouts. Here I stop to replenish my groceries. While waiting to be checked out, I notice that the woman ahead of me has quite a large load and accordingly carry it out to her car for her. On my return I am surprised to have the proprietress remark, "No one around here would do that! Where're you from?" Coming from where I do, it is difficult for me to reply to her without sounding as if I considered myself the embodiment of cavalier gallantry with overtones of George Washington and Robert E. Lee, and I fear I simply succeed in sounding as if that were how I was trying not to sound.

It is a curious thing. You could find as many deplorable specimens of the human species in Virginia as you had a mind to; and with the Old Dominion's glories it is absolutely impossible for me to claim any slightest connection. Yet I am aware that my sensations on driving across the country with those chaste black-and-white Virginia plates are different from what they would be with, say, New Jersey plates. From this, the depressing conclusion is to be drawn that if you give a human being any excuse whatever for a sense of distinction he will fasten on it, which is to say that *I* will.

The circumstances of this trip may be mitigating, however. As it goes on and I look more and more travel-worn, I find I am imputing a superior and condescending attitude to the occupants of the big new sedans alongside me in traffic. There is the prosperous-appearing man in clean white shirt and well-pressed suit behind the wheel and the reasonably personable, beauty-parlored, well-groomed woman with quite creditable, smoothly hosed legs beside him, a token of his success. And there am I in my caboose, a homeless-looking itinerant, devoid of consort or any credentials of position, the sort of person to take no notice of lest he presume. Incredibly, the imagined regard in which I am held actually colors my view of myself—and I have a glimmering of the handicaps that must be overcome by those whom society casts from the start in an inferior role. "You know what that bloke is?" says my disrespectful inner voice, speaking of the driver of a new Oldsmobile beside us, and, as it is apt to, in a lower-class English accent. "He's part owner of the local lumber-yard, and he's not only got that wife with the blonde-rinsed 'air but also color telly and a garage door that opens when he beeps his 'orn. No wonder we're in awe of 'im." I am not in awe of him, but when in towns I am beginning to acquire, just around the edges, the self-regard of a vagrant. . . . A vagrant with Virginia plates, though.

Burns is almost an oasis, with trees, though barely with them, I should say, and long-haired teen-agers in a Corvette. East of it—and you never know what to expect—the plains are standing in water, apparently not just from a cloudburst, for there are Mallards on them, Red-winged blackbirds, shorebirds, Eared grebes and a Wilson's phalarope. The grebes, with black foreparts and backs and red eyes at the apex of triangles of golden plumage covering the sides of their heads, could have been fabricated by Fabergé, those deft workers in precious metals and jewel-like enamels for vanished royalty. The largely white-and-gray phalarope—an inland member of a triumvirate of swimming sandpipers that otherwise frequent the high seas and breed on Arctic coasts—is scarcely less a work of art, with the black of its needle bill continued in a fine black line that widens through the eye and down the side of the neck, turning chestnut. And I am brought up against the problem

I am no nearer solving than when I saw my first Golden-crowned kinglet at the age of twelve, which is how to respond to such exquisite contrivances of Nature's. One cannot collect them or caress them, as men have been known to collect and caress beautiful girls.

On the outskirts of the village of Buchanan is another "Oregon Geology" sign. This one informs you that you are at "the northern limit of the Great Basin, which has no exterior drainage," and by an outline map shows it extending to southern California. So here is where you leave that bourne from which no waterway emerges.

To render things their due. . . . Perhaps if one were a painter one could fulfill the obligation one feels. I understand and envy the water-colorist who has produced a full portfolio of railroad stations—one of the happiest forms American architecture has taken. A beautiful job he has done, too. The mountains from U. S. 20 reawaken the perennial need I feel to *make* something of these ranges of diverse origin, to give them recognition in their variety. Is it a matter of rendering unto God the things that are God's? In the north are the snow-capped ranges of the Blue and, beyond them, the Wallowa Mountains; remains of the original Rocky Mountain chain, they are cradled in the fingers of the mitten-shaped plains. Rising all by itself far to the south in the Great Sandy Desert, like a displaced Arctic island of towering height, snow halfway down its sides, is a range that turns out to be the Steens Mountains, a fifty-mile-long block of layered lava uptilted a mile above the plateau. These make me recall how as a youngster on trips between New York and Georgia I used to imagine working on museum dioramas representing the continent's various land-forms and natural habitats.

But to be a painter: that would be it, I think. Were I a water-colorist like Ranulf Bye I should do a complete series of the types of North American mountains. The work would be performed under great difficulties. The colors would dry on contact with the paper before the Panamints, freeze in the Alaska Range. But if I painted with the skill I should surely paint with if I had it, the results would justify all hardships; that is how good they would be, combining science and art!

With all the skill in the world, however, it might not be possible to render plausibly the hills by which the Malheur River passes. They seem themselves too much the product of a conscious artistry, so much so that I tend to become incoherent.

The fertile valley contains the town of Juntura, which is sur-
rounded by hills that look as if they . . . the rain had carved them
out of huge cakes of green soap. A laval [a word I am told does not
exist] *bluff across the creek up which we're traveling, there are*
almost faces there. You have slits for the eyes and the mouths;
they're almost formed into human features. The mountains or
rivers . . . I've never seen anything like the interlocking, water-
molded cakes of soap that tower, oh, hundreds up to thousands
of feet above us. They keep on as we go up the river, mile after
mile—huge things. Many have bands around them of exposed vol-
canic strata. And now these big mountains crowned by volcanic
strata are sending out spurs. They are also mounded and smooth
as molded soap. Such beautiful structure of . . . sheer structure
of the land, I think I have never seen. Henry Moore would go wild
over it. The green on the hills forms a kind of bloom on the brown
or reddish-brown or liver-brown earth. . . . Here are men, women
and children fishing in the mountainous, pretty little streams,
pretty little river flowing along merrily through these elephantine
earth-forms. The rock is now beginning to come out in ramparts
and balconies and dikes, protrusions of castles, often chartreuse
with moss against the bare, brownish-red rock, with the late after-
noon sun bringing out the strata. Tremendously picturesque. I
should not be so stirred up if these scenes were more renowned. I
have never heard of them. The Malheur Mountains?

All of a sudden the hills are now all of tuff. There are buff or
cream-colored tuffs with the green over them. And farther on the
hills are white. ["Now you take that double one over there," says
that uncultivated and impudent English voice. "A very fitting and
proper name for it"—the word comes out almost as *nyme*—"and
one to give honor where honor is due would be Fanny Hill.
What?"] *It's hard to say whether a magpie is more like a jay or a*
crow, but to see that wonderful contrast of black and white, with
the green iridescence, like a black rooster's hackles at the base of
the primaries and tail. . . . They seem sort of to float in the air.

Nyssa, on the Oregon side of the Snake, has the same name as
my older daughter, but otherwise seems farther from home than
any other town so far. The vacancy both of the arid West and of a
Sunday evening possesses it. Only the cafés are open; there will be
no postcard from one Nyssa to the other. Of the few loiterers and
passers-by, most, to my surprise, look like Mexicans, a few like

Indians. It could be a motion-picture set on which the extras are only desultorily beginning to assemble. The fertile lands across the river are a different world. Aware that I have not had a bath since Oklahoma, I put up for the night at a motel on the outskirts of Caldwell after dinner beside a swamp from which strange birds and frogs are calling.

It is in this area that the Snake, having crossed southern Idaho from its sources in the mountains of western Wyoming, turns north to Washington and its eventual juncture with the Columbia. The gorge it has cut on the way through mountains of uplifted lava ten times older than that of the rest of the Columbia-Snake Plateau reaches a depth greater than that of the Grand Canyon. Hell's Canyon, otherwise the Grand Canyon of the Snake, came fairly by its name. Its discoverers, a party in the employ of the fur-dealer John Jacob Astor, were the first to cross the continent after the Lewis and Clark expedition, which they followed by seven years. They had been trying to descend the Snake but, defeated by "the accursed mad river," which tore their canoes apart and drowned two of their number, they took to the desert north of the river, only to find themselves, debilitated by days of hunger and thirst, with the most terrible of all the Snake's many hundreds of miles of canyons to deal with. "Frozen by cold and snow, blinded by fog, and crazed by hunger, the Astorians wandered through the nightmarish chasm," as *American Heritage* recalls. "Men died, and others became deranged." Eventually, after eating their horses and dogs, "most of them straggled on to the mouth of the Columbia, more dead than alive." Men did not take the continent for granted in those days. Or for many thereafter. . . . But time does not allow me the satisfaction of viewing the basaltic jaws of this mile-deep maw and obstacle to the easy conquest of the land. As always, I must hurry on.

Bathed in early sunlight, even an unexceptional town like Meridian—which does have trees, however—seems to partake of a universal grace. There is nothing like being abroad under fair, mild skies when the life of town and countryside is just getting under way and fatigue, habit, disenchantment, and rancor have yet to resume their sway over mankind. Even the signs for the shops seem redeemed by a general cheerful innocence. But like all the fruits of life, the joy of early morn must ordinarily be got at through a disagreeable husk, which in this case is the almost inhuman difficulty of getting up to discover it. Herein lies a good reason for being occasionally uprooted from one's routine, as by travel, and thus freed partially at least from the inertia that battens on it. . . . Beyond the irrigation canals, junkyards, and truck depots of the outskirts of smog-bound, neighboring Boise, there is much to be said for the rolling, bare rangeland of grass and sagebrush that goes on for unchanging miles, the snowy peaks of the Owyhee following along in the south.

Are you ever out of sight of mountains westward of the Great Plains? I do not know where. And time after time I say of them: these are incomparable, these are supreme; and so they are, each time, for what they are. From U. S. 20, the spectacle is of the Northern Rockies rising from the Snake River Plains and the epic contrast that unfolds, kingdom of basalt against kingdom of granite.

The lava of the Snake River Plains is younger by millions of years than that of the rest of the Columbia Plateau, and vast fields of it along the highway might just have solidified; it resembles overcooked, crusted fudge or gigantic, dried cowpats. On the north, however, are enormous barren basalt mountains. Behind these the Sawtooth Range of the Northern Rockies comes first to view, fitfully, its sharp white peaks very distant. Sun Valley is among them. Then—*northeast of Shoshone we are approaching those mountains in the north and it is a tremendous sight to see them grow up from the horizon. They extend almost all across it, very jagged peaks, and their snow mantles brilliant in the sun. The rise of the Sierra Nevadas from their base is incomparable, but nothing can equal these Rockies for the height at which the peaks stand above the valleys—for their magnificently rugged and dramatic profile. The ones right ahead are apparently the Lost River Range, of which the highest is the highest in Idaho—12,662 feet.* I refuse to spoil it for myself by acknowledging the name the local buffoons have given it.

These are the forged-rock Rocky Mountains, analogous to the Blue Ridge and other escarpments on the seaward side of the Appalachians. Hewn in large part of granite batholiths, they stretch on through northern Washington and western British Columbia to reach their climax in Mount Denali of the Alaska Range, the tallest mountain north of Chimborazo in Ecuador and one said to stand higher above its immediate base than any other in the world. (There is an analogue to the sedimentary Appalachians, too, in the eastern ranges of the Northern Rockies that begin in Montana and end in the Brooks Range of northern Alaska.)

Seen beyond the outcroppings of Stygian-dark, earth-bound basalt, the Rockies' ascendant, snow-draped peaks, beneath the white clouds that rest above them as on a sea of light, seem ethereal. The contrast grows as the worn, splayed basaltic mountains gain in stature—Plutonic outgrowths deep-olive in color under thin grasses. The foreground grows more forbidding as you approach Craters of the Moon, the raw lava transforming it into the semblance of a dumping ground for old asphalt or of dark earth gouged and banked by bulldozers. The Rockies, seen exalted by light in gaps between the basaltic formations, are like the realm of Ariel glimpsed from that of Caliban. But wait. An extraordinary beauty begins to be revealed in these basaltic mountains of the night. In their now grand proportions they have the smoothly sculptured form of the huge rounded hills of the Malheur of yesterday. One rises into the zone of snow, its dome white.

We're climbing up into these wonderfully shaped basaltic mountains. One has a broad peak from which gigantic spurs radiate out, smooth as seals. They're tremendously majestic. It is as if they had been ennobled by a tragic destiny. . . . No, really that is too much. But it is how they affect me.

Nearer around one the grim disorder grows. Piles and windrows and fields of broken and pulverized lava spread out even farther with the Craters of the Moon National Monument. Cones of black lava grit, like huge piles of coal, rise before you. The scene is the darkest I have ever seen. As you go on, the heaps of lava become ever more jagged and nightmarish. A seven-mile loop road takes you among the craters, some of the "spatter-cone" type, formed of blobs of pasty lava. Parts of the wall of one of the craters, carried away by the upwelling streams of lava, stand some distance off like monstrous hunks of devil's-food cake. These, and the other scraggy, clinker-like rock were semi-solid lava to begin with. The lava that was hot enough to flow freely hardened into glaciers of rock like congealed black dough. The grit was from hardened lava froth.

Much of the earth's surface had its origin in scenes not dissimilar to these, if generally on a much grander scale. Conceivably all of it did, including the oceans—condensed from the huge quantities of steam in volcanic eruptions. So you gaze rather appalled on this extraordinary panorama of dark desolation, cruel in all but intent. And you marvel at the plants that have ventured into it. Even after 1,600 years—evidently about the length of time since the last eruptions—much of the landscape is devoid of any green, the lava looking as if it might just have cooled. The older flows have been well vegetated; what is so striking is to see the little Limber pines—those that have not died at their posts, as many have—growing here and there from otherwise sterile volcanic cones and among the younger blocks of lava.

But there is a troubling aspect of the scene, too. Though I do not face it and am soon put out of mind of it by other sights along the way, it is there and it touches a fundamental conflict in my view of the natural world. It is a conflict, I learn later, that Konrad Lorenz shares, which should surely make it excusable. In an observation that puts the difficulty well, the distinguished ethologist says:

If you were to ask me if I'm a monist or a dualist, I would reply, "The devil if I know." When I look with emotion upon the inorganic world around us, the beauty of a sunset, I think I'm a monist. At such a time I am convinced that there are universal laws that reign over the entire universe, and that among them the laws of life are merely special cases. But when I see the struggle of organic life, so fragile, so vulnerable, against the eternal forces of the inorganic world, my vision of the struggle is something like a photograph of the Galápagos Islands: an immense torrent of frozen lava in the midst of which is a hole no bigger than the palm of your hand—and from this tiny hole rises a minuscule flowering cactus!

That is how it is. The little Limber pine, bright and sensitive and venturesome in the chaotic jumble of lava, makes you think of life as what counts, life the touching and heroic assertion of spirit in a brutal and soulless universe. Then you see the mountains, noble in their proportions, soaring to their radiant heights, and it can only be that a central impulse and conception governs and harmonizes all.

And of all the mountains that so greatly express our aspirations, and perhaps a spirit of striving that is in the cosmos as a whole, the ultimate, I think as I reach Rexburg and turn north for Yellowstone, must be those far off in the east—*impossible peaks*, I exclaim: *the Tetons.*

It was Yellowstone's geysers, hot springs, and boiling mud pots that primarily led to its preservation as a National Park—the first of all and still, with over 3,400 square miles, the largest. The first white man to visit the area and report what he had seen, a well-known trapper and member of the Lewis and Clark expedition named John Colter, who entered it a year after part of the expedition under Clark had descended the Yellowstone River just to the north on the return from the Pacific, was heard with disbelief. This is not remarkable, for nowhere else on earth is there such a display of geysers as Yellowstone's three thousand. Yet I find that the actuality, if not harder to credit than the reports—after all, you cannot reject the testimony of your eyes and ears—is much less readily taken in stride.

But how am I going to fare in Yellowstone, and what be able to see? The snow blanket descends the Yellowstone mountains and is a foot deep in the Targhee National Forest, into which the highway ascends up the North Fork of the Snake on the way to the National Park. The forest is of Lodgepole pines so slim of trunk they look as if they had been stretched out.

Unexpectedly the highway comes out on a high pond in the woods on which are two swans. An instinct tells me I am seeing my first Trumpeters. And so I am: they are solid black of beak and face. Moreover, a sign says "Home of the Rare Trumpeter Swan" and explains that the number of the species had increased from one hundred in 1930 to seven hundred by the end of 1965. Once the Trumpeter's nesting grounds extended all the way from the Yukon in Alaska to the prairies of Indiana, but traffickers in feathers and flesh reduced its flocks to remnants in Yellowstone and British Columbia numbering, according to the Bureau of Fish and Wildlife, less than seventy. While the best that protectionists can usually achieve today is to retard the pace at which everything not human is being reduced or destroyed, the number of these magnificent birds is now in the thousands, and we are spared—for the present—another ineradicable blot on our dark escutcheon.

With any break in the National Forest comes an eruption of commercialism. Most of it is aimed at the pleasure-bent who, having come so far, are looking for more than unimproved wilderness and views of mountains basking under flotillas of white clouds in a blue sky. There are, for example, Mother Goose Village and a Dinosaur Safari. The latter is in West Yellowstone, a town of lodges and motels at the entrance to the National Park. All these but one appear to be closed—and something tells me I am better off here in mid-

May, snow or no snow, than I should be in summer. By then I have discovered that at least some of the roads in the park are open.

One of these is to Old Faithful, where there is a campground. The road takes you past layered and pillared cliffs and buttressed ridges of gray-grown rhyolite; along dark rivers of glassy water so cold it floats lumps of snow; by that astonishing forest, which I'd swear has gone on for fifty miles now, a perpetual wheatfield of slender Lodgepole pines; and among the hydrothermal phenomena.

My *good*ness!

In every quarter the earth is steaming through innumerable fissures. This is the Lower Geyser Basin. With the last of the daylight I have a tour of the boardwalk that leads through it. Vapors are rising on every side. Among the first of the boiling springs is a funnel-shaped pool of heavenly blue. Near by, boiling mud is leaping up and falling with a *plop, plop, plop;* it makes you think of a dwarf jumping up and down in mirthless satisfaction. Muddy red water, half mud, half water, is spouting two or three feet high. There are spray geysers and scalding water flowing over the shelves of white or coral-tinted travertine it has deposited. The forest is loud with the hiss of geysers you cannot see. One sounds with the steady roar of a steam locomotive about to get under way.

Child as one is of an age of manufactured effects, one must make a point of recognizing that these displays are not what might be seen at a World's Fair issuing from concealed pipes. Man has nothing to do with them. Not far down is a mass of cooling but still sizzling rock with which the flowing ground water is coming into contact, and a knowledge of this makes the earth seem very much alive. One feels as a sophisticated Greek or Roman might have if, after going for years through the forms of religious observance, he visited a shrine and discovered that no dissembling priest was in the oracle's place but a veritable god speaking in a god's accents and capable, for that matter, of shaking the *terra firma;* the tremendous rock slide below Mount Jackson and the huge blocks shown in a nearby exhibit to have fallen from it are token of the earthquake of 1959. (A noble earthquake it must have been.)

It is hard to believe I am alone, but looking continually around I see no one. If I trusted my rather eerie feelings I should say I was in a company, right enough, but an invisible one. . . . However, there is reassurance. Were I a votary of the earth gods—and I cannot swear I am not and am certainly not going to *here*—I should take it as a mark of exceptional favor that in this place, among these geysers, I am vouchsafed my first sight of a bird that may be the country's loveliest. It alights on a bare branch near by, a creature of fairy-like delicacy and mildness and of an azure matching the evening sky behind it—without the red breast of its eastern cousin. It is a Mountain bluebird.

The campground at Old Faithful is closed—as, I learn, are all others in the park until June 1. With darkness having fallen, this is very awkward, for the rules are stringent against lying up overnight anywhere in a National Park but in an authorized campground. What to do? What is that camper-truck doing at the gasoline station (closed) near the lodge? A young man answers my knock on his door and tells me he has a Ranger's permission to stay there overnight. How suddenly different the situation! It turns out that he has lost his job but before binding himself to another is wandering about the country seeing what it is like. There would be much to talk about, but the evening is too far along for it. I park beside him and turn in after a late supper by the glare of the gas-mantle lamp, warmed both by its heat and the motor's. At three-thirty, having been aroused gradually, against last-ditch resistance to acknowledging it, by the penetrating cold, I am sufficiently alarmed by the possibility of the engine's freezing to get up and run it for a while. The result is that, with a tarpaulin for extra cover, I oversleep for the first time on the trip, not waking until six-thirty. It is so cold the windshield is frosted inside as well as out—the altitude here is above 7,300 feet—and I do not tarry over dressing. Setting off for a run after breakfast in the direction of Old Faithful, I am in luck, reaching the site just in time to be one of half a dozen watching the great geyser go off.

Again, what you see registers on you first as an engineering achievement; anything you have ever seen in the least comparable has been. Accordingly, with the counter-realization that this prodigy is born of a repository of the earth's primal heat without external intervention, the awesome phenomenon gives you even more pause. You are seeing something that should not be, as a ghost should not be. And it is awesome enough, that uncannily mounting white fountain. Up and up it goes, triumphantly, as if to confound the unbeliever. At more than fifteen stories high it holds its pitch, protracting the impossible. Even on subsiding it keeps leaping and falling for a spell at lower heights, not to let you think it unable to repeat the performance. And not only do you see it for what it is in itself, but, as you do the Grand Canyon and the redwood forest, more impressionably for knowing that in all the world there is nothing else of its kind to equal it. In the freezing air, the white plume lifted with such stunning power and all the great quantities of steam issuing from all over the neighborhood must be at their most spectacular.

"Our whole party was wild with enthusiasm," wrote Second Lieutenant Gustavus C. Doane, co-leader of a semi-official expedition to Yellowstone in 1870, whose report, confirming earlier accounts of the area's wonders dismissed as fantasies, had much to do with its designation as a National Park two years later. I have to forego the cascades of stone deposited by flowing water at Jupiter Terrace, the cliff of volcanic glass and the petrified forests of still-standing trunks. But what I am able to see of the snow-bound park is enough to explain the effect on its explorers: the Morning Glory Pool, turquoise in its depths, rust-colored along the margins of what would be the petals; the thirty-foot-wide Sulphur Cauldron of grayish-yellow waters boiling away with the sound of waves breaking idly on a rocky shore and emitting clouds of choking steam; the broad Yellowstone River pouring down its great falls, 100 feet in one stage, 300 in the other, in wraiths of vapor, its roar filling the gorge it has cut through the rhyolitic lava; the sharp-edged peaks and ridges of the Absarokas, blue under the morning sun across the frozen surface of Yellowstone Lake—all in addition to the geysers. Yet what is to me most special was to those first enthusiasts commonplace: the animals.

In the flat, grassy valleys, elk are grazing, as many as fifty in a herd. Grayish-brown like the rocks but for their buff behinds, they move off with a slow, uncertain dignity if you stop, or even jog a little, head high like camels'. One bull still has an antler left and another off by himself is growing some new ones. . . . And can it be? With some elk beside the dark Firehole River are two bison! What massive animals they are, how high-built, and head and underparts almost black.

In the morning, while I am watching the elk on a marshy plain, along the boardwalk that crosses a corner of it, a coyote goes trotting. To my joy, it decides to come back and have a look around. An elegant, poised creature it is, slim of muzzle. Only about 150 feet away, it relieves itself on a rock, then resumes its course in an even, loose gait that looks as if it could be kept up all day. . . . Now here comes another, down the same boardwalk. And the second stops and relieves itself on the same rock. Ahead of the first, two Canada geese take off with low, warning *honks,* alert in every nerve, and put down again a short distance off on a little pond. To think: here are waterfowl less apprehensive of me than of another animal!

So it is that after five thousand miles I come to a vignette of the continent that was, in its morning innocence. In a few other preserves it could be duplicated, but for the rest it is gone, gone in one short final century of the spanning of the country by the railroad. The shaggy bison I see on my way out of the park, standing all by himself but for a Canada goose near by, his head down, ruminating, could hardly be aware of what once had been. He has no memory of a time when the herds of his kind stretched from horizon to horizon and the flocks of migrating waterfowl streamed the width of the sky, when the land teemed with life, was clamorous with it, and each creature was perfected in its role by the very enemies that threatened it and, in being tested and ever on its mettle, knew thereby the sharp savor of living. But if the big bison cannot remember what used to be, he must still have instincts attuned to the sight of the high-humped host of his kind like the waves of a dark and woolly sea, the rich, warm scents, and the rumble of the earth beneath the thudding hooves.

Old fellow! You know that where comfort and the pulse of excitement should be there is nothing, and your heart is heavy—though no heavier, I promise you, than mine is for you and for all that is gone. . . . The old bull stirs . . . but only to turn his back and walk slowly away.

11

FROM GRAND TETONS
TO FRONT RANGE

The Tetons rise almost on the southern border of Yellowstone; the two National Parks are only a few miles apart. In terms of the mitten-shaped Central Desert, they are at the nail of the thumb— that is, at the tip of the Snake River Plains. Like the Sierra Nevada, they are a fault-block range, the two being at opposite frontiers of the Basin-and-Range Province. While only forty miles long, they are composed of granite and gneisses far antedating any rock in the Sierras, a section of the ancient Continental Basement having been heaved up to form them, as it was to form the crests of the Central and Southern Rockies. Like all the high mountains of the West, they have a configuration sharpened by the glaciers of the Pleistocene ice ages. Composed of snow falling inexhaustibly and compacted by its own weight, these rivers of semi-plastic ice plucked off rocks frozen to them as they sagged away from the mountainsides against which they were formed, and the process was continually repeated as snows filled with new ice the gap thus left and more rocks were pulled from the face of the cliff by the sagging glacier.

Having taken due cognizance of the facts, I think I have to say that of all the mountains I see on this trip, the Tetons are the most thrilling. On the other side of Lake Jackson—a long body of water impounded behind a glacial moraine in the fault-block trough east of the range—they soar up dizzily without preliminary foothills. From the groves of poniard-slim Blue spruces, massed like blue-green crystalline stalagmites, you gaze across the ice at the array of clustered, deeply chiseled, pyramidal peaks flung skyward from the flat valley to the more than 13,700-foot-high summit of the Grand Teton; and, fretting over the necessity of putting off a closer approach to another time (if you are in my shoes), you cast about in your mind for a likeness. Monstrous seas of rock gale-tossed in haphazard, foam-decked, peaking waves? Yes, they have the reckless, upward sweep of line of cresting waves, but no waters ever achieved such jagged shapes, no foam the whiteness of those snowfields. Less excitably, and with the Pleistocene age in my mind, I even think of the heads of a herd of giant mammoths sloping steeply up from base of trunk to narrow crown. But what the Tetons most resemble when you can see the range in its entirety, as from a high pass twenty miles to the east, is, I think, a mighty conflagration, of flames of rock and snow.

"The Grand, Middle and South Tetons [were] called the Trois Tetons by trappers and explorers of the early 19th Century," the National Park leaflet tells us demurely without saying why. To the Spanish, carrying the Cross over the carnage of massacred Indians, the snow of the Okus aglow from the red sun was the blood of Christ; to the French, far from the boulevards, the eminences dominating the range that gives birth to the Snake River were breasts. The names Sangre de Cristo and Tetons tell us little or nothing of the mountains on which they were bestowed but a good deal about their originators. Men see in things what they bring to them.

And what do the American people bring to mountains? Of what is it most consistently reminded by them? The answer is: of successful men. Our idea of what to do with mountains is to use them as pedestals for reputations. Having mountains named after them is the reward we have habitually held out to men who distinguish themselves.

Witnessing a stellar performance, Americans have an urge to participate in the star's triumph—to be part of the act. This is a view I recently heard ventured by a participant in the "Texaco Opera Quiz," that delightful feature between the acts of broadcast productions of the Metropolitan Opera; the question had been raised as to why American audiences applaud so boisterously, crashing in regularly after arias and drowning out the concluding bars of operas and symphonic works. The answer would account for the cult we make of public figures, the streams of publicity about them we produce and consume, the efforts we make to touch them when they appear in crowds—and our addiction to naming landmarks after them. Long before history has had a chance to decide whether they deserve any honor at all, we rush to affix the names of the prominent—outstanding politicians especially—to bridges, cultural centers, airports, public buildings, highways, and naval vessels. These at least are of human creation and transient. But we are equally unsparing of that which is not and, in human terms, lasts forever: mountains.

The Scots may look up to Ben Dearg and Ben Macdhui, the Welsh to Eryri ("Eagle's Place," denigrated as Snowdon) and the Brecon Beacon, the Irish to Carrantuohill and Lugnaquilla, the English to Cross Fell and Wear Head, the Germans to the Zugspitze and the Feldberg, the French to Mont Blanc, the Vignemale, and the Puy de Sancy, the Swiss to the Weisshorn, Matterhorn, and Finsteraarhorn, the Austrians to Grossglockner, the Greeks to Olympus and Kiona, the Spanish to the Pico de Aneto (of the Maladettas) and Monte Perdido, the Italians to Monte Rosa and the Gran Sasso d'Italia, the Sicilians to Etna, the Mexicans to Orizaba and Popocatépetl, the Guatemalans to Tajumulco, the Costa Ricans to Chirripó Grande and Irazú, the Ecuadorians to Chimborazo and Cotapaxi, the Peruvians to Huascarán and El Misti, the Bolivians to Illampu and Illimani, the Chileans and Argentinians to Aconcagua and Tupungato. But we Americans? The roll call of the summits that give our country grandeur, on which we have officiously set our stamp, has all the poetry of an index to a high-school history or the roster of a chamber of commerce. Whitney. Mitchell. Cleveland. Elbert. Morgan. Borah (highest in Idaho). Long's. Humphrey's. Taylor. Adams. Washington. Moran. Marcy. Wilson. Hyndman. Mansfield. King's. Hayden. MacDonald. Zirkel. Etc., etc.

Well: I have that out of my system. Or almost. There is still McKinley. McKinley is the finish. Denali, it had been, "the High One," the 20,320-foot Home of the Sun to the Alaskan Indians. Then, in a magazine article, a self-important prospector, with no known claim on the nation's consideration or any motive but the crassest, coolly supplanted the euphonious and noble name of the continent's grandest mountain with that of the stodgy defender of the gold standard then occupying the White House. That was all it took. The American people scurried bleatingly into line, proclaiming Mount McKinley. What a nation of peasant slaves!

But, oh, the names that are borne by mountain ranges, rivers, and other features of the land that the politicians, the politicians' claques and the civic-minded have left alone! Full of the sap of the country, sweet and bitter, they are names acquired from the Indians or given by the early white men who lived the life of the land: the Appalachian, the Allegheny, the Adirondack, the Catskill, the Ouachita, the Ozark, the Panamint, the Wallowa, the Owl's Head, the Bitterroot, the Last Chance, the Medicine Bow, the White Cloud, and the Shadow mountains; the Shenandoah, the Susquehanna, the Monongahela, the Juniata, the Mohawk, the Hoosatonic, the Potomac, the Chattahoochie, the Apalachicola, the Atchafalaya, the Santee, the Niobrara, the Purgatoire, the Cache la Poudre, the Belle Fourche, and the Sweetwater rivers; Bitter Creek, Crazy Woman Creek, Hungry Creek, Doe Run, Bull Run, and Roaring Run; Deadwood, Deadman Pass, Deadhorse, Dead Mule Canyon and Stud-Horse Canyon and Wild Horse, Hellgate, Bone Gap, Wolf Pen, Bear Wallow, Possum's Trot, Blacklick, Big Piney, Lonesome Stony, Deep Step, Powderhorn, Blooming Rose and Dewy Rose, Rising Fawn, Rising Sun and Sundance, Hungry Mother, Forks of Buffalo, Broken Bow, Warrior's Mark, and Sweet Annie hollow. Even some mountains have escaped: Katahdin, Monadnock, Graylock, Winespring, Hawksbill, Spruce Knob, Fair Weather, Knife Point, Elkhorn, Sleepy Cat, Grizzly, Cloud's Rest, Lone Cone, Stony Man, and Old Baldy. There is music in them all, and in none is it purer, to me, than in the name of the range forming the major tusk of the elephant's head of the Central Rockies, the Wind River Mountains.

U. S. 287, on its way southeastward to Laramie and Denver, parallels the range but at a distance of thirty or forty miles. It does, however, stay close to the Wind River itself, from the stream's source below Togwotee Pass, thirty miles on from the Tetons. Over 9,600 feet high and on the Continental Divide, the saddle is strategically situated. You not only pass here from the valley of the Pacific to the valley of the Atlantic; you also take leave of the volcanic West. The last you see of this are frontier battlements which, excluding the great cone volcanoes, may be the most imposing laval highlands in the country. (The unauthorized adjective seems to fill a need.) "Palisade Rock Formations," the road-map says. And they are that—super-terrestrial edifices of story on story of vertically scored, dark-mauve rock, the monumental remnants of a plateau built up by successive layers of welded rhyolitic tuff, each from an eruption that rained fire on the earth beneath darkened skies. Standing high above the snowy spruce forest, up to nearly 11,900 feet—Lava Mountain, one of the nearest, a huge butte of horizontally banded minars—they are almost scalp-tingling. If you were not somewhat habituated to the West you would feel they belonged to another planet.

In the open, grass-and-sagebrush country to which you descend from Togwotee Pass you would certainly feel that this could not be the United States. It is too vastly roomy and lost, its exotic structures too difficult to relate to the familiar. And what *is* it? Küchler calls it "Wheatgrass-Needlegrass-Shrubsteppe." But it is not the mountains, it is not the plains.

What it *is* is a basin, so called, and one of those that separate the parts of the Central Rockies and the Central Rockies from the Southern Rockies. The basins are valleys in which sediments have accumulated in such quantities that they have come to account for more of the topography than the mountains from which they were stripped, as in the Basin-and-Range Province. Accumulating and turning to rock in their turn, the deposits have been cut down by streams and the new sediments spread over the Great Plains. As on the Colorado Plateau, the land stands at various levels and you pass cliffs and bluffs, sometimes huge escarpments. The carving and colors are arresting even by Western standards. *On the left, worn-down hills of alternating brick- and sand-colored strata. . . . We're now going through a real canyon of brown-red sandstone from top to bottom, stratum after stratum. Great red-sandstone walls rising right up from the car, right up from the road beside the car. Over on the other side of the Wind River there are various shades of lavender strata under a kind of sandy, pea-green topping.*

Strange and somehow arbitrary the scenery may be, but it is Wyoming and a part of Wyoming in which America, in a manner of speaking, stands face to face with itself. The range of high hills, grassy-flanked, topped by black forest, that accompanies the highway on the right, concealing the Wind River Mountains, is evidently grazing land. Not without justification does Wyoming sport a bucking bronco on its license plates. It is the heart of the ranch country. Several times herds of Herefords block the road; I pick up their incessant bawling on the recorder as I try to push a way through them. A real cowpoke, riding loosely on an energetic pony, is trying to shepherd the largest herd and acknowledging his difficulties with a wry smile and a shake of the head. Two girls are riding on the outskirts of the herd. One in light blue, tapered trousers, is probably an Easterner. The other, whose blue jeans, incongruous horn-rimmed glasses and unconcerned whistling suggest that this is the ordinary thing for her, could well be the rancher's daughter. And probably it is a small rancher who has to take in paying guests to stay in business.

In Lander, one of those Western towns open to sky and sun, and set in a comparatively green countryside, a scattering of figures in ranch-style attire is in evidence, among them a big, stocky, fat Indian talking to an elderly white man leaning against the front of a café. The women and girls, however, are conventional metropolitan America; provincialism in dress is not what the fair sex usually aims at. You read that Lander used to describe itself as "where the rails end and the trails begin." An outfitter for hunters drawn to the Wind River Wilderness, it was formerly also the haunt of George LeRoy Parker, a Mormon cowpuncher who became, one might say, the *beau ideal* of outlaws under the name Butch Cassidy. Cassidy was the light-hearted leader of a band that plied, it is written, from Mexico to Canada and from the Pacific to the Great Lakes yet he never, in all these depredations, killed a man. The passing of an America born with the Lewis and Clark expedition a century before was signalized in 1902 when Cassidy decided that the West, his West, was finished and sailed to South America. Well, times must change. Yet one may hope that Cassidy did not, as the report had it, put a bullet through himself in 1909 in order to avoid surrender in a twelve-hour battle with the Bolivian cavalry but lived to return to Lander, as some say he did in the 1930's, to reclaim the seventy thousand dollars he had once cached in the Wind River Mountains when closely pressed by a posse.

On the way to Lander you pass the grave of a Sacajawea, pronounced by Wyoming authorities the same Sacajawea whose meeting with her Shoshone kinsmen was so providential for the Lewis and Clark expedition. Near it is the grave of the Shoshone chief, Washakie, who, though born before the expedition, yet lived to within two years of Butch Cassidy's departure. Washakie, whose single-handed combat to the death with a Crow chieftain may have given the name Crowheart Butte to the great eminence across the Wind River from U. S. 287, cooperated with the whites and was rewarded by a vast reservation for his people. This you pass for fifty miles on the way to Lander, seeing an occasional ranch house or group of shanties. At least you pass what was left after the United States Government thought better of its generosity and relieved the Shoshones of the more fertile part of their reservation, the valley of the Popo Agie, in which Lander is located.

Shoshones and Crows, and the more warlike Sioux, Blackfeet, Arapaho, Cheyenne, and Bannock—Wyoming was the hunting ground of all, and a major battlefield in the generation-long, relentless operation of breaking the Indians' hold on their lands. The map is dotted with the sites of forts of a century ago, three around Lander. You understand why the struggle began early here and continued with a savage intensity. That is after you have ascended nearly a thousand feet to a tableland so high the snow is still on it in mid-May and you can see at last behind you the tremendous, crinkled mass of the Wind River Range, its high peaks jutting through snowfields glistening like vanilla icing in the sun. For many miles thereafter you have barren ridges of earth-brown, deeply etched sedimentary rock on the north. These begin to shape up into peaks. One more prominent than the rest is deeply cleft. A sign tells you that it is Rattlesnake Ridge and that it served as a landmark for the immigrants' wagon-trains. And there, where the Sweetwater River flows beneath it, was the stage stop for the Pony Express in '60 and '61.

You have reached the California-Oregon Trail and its crossing of the Sweetwater on its way to South Pass. That famous, 7,550-foot-high crossing of the Continental Divide south of the Wind River Mountains is forty miles to the southwest. The pass is actually a twenty-five-mile-wide valley-plain and is said to be so furrowed with old wagon-tracks as to resemble a grass-grown, plowed field. Between 1840 and the completion of the railroad in 1869, 300,000 went westward over the trail, strewing it with tools, trunks, and furniture they could carry no longer as the going grew tough here in Wyoming. The Indians saw the rivers of caravans, read the portents aright and responded accordingly—and in the end, of course, futilely. But of those who traveled the trail, 34,000 fell to sickness, accidents, and arrows and were buried along the way. So one reads in the Works Progress Administration *Guide* for Wyoming.

A little farther on, paralleling the Sweetwater, the highway passes near "Historic Three Crossings Station," of which the *Guide* has this to say: "It was to this station in 1860 that Bill Cody, 15-year-old Pony Express carrier, rode from Red Buttes on the Platte, 75 miles away. There he found that the rider of the 85-mile stretch to Rocky Ridge had been killed. Cody thereupon, without resting, rode to Rocky Ridge and returned to Red Buttes, with eastbound mail, on time. This 322-mile ride is the longest on the records of the Pony Express." Such was the high endeavor called forth by the daring ideal of that wild, cross-country relay race; for that was what it was —an idea, an impractical, vaulting, really impossible idea. The Pony Express was pure adventure, owing nothing to any mechanical reinforcements of human heart and stamina, and it aroused the national imagination in its day as its memory does now. But, having endured only eighteen months before the telegraph supplanted it, it has vanished almost without a trace, as have the wagon-trains, the raiding Indians, the badmen. You would suppose that nothing had ever happened in this remote, unsettled country.

The highway turns south for Rawlins before a massive formation of snowy peaks called the Ferris Mountains. These mark the beginning of a new component of the Western Cordillera. If you picture the Southern Rockies as a goat's head, these are the detached tip of the western horn formed by the Medicine Bow Range.

On the last forty miles to Rawlins we've been passing mostly barren country, barren flatlands partially—very partially—covered with sagebrush, and the mesas on the side with tilted strata—bleak, uninhabited country. You can see in country like this, though, why people are so captured by the Western sky. It seems to go on to limitless distances beyond the already extremely distant horizon. For the last two days it's been a marvelous sky, very deep blue overhead and paler toward the horizon with flotillas of snow rafts riding on it, as the clouds seem to be, all more or less on a level and receding to that tremendously remote distance beyond the last hills. . . . Deciding that any country is dull may be premature. On the rolling sagebrush plains east of Rawlins are half a dozen Pronghorns. Tranquil as a domestic herd, they are beautifully patterned in fawn and cottony white and dainty on their long, brittle legs. Where the country seems hopeless, you may expect to find it left to the aborigines—the wild animals and the Indians.

"Medicine Bow. Population 392." Ugh. A dusty plains village, it is as dreary a place just before sundown as I have seen, even with the treat of a telephone call home to give it an aura. Why does it stir something in memory? A sign by the dingy Union Pacific Rail-

road station explains it: *Home of Owen Wister's "The Virginian."*
So this is it, this is where that epochal addition to the world's literature of romance, the Western, began, and with it a billion persons'
picture of a major part of the North American continent. But what
a drab birthplace! The thought of it preoccupies me during dinner,
for which I stop a short distance down the road to catch the last of
the daylight.

A touching figure the Virginian was, in retrospect and against the
background of the bare, bleak plains, unrelieved in the expiring
light except by some low ridges on the horizon. For most cowboys
the life can only have been a meager and a hard one, however unconfined: fourteen or fifteen hours a day or more in the saddle
breathing the dust of the herd in the parching summer heat, riding
the fence line all alone, all day in the winter blasts so cold the tears
would freeze on the eyelashes. No wonder they sang to themselves
and their songs have a bit the air of whistling in the dark. But did it
mean something to them, as demonstrably it did to the riders of the
Pony Express, to know they were living an idea? *Did* they know it?
They would have known it, certainly, once Owen Wister and his
fellows had fixed the figure of the cowboy in legend. The immigrants to Oregon and California surely were aware of taking part in
an epic—the crossing of continental wilderness. They knew they
were living an idea. Americans have known it, in the great chapters
of our past. Those who came first to our shores knew it; they were
not merely settling a new world but bringing one into being. Those
who fought the Revolution knew it, for they had set forth the idea
for all mankind to read. Both sides in the war of 1861–65 knew it,
else they would not have fought as they did.

But they have all gone, and the Virginian with them, worn down,
broken, ultimately destroyed by the years, if not cut down before.
And I . . . I have come to Rock River (Elevation 6,892). Rock Bottom, it might be called. Here at a so-called trailer court I am al-
lowed to park overnight for a dollar—fortunately, there being no
alternative. A walk quickly encompasses the town's resources—a
tawdry collection of gasoline stations and third-rate cafés serving
local truck-drivers and a couple of comparable hotels, in the muddy
back yard of one of which I am parked.

"The trapper, the explorer, the pony express rider and the cowboy may have passed over the hill," says the Secretary of State at

Cheyenne in a foreword to the Wyoming *Guide,* "but the sunset against which the pioneers saw him silhouetted still flames over Wyoming in scarlet and gold." It is a curious assertion.

The sunset still flames, true enough, and over the United States as a whole. But, merciful heavens! After all the indomitable hopes, the incalculable energies expended in the service of heroic conceptions, the suffering, the loneliness, the anguish and the dying right and left, after the fearful price paid by the aborigines of the land that we might be accommodated, after all the wealth amassed, should there not be more to show for it in the America that meets the eye? Can justification for all that went before be found in the America portrayed in the advertisements and on the television and motion-picture screens? Yes, yes, there is of course a great deal beyond the picture presented by the salesmen of commodities and the entertainment industry—though I am not sure who speaks with more authority than the agencies which have billions at stake in presenting us as we like to see ourselves. But travel the highways and you cannot help asking yourself if this is what it all comes down to, this succession of monuments, squalid or grandiose, to getting and spending. You wonder how it is we have created so little that begins to match the natural splendors of the continent or that speaks of what is lofty and stirring in our own history.

American communities do, it is true, seem in general rather more disposed than otherwise to preserve the remains of the past, provided that the getting and spending are not thereby significantly impeded. And with the tourist business being what it is, they are likely to be promoted. In addition to the steam locomotives and historic houses saved from oblivion, "Frontier Days" celebrations seem to be common among Western towns. In Laramie, where I look with respect up a street of fine, substantial masonry mansions of the past century, some built by English cattle barons, shop windows display garments and paraphernalia of the Old West and a chuck wagon is drawn up by the curb. Wyoming relinquishes the idea of itself with reluctance. Entering Laramie from the south— by which I leave it—you are welcomed to the city by a large billboard depicting a horse and rider. Yo're in cowboy country now, Pard: home on the range. Behind the billboard a Portland cement plant is pouring out buff-colored smoke visible from miles away, and behind this are what seem to be squatters' colonies and a vast automobile junkyard. "Time cannot change or diminish the gifts that Nature has lavished on Wyoming," says the Secretary of State, writing in 1941, when things may have looked a little different. "Time has not changed—it will not change—the brightness of our sunshine, the pureness of our air, the music of our refreshing breezes, the majestic grandeur of our mountains, the beauty of our lakes and rivers, the inspiration of our great forests. . . ."

At intervals behind the dark, low ridges in the middle background you see the tops of higher mountains. They look like the backs of white dragons. Those are the Medicine Bows, on the way to Laramie. South of Laramie, beyond the State line and the blocky ruins of red granite ridges and outcroppings weathered gray, resembling the remains of ancient castles, beyond the mesas of red sandstone facing them, U. S. 287 takes you south toward Denver within view the whole way of the Front Range of the Rockies, which looks out across the Great Plains. And from here the image of white dragons presents itself forcefully indeed. So it must have presented itself to the early comers. They were of course glad to see the serrate wall rise slowly on the horizon; it was what they had come for—in the 1820's and 1830's for the beaver the mountains harbored, after 1858 for precious metals.

But if the treasure was to be gained, it had to be on the mountains' own terms, and it must have been clear that these terms would not be trifling. Even today, with everything made easy, a little imagination tells you how puny and feeble human enterprise must have seemed to be pitted against those mountain guardians of the golden promise of the West. From the highway to Longmont and Boulder, the Front Range rises behind a succession of forehills dark in shadow, parts of it half obscured by gray mists of rain, some of its snowfields gleaming in the brilliance of the sun beneath cumulus clouds bursting with light, and it looks all of what it is, the beginning of a wilderness, surpassing any, of enormous peaks and ridges. With 180 or more summits over 12,000 feet above sea-level, more than 110 of these above 13,000 and 40 above 14,000, Colorado embraces North America's most formidable assemblage of mountains.

Few battles of modern times can have taken such a toll of the combatants as the Mountain Men paid in lives for their packs of pelts. What men will endure for money! one is inclined to exclaim piously. But that cannot have been it—not, certainly, if there is the clue I think there is in the testimony of an English observer, who died at twenty-seven in 1848. Writing of a typical pre-arranged ren-

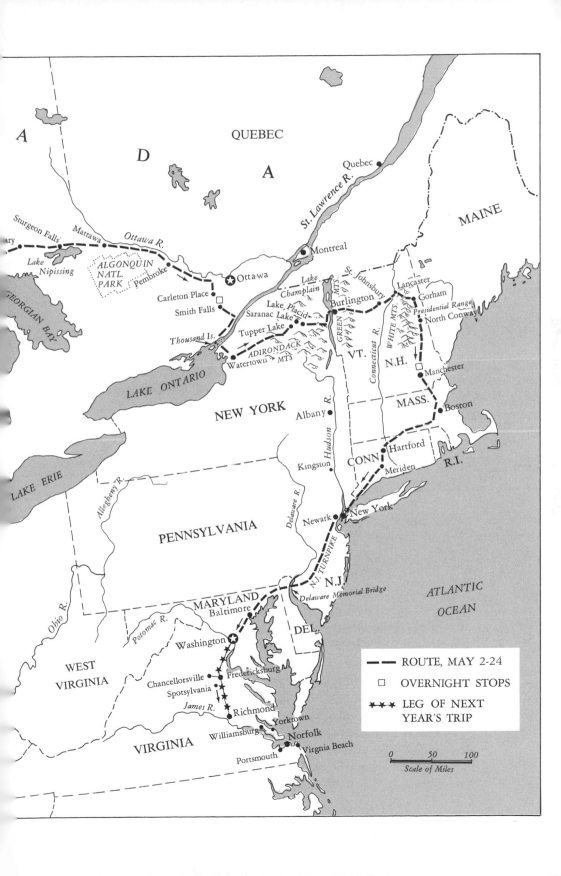

CA NA DA

QUEBEC

Quebec

St. Lawrence R.

MAINE

Sturgeon Falls
Mattawa
Ottawa R.
Lake Nipissing
ALGONQUIN NATL. PARK
Pembroke
Carleton Place
Smith Falls
Thousand Is.
Montreal
Ottawa
GEORGIAN BAY
LAKE ONTARIO
Lake Champlain
Lake Placid
Saranac Lake
Tupper Lake
Watertown
ADIRONDACK MTS.
St. Johnsbury
Lancaster
Gorham
Burlington
GREEN MTS.
WHITE MTS.
Presidential Range
North Conway
VT.
N.H.
Manchester
Connecticut R.
MASS.
Boston
NEW YORK
Albany
Hudson R.
Kingston
CONN.
Hartford
Meriden
R.I.
LAKE ERIE
Allegheny R.
PENNSYLVANIA
Delaware R.
Newark
New York
N.J. TURNPIKE
N.J.
Delaware Memorial Bridge
ATLANTIC OCEAN
Ohio R.
MARYLAND
Baltimore
Potomac R.
Washington
DEL.
WEST VIRGINIA
Chancellorsville
Spotsylvania
Fredericksburg
James R.
Richmond
Yorktown
Williamsburg
Norfolk
Virginia Beach
Portsmouth
VIRGINIA

ROUTE, MAY 2-24
◻ OVERNIGHT STOPS
✶✶✶ LEG OF NEXT YEAR'S TRIP

0   50   100
Scale of Miles

dezvous at which trappers sold their packs to the agents of the fur companies and in turn bought inferior supplies from profiteering traders, George Frederick Ruxton recalls:

The rendezvous is one continued scene of drunkenness, gambling, brawling and fighting, as long as the money and credit of the trappers last. Seated, Indian fashion, round the fires, with a blanket spread before them, groups are seen with their "decks" of cards, playing at euker, poker, and seven-up, the regular mountain games. The stakes are "beaver," which here is current coin; and when the fur is gone, their horses, mules, rifles, and shirts, hunting packs, and *breeches,* are staked. Daring gamblers make the rounds of the camp, challenging each other to play for the trapper's highest stake—his horse, his squaw (if he have one), and, as once happened, his scalp. "There goes hos and beaver!" is the mountain expression when any great loss is sustained; and, sooner or later, "hos and beaver" invariably find their way into the insatiable pockets of the traders. A trapper often squanders the produce of his hunt, amounting to hundreds of dollars, in a couple of hours; and, supplied on credit with another equipment, leaves the rendezvous for another expedition, which has the same result time after time, although one tolerably successful hunt would enable him to return to the settlements and civilized life, with an ample sum to purchase and stock a farm, and enjoy himself in ease and comfort the remainder of his days. . . .

It must be that that was just what the trapper in his heart meant to avoid at all costs and that the regular dissipation of his earnings was his means, doubtless unconscious, of ensuring that he would succeed—as it was too with the prospectors like Shorty Harris, who managed to have nothing to show for his killing on the Bullfrog Lode. There are men whose needs nothing will satisfy this side of the loneliness of the wilds, the demands of which, however severe, are very different from the demands of human society. One remembers also the miners of whom the New England woman of the Feather River Canyon wrote that they would give up a claim "by which, if they pleased, they could lay up more in a month than they could accumulate in a year at home" and "will wander off in search of better 'diggings.' "

However, I have come to suspect that in the pursuit of gold, which above all else supplied the incentive for the arduous and death-dealing exploration of the New World, a special incitement is at work. Gold is highly prized by society, the synonym of value. It is heavy, imperishable, and richly, lustrously beautiful. It is rare but not beyond discovery by persistent quest. It is found in places peculiarly expressive of Nature—in mountains and streams. These attributes in combination make gold, I think—the ultimate object of search—powerfully symbolic. For men of active natures and strong urges, I suspect it can come to stand for the meaning of life, to be won against all hazards, Nature's quintessential secret, in the mastery of which fulfillment is to be achieved. And of course when it is found and does not resolve the dissatisfactions, larger strikes must be sought. There is no end.

I have my own objects in life to think of, however—and whether, whatever exactly they may be, they will prove in the end, any more than gold, to resolve the excitations the heart is subject to remains to be seen. Meanwhile, I envy the prospectors at least in that their searchings saw them initiated in the country their hopes brought them to whereas I am snatched from one place to the next, leaving each still a stranger to it. Resisting the terms of the bargains one enters into with life is self-destructive futility, as I know, but the knowledge does not lighten my sense of guilt in breezing in and out of the temples of the Great Spirit. In time I shall have to make amends by taking up the pilgrim's staff, which is to say the hiker's pack, and walk the most arduous trails I can find. For the present I show my good faith by continually consulting the parti-colored Geological Survey map and studying, each evening, the lesson for the day ahead in the texts I have brought, which may mean poring five times over a critical passage. In doing so, I learn things Jim Bridger never knew for all his half-century as trapper and guide in the West, and would have been bored to death by; things that Jedediah Smith, who rediscovered South Pass in 1824 and opened the way westward from the North Platte, would have indignantly repudiated as contrary to the Bible he habitually carried.

The map shows the Front and Rampart Ranges narrowly bordered by blue on the east, which represents late Paleozoic sedimentary rocks. These take a more dramatic form than you might expect. Slabs of varying size—and hugeness—they stand in some places at the angle of artillery pieces set for maximum range, in others nearly vertical, as in the Garden of the Gods at Colorado Springs, where they are of red sandstone. You see in them remains of the layers of soft rock, many thousands of feet thick, that once blanketed the region and wore away as they were uptilted in the buckling of the earth's crust that took place between 50 and 100 million years ago. Up from below these came the harder, forged rock of the continental basement, although this did not stand fully exposed until perhaps 30 million years ago or less.

Pink and olive-green are the Front and Rampart Ranges on the map, meaning that they are of fairly old and very old pre-Paleozoic igneous and metamorphic rocks. Expecting rocks of such venerability to be a moldy gray, and forgetting that rocks age only on the surface, I am amazed at the splendor of those through which the highway up Big Thompson Canyon to Estes Park has been cut. The schistose rocks glisten like sheets of silk. Plates of mica and feldspar crystals sparkle like cut glass. The bright gray, pink, and red granites and gneisses, all juxtaposed and cut by dikes, are like varicolored candies.

The gorge cut by the Big Thompson River—and it must have been Thompson who was big, for the river is a mere dozen feet across—could have been designed to enhance the visitor's susceptibility to what awaits, like the massive statuary before the royal court of the Pharaohs. Narrow and twisting to begin with, its walls of dark, split, and crumbled rocks five or six hundred feet high, if my guess is right, the defile opens out as you proceed to permit you to gaze up at the sentries of the Front Range—steep, pyramidal foothills of gray rock partially cloaked in pine forest. Austere retainers they seem, whose notice the human encroachments on the canyon are far beneath, outposts whose span of attention is measured in geological ages.

Estes Park, to which you climb from 5,000 to 7,500 feet, is not, as I had once thought, a park in the conventional sense but one of the high basins ringed by peaks called parks in the Southern Rockies. It is also a town and one pretty much like others consecrated to vacationers with the difference that around it, in aloof and spectacular sovereignty, are the granite icebergs of the Front Range, and of Rocky Mountain National Park.

A few miles beyond the entrance to the park is the start of Trail Ridge Road, which crosses the 410-square-mile reservation and, so the Park Service says, is "the highest continuous automobile road in the United States, reaching an elevation of 12,183 feet." It faces me with my shame all over again. I ought, indeed, to be dumped out on the Colorado Plateau, to have to cross the continent on foot. It is not right to sail effortlessly over the crests of these mighty ridges.

As it turns out on this occasion, I need not have worried excessively for the road is closed after only six miles. The plows have been all the way through but a workman tells me that a few days back a blizzard with winds of a hundred miles an hour had struck, and I suppose other such sudden storms are feared. Yet it is so warm today even at two miles' elevation that it seems entirely out of order to be filling an icebox from a snow-bank. (I am, it is true, to be back here again the next summer with my wife and daughters and be able this time to drive the whole way on Trail Ridge Road, over the summit and on across the Continental Divide. But then too there are limitations on how much one can see of the park, and of a kind Jim Bridger never dreamed of. Every campground is filled for the four-day week-end and one must move on.)

Trail Ridge Road zig-zags higher and higher, with every turn presenting Olympian panoramas which must be supreme in their effect of all I have seen, other than the Grand Canyon. It is the sheer scale of the range that is so overpowering. The towering wall of the Sierras and the Tetons' magnificent torches of stone are unsurpassed for drama. But here the downward swoop of enormous valley that the skidding vision plumbs and the wall of the amphitheater on the other side up which it sweeps almost make the heart skip a beat, like the plunge and rebound of a roller-coaster. They do, certainly, if you are by yourself and driving with one hand above the drop-off while ransacking your vocabulary for words adequate to the range's scope.

By an optical effect, the mountains appear to grow higher as the road climbs. So above all does the double peak a bare ten miles to the south, at the edge of the Front Range, which, rising above the shoulders of its auxiliaries to a height of over 14,250 feet, reigns over all with an imperial calm. Nesotaya to the Indians (if that is a fair transliteration of the French transliteration Nesotaieux), it was The Guides—and a landmark—to the pioneers, who ignored the branding of the mountain in 1820 by Major Stephen Long's party with the commander's name. The hollowing out of the slopes by the Pleistocene glaciers has given the immense humps of mountains sharp crests and ridges, and their sculpture is accentuated by the snow that fills the crevasses and clings to the leeward sides. *To think of the forces that lifted these masses of stone from miles underground to almost three above it stuns the imagination. . . . Everything you feel about mountains you feel here as strongly as you probably could, the sublimity and profundity of their repose, the sense of their looking beyond you to unfathomable reaches of time.*

The summits give the impression of having pushed up through the blanket of forest. The dusky-green pelage of the troughs laps up the concave, higher slopes, like waves running up a steep shore. At about 9,500 feet on Trail Ridge Road the aromatic Blue spruce and the aspen still bare in mid-May but for the hanging catkins abandon the field to the shock troops of the conifers—Limber pine, Engelmann spruce and Subalpine fir. With increasing altitude, these yield by inches to the savagery of winter gales. At Rainbow Curve, the tallest is only ten feet. Beyond, the grimness of the struggle is attested by the plight of the survivors, which stand, plucky to the last, like battle-tattered standards with only strips of the bunting streaming out to leeward from the staff. More and more, the foliage hugs the earth. In places, it looks as if it had simply been poured out over the ground in liquid form. In others, the mats of Engelmann spruce remind you of a raft with one upright, ravaged little tree above it like a mast with shreds of sail clinging to it.

Treeline, the transition from Hudsonian Zone to Arctic, comes on the average at about 11,500 feet. Above it, even the height of summer sees a plant growth only two or three inches high clothing the slopes below the bare rock and persistent snow-banks. This is the alpine tundra (a word of Lapp origin for treeless, Arctic plains), of which there is more in the mountains of Colorado than anywhere else on the continent below Canada. A dull, brownish-green at a distance, it resembles an impoverished, close-cropped pasture on nearer view. But among the drab grasses, sedges and lichens—some of these yellow or orange, however—is a jewelry of flowering plants that captivate anyone not wholly inaccessible to beauty and the charm of life. The alpine flowers are the pixie-children of the plant kingdom which never grow up. Asking so little of the world they can troop with felicity where their grosser relatives would fail and die, they seem touchingly gay and have a child-like disproportion, often, between large blossoms and small infrastructures. The flowers of the forget-me-nots, of the intensest blue, some of white, are only a quarter of an inch across, but there are full-sized lavender asters with yellow centers and full-sized pale lavender phlox both growing from mere pincushions of foliage, and conventional buttercups also on dwarfed plants. The five-petaled flowers of the Alpine sandwort spring from small, flat mats of minute leaves, and the little Rydbergia is almost ludicrously top-heavy under its two-inch-wide sunflowers—the largest of all alpines—and the Sky-pilot scarcely less so with its clusters of lilac trumpets.

How do they manage? Where the flowers of the severest deserts characteristically cope with adversity as annuals, surviving as seeds between rains perhaps years apart, the alpines are almost all perennials and contend with the brevity of the season by forming flower buds before summer's end, carrying them over the winter and bursting into bloom at the first mildness. And they are their own fur coats against the wind, their fine foliage in compact cushions or mats. Moss campion—and what a charming name it has!—is an extreme, with foliage, as the name implies, of mere filaments; and it thrives around the whole northern hemisphere. All the same, you feel that an elfin magic must account for it when you see it starred with little pale-orchid flowers in the fellfields. (This seems to be the name given the high barrens of rock shingle, battle ground of mountains and elements where the rock has been splintered and resplintered by the frosts.) You could believe, way up on a fellfield, that this is how the earth will be when the sun's warmth has begun to fail and life to ebb. And the impression is not much mitigated by a Horned lark with bright-yellow throat which utters a plaintive, questing note from the tundra, as if it had once been seeking its vanished kind but now is absently repeating its call without remembering the occasion for it.

There seems to me an undeniable fellowship of life. The bonds, let it be granted, do not seem very close to one being harassed or done to death by other living creatures, be they mosquitoes, bacteria, or man-eating tigers. I think of mosquitoes because after leaving Rocky Mountain National Park on our family camping trip and endeavoring to put up in the lush vale of the Little Laramie River, we are beset by such swarms of the little blood-suckers as I have never seen before, except once on military maneuvers in southern Georgia. To escape them we have to drive up into the Medicine Bows to a campground where there are still piles of melting snow—and, thronging the soggy meadows below them, yellow trout-lilies called Snow-lilies and Marsh marigolds of waxen white petals and yellow centers like little water-lilies.

Having one's blood feasted on by insects is peculiarly repellent. Yet I recall how a fellow squad-member of mine at the Army camp in Georgia watched a mosquito with evident satisfaction as it gorged on his arm. He was a man of noticeable good looks though with a rather large jaw—unless it was simply that a saturnine grin so often gave it prominence; his attitude toward life was one of omnivorous acceptance and comprehensive irony. "Poor, starved, wizened, cold little thing!" he declared, cocking an eye at me, whom I think he considered a person never difficult to get a rise out of. "Think," he went on as the insect swelled up into a small red lantern on his arm, "how she must be frantic with ecstasy as she feels that good warm blood fill her shrunken little tummy!"

And probably it is fair to interpret an insect's primal urges in terms of our own. At any rate, other organisms, including those we see as most malignant, are only obeying, helplessly, compulsions about which they have as little choice as we about those that give us scant respite—less choice, indeed; man, and nearly man alone, is guilty of gratuitous aggressions. They, like us, have all they can do to make it. All living things are in much the same clutches, and if we must prey on one another to survive, it is because our needs and urges are so similar, and so relentless.

So when you see life at the edge of existence, in the high fellfields or poking through a frozen torrent of lava, you can hardly fail to feel the sympathy that goes out to kin. You may feel it, too, though for different reasons, if you stop at one of the scenic turn-offs from Trail Ridge Road below treeline. Creatures eager to claim kin with *you* are waiting. Chipmunks and ground-squirrels scurry about the retaining-walls, nervous, quick, and hungry. And unmistakably looking to share your provisions. The ground-squirrels are similar in color to the chipmunks but have sharper muzzles and four dark stripes down the back in place of the chipmunks' two and are smaller. The chipmunks get the lion's share. Some will take graham crackers from your hand quite fearlessly. Clark's nutcrackers—small, stiletto-billed crows, gray and white with black wings—come within a few feet for what you may give them and glide away down the slope of the abyss with a sangfroid that turns your own sang a bit froid. Equally forward are the Gray, or Canada, jays, which with their short bills and puffy feathering make you think of overgrown chickadees. At lower levels, magpies and paradisiacal Steller's jays swoop down out of the trees for scraps.

It almost hurts to see wild creatures so tame, for you cannot but think that this is how they would be everywhere but for the men with guns—men and boys—who have nothing better to do than skulk after them, moose and owl, squirrel and robin, legally or illegally. ("Today . . . anybody with a fat belly can safely shoot the animal down from a distance," said Adolf Hitler contemptuously of Herman Göring's addiction to the hunt.) With all the suffering and death that is inescapable, you would think that human beings would be revolted at the thought of killing for pleasure their already hard-pressed fellow beings. But no: man is the animal from which all others above a hummingbird's size, exclusive of those he has bred for his own use, flee in apprehension or terror, and he is the only one.

My last sight of the Western Cordillera is at evening after an interlude unique in the trip—dinner, and a large and gratifying one, at a restaurant in Boulder as the guest of a most agreeable lady whose son-in-law I have the good fortune to be. When I set forth again, the sun has sunk to the mountaintops, its rich light flooding the fertile intervening farmlands. Everything seems to transcend itself: the fields of a deep green in an orange glow; the archipelagos of clouds, clouds dark and menacing, and white clouds, swelling sphere on sphere, which seem the embodiment of hope; and, matching the brilliance of the snowiest cloud in its frosting, the Front Range culminating in double-headed Nesotaya enthroned like a monarch with arms outspread. The cohort of mountains seems to stand guard as in the past before a West you look back on as still a land of promise, unrealized, still not altogether reduced to human dimensions and possessed, still offering that second chance it is human of us always to be seeking.

12

THE NORTHERN
PLAINS

I have had enough driving. I can tell that even without the pain
that afflicts me a quarter or a third of the time, as of a knife-blade
buried between the left shoulder and the base of the neck. In three
days I could be at home again. But by driving straight back I should
miss out on too much; I am not going to repeat the mistake I made
in turning back too soon from the Pacific Coast. So, with darkness
coming on, I set a course that will take me north through eastern
Wyoming and to the Black Hills and Badlands of South Dakota.

My expectations of a sleeping-place between Fort Collins and
Cheyenne being not high, I am the more enchanted by a rest area
that turns up just within the Colorado line. It is well off the highway, clean, grassy, and tenantless, with nothing beyond it but the
vast starry silence of the Great Plains. There must, I feel, be something to counterbalance the charm of the spot; one is seldom al-
lowed to possess, unalloyed, the contentment of soul that comes to
me on stepping out of the bus. And it seems there is: I have neglected to fill the plastic jerry-can and shall be strapped for water in
the morning. But from a night of deep sleep I awake to find a
drinking fountain near by! Heaven knows what the source of the
gushing water may be, but I feel it only fair to retract some of the
harder words I have had for highway departments.

The morning is all that the night promised—the only mild night
since Death Valley. It is balmy and windless, and under a warm sun
the plains, grazed to the nap of a golf course in winter, roll away

into the distance. From the top of protruding sandstone slabs, mead-owlarks blurt their warbled whistles, stirred by the bright and spacious new day. At the end of the rest area, an arresting assembly of such slabs is identified by a descriptive sign as "Natural Fort." I learn that I have spent the night with history. In 1831, a band of 150 Blackfeet, pursuing the bison herds driven by drought from the tribal hunting grounds, met 600 Crows, whose enemies the Black-feet were. Emboldened by superiority of numbers and egged on by twenty white trappers accompanying them, including the half-Negro Jim Beckwourth, the ordinarily not-very-warlike Crows at-tacked. The Blackfeet fell back on the Natural Fort, but their doom was sealed by the odds, and one by one they were killed to the last brave.

Is it possible that the sites of death exert the hold on us they do because unconsciously we anticipate that at the very end dying is like the blissful moment of drifting off to sleep after a wearisome day? I doubt it. Because we see in the finish of human lives the end of turmoil, at least their share of it? Or maybe it is that our com-miseration with the dead sharpens for ourselves the tang of being alive: *they are done for, while we have this day before us, and all our tomorrows. . . .* Anyway, I wander among the stones of the stronghold, conceiving of the possibility, clearly nonexistent, of turning up a relic of the fight and making contact with those poor fellows who saw their companions fall one by one and knew that no escape was possible.

For two hundred miles northward the close-cropped rangeland, split-pea green in color, accounts for all the earth from horizon to horizon, its contours, as in Texas, those of a nearly spent swell. Sometimes there are low, sandstone escarpments, bluffs or buttes, occasionally a little slough or creek bottom. Where there is a creek (Horse Creek, Bear Creek, Rawhide Creek, Old Women Creek) its course across the plains is traced by a line of cottonwoods and wil-lows. The most important—though nothing about it recalls those several hundred thousand who trod its banks westward—is the North Platte, at Torrington, a livestock center with a big beet-sugar plant. Agriculture through here must be dependent on irri-gation; for a while we go along the Interstate Canal, which is twenty feet wide with banks above the plain. But whatever else, after the early-morning calm, there is the wind—and my complaints about it. *These blasted side-winds. . . . No cars on the road at all. . . .*

You have to fight this wind all the way. . . .

There's a terrific wind on the port bow. It's no wonder the poor little bus is having such a hard time.

But the chubby, pretty little black Lark buntings with white wing-patches and tinkling songs are back, and Killdeers here and there show their white-striped wings and rufous lower backs as they fly effortlessly off. The Killdeer and the Mourning dove, I have come to think, are our truly national birds.

And there is the veritable greatness of the Great Plains. No other landscape I know is so connotative of infinite reaches. The drama that the mountains provide farther west is here the function of the clouds. The clouds *are* mountains, or build up like mountains, only such exalted mountains as are never to be known outside the realm of pure spirit, and mountains that do not bound vistas but only suggest farther distances beneath and beyond them. *I had been thinking what a beautiful scene it was here, with the short-piled green rangeland, the sandstone outcroppings like palisades, the very low ridges on the left peppered with conifers, and the ice-floes of clouds leading way off overhead, leaving part of the plains in sun and part in shadow, when three more delectable little Prong-horned antelopes appeared, catching the sun, lovely fawn and white, a buck and two does with prominent dark eyes and white underparts and white patches on their behinds. They went off in a sort of even canter, evidently not very alarmed.*

"Watch out for deer, elk and bison on the road," warns a sign in Wind Cave National Park, on the southern fringes of the Black Hills. Nothing is said of prairie-dogs, but there is a village of them bustling with activity; ground-squirrels, they remind one of little pigs as they chase one another about among the mounds. And there are more Pronghorns the color of toasted marshmallows, grazing contentedly but ready to go off like springs. The silvery green of the high grasslands and the black patches of Ponderosa pine forest make it the most attractive country of the day. According to a second sign, there are three hundred bison in the park out of a total of about five thousand remaining in the country as a whole. And five of them come into view around a hill, heavy-headed, short-necked, shaggy—living monuments. It requires only the sight of them to bring back, as in the turning of a page, the North America that Lewis and Clark knew, "the whol face of the country . . . covered with herds of Buffaloe, Elk & Antelopes," and "so gentle that we pass near them while feeding, without appearing to excite any alarm among them": the herds, the Indians who followed them, and the wolves that "go in droves by night, with dismal yelling cries," as Mark Catesby wrote sixty years earlier —actually a clear, spine-tingling singing according to those who have heard the wolf's howl without animus.

You realize how empty the plains are. Are there cattle? I do not notice. Now and again we pass collections of ranch buildings in a clump of trees with the usual windmill and perhaps a field bright with sprouting grain. But the chief impression made by the wind-swept grasslands, on through South Dakota, is of unnatural life-lessness and vacancy.

The plains were the last frontier south of Canada. While one is apt to picture the frontier as having been pushed ever westward from ocean finally to ocean, it in fact leapt from the middle of the country to the Pacific in the 1840's. From then on, the Far West was infiltrated piecemeal, leaving the broad expanse between the lusher prairies and the Rockies a no-man's-land, or no-white-man's-land.

It was the cattlemen who moved in first. They got their start in southern Texas when it was still Mexico, and they gradually spread, bringing the culture of the *vaquero* with them, his etymology—his lariat, corral, bronco, mustang (*mestengo*), and rodeo —his broad-brimmed, high-crowned hat and fancy accouterments and his total commitment to the saddle. The era of the cattle drives began in the 1840's and after the interruption of the Civil War was in full tide until the early '80's. The trails ran to the railheads of Kansas (the famous Chisholm to Abilene), Missouri, Nebraska, Wyoming, and even Montana. The longhorns came by the thousands and tens of thousands, to a total of millions. With them came the cowhands, thirsty and rambunctious, and the outlaws, to duplicate in the cattle-trail towns the hell-raising of the mining camps and the show-downs of badmen and sheriffs without which the American legend would be unrecognizable. But, as that staunch daughter of the Nebraskan sandhills, Mari Sandoz, observes:

It was soon discovered that longhorns grew larger in the more rigorous climate, the more nutritious range, of the upper Plains, the meat worth more per pound on the market. As fast as the Indians were driven out the ranchers moved in. With their armed cowboys a private military, they spread over the public domain as though taking a kingdom, and held it as long as they could by gun and rope against the settlers, the legal claimants. For a long time the leading cattlemen held the range against the highest courts of the country.

The bloody strife over the slavery issue in Kansas and Missouri in the '50's, which hatched John Brown, was duplicated on a wider battlefield in the '70's and '80's and even into the '90's in the contest for the plains and prairies between the cattlemen and the wave of immigrants come to acquire farms in the public domain under the Homestead Act. In one of the most notorious incidents, the cattleman Print Olive, up from Texas with his brother, each with a string of murders to his credit, captured two of the leading settlers of the Sandhills after provoking trouble and, to intimidate the others, had his gang hang them, douse them in oil, and set them afire. In the Wyoming territory, to eliminate the center of settler resistance at Buffalo, the big ranchers even imported a force of gunmen recruited by an offer to pay five hundred dollars for every settler killed, but in this case the battle was won by the settlers.

In the struggle for the last potentially important agricultural lands not yet taken up, the avid settlers were matched not only against the strongarm men above and beyond the law; there were also the operators and manipulators ready to take advantage of the law's blind spots to acquire for their own profit vast tracts intended for the homesteader. The prospective settlers' lack of resources and the need, usually, of more plains acreage to support a farm family than could be obtained free under the Homestead Act played into the hands of the speculators. The ranchers also corraled large holdings through the use of dummies—proxies who took title to land as supposed homesteaders. Tens of millions of acres had been granted the railroads along their rights of way to encourage them to build; these the companies usually offered at exorbitant prices or held off the market—tax-exempt under the law. With all the riches put in their way to be scrambled for, fought for, finagled for, it is probably remarkable that the American people have been able to settle down as well as they have.

While possession of the grasslands was in hot dispute, there was never much question as to who would be dispossessed of them.

The discovery of gold in the Black Hills made clear that the Sioux, who had been promised them in perpetuity, would be evicted. The Sioux, whose mounted braves made up what has been called the finest light cavalry ever seen, resisted. But following their defeat of Custer at the Little Bighorn in 1876, the Army was reinforced, and in 1877 Sitting Bull was compelled to retreat into Canada while Crazy Horse surrendered—only to be bayoneted to death by his captors. It was in that same year that Chief Joseph led six hundred of his Sahaptins in a fighting retreat of thirteen hundred miles from the Wallowa Valley of Oregon across Idaho and Montana only to be halted, with but fifty of his warriors left, just thirty miles short of Canada and safety; here, on the Yellowstone, he made his final, moving declaration to the white generals, offering them his rifle: "I am tired of fighting. . . . My people ask me for food, and I have none to give. It is cold, and we have no blankets, no wood. My people are starving to death. Where is my little daughter? I do not know. . . . Hear me, my chiefs. I have fought. But from where the sun now stands, Joseph will fight no more forever." In 1879, Dull Knife's fleeing Cheyennes were pursued for a fortnight across the Nebraska plains, the corpses of those killed left frozen in the sub-zero cold of January, and almost totally destroyed. Between the two events, in 1878, the peak of the slaughter of the Passenger pigeons was reached at the huge breeding colony at Petosky, Michigan, from which, it was said, five freight-car loads of birds were shipped every day for a month. Within five more years, the bisons' hosts, numbering how many millions no one knows when the railroad first spanned the continent in 1869, were reduced to a few hundred individuals.

The end of the Indian fighting came in December 1890 at Wounded Knee, south of the Badlands in South Dakota. Here the 7th Cavalry avenged Custer by turning its Hotchkiss machine-guns on Big Foot's band of Sioux, which had surrendered and were in process of being disarmed; the excuse was that some of the 150 braves had fired on the 2,500 Army troops. The Indians, among whom were 250 women and an uncounted number of children, nearly all were slaughtered.

Behind this massacre, it would seem, was the fear among the whites of a general Indian uprising incited by a new creed which promised the coming of a messiah and the restoration to the redman of all that had been taken from him. The cult was expressly pacific and nonviolent, a fantasy embraced by a desperate people deprived of any other hope, and was in no sense a threat. Its most overt expression was in the Ghost Dance, in which the participants danced for hours, daylong, to the point of hypnotic seizure. As one of them explained:

When I fell in the trance a great and grand eagle came and carried me over a great hill where there was a village such as we used to have before the Whites came into the country. The tepees were all of buffalo hides and we made use of the bow and arrow, there being nothing of White Man's manufacture in the beautiful land. Nor were any Whites permitted to live there. The broad and fertile lands stretched in every direction and were most pleasing to my eye.

Rather than having their lands restored to them, the Indians now even had taken from them the last of what they had had. Beginning in 1889, Oklahoma was opened piecemeal to white settlement, which is to say to wild races for possession. The land-grab here reached its ultimate expression. The first free-for-all, as John A. Hawgood notes, "not only brought over 60,000 pioneers into the [Oklahoma] District in one day, but also conjured brand-new cities into existence in an afternoon." And so it went in other parts of Oklahoma as these were declared open between 1889 and 1893. It was in 1893 that the last shipment of Passenger pigeons to the market took place.

Procedures against the Gray wolf of the plains produced more gradual but equally decisive results. In the elimination of animals competitive with stockmen and farmers, or considered so, even the prairie-dog has not been overlooked. Though an occasional little striped ground-squirrel runs across the road in front of the oncoming car—a swatch of fur, you think it, pulled by a string across a corrugated surface—one may drive for hours without seeing a prairie-dog. At least I do. Yet we are told that one prairie-dog town alone, in Texas, was estimated at the turn of the century to embrace 25,000 square miles and to comprise 400 million inhabitants. Today, where a few survivors set up a colony, the rancher who owns the land—or if it is federally owned, leases grazing rights from the government (on terms that rob the public)—may be counted on to call in the eradicators of the Department of the Interior to clean it out. Prairie-dogs are fed poisoned grain and coyotes destroyed by bait that releases a lancet to inject their mouths with cyanide—by professional poisoners paid by the taxpayers, who have no voice in the matter.

The beef cattle that replaced the bison are more and more today,

I read, crowded into feed lots, "where livestock is scientifically bred and fattened for slaughter," according to *Time*. Pointing out that on open ranges "the land could absorb the excrement; natural processes converted it to fertilizer," *Time* reports that "because most feed lots are situated near lakes, rivers or streams so that livestock can be watered, rain can cause heavy manure runoffs that in turn pollute the water supply. Waste materials equivalent to those produced by 100 million people, for example, have been measured in the Missouri River between Omaha and Kansas City." Such lots, crammed with Herefords, are certainly a feature of Colorado east of Fort Collins, as I learn on the family camping trip next year.

So I am inclined to think that as I roll along through eastern Wyoming and South Dakota I really do see few cattle—only the spacious plains and the emptiness that keeps one reminded of all that is missing, which no Ghost Dance will bring back.

These Black Hills, now that we're in them up around Custer, are a good deal like the foothills of the Front Range, though they're not as high and are spaced farther apart, with great monoliths of the basement rock upthrust and heavily scored and carved, very gray and old-looking. Look very pachidermal, too. . . . Heretofore the blackness of the Black Hills has consisted solely of Ponderosa pine, but now as we're approaching Mount Harney there are some beautiful White spruce [a colony of the silvery-needled, modest-sized tree isolated by hundreds of miles from its vast Canadian range]. *Mount Harney* [the highest of the range at 7,242 feet] *is a dark, forest-covered, scalloped ridge. Doesn't look very tall, really. It's the whole formation that's elevated, I suppose. . . . Four thirty-five, and down from the Black Hills uplift toward Rapid City; I hope that's where this double-lane highway goes. And I hope away from Monkey Island, the reptile gardens, side-shows, and other elevated entertainments. . . .*

And down, down it is to Rapid City, which is an array of little houses spread out over the plains, the usual commercial district.

After the Black Hills' hortative tabernacles of tourism and Rapid City's supermarket-and-gas-station strip, regaining the rangeland is a relief. But there is no getting away from the billboards, particularly those of the Wall Drug Store. These have been going on ever since Wyoming, for a hundred and fifty miles, I should say. Their pitch is jocose, expressing a monumental self-satisfaction. And they have become unendurable. "Let the dirge for America be a Nervous

Wreckuiem," I say to myself. By the time I reach the town of Wall I have worked myself up to an intensity of outrage which cannot, with self-respect, simply be swallowed. So I pull up in front of the accursed emporium and go in.

It turns out to be virtually a department store, and well patronized, with all kinds of gear, especially of a Western character. The most senior-looking of the staff is a gray-haired man talking on the telephone behind the films counter. I stand by in a state of controlled simmering until he has finished.

"Do you know where the manager is?" I ask tensely.

He is the manager.

"I want you to know," I say in a carrying voice, but one trembling with rage, "that you and those like you are more dangerous enemies of the United States than the Communists. Here we've been given this magnificent country and all you can do is prostitute it with your miserable billboards across half the state."

He could not have looked more flabbergasted if I had turned into a rhinoceros before his eyes. Aware that all the business of the store in our vicinity has stopped and that everyone is staring at us, transfixed, I see the astonishment in his face give way to the flush of fury.

"You get out of here!" he cries. "We don't want your kind here!"

But the satisfaction my expulsion might have been expected to afford is denied him. I am already halfway to the door. Aware that he has failed to recoup face, he follows me to the street. The last I see of him, from the bus, he is writing down my license number.

In my mind, I am a belligerent sort of fellow, but when, as happens, alas, a little too often, I carry contentiousness into real life, I feel afterwards none of the swashbuckler's heedless indifference but rather a nervous gloominess. In this case, moreover, in the deepest hinterland—and if you go much deeper than South Dakota you start coming out the other side—I think it not improbable that the police, responsive to the town's leading commercial interest, will come after an outside agitator who has blasphemed the national religion, private enterprise. All this doubtless colors my impression of the Badlands, which begin directly after Wall. What counts for more, however, is the lateness of the hour and the earliness of the season: it is sundown and only three or four other cars are on the road, the last a police car from which I am looked over as it passes. If I have ever been in an eerie place or seen a Realm of the Dead, it is the Badlands.

You descend to them, for they have been excavated out of the plains by the run-off of rains channelized in the White River and its tributaries. The grim and still-continuing work of erosion has exposed the world of the Oligocene, buried for 25 million years under the sediments washed down from the rising highlands to the west and under volcanic flake and grit from the same direction. For 15 million years, before the Rockies had achieved sufficient stature to intercept the rain clouds from the Pacific and bring drought to the land to their east, the area had been a marshy flood-plain harboring saber-toothed cats, small camels, giant pigs, two-foot-tall proto-horses, and huge rhinoceros-like titanotheres.

The Mako Sico of the Indians, *"les mauvaises à traverser"* of the early French trappers, the Badlands in any language have from a distance the configuration of wet plaster from which a trowel, laid flat on it, has been yanked, raising sharp-edged ridges and pin-nacles concave in slope. As the road goes down among them, seem-ing to drop a good thousand feet before the finish, you see that the monstrous structures are banded in various rosy and gray-sandy hues. Below, more intense colors appear. The deeply scored, hollow-sided peaks and domes, buttresses and compound buttresses of hardened clays at which one stares up aghast include strata of true rose color, and a yellow almost like a yellow sherbet, even a dull orange. But they take me back to a youthful nightmare in which I am locked up at night in the Egyptian wing of the Metropolitan Museum among the tombs, the sarcophagi and the sightless stone figures of extinct Pharaohs and of Nilotic gods of the dead, all in the most terrifying state of intermediacy between death and life. The Badlands are indeed like a necropolis, a sanctuary of dead rulers seventy feet high, still enthroned.

These shapes rising on all sides, so many of them looking like headless beings with arms extended, gripping the ends of the arms of their seats. . . . These headless trunks of plaster all put out ex-tensions toward the road that seem to end in hands or clenched fists, like enormous, disproportionate arms, as they seem to be, ex-tended like the arms of the Sphinx, toward the road. Very much like the Sphinx eroded away, with the heads eroded off. . . . I feel very much alone with them.

It is when I am just leaving the National Monument that the police car comes by. (The Badlands themselves go on for about a hundred and twenty miles, with a breadth of from thirty to fifty miles.) I cannot deny that I am relieved to see it go.

I still feel on edge from the anger I had worked myself up to. How is one to handle one's animosities, when almost invariably they leave one feeling worse than they do their objects, who seldom even know of them? Perhaps one should learn not to judge others. What a relief it would bring to give the human race *carte blanche* in one's mind! How much one would spare oneself if one were all-charitable—the amnesty presumably to include also oneself! Or if one fell in with that bland and genial attitude toward the public of popular magazines, politicians, advertising agencies and television stations by which people are *good,* especially American people. Or if one declared once and for all with the Moral Rearmament musical *Up With People!*

But *all* people? The people who plaster the country with billboards? The people who empty their garbage on the countryside? The people who poison rivers and put hills through meat-grinders? The wholesale killers of beasts and birds? The machine-gunners of Wounded Knee, the soldiers who murdered Osceola, Cochise, and Red Sleeves under flags of truce, the townsmen of Fort Grant who lynched eighty-five Apache prisoners of the Army? Not to mention thieves, swindlers, extortionists, kidnappers, murderers, rapists? Up with me if I commit the enormities I am capable of?

No, it is too much for me.

"The way to manage it," says that voice from within, "is to be persuaded that everyone gets what's coming to him in the end. Why," it cries, "if I could be sure of that, there's no lying, vandalizing, embezzling, purse-snatching, scoundrelly whoreson knave in all Christendom but I could love him! Just so long as I'm bloody well certain he's not going to be let off a thing! . . .

"But what's this we're coming to? Kadota. It looks like Kadota, South Dakota, for the night. But what improvements on Eden will it have to lay before us?"

What it has, and what I am very grateful for, is a space beside a small commercial hotel which the proprietress says I may park in overnight, and for no charge. Unfortunately, however, the yard is so brightly lighted it is like day inside the bus and I have to have a cover over my eyes to get any sleep at all.

By the morning's first coffee after breakfast, having turned due north for Pierre, in the middle of the state, I am near the great divide of the 100th Meridian. The plains are growing greener with fields of stubble-high shoots of new wheat. Few signs of human habitation appear, however, and not a tree is to be seen. But the Lark buntings are not oppressed by the bareness. For lack of perches, the little pied birds sing on the wing, rising twenty or thirty feet, then coming down with their wings in a broad V, like toy airplanes descending.

Out for a run down a side-road, with a rather cold wind blowing but no other sound except the singing of the Lark buntings. The song starts with the twangy notes of a Bobolink, then has a sort of canary-like reiterated note and a snatch like a Song sparrow's. Otherwise there's just this great silence and the low rolling hills receding into the remote distance, all smooth and pale green, as if the land had been made and finished and then everybody had left it for good.

On the outskirts of Pierre, a not unpleasant town with trees coming into bloom, the Missouri suddenly appears between rather low, green-wooded banks, freighted with silt and legend. (Just upstream, it disappears in a long impoundment behind a dam, as it has disappeared over a large part of its length. The great Missouri, which once flowed free across the northern plains 2,600 miles to the Mississippi, is now a chain of captives fat in their immobility.) On the other side, driving north along the 100th Meridian, the country flattens out. The monotony of it must dishearten the most ardent partisan of the continent.

The fields go on and on. We've evidently got hours more of bucking this apparently endless wind before we turn east. The grass tugs at its roots, as if striving to be off with the racing air, off for somewhere. . . . You'd think at least they'd plant some hedgerows. But nope. Not a shrub anywhere to be seen. Occasionally a group of scrawny little trees sending up three or four little trunks from the ground, but nothing else. Nothing but grass and produce of one kind or another: wheat, I suppose, but not much of that. A red barn with flanking sheds, a few other red outbuildings, a white house dwarfed by the barn, some cylindrical enclosures of corrugated sheet-iron: that's the typical farm. With some trees around it, which aren't in leaf—haven't even started—and a windmill. And wind. . . . We pass a disk-harrow that takes up three auto-widths on the highway, pulled by a tractor with a glass-enclosed cab.

It comes to me that in six thousand miles I have not seen a farmer. In my boyhood it would have been inconceivable that there would ever be no more farmers, but the inconceivable has come to pass.

There are agrobusinessmen who operate machinery on huge tracts, but there seem to be few proportionately even of them. And has any but the older of them ever held the reins in a buggy, driven horses to the blacksmith's, pitched hay onto a rick, spread manure with a fork, turned a cream separator, mixed mash for cows and chickens with a shovel, hoed corn, milked a cow by hand, or followed a cultivator or plow between the handles? I doubt it. Could they harness a team?

Whether as a farmer or engineer of gang plows and combines, I think it would turn me despondent or savage to have to live on these bare, level plains. But three middle-aged men at a service station where I stop seem neither, but, rather, altogether human and considerate. Two of them go to work on the bus. "Isn't this pretty windy country?" I venture. They are quite whimsical about the wind. Even cheerful. I ought to be here in the winter! "One thing. When we have snow, there's usually enough wind to blow most of the range clear."

But one never knows. In an hour or so, having taken a right-angle turn out of the teeth of the wind, I am lamenting the need to hurry on. What one can be sure of is that however monotonous the landscape in any part of the continent, it is evolving into something else. The first evidence of change had been in the small boulders appearing in the fields north of Pierre. They are left-overs of the ice-sheet, which reached to the Missouri River; the Missouri is where it is, in fact, because it flowed along the front of the ice-sheet, carrying off the melt-water. From now on, through Canada, which was buried two miles deep under ice, down to New York City, where the ice stood as high as the Empire State Building, the surface of the earth is the work of the Pleistocene.

In its massive, probably scarcely perceptible, all-annihilating advance down from the north, the ice-sheet gouged hollows in the land, while in its retreat, many thousand years later, it left valleys blocked by the spoil. The result is that everywhere it stood there are lakes, of which the ten thousand claimed on Minnesota's license plates are only a small fraction. Among them are lakes the largest in the world, if you do not include the Caspian Sea. Eastward of the Missouri in North Dakota the sloughs and ponds multiply. The colors of the still-wintry prairie are those of the Continental uniform in the Revolutionary War: buff of last year's grass and blue of water. With the sun behind you, the lakes are almost indigo, even the pools of standing water on the plowed fields. Could it be the effect of the black—and very fertile—soil of the eastern Dakotas? This itself is a deposit of the ice-age, plus ten millennia of accumulating humus. It is a landscape of buckskin studded with lapis lazuli; and each of the jewel ponds is the home of Western grebes, Black terns, Lesser Scaup ducks, Shovelers, Blue-winged teal or Yellow-headed blackbirds. The swan-necked Western grebe is a new one to me, but there is no tarrying.

It is true, I am thinking: farming as it has been since man exchanged hunting for planting is finished. In the space of my lifetime the American people have pulled their roots up out of the soil, as have other industrialized peoples. Their condition is in this respect without precedent in history. Those who fought the long, ruthless struggle for the American land would doubtless be astonished to know of the flight from it of their descendants. You cannot help wondering what this uprooting may forebode. At the same time you ask yourself if anyone not living on a traditional farm has any right to lament the change. It is all very well to respond to the appeal of Nature, but how must Nature look to those who live at grips with it, dependent on its hard-won bounty? With this question, there comes before me the disquieting figure of Emma Bovary, as it has come before me not a few times before.

Madame Bovary was the inveterate romanticizer whose pursuit of the illusory to the neglect of the real and attainable good destroyed those who were closest to her after leading to her own untimely and agonizing death—the most horribly portrayed in all literature, I should think. (At whom, or at what in himself, was Flaubert getting back? one wonders.) There is a judgment propounded in the characterization of Emma that lies cruelly in wait for those who make much of Nature. As a young girl, Emma had dreamed of knights and troubadours, or chatelaines leaning from turret windows and noble lovers who would bear her away to untroubled bliss in perfumed gardens. "Had her childhood been spent in cramped quarters behind some city shop she might," her creator observes, "have been open to the lyric appeal of nature—which usually reaches us only by way of literary interpretations. But she knew too much about country life: she was well acquainted with lowing herds, with dairy maids and plows." Those are uncomfortable lines.

One may clutch at the evidence of Gustave Flaubert's phrase—

"lowing herds . . . dairy maids and plows"—that he himself had had small acquaintance with farming. (And he had not, we read, having been a city boy, though "he loved the country, and Paris was extremely distasteful to him.") But chiefly I rely on John Muir for the defense. (Now the whole truth of his importance to me is out.) Muir was farm-bred in Scotland and Wisconsin in the 1840's and '50's and knew farming at its hardest. Yet no one had a greater ardor for Nature. His remarkable talent in mechanical invention might well have made him a fortune in industry, yet he chose the companionship of mountains and forest—and having done so was also capable of returning to farming when need arose, and with conspicuous success.

I can also take cover in the reflection that I have known something of farming too. I was only a summer farmer, in my teens, but it was an unaccommodating farm, small and stony, close to, and of the kind associated with, New England. The hours were long, the work hard, the food, alas, execrable. So when I asked myself, as I did at that time, how I thought I should take to farming as a life's occupation, I was under no illusions about it. (One is fortunate enough to be able to remember a few details of this kind about the past that may bring back the kind of person one was then.) My answer was that I thought I could take to it very well provided others were living the same kind of life. This was of course a large reservation, one that many a farm youngster has shared and thus been found less than immune to the pull of the city's excitements. All the same, it is not as if I had no acquaintance with lowing herds and plows (I did miss out on the dairy maids) or, having known them, found them insupportable.

But it makes little difference that one may have some license to speak of life on the land. Whatever the signs may be of the kind of sequel our desertion of that life could portend is immaterial too. Our independence of the land will continue to grow with the advancement of technology, and nothing can arrest or reverse it but a disaster to the civilization we are busy elaborating.

With every eastward league, average rainful is gaining. The arid plains have yielded to the moister prairie. A little tumbleweed has collected against a fence eighty miles west of Fargo and the Minnesota line, but the Lark buntings have disappeared. Grackles have replaced the smaller, shorter-tailed Brewer's blackbirds, so common through the West, and the last magpie was yesterday. I am passing from the Western to the Eastern gravitational field. Within forty miles of Fargo, trees have appeared along the fencerows and there are more in the farmyards. In another thirty miles the country could be called handsome. Protected by windbreaks of as many as four lines of trees, which like the shade trees are just coming into leaf, the farms with their spruce houses and huge barns are like islands in the black sea of the newly turned prairie. You wonder if the owner, seeing his prospering demesne, the creation of his toil, in the full, deep radiance of the setting sun's level rays, does not feel the same inexpressible sense of accomplishment and beatification as a painter who has brought a work of art into being.

"Death is sweet when it comes in its time and in its place, when it is part of the order of things, when the old peasant of Provence, at the end of his reign, remits into the hands of his sons his parcel of goats and olive-trees in order that they in turn transmit them to their sons. When one is part of a peasant lineage, one's death is only half a death. Each life in turn bursts like a pod and sends forth its seed." But even if I had *Wind, Sand and Stars* with me, instead of merely remembering the sense of the passage, I could hardly present myself at one of those farms and ask if this were in truth how it was. I am not sure how the owner would take to being addressed as a peasant, either.

Fifteen miles inside Minnesota, hardly daring to believe my good luck, I find that the campground at Buffalo River State Park is open and designed to prescription, in a woods above a stream, secluded and nearly unoccupied.

13

THE NORTH WOODS

The fee in the State Park is two dollars, but that is not too much to pay for a night of blessed quiet in which I do not wake once. I could even have a much needed shower in the morning, but the temperature inside the bus is thirty-five degrees and I am not man enough for it. The advantage is that I am ready for the road by five minutes after seven.

In the trees by the Buffalo River there is a Blue jay and at Detroit Lakes, a small industrial town forty-five miles inside the state, a Civil War memorial. By then, too, the prairie has yielded wholly to woodland. We are back in the East. Soon, by all appearances, we could be all the way back. The dark woods of White spruce and Balsam fir chalk-veined with Canoe birches reflected in the numerous cold ponds are those of Maine. So are the occasional clapboard houses and old barns, and the men in red-and-black plaid lumberjacks who look as if a little shrunken from habitual cold, though sturdily built, certainly. A hundred miles has brought a different world.

The woods go on for many miles but obviously are come-backs from a thorough cutting-over. It occurs to me how much longer it must take a northern than a southern forest to recover from a lumbering, with so short a growing-season. . . . Remer has the bare look of a Western town, but the bareness is a cold-weather, not a sun-stricken bareness. Some kind of auction is going on. The people gathered around look like *good* people but people who have had a hard, hard life. And they are bundled up in quilted jackets—on the twentieth of May! And need to be. You would hardly know spring had begun. The deciduous trees are still bare, though the Quaking aspens—for we have entered their great range—are green-budded. The sky-blue waters, celebrated in song, are sky-gray waters under a leaden overcast. A few drops of rain are on the windshield, though the outlook would seem to be for snow. Those who stand by this country, resisting the pull of the city, the Southwest, California, and Florida, have my respect. The winters must be desperate, such farms as there are look as if they could not return a great deal on the labor they would take, and money up here cannot be easy to come by. The numerous signs to lakeside resorts remind you that as people abandon the soil (and farther south in Minnesota and across northern Wisconsin and Michigan I am struck the next summer by how many fields the woods are closing in on and how many barns the size of railroad stations have been left to sag and molder) they reflood the country on week-ends and summer holidays in pursuit of recreation, in a diastole and systole of heavy-laden station-wagons, pickup trucks with camper bodies, trailers, and towed boats. But the vacationers remain outsiders, on leave from the Organization. It is the Organization, not the land, that they have to serve, to understand, and to make sure of their accommodation to.

Of course, you do not have to be much of a realist to appreciate that without the vacationers' dollars, probably not many of those who remain behind in such places as northern Minnesota could make a go of it. One way or another, almost all of us become Organization men, which is to say contributors to and beneficiaries of the exacting and munificent great American economy—even the Navajos, who are learning to develop the resources of their reservation. ("The Ghost Dance movement of 1890 died at Wounded Knee, and with it died . . . the last futile attempt by the American Indians to retrieve the old ways," says Peter Farb in *Man's Rise to Civilization.* "From that time on, Indians turned to movements that sought accommodation with whites.") We are all bound, and by the strongest of bonds—our self-interest—to that aggregation of industrial corporations, governmental agencies and private institutions, all interlocking, which increasingly *is* the United States and which puts power in our hands to order our surroundings to our liking. But you do not have to be one who constitutionally takes a dark view of human affairs or an alarmist about nuclear war to suspect that those whose descendants have the best prospect of being here in the long run may be those who owe it least.

In late morning the road crosses a hundred-foot-wide river gliding carefree along between marshy banks, unwitting of the great destiny awaiting it; and it is the Father of Waters.

Beginning fifteen miles the other side of the Mississippi, events of more than 1,000 million years ago were to make a great difference in things today. Sediments accumulating at the bottom of an obscure and forgotten sea of that time contained large quantities of iron compounds. These sediments were converted into rock which later was metamorphosed into the harder taconite. This, in turn, where subsequently exposed in outcropping ledges, was subjected to a leaching that dissolved nearly everything but almost pure iron oxide. Thus, the Iron Ranges of Minnesota, the most productive iron fields in history. Utilizing the open-pit method, men have been mining these deposits since the 1880's. Along U. S. 169, which skirts the most important of the ranges, the Mesabi (from the Chippewa word for *great*), the excavations and the mesas of spoil go on for fifty miles; "man-made canyons and mountains," an official sign calls them, and it is not far wrong. The spoil is sand-colored, in some spots golden, to deep reddish-brown verging on magenta and even blue, the ore in the little strings of gondola cars on railroad sidings a dark red-brown, almost black. (No work seems to be in progress, perhaps because it is Saturday afternoon.) Beyond the comfortable little town of Nashwauk, on the very edge of a pit, I have lunch at a "wayside" overlooking one of the earlier diggings, a canyon seventy feet deep in almost purplish-brown slaty rock. A sign declares that the Mesabi has so far produced 2.37 billion tons of iron ore—which is a lot.

The surgery that has here been performed on the earth—and that is what it makes you think of—is comparable with changes wrought by geological forces. You cannot but be impressed by what our little species can do, and by what is represented here. Out of this matrix came the American Steel Age—came the rails that criss-crossed the continent and the huffing locomotives, came the fleets of the Merchant Marine and the Navy, came all the guns, came the machinery, came the girders of factories and skyscrapers, came 200 million motorcars, came also (which I should sorely miss) bicycles, hand-tools, and surgical implements. But the rich ores of the

Iron Ranges have about run out, as rich ores of other metals in our country have been running out and inevitably will run out everywhere. By the time you turn north out of the Mesabi at the town of Virginia you have a vivid idea of what is in store for the earth as mankind in its mounting numbers and spreading industrialization is forced to exploit poorer and poorer ores, which is to say to dig out and "process" ever huger amounts of rock for the same return.

Ely, where the highway turns back to the southeast, is virtually the end of the line, the jumping-off place for the roadless country to the north comprised in the Boundary Waters Canoe Area (which makes up half the 3,125-square-mile Superior National Forest) and the even larger Quetico Provincial Park, which adjoins it in Canada. The Quetico-Superior region is part of a forest land laced with rivers and lakes, and so copiously it could almost be considered a crowded mass of islands in a fresh-water, inland sea. Only somewhat less well watered, this land, moreover, stretches on to the neighborhood of Hudson Bay and the Barren Lands of the Arctic, growing ever wilder beyond the several roads and railroads that cross it north of Quetico Park. In the Boundary Waters Canoe Area logging is prohibited, but copper-mining interests hold leases in it, putting its future in jeopardy. It is still true wilderness today by my criterion, however, and the only one remaining in the original forty-eight states except for nearby Isle Royale in Lake Superior, for these are the only areas still harboring that magnificent and supreme expression of an untamed continent, the Gray wolf. (This is before the electrifying tidings of the reappearance of wolves in Yellowstone.)

"There was a great satisfaction in knowing that the wolves were in the country, that it was wild enough and still big enough for them to roam and hunt," says Sigurd Olson of "a beautiful night for travel" in the Quetico-Superior country he has celebrated for so many readers as *The Singing Wilderness*—"twenty below, and the only sound the steady swish and creak of my snowshoes on the crust." There would be such a satisfaction for me, surely. "I knew, as I hiked along that night," he recalls, "that I was being watched, a lone dark spot moving slowly along the frozen river. . . . Then, far ahead, . . . two shadows broke from cover and headed directly down the river toward me. I stopped, slipped off my pack, and waited. Nearer and nearer they came, running with the easy, loose-jointed grace that only the big timber wolves seem to have. A hundred yards away they stopped and tried to get my wind; they wove back and forth, swaying as they ran. Then, about fifty feet away, they stopped and looked me over. In the moonlight their gray hides glistened and I could see the greenish glint of their eyes. Not a movement or a sound. . . . As suddenly as they had appeared, they whirled and were off down the river, two drifting forms against the ice. Never before had I been that close, possibly never again would I see the glint in timber wolves' eyes. . . . Once more came the long howl, this time far back from the river, and then I heard them no more."

State Highway 1 across the northern beak of Minnesota could hardly be expected to afford the sight of a timber wolf. An encounter like Sigurd Olson's has to be earned (and I wonder if shooting one of the human riff-raff who run wolves down in airplanes and kill them would serve). However, a Black bear does go humping off into the trees ahead of me, evidently not much frightened but taking no chances. It is woods all the way across—National Forest. In some parts the Canoe birches stand like bristles on an upturned brush, their budding, raisin-colored tops like lint. Among the spruces, firs, and aspens are somber Red pines and little Jack pines, short-needled as Pinyons—altogether like Maine. And most gratifyingly, the ancient rocks of the Canadian Shield have shouldered their way through the surface, bulging masses of stone, gray to dull, pale pink, some banded and veined. They make you think of whales up for a breather from the immemorial depths of geologic time.

Six o'clock, and at the end of a long down-grade comes a sight that almost startles the life out of me—a great, gray mountain range where there is none. But it is Lake Superior. The other shore—in view here at the narrow western end of the lake—is uneven in profile and gives it an irregular ouline, and I had mistaken the horizontal surface for a vertical one. Along the lake are humped hills. I have come at last to the beginning of my Archaean Hills—the oldest of the continent: old in rocks, old in deformation (the folding and compression to which rock-strata are subject in the gestation of mountains), old in topography, as Philip B. King of the U. S. Geological Survey writes. Leaving the bus and scrambling up and down slopes through the woods for a photograph, I come to a high point from which, across a small bay, there is a view of the hill before me ending in a sheer cliff above the water. Ring-billed gulls evidently nest on it, for several are sailing across the rock face and the air resounds with their yearning, threatening, jubilant *klee-ah, klee-ah!* In this setting, they might be the progeny of a dawn world.

While the sun seems oddly on the verge of setting the whole time, I have a two-hour drive along the lake to the last campground in the United States, in Grand Portage State Forest. The woods go on, sparse and northern-looking, seldom interrupted, though there are cabins and trailer-homes in them. A town, Grand Marais, "welcomes you to the land of the *voyageur*," and a plant of the Erie Mining Company with its own harbor—"Taconite Operation," says a sign —has produced a huge plateau of material black as coal. The lake is to be marveled at. The last suggestion of a farther shore has disappeared and you might be looking at the ocean. But there are no whitecaps and the waves break without foam on the rosy shingle. Plants, moreover, to which brine is lethal, grow to the edge of the water.

The campground has so remote a feeling, with the sun sinking at last behind the spires of the spruces and the chill of night already descended, that I am surprised to find it open; surprised and greatly relieved, even though no water is available. A book with dinner gives the illusion of company, as usual. It is, however, a lonely spot. The deepening blue of the sky fades into a warmthless apricot above the vanished sun, before which the small spruces stand like black witches in tall, pointed hats. I learned long ago to make do with solitude as needs must be, but I have to admit that chill northern evenings that find me alone tend to test my morale. But this is not an occasion when the test is very trying. Woods, though they can be very black, are yet not like a dark city street with a few naked lights in empty offices, and my lot at the moment, as at most other moments, seems a great deal better than I deserve. Yet circumstances such as these do raise the question: *is* one alone?

As I think I have confessed, I am apt to feel aware of a Presence in Nature, sometimes more strongly than at others. It is one I feel an indefinable reassurance in acknowledging and have an instinct to honor and revere, and to celebrate. But whether my feeling testifies to anything outside myself, whether it is a mere reflection of an inner need, I have no way of knowing. To be on surer ground, I let D. H. Lawrence speak for me. Writing of the Etruscans, he made an observation which for me has been hauntingly illuminating, even for one from that percipient source: "From the shadow of the prehistoric world emerge dying religions that have not yet invented gods or goddesses, but live by the mystery of the elemental powers in the Universe, the complex vitalities of what we feebly call Nature." I believe I should have been at home among those dying religions, which I am not sure have altogether died.

And the purpose of Nature?

Here I am among the Archaean Hills. I have seen some today and shall see more tomorrow. And am I vouchsafed any special revelation by contemplation of these veterans of lost pasts which I have had in my sights since leaving home? Of course not. None beyond that which I seem to find in the plumbing of geological time and the processes of the earth wherever manifested. And that is a strengthening of the conviction I have come to that the Cosmos is to be seen as a work of art, one which, like any work of art, is its own justification, needing no other. Or so I can readily believe— and certainly I have no way of divining further meanings or aims or even conceiving what they might be. Geology . . . I am wrong in saying that it strengthens my conviction as to the nature of the Cosmos; what it does is enormously expand the frame in which I see it, even to lengths that paralyze my imagination. Sculpture and painting in motion, epic poetry, drama, dance, music, a symphony of rhythms of every tempo: such is Creation. Only so regarded has it for me the unity and internal consistency we seek in it, is it explicable. It is art that reason and science enable us to understand, as far as we do understand it, and that our own arts make us conscious sharers in. And must it not be that our greatest works of drama, music, and painting, which thrill us with their conception, have been implicit in Creation all along and tell us something of its character, if all the constituents of Shakespeare, Bach, and Michelangelo were present when these Archaean Hills were formed?

Awakening at four in the early northern dawn, I am up at five and soon, with breakfast in me, am full of the new day's hope and confidence. The temperature in the bus to begin with is thirty-four degrees, which means it can be no more than twenty-eight outside. At six-thirty I am away for an exceptionally early start, not sorry to have the warmth of the motor.

I am still scrutinizing and trying to absorb the character of the Archaean Hills, which, rather steeply domed, run out into the lake in peninsulas; one of them, fifteen miles inland, I see is 2,300 feet high, the highest elevation in Minnesota. But the country I have come to stands for other things than the primordial highlands. Of these others there is a reminder in the town of Grand Portage, the last in the United States. Its name refers to the nine-mile portage, beginning here, by which the voyageurs reached the Pigeon River above its falls and were able to ascend the river to the network of waterways—the Quetico lake country and beyond—to the west and north. The portage was first used by the indefatigable French pioneer fur-trader and explorer, the Sieur de la Vérendrye, in 1731. Within three years the French in their canoes had reached Lake Winnipeg and had established a post on the Red River, which drains into it from the Dakotas, and had the plains before them. At that time, our own settlers had not gone much beyond the Connecticut River in New England and were only just pushing up the Mohawk from the Hudson and down the eastern valleys of the Appalachians.

It is rather a shock to recognize how far ahead of us the French were in the drive to the west. We and they started neck and neck. Samuel de Champlain founded Quebec in 1608, the year after Jamestown's ill-starred birth; but where the falls of the Potomac were as far as Captain John Smith was able to press his explorations, Champlain had within seven years ascended the Ottawa River (which enters the St. Lawrence from the west at Montreal) and reached Lake Huron. And that was five years before the landing of *Mayflower*. In 1634, Champlain's lieutenant, Jean Nicolet, led his paddlers into Lake Michigan. (The object of this strenuous western push was the Pacific Ocean and the wealth of the Orient. On reaching Green Bay, Nicolet donned a garment of Chinese silk "all strewn with flowers and birds of many colors" as appropriate for his meeting with the Winnebagos, the "People of the Sea," and quite likely subjects of the Grand Khan, to whom Nicolet was an accredited emissary of King Louis XIV.) In 1673, the trader Louis Joliet and the missionary priest Jacques Marquette reached the Mississippi from Green Bay via the Fox and descended "this so renowned river" to the Arkansas. Their voyage the Sieur de la Salle completed in 1682 and from the Mississippi's mouth claimed all the lands drained by the world's longest river for the king who that year moved his court to the new palace at Versailles. By that time, adventurers from the Virginia colony had managed only to cross the Blue Ridge.

And therein, of course, lay the difficulty—the Appalachians. From the English colonies in the northeast, the only river leading westward was the Mohawk, and that sole corridor through the mountains, by the time the English had acquired New York from the Dutch, was blocked by the hostile combination of French and Indians. From the settlements to the south, the rivers narrowed and grew rougher with every league westward across the rising Piedmont and, if they broke through the Blue Ridge or its northern equivalents, wound hopelessly, torn by rocks, back into a maze of mountains. Through the ranges that rose, one upon another, athwart the way to the Mississippi Valley there was no passage but the most toilsome, afoot. For the French, a system of waterways requiring only short portages led from the mouth of the St. Lawrence to the foothills of the Northern Rockies, only a few hundred miles from the Pacific. (This it was that led to the crossing of the continent by Alexander Mackenzie, in Canada, a decade before Lewis and Clark.) It is significant that the South Carolinians, who were close enough to the lower end of the Appalachians to round their terminal spurs, were highly successful in the pursuit of trade westward through the wilderness, even without benefit of water roads. Within twenty years of the founding of Charleston in 1670 they had driven the Spanish out of the way and were leading pack-trains of a hundred or more horses on year-long trading expeditions for deer hides to the Creek, Catawba, and Cherokee villages deep in Georgia. By 1700, some of the more than fifty thousand hides they were sending yearly to London came from tribes across the Mississippi.

Skins were also the business of the French, but beaver pelts primarily. Plying the waterways of Canada were licensed traders and, generally well ahead of them, those unlicensed, called outlaws—*coureurs de bois*—by jealous officialdom and the scandalized Jesuit fathers. These were adventurers who took to the wilderness as to a native home with a capacity for meeting it on its own terms that you feel must have been latent in certain European strains since the days when Europe itself was mostly trackless forest. Like the "Long Hunters" of Tennessee and Kentucky who came later and the Rocky Mountain men of the past century, the *coureurs de bois* mastered Indian craft while retaining the trained intelligence and acquisitive drive of the whites. They learned the ways of the forest, river, and muskeg and the animals that inhabited them and how to handle the tricky, fragile birchbark canoe and even how to make it. With only the clumsy wheellocks of the day, later flintlocks, between them and certain death they would embark gaily for the wilderness, heading for waters no white man had ever seen. They were drawn by the lure of gain that was chancy, by the spell of the majestic and beautiful solitudes, above all, no doubt, by the freedom where the only restraints were those of one's own physical limitations and the precious few that conscience imposes in the absence of fear of detection. It was prowess, daring, and endurance that saw them through—when they did come through—brought them food, filled their craft with pelts, perhaps left a human corpse or two behind them, and won them Indian girls to share their blankets— and add a fecund new strain to the sparse population. To posterity, which will, within limits, forgive anything but lack of spirit in those who pass across the pages of history and is indulgent of vices among them it sternly censures in current practice, the *coureurs de bois* are an appealing breed, as appealing as they were valuable to New France. Moreover, when the ice was off the rivers in the spring and, bending to their paddles, tanned almost as the savages they brought with them, long-haired and buckskin-clad, they swooped down on the staid and churchly villages of Quebec and Montreal to fling away their profits in boisterous carousal, they seem to have had an appeal to contemporaries, at least to the youngsters of the town—or their way of life did: enough to fill their ever-thinning ranks with recruits.

Yet not many immigrants from the mother country were attracted to New France. The French in Canada were spread too thin for the inevitable contest with the British. And they had not only the firmly based and populous English colonies in the south, from Nova Scotia to Florida, but the British also on their northern flank. In 1670, Charles II had made the Governor and Company of Adventurers of England Trading into Hudson Bay "absolute Lordes" of all the lands draining into the bay—more than a million square miles. It was—and this was illustrative of the costs of the maladministration of New France—two *coureurs de bois* who, bilked by the authorities at Quebec of most of the furs they had garnered on a foray to Hudson Bay, had interested the British king in the rich rewards the area promised. When the French, sixty-four years later, followed the route from Lake Superior to Lake Winnipeg and the Red River pioneered by la Vérendrye, they put themselves in a position to intercept the trade of the now well-established Hudson's Bay Company.

With the French defeat in the Seven Years' War, Canada and the lands between the Appalachians and the Mississippi passed into

British hands. So, of course, did control of the fur-trade. But where the French had been pre-eminent, their collaboration in the trade was still indispensable; without, especially, the French Canadian canoemen called *voyageurs,* no trade goods would reach the interior, no furs come out.

The fur-trade—the economy of French Canada—rested on that marvelously engineered Indian creation, the birchbark canoe. Fabricated of strips of the bark of the powder-white Canoe birch up to thirty feet long stretched on a frame preferably of light, strong White cedar and sealed with spruce gum (which had to be renewed at least once a day), the canoe was made in several sizes—and never by anyone as skillfully as by the Indians. The largest, derived from war canoes, were giants up to thirty-five or even forty-five feet long and as much as six feet in beam. Capable of carrying eight thousand pounds of cargo, they were yet light enough for two or three men to shoulder on portage. With crews of up to fourteen, these *canots du maître* were used on the voyage from Montreal to Grand Portage—almost a thousand miles even by the Ottawa River cutoff. Here the cargo—trade-goods—was back-packed upstream to waiting *canots du nord,* twenty-five-footers, on the average, with a crew and a capacity about half that of their big sisters, suitable for further hundreds of miles on constricted and often turbulent waterways.

Perhaps no commercial operations of such scope have ever depended on so slight an agency as the birchbark canoe—for, as Bernard DeVoto says, the fur-trade, freed of the shackles of French officialdom, was "the first North American business that required large-scale organization." Equally, it seems likely that no such frail craft have ever carried more robust crews. The *voyageurs* were huskies who day after day could keep the canoes surging forward at six knots (with no current or wind to buck), resting only at prescribed intervals to smoke their pipes. But the paddling was only part of it. Between Montreal and Lake of the Woods by the Ottawa River route there were ninety portages, and at these, through bogs or over steep rocky ledges, the *voyageurs* had to pad with two ninety-pound sacks of cargo on their backs connected by a strap passed over the forehead. As Bernard DeVoto wrote:

The skill of the *voyageurs* was to take through the boiling water of the *saults* a craft which a moccasined foot could puncture and a second's contact with a snag or rock would rip apart. In big rapids few who were upset lived to swim ashore or be pulled out by their companions. Small wooden crosses clustered on the shores at such places, voices cried out of the water at night, and the rivermen appeased the saints and the Indian deities alike by many kinds of amulet and incantation.

The empty waters of Lake Superior—and I do not think I see a single craft on them during the whole day I spend passing around the northern side of the lake—invite you to call back those voyagers of two centuries ago. One is to imagine hearing their voices in a lilting chant of peasant France before they sweep into view around a headland. Then here they come, the big *canot du maître* brightly painted at the buoyant, upcurved bow, dripping paddles glistening red as they lift in unison, red knitted caps cocked over swarthy faces animated even in the strain of the effort, the short work-shirts of the paddlers bound round with a woven sash of riotous colors. The canoemen were proud of their strength, competing in the number of sacks they could carry on portage; proud of their skills, which they passed on to their sons. While they toiled and risked their lives for a pittance of pay and rations of dried corn or peas boiled up in a big pot with salt pork or bison tallow, they were conscious of living an idea, a tradition; their distinctions of dress and ways and song and their camaraderie made that evident. They knew who they were. They were *les voyageurs.* And they were of gay heart and full of life.

It is seven-thirty when I cross the Pigeon River, which is broad and placid after its emergence from the low wooded hills behind it. The country on the Canadian side is more sparsely settled, tourist accommodations are much fewer. U. S. Highway 61 has become King's Highway 61 and the next Esso service station is Royal Esso Service—changes, I have to confess, that for complicated reasons I rather take to.

A plant of the Great Lakes Paper Company, Limited, pouring out huge plumes of smoke and the sour smell of wood pulp, marks the outskirts of the combined city of Fort William and Port Arthur. This is the only town of consequence before Sault Sainte Marie at the eastern end of the lake, 432 miles away. (With Duluth, at the other end, 180 miles behind, it strikes me as a very big lake indeed.) Steering a way through it is like trying to get through a city at home in 1935, when streets were for local traffic only. For the rest, the difference between the Canadian city and its American counterpart is distinct, but subtle and difficult to put the finger on. The small houses here, blocks of them, of two stories and gabled roof, are of a more traditional style, and the faces on the streets are indefinably British. Two schoolboys, with almost bobbed hair and collars reaching nearly to their ears, have that lifted-nostril, fined-down look of some English youngsters. A nice-looking young man is pedaling my way on a bicycle with a bit of cardboard behind the seat lettered "Victoria, B. C.," the like of which you would hardly look for at home. There is less prosperity evident and things are less overwhelming, especially in the way of advertising. I must say I like the diminished insistence. Of course, however, it is a Sunday morning and still rather early. . . .

The danger of solitary speculation is that it leads to the elaboration of all kinds of theory on the slightest basis of observed fact, with no interlocutor to call the speculator to account. Rolling along Route 17, the Trans-Canada Highway, here an asphalt road colored old rose by the aggregate used in it, a pink granite of which there are conspicuous outcroppings, I come to the conclusion that what is striking about the United States from the vantage point of other countries is the ferment of expectation in which its population exists. The present is for us only the stepping-stone to a more generously endowed future—so let us get on with it. The present hardly exists for us. This creates a marvelous medium for the culture of progress. It is probably also what makes us on the whole neglectful of our surroundings and tolerant of their abuse by commerce and industry; these, being agencies of the future, are not to be impeded. Never mind what things look like; we're only passing through to the bigger and better. Only the life on the make is an acceptable life, and there is no contentment in making the most of your present situation and circumstances, or of yourself in them.

I cannot say that an American customs official at the minor Pigeon River post at seven-thirty of a Sunday morning would not have been as pleasant as the Canadian. I may be entirely mistaken in suspecting that his outlook would have been colored by the inequity that placed him in such a spot at such a time and by impatience for a future in which it would be rectified—had *better* be rectified. But I doubt that his manner would have been quite that of the Canadian who, having had my word for my origin, destination, and innocence of firearms, stepped back and looked me in the eye, the representative of the Dominion of Canada admitting a

guest to his country, standing in place of the Queen, whom circumstances prevented from officiating at the occasion. "You're *on* your
way!" he declared with gracious warmth. "Have a *good* time!" At
seven-thirty on Sunday morning.

I went off repeating the words to myself appreciatively. Occasionally during the day they recur to me. "You're *on* your way! Have
a *good* time!" He pronounced *good* to rhyme with *brood*.

It is odd to think that a bit of this to-me-nameless Canadian will
remain with me for life, going wherever I go.

"I must tell you of a time I was crossing the border into Canada. . . ."

Apart from the Blue Ridge Parkway, the Trans-Canada Highway
around Lake Superior is the longest road of virtually uninterrupted
natural beauty I have ever seen.

*We're skirting Nipigon on a high road that looks across the roofs
of the little town and the narrow bay on which it is located. . . .
There are continual hitch-hikers on the road. You get the impression that half the skimpy population is either hitch-hiking or fishing.*

*We're now, at ten-thirty, rounding the northernmost little bay
of the lake, just above the Nipigon River, which opens out into
a beautiful broad bay between low-lying banks forested with olive-
green spruce and fir, pale-green aspen and white birch. This is the
farthest north of the expedition. . . . It is stunning country, with
these high, rugged hills extending to the shore, and then ridges running well out into the lake. In many of the road-cuts you see the
most arresting combination of brick-red strata alternating with
putty-colored strata. We're passing through deep cuts in mountains
of pink granite. . . .*

*Patches of snow in the shade up here; "1,356 feet above sea-level,"
it says at a pass here. . . . From a place where the snow had been
melting down the side of a cut and freezing I chopped off enough
ice to fill the icebox. . . . A truck turned over on its side at the top
of the pass. He's probably the one who sailed by me this morning.*

The rock ledges are as smooth of surface as if washed by eons of
seas, but the planing and polishing agent was of course the ice. One
thinks of the ice-sheet as having descended from the Arctic, scraping
the land bare in its progress and then holding it a lifeless captive
beneath its crushing weight—sufficient to depress the earth's crust—
for twenty or thirty thousand years. And so it did. But one has to

remind oneself that in the past two million years or so there have
been four such visitations, with time enough in between for the
land fully to recover and all memory of the ordeal (if memory
existed) to pass away. (Why any of the ice-ages occurred, or if another is in store, no one really knows.) Were those lands created
off the coast by the scourings of the fourth ice-sheet—Cape Cod,
Martha's Vineyard, Nantucket and Long Island—created three times
before by the other ice-sheets, only to disappear each time? (Some
of Martha's Vineyard, actually, was present throughout the ice-
ages.)

It is hard for me to think of the inexorable, brute advance of the
ice and its long, lethal dominion over the north without a feeling
of horror. Yet the transfer of water from the oceans to the ice-sheet,
which lowered their level by several hundred feet, must have redeemed from the sea not a great deal less land than was lost to
the ice. The Pleistocene period, moreover, was a time of magnificent fauna. And when the ice retreated—only ten thousand years
ago the last time—it left a country much more hospitable to life
in its lacework of lakes and rivers.

The greatest sufferers must have been the mountains. Against
these the ice pressed until, with accumulating power, it was able
to gouge a passage through and between them, until finally it over-
rode all but the highest. Some of the hills overlooking Lake Superior are encircled by cliffs like broad headbands that must mark
the ice's work. Some are ridges ending in precipitous southern
slopes above piles of rock stripped off by the glacier as it overtopped
them and glided down their far sides. The wonder is that so much
was left of the Archaean Hills by the mass of ice that four times
scraped over and by them on its way to the line of the Missouri and
Ohio Rivers.

If the bare rock of the hills is mostly a dull gray on its worn
surface, it is dazzling within, where the highway has laid it open.
The tape resounds to my exclamations over the rocks: nearly black
and nearly white rocks; bologna-colored granites and granites like
strawberry whip; dark-gray and pale-gray gneisses banded narrowly
or broadly in various shades of pink, or swirled in pink or white.
Unbelievable. And this is the continental basement, as much as a
billion or even two or more billion years old—maybe half the
planet's age in places! For miles, greenish-gray schists, marbled with
quartz, are bright green on their cleavage faces, presumably from

chlorite but looking as if painted. One is loath to think that but for the blasting for the road the colors would never have been revealed and that they are destined to be lost with weathering. The rocks used for a highway fill are almost as bright as pastries, and it is very like a child in a pastry shop that I scramble among them for trophies—specimens, I call them.

Of the flags I have seen flying, most are of the new red-and-white maple-leaf design. Among them, however, are a few red ensigns, with British union. Inasmuch as these had been retired, I thought, in deference to *Québecois* sentiment, I ask a shopkeeper about it. "Oh, there are hold-outs," he replies impartially. "I can tell you which we'd floy, gaffer," says a voice within me, so distinctly, albeit without authorization, that I almost expect the shopkeeper to be startled. It is true, though, that giving up a symbol to which long association adheres is difficult. And new flags are apt not to be very stirring. Why a maple leaf, moreover? The Sugar maple—the one honored—is indigenous to Canada only in the extreme south-eastern part. By contrast, the White and Black spruce, Quaking aspen and Canoe birch together blanket the country below treeline, overlooking the Atlantic from the capes of Newfoundland and the Arctic Ocean from Alaska. *There* would be trees for Canadians to celebrate!

After a run along the shore in Agawa Beach Park, at the eastern end of the lake, I have dinner overlooking the water. The air off the lake is bitter, and the sound of the waves is like that of the waves on an ocean beach but shorter, quickly hushed, without the seething aftermath. The trees crowding the rocky promontories, facing the setting sun, are like an army brought to a halt, frustrated.

I have been astonished at how unchanging the country is over such distances. And of course I have seen the merest corner of it. For hundreds and many hundreds of miles the lake-studded forest fans out over upper Canada, growing wilder and more diminished with lowering temperatures. It is to these harsh reaches of ferocious winters that the wilderness has been reduced since it met the first settlers on the Atlantic shore. From the lands from which it has been thrust back have vanished also the animals it harbored, two-legged as well as four-, white as well as red men.

It comes to me that the French and Indian wars, as we call them, were among other things a contest between those whose medium was the wilderness and those who were set on supplanting it. As

Ray Allen Billington, a student of the frontier, expresses it (so I learn after my return when I set about to bridge the wide chasms in my knowledge of our history), "The frontier process can be roughly visualized in terms of two loosely defined groups. One—made up of fur trappers, missionaries, herdsmen and others whose enterprise depended on preserving the wilderness—was interested in *using* nature. The other—comprised of farmers, speculators, town-planners, merchants, millers and a host more whose profits depended on advancing civilization—was bent on *subduing* nature." It was these two interests that stood at swords' points when, on the defeat of the French in 1763, the English Crown sought to preserve for the Indians, provisionally, the trans-Appalachian forest lands it had acquired, which its American subjects eyed covetously.

The division went back far beyond that, however. In the motives that brought the white men to the New World to begin with there was an irreconcilable dichotomy. Side by side with a driving passion for gain or for land on which to bring a new society into being was an urge to redeem the aborigines from "darkness and miserable ignorance of the true knowledge and worship of God," to quote the letters patent establishing the Virginia companies of London and Plymouth. Consideration for the Indians in this world or the next did not long remain a guiding consideration anywhere, of course. Nevertheless, while some missionaires resorted to conversion by fire and sword, many befriended and defended the natives, from Brazil to Canada, often at a high cost in self-sacrifice and in hero-ism. Yet the price they exacted was high, too: the relinquishment by their protégés of their gods and their cultural de-Indianization. And those other champions of aboriginal America, the trappers? It was not a concern for the wilderness or even a minimum self-interest on their part that saved the beaver from extermination at their hands; such considerations, if not beyond them, were be-yond their ability to act on. It was competition from South Ameri-can nutria and the fall from fashion of the beaver hat.

All the same, a century ago, even before the frontier was pushed back into Canada, a genuine and, for the first time, disinterested concern for the preservation of wild America did begin to make itself felt among us. Its first great achievement was the setting aside of the Yellowstone wilderness for preservation, an event that took place even before—four years before—the Sioux had shot their bolt at the Little Bighorn. The aim of the conservation legislation passed since then has been primarily, as it is usually explained, to serve the recreational needs of the American people. And no doubt this is correct—certainly if we take recreation to include relief from the tensions of modern urban living and the sense of renewal to be realized among wild mountains, along forested rivers and by the still-untamed sea, of which the conservationists speak eloquently.

But I believe that conscience and a profound foreboding have been at work among us not much less than concern for our personal benefits, and in many cases more. Some at least of the natural splendors protected in the forty thousand square miles of the National Park system will be visited by only a small minority of Americans. Few of us whose representatives have bestowed official favor on scenic rivers and legislated the permanent protection, as such, of an initial 43,750 square miles of wilderness (with more to be added) will ever take a canoe trip or camp beyond a good road. A national, indeed international, effort was required to give twenty-one Whooping cranes—all there were left in 1952—a chance to bring the species back from the brink. (The long stretch of country between their breeding-grounds in the bogs below Great Slave Lake and their winter quarters on the coast of Texas had to be blanketed with appeals for their safety; a group of farmers in Saskatchewan dissuaded from carrying out a vow to shoot them all to prevent further expenditures on them; an oil company persuaded to restrict its drilling in the vicinity of the wintering flock; the Air Force brought to forego use of an adjacent island as a bombing-range.) Yet few Americans will ever see a Whooping crane. Almost none will ever see any of the birds-of-paradise in the high forests of New Guinea that owe their lives to a Congressional ban on the importation into the United States of wild birds' plumes. Most would be only repelled if they *should* see a Gila monster, a clumsy, uncouth, and venomous lizard of our Southwest. Yet, in a stellar example of what I have in mind, the elected legislators of Arizona have given the unloved but individual reptile the protection of the laws.

For many of us, an America without tall timber and high rocks where man is an interloper and can hike all day without meeting another of his kind would not be an America at all; and it is of secondary importance whether we ourselves ever venture into such unconquered domains. What matters is that they be there and we know it. Without them, the country's atmosphere would not have the *timbre* and resonance it has now. A man in total darkness can tell by the acoustics, by the quality of sounds and of silence whether he is confined in a small room or is at large beneath the sky, whether he is trapped or free. Yet even more than this, I think, enters into the protective urge that the continent and the remnants of the life it supports have been causing to stir in us. The catastrophes we have brought upon them have left us in no doubt at all that their fate is in our hands, in the sense that there is no part of them that we lack the means to destroy and is wholly safe from our exercise of those means. Where natural laws once prevailed, our own dictates now rule. We have brought off a revolution of enormous dimensions, and now we are learning what many a revolutionary has found, that power, while it looks altogether inviting to those who do not wield it, has a very different aspect when it has been achieved. The excesses to which revolutionary regimes are notoriously prone may well be prompted by a failure of nerve before the magnitude of the responsibilities they have taken on. And we have supplanted no mere temporal princeling, no mere junta of men no better than ourselves. To the reach of our grim powers of destruction we have replaced the sovereignty of Nature, or, as Thomas Jefferson had it, of Nature's God, with our own.

Shaken by the signs that already we are making trouble for ourselves by our recklessness of rule, we have very sensibly called up the scientists, who have some knowledge of the workings of the realm we have usurped. Their warnings are very stern indeed. At the present rate we may fatally deplete and poison our environment, putting an end not only to what passes for civilization but possibly even to our kind.

No one gainsays them. Yet what technology hath wrought, cannot technology unwork? Most of us would probably concede it that capacity, as far as physical phenomena go. And, while ecologists admonish us that all life on earth is a single web from which no strand may be eliminated with impunity, few of us probably are persuaded that our prospects on earth would be imperiled by the extermination of the Gray wolf, Bald eagle, alligator, leopard or Blue whale, least of all the Gila monster.

Yet we are responsible for them. I think the meaning of our accountability has dawned upon us. Those who supplant a king assume a king's responsibilities, those who supplant a God a God's. We may be insensible of *noblesse oblige*—being worthy of one's advantages—which to the high-minded is the ultimate sanction. But we know in our hearts, in our bones, without having to guess at the mechanism involved, that responsibilities cannot be evaded without incurring a reckoning strict in its exaction of an eye for an eye, a tooth for a tooth. And the responsibilities we have lightly shouldered are awful indeed. They embrace the whole community of plants and animals, bewildering in their numbers and variety, each a marvel superlatively modeled for its role by the creative energies of some billions of years, the whole breathtaking, humbling, in the fertility and daring of its artistry. And *living:* each species an expression of that incomprehensible vitality we all share and share alike. We are aware how we have laid waste about us, vandals undoing the work of Creation. And we know that it is precisely for our kind of high-riding, heedless arrogance—for *hubris*—that Nemesis lies in wait.

14

THE NORTHEAST

After driving in the dark through the city of Sault Sainte Marie, the name of which I find I did not know how to pronounce, and looking in vain for a camp-site, I settle for a cabin on the outskirts. It costs five dollars and may be worth three but does offer a shower—my first since Idaho.

The next day is one of ever more agreeable landscapes, with a poor start and the interruption of an all-time nadir after 180 miles. Up to that point, with the road most of the way never far from the Georgian Bay lobe of Lake Huron, it is mostly inferior woods and struggling, straggling farms with now and again a big old abandoned barn of vertical siding. Then come the environs of Sudbury, which not even Death Valley or the Badlands can equal for desolation. For mile upon mile there is nothing but the stubs of worn-down mountains stripped of cover to the bare rock, fragmented and blackened. Nothing grows on them. Between their remains are barren, poisoned-looking mudflats. At Sudbury itself you see the explanation: huge smelters with tall chimneys pouring an evil-smelling white smoke into the air. Canada leads the world in the production of nickel, and this is where it comes from. You could imagine yourself arrived at some dreadful mortuary of hills, a place to which mountains shrunken and failing with age repair to give up their ghosts and be incinerated. The crematorium extends for eight or ten miles beyond the city, before the woods begin to reassert themselves.

At Sudbury, as in the Mesabi, you see practical geology. The rocks of the Canadian Shield, which, incidentally, is two-thirds the size of the original forty-eight states, are mostly granite and gneisses of no interest to the extractive industries. But widely distributed among them are strips and patches of two series of rocks (a series consisting of rocks formed in the same region in the same epoch) comprising metamorphosed lavas and more or less metamorphosed sedimentary rocks, which contain most of the important metals and are especially rich in iron, nickel, copper, and silver. All the way from Sault Sainte Marie the highway has passed exposures of the older of the two series, the Keewatin, which includes some of the oldest rocks of the Shield. The broad-backed outcroppings were planed down and smoothly grooved by the passage of the ice-sheets, but in some of the hills around Sudbury the ends of tilted strata are revealed, very unlike the confectionery but solid rocks of yesterday and those to come.

At Sturgeon Falls, while the bus is being lubricated, I stop by a rather dark little café for a bite of lunch—my second meal in a restaurant since leaving home. And here suddenly, behind the counter-bar, are French Canadians, a man and a woman. What is it about them—about the French? Is there a human warmth in their regard? No, it is not warmth or humanity especially, but in their half-smiles there is a faintly ironic, very pleasant recognition of our common humanity, as if on that basis we were known to each other. And there is that quality for which there is only a French word, *insouciance*. Instead of butting head-on into life, the French seem to deal with it glancingly, suggestively, in a way that I suppose is implied in the word *style*. "In this matter of life and art it is not the Why that matters so much to our happiness as the How," Conrad observes. "As the Frenchman said, '*Il y a toujours la manière.*' Very true." For a Saxon type, chronically struggling in the toils of substance, the French are a fascination and tantalizing relief. If I have to have an inner voice to do me discredit, I think I should find it less objectionable if it were French. ("If you ahsk me"—the intonation is almost Cockney—"I'd say the French were veddy nice to visit, but I shouldn't care to be one!")

"Yess. . . . And for drink Monsieur will have . . . ?" And, looking gratefully up at the young woman, I reply as nearly as I can in consistency with the gallantry that has somehow been imputed to me.

Beyond Sturgeon Falls, the highway skirts Lake Nipissing, which was an important link in the canoe route from Montreal. On the west, the lake drains via the French River into Georgian Bay and Lake Huron while on the other side an eastward-flowing tributary of the Ottawa River rises only a few miles distant; it is almost uncanny how the water road westward worked out for the French. Within an hour one is in Mattawa, a town with fine old red-brick, gabled houses, on the Ottawa itself.

This is as beautiful a river to drive along as I have seen, half a mile wide, it seems, and a deep blue under the cold blue sky, with the wooded ridges of Quebec, gray and dark-green in patches, forming the far shore. The Trans-Canada Highway follows it for nearly a hundred miles, and all of it would be wholly enjoyable but for the traffic. It is the Queen Mother's birthday, I am told, and the population, wherever it comes from—for the towns are small and far between—has taken to its cars. Doing sixty-five on the somewhat jouncy, uphill-and-down highway, these pile up behind me if I do not hustle or get out of the way.

At Pembroke, some ninety miles short of Ottawa, the highway leaves the river and takes you through fruitful-looking farmland with big barns, well-kept houses and very sizable deciduous trees— the first in I do not know how long. After I turn due south for the United States at a small river rather confusingly called the Mississippi, the countryside grows more and more like the eastern Piedmont of Virginia. Old-fashioned, red-brick, and field-stone houses look serenely out on fields of pleasantly irregular topography and stands of trees, even a split-rail fence or two. At Carleton Place I could imagine myself among the harmonious, closely-ranked, time-steeped buildings of Leesburg, but this is a larger town, with more substantial public buildings of stone and an enviable river dividing it—still the Mississippi.

The Good Land, one could well call it. And it is more than that where it overlooks the St. Lawrence. I come to the river at seven-thirty the next morning, having spent the night in a grassy area behind a service station at Smith Falls. And what a river it is! Broad, blue, and majestic, it is all that the Mississippi (the big one, that is), ought to be. It even has wooded islands rising in it, some with houses and boat-landings, some only outcroppings of rock supporting a stand of conifers; these are among the so-called Thousand Islands. Back from the shore and the gnarled rocks of the Canadian Shield, dairy cattle graze. With the trees sprouting their new raiment, it is idyllic, this combination of a pastoral countryside and a great waterway opening out upon the seven seas. If it were not for the winters. . . .

But if one braved the winters and settled in Canada, would one discover in time what it is to be a Canadian? With everyone I have spoken to since the Pigeon River I have found myself trying to decide to what degree he was American, to what degree British —or French. (In upper Canada it would be Indian.) All my life I have lived in the adjoining country and I have no idea whether there is a Canadian personality, or what the Canadian consciousness may be, or Canadianism. (Which has not, however, prevented my presuming to include the Canadians in the "Our" of this book's title.)

But, for that matter, what is it to be an American, or, to be correct, a United-States-of-Americanian? (At least the Canadians have a name for their nationality. In only two nations is such a name lacking, and it seems to me far from insignificant that these are the U.S.A. and the U.S.S.R.) The question is one to mull over, and when one has done so long enough, one comes to a paradox; or I do, and a not reassuring one.

This, the last day of the trip before the final heading for home, is also to be the longest—530 miles—as a consequence of my undertaking to obtain a picture in my mind of the three major mountain ranges of the Northeast between 8:30 A.M. and sundown. This is next to not seeing them at all, but I had said a week ago I should be at home by the evening of the twenty-fourth, barring accidents, and I cannot bring myself to extend the trip by another day.

"The grandeur of the Catskills, and the loveliness of the lake-region of Central New York, are both surpassed in the great Wilderness of Northern New York, the Adirondack, where the mountains tower far above the loftiest of the Catskills, and where the lakes are to be counted by the hundreds, and are not surpassed in beauty even by Lakes George, Otsego, or Seneca." So wrote a contributor to William Cullen Bryant's *Picturesque America*, Robert Carter, in 1874. "This remarkable tract, which thirty years ago was known, even by name, only to a few hunters, trappers, and lumbermen, lies between Lakes George and Champlain on the east, and the St. Lawrence on the northwest. It extends, on the north, to Canada, and, on the south, nearly to the Mohawk. In area it is considerably larger than Connecticut, and, in fact, nearly approaches Wales in size, and resembles that country also in its mountainous character, though many of the mountains are a thousand or two thousand feet higher than the highest of the Welsh." And, "They are wild and savage, and covered with the 'forest primeval,' except the stony summits of the highest, which rise above all vegetation but that of mosses, grasses and dwarf Alpine plants. These high summits are thought, by geologists, to be the oldest land on the globe, of the first which showed itself above the waters."

In absolute terms, the Adirondacks are incomparably older than Robert Carter, with his picture of universal waters, probably had any conception. Even twenty years later, a leading American geologist, Clarence King, was asserting that "we have no warrant for extending the earth's age beyond 24 millions of years." In relative terms, however, the Adirondacks *as mountains* are—contrary to a still common misconception—vastly younger than the Appalachians, of which, of course, they are not a part. They are, it is true, composed of a series of rocks belonging to the Canadian Shield which were the foundations of mountains that reigned sometime between 800 million and a billion years ago, the Grenville. But those mountains had been leveled by time, their bases submerged in the sea and overlaid by sedimentary rocks before a slow up-warping of the earth's crust long, long afterward, culminating no more than 25 million years ago, raised them thousands of feet again. Exposed to the elements, which stripped away the sedimentary-rock covering as they arose, and to the later passage of the ice-sheets, they were carved into the mountains we know as the Adirondacks.

On State Highway 3, you enter Adirondack Park within forty miles of the nearest point on the St. Lawrence. ("Park" is something of a misnomer, for of its 8,750 square miles, considerably less than half is in public ownership and restrictions on the use of the rest are few.) Ridges of bulbous outcroppings of the basement rocks have already begun, and there are spruce and fir from the start—for the Adirondacks are clothed in the largest expanse of North Woods in the eastern states outside northern Maine. But approached from the west, the range acquires stature only slowly; the up-warping was greatest on the other side. Trilliums are in bloom—three-bladed white pinwheels—and, where I have a run at about 1,500 feet, the dainty yellow Trout-lilies, each suggestive of a little snake's head, striking downward, if the image is not wholly out of order for so demure a flower. . . . I am with myself as I was when my parents brought me to the Adirondacks for a week when I was twelve and I tramped about through the dark forest and over the open, winter-racked heights in a rapturous satisfaction at being in the spruce-filtered northern air among such powerful protagonists of the northern wilderness. Beyond a certain age you look back on yourself in youth as someone who has died with his promise—which you were not aware of at the time and would be hard put to it to define now—cut off.

From Tupper Lake, fifty-odd miles inside the park, you see the major summits clustered in the east. Real mountains they are, more rugged in form than you would expect of any in the East. Beyond Saranac Lake, from the north at Lake Placid or from the still charming valley-village of Keene farther on they appear a wild sea of mountains, with craggy, broken, steep rock faces showing through the mantle of mottled coniferous forest and stands of birch covering whole sides of them. Forty-six are approximately four thousand feet or above—and there is a fraternity of persons who have climbed them all, called the Forty-sixers. They culminate in Mount Tahawus—"Who Splits the Clouds" (or Marcy, as it has become by general, but without my personal, consent). Tahawus stands 5,344 feet above sea-level and on May twenty-third is still etched with snow at its summit.

"Elsewhere are mountains more stupendous, more icy and more drear, but none looks down upon a grander landscape, in rich autumn time; more brightly gemmed or jeweled with innumerable lakes, or crystal pools, or wild with savage chasms, or dread passes. . . . A region of mystery, over which none can gaze without a strange thrill of interest and wonder at what may be hidden in that vast area of forest." So wrote Verplanck Colvin, who in 1872 had been appointed superintendent of a topographical survey of the mountains and spent twenty-eight years exploring them. The awesome qualities of the Adirondacks seem always to have taken hold of imaginations. An early investigator of Ausable Chasm quoted by Robert Carter wrote, "The whole prospect, except the rocks, was dark with thickest, wildest woods. As we rode slowly through the still narrowing gorge, the mountains soared higher and higher, as if to scale the clouds, presenting a truly terrific majesty. I shrank within myself; I seemed to dwindle beneath it. Something alike to dread pervaded the scene. The mountains appeared knitting their stern brows into one threatening frown at our daring intrusion into their stately solitudes. Nothing seemed native to the awful landscape but the plunge of the torrent and the scream of the eagle."

There were indeed depths of intimidating wilderness in the Adirondacks in that day; and it was a time, too, of a Byronic romanticism about mountains (not that I am one to say that time has passed). Furthermore, it was a time of growing urbanism and ugly industrialism. *Adventures in the Wilderness,* written by a young Congregationalist minister from Boston, William H. H. Murray, in 1869 started an Adirondacks-rush with its accounts of the abundance of game ("With a guide who knows his business I would undertake to feed a party of twenty the season through and seldom should they sit down to a dinner lacking trout and venison") and of the salubrity of the air, with the "pungent and healing odors of the conifers," capable of putting sixty-five pounds on a dying consumptive in five months and turning him "bronzed as an Indian, and as hearty." Such panegyrics, and Murray's was not the first, bore their inevitable fruit. Colvin wrote bitterly of it: "Where first one comes, the next year there are ten, the year after, fully a hundred. Hotels spring up as though by magic. . . . The wild trails, once jammed with logs [tree trunks], are cut clear by the axes of the guides and ladies clamber to the summits of those once untrodden peaks." Even Colvin could scarcely have foreseen the time, however, when more than two million camper-days a year would be logged at State areas in the Adirondacks (according to a contributor to *Audubon Magazine*) and more than 140,000 be turned away.

Thanks to men like Verplanck Colvin, the legislature at Albany in 1885 created an Adirondack Forest Preserve of Crown lands that had become the State's at the end of the Revolution. The Preserve, comprising 3,750 square miles in tracts that form a patchwork within the Adirondack Park, is protected by an article in the State Constitution providing that they "shall be forever kept as wild forest lands" and that no "timber thereon be sold, removed or destroyed." Article XIV has not, however, prevented the construction of Interstate 87, the "Northway," straight through the eastern side of the park. It is a bleak precedent, with the incidental result that the Adirondacks are now to be brought within a half-day's drive of New York City. But of course there is nothing unique in the situation of the Adirondacks. The specter of Yosemite on a summer week-end stands over all parks.

And what would one have? In a country where popularity is the criterion of value and the determinant of the survival of public lives, products, and institutions, one would hardly wish unpopularity on the parks. Yet what if their popularity threatens the loss of the very attributes that led to their protection? Exclusion of private cars from parts of Yosemite Valley has already begun and will have to follow in other parks. Beyond that, one may hope that if the parks are overrun and become mere playgrounds for people, adjuncts of all that the visitor had sought to get away from, an appreciation of what they are meant to offer of a still ascendant, harmonious and mysterious Nature will lead to irresistible demands for vastly more parkland. But if in the long run the great natural assets of our country are to be saved it will be because we have come to recognize that they are the property, if of anyone, of society, future as well as present. It will be because we have not only stopped the squandering and abuse of the lands, resources and waters by private industry and bureaucratic agencies but have undone the carving up of our beaches, mountains, lake-shores, and riversides into private lots and undertaken to redeem them from the rash of homesteads—shacks, cottages, and villas—and attendant commercial dispensaries by which today, in the general rush to grab for oneself a bit of Nature at its most inviting, the loss of all for everyone is threatened.

Meanwhile, a transient crossing the northern Adirondacks can at least tell himself that large areas of the range remain roadless and that the forest has gone a long way to recovering from the sacking it was already beginning to take from the lumbermen when Robert Carter wrote. It seems remarkable to me that the park is in general as unspoiled as it appears; even Lake Saranac, in the major resort area, is still largely wooded.

Following the signs to the ferry across Lake Champlain at Essex, I discover what none of them had disclosed, that it has not yet begun operations for the summer. What is worse, I also learn that the next of the infrequent ferries from Port Kent, twenty-three miles farther up the lake, leaves in half an hour. On an Interstate, there would be no difficulty, but State Highway 22 proves to be just as I knew it on many a drive, especially many a snowy drive, through Westchester County in my Model A two-seater. That is to say, it is a modest road in no hurry, curving accommodatingly to the terrain and seeking out pleasant vistas—just what a road should be, in fact. Regretfully, I do it great violence, and also the bus, which is desperately unsure of itself on tight curves at high speed.

As it is, they have to hold the ferry when they see us coming.

Ah, but it is agreeable with the emergency behind one to sit over tea and graham crackers and peanut butter out on that beautiful body of water. Lake Champlain is like the St. Lawrence, even having a few islands in it, but is bordered by mountains. On one side are the rampant Adirondacks, multi-peaked, seeming to rise right up from the lake, on the other, less imposing because less close, the more even ridges of the Green Mountains, northern counterpart of the Blue Ridge.

The hour's crossing disembarks you in Burlington, the "Queen City of Vermont," up through which you climb steeply to find yourself passing along a street of magnificent houses. Dating, evidently, from the 1880's for the most part, these are of white clapboard or brick, all constructed with a cabinetmaker's pride and care, all huge, under even huger elms and behind sumptuous lawns. If in the eyes of my forebears the Yankees were adept to a fault in the making of money, no one has been able to condemn them for not knowing how to spend what they made. Perhaps the New England winters arrested any tendencies to profligacy— they would in my case—and taught the value of sound investment. But I think it must have made a difference, too, that in the past, and not only in New England, those who built did so as members, and generally consequential members, of a social organism, a community. They built, accordingly, with a keen sense of responsibility. They built also in an architectural tradition—which means in a style that had gradually evolved and hence was an honest one, for falsity will not stand the test of time.

In all parts of New England I have seen where the past has not been swamped by the traditionless, styleless building of the present there are these admirable, even noble, if often simple, *virtuous* houses. And it is true of the strip of Vermont I see following the Winooshi River eastward from Burlington on U. S. 2, which I note is the northernmost of the transcontinental highways in the United States.

The road winds around this beautiful countryside in a charming but not very expeditious way. The Winooshi Valley is rather narrow and is occupied by apparently thriving farms, with hilly green fields and the wooded, greater hills right behind them. . . . This Vermont countryside, such as the valley of the upper Winooshi, must be as beautiful as any in America, with the great hills sloping back and rearing up behind the rolling green valley, where these fine New England houses are, which were built with so much respect for the world one must live in, and the mountains softened by the smoky-looking deciduous forest, contrasting with the sturdy, dark-green conifers that form groves on the slopes.

In the lowlands the new foliage is pale gold, in the mountains below the higher elevations the color of goldenrod just before it blooms, and so bright and shimmering in the sun that the mountains look as if they had snow still clinging to them. It is that most precious of all the moments of the seasons, when the earth for the first time, still in incredulous surprise, is entrusting herself to spring like a young girl in love in the dawning, still tentative but exultant knowledge of her emotion's requital. When you think of this return of life on the mild southern breeze, under the warming sun, the sudden sprouting of green and gold across the dead and sodden landscape, the sleighbells of the Hylas piping miraculously in the cold bogs, and every day bringing new birds to add their remembered songs to the heart-liberating medley— when, as I say, you think of all this coming to pass at the very time it seemed most unlikely the New England winter would ever end, *could* ever end, you have, I believe, part of the explanation of the deep and informed appreciation of Nature that first found words in America, printed words, in New England.

Another part is at hand for anyone who exposes himself to the New England countryside and discovers its pure and inexhaustible beauty, of which the secret is the astringent northern air and New England's sculpturing—its geology. There are verdant, hospitable valleys, but they are valleys hemmed in by hills and in much of the country by rugged mountains. And these ever-present highlands, stripped to the unyielding rock by the glaciers where they are steepest and boulder-strewn by that same agency, like the whole of New England, thrusting their granite pediments out into the North Atlantic, not only provide the major elements of New England's picturesqueness; they have set a limit to man's easy exploitation of the land and preserved much of the section's natural character. They also, it is true, necessitated the emigration westward of the surplus sons and daughters of the once multitudinous New England families. No less truly, they turned New England to the sea, to fishing boats that plied the Banks, to the whalers that ventured from northern ice to southern ice and to the clipper ships that ran beneath clouds of canvas over all the seas of the earth, to the abiding glory of New England's name.

If, in Van Wyck Brooks's phrase, there was a flowering of New England, as surely there was, it was partly for the reason that many a plant has flowered profusely; New England was pot-bound, pot-bound by topography and climate, as, paradoxically, it was stimulated by both. America owes a great debt to the New England winter, more than I should have been prepared to concede in the years I was enduring it. And yet . . . I sometimes wonder if the New Englanders used those intellects sharpened and fortified with reading during the long, snow-bound evenings to think things through when they turned their backs on the land and, with consequences later fatal to their shipping, decided that favoritism should be shown the factory. It was a momentous step the New England capitalists took when, in combination with their fellows in other sections, they succeeded in having Congress require every citizen—every farmer, every planter, however poor—to pay tribute to the manufacturer, however rich. The protective tariff of 1828 demonstrated that "free enterprise" was a phrase to be invoked by capitalists when it suited their interests, rejected when it did not. It established the principle that an economic interest strong enough to bend the federal government to its purpose was entitled to rig the market in favor of its product. And it caused the first flare-up of the instinct of self-preservation on the part of the South as such. ("The Union—it must be preserved!" Andrew Jackson declared in a toast, looking John C. Calhoun challengingly in the eye. "The Union," the South Carolinian echoed, "—after our liberties, most dear!") The Civil War saw the conclusive defeat not only of the South by the North, the slave-holder by the employer, but also—I was taught at a New England university— the landsman by the industrialist.

We've come to the head of the Winooshi Valley and are ascend-

ing to a pass of some kind through forest where Canoe birches have put in an appearance again. . . .

We seem to be on top at a town called West Danville. There's a lake up here with houses around it, but how there can be a lake in a saddle, I don't know. You can see the White Mountains off in the distance, rather dim. It is for the highest group of these, called the Presidential Range, that I am heading, the Kan Ran Vugarty of the Indians—a name that, according to their historian, Stearns Morse, couples "their whiteness and their soaring grace in one figure implying the whiteness of a sea gull." The range, gathering its forces in central New Hampshire, extends about a hundred miles northeastward well into Maine. Where it rises to its supreme elevations, it represents the ultimate expression of the Appalachians north of North Carolina, although solitary Mount Katahdin standing at a height of nearly a mile above sealevel in north central Maine runs the higher of the Kan Ran Vugarty a good second.

Down, down, down to St. Johnsbury, which spreads up into the hills. It's on the Connecticut River, which forms the border with New Hampshire. There's an old mill down here at the bottom, an old New England factory. An historical sign says, "First American Platform Scale. . . ." St. Johnsbury's NOT *on the border* OR *the Connecticut. The shadows are lengthening ominously and we've got a good way to go yet. I wonder how I'm going to see the White Mountains by daylight and how possibly I'm going to get to New York by noon tomorrow—*to keep an appointment I feel I must.

On high ground coming into Lunenberg you can see Mount Washington and its neighbors standing up like the Front Range of the Rockies, Mount Washington being well mantled in snow, the others less so. (At this time I have yet to learn the great mountain's native name.)

Now, at six thirty-five, we are *crossing the narrow but very pretty Connecticut and entering New Hampshire. Driving east on U. S. 2 out of Lancaster you head right toward those grand, humped mountains. There are three that stand out as the tallest with the most snow on them. . . . You get a wonderful look at them broadside as you drive along here, these big ones form . . . clustering together, forming a group, I suppose actually a ridge. . . .*

We're heading north to go around the range in that direction at seven o'clock. It looks as if we can cut off a triangle with Gorham as the apex by taking the Dolly Copp Road, a short-cut. . . . The Dolly Copp Road, which started out as broad and paved has became the opposite. I hope it's all right, I hope it saves time. . . . I think this is a mistake. . . .

Back we go with a loss of a precious five minutes in this race with the sun. . . . Will the Mount Washington auto road be closed? I hope to be able to get part way up it anyhow. A road for carriages, from which the present road has evolved, was put through to the top of the mountain, up the eastern side, between 1855 and 1861, to be followed eight years later by the well-known cog railway up the western. Opposed as I am to the degradation of a mountain by any construction carrying people up it, if a road is there and the opportunity to reach the top by other means denied me, then up the road I go if I can.

For the last time we turn south, this time on New Hampshire 16, the White Mountain Highway. . . . You get just as sensational a view of these mountains from the eastern side. You have Mount Washington in full view here as you drive along the side of its slope. It just goes up there, up and up and up, to a rounded summit, slightly pointed, it would seem from here on the southeastern side, a great, smooth summit. . . . Gosh, I believe the automobile road is *open! "Eight miles to sum—" Oho. "Closed." . . .*

I talked to the man at the gatehouse and they won't let me go even part way up. It seems they're working on the road: it's been washed out in places.

This is a much greater disappointment than the tape would indicate. At 6,288 feet, old Agiochook, hoary monarch of the New England skies, stands 5,000 feet above its base and nearly 500 higher than its nearest rival, the highest point between the Black Mountains, 800 miles to the southwest, and the giant range of the upper coast of Baffin Island, 1,800 due north.* On a clear day it is said that from the summit you can see the greater part of the New England highlands—across Vermont to New York, far into Canada and Maine, to the coast and beyond, and south to Massachusetts. "There is no ship arrives in New England, either to the

---

* This, like its southward extension in the Torgat Mountains of the coast of Labrador, seems to have been raised by a faulting of the Canadian Shield, which also apparently dropped a section of the Shield to separate Greenland from the continent.

west so farre as *Cape Cod* or to the East so farre as *Monhiggen*," wrote a voyager of 1628 in the first reference to Agiochook, "but they see this mountaine the first land, if the weather is cleere." The view I have had of it, white-domed, dark-caped in spruce and fir above the budding deciduous forest cloaking the lower slopes in mail of radiant scales, has only made harder my having to pass it by.

Agiochook is commonly referred to as an arctic island above New England, and it is that. The rocky, treeless heights of the summit actually extend along the lofty ridge for twenty miles, and they include three icy lakes. However, it is not altitude *per se* that puts the crest above timberline; trees grow three thousand feet higher at the same latitude in the Rockies. What the forest cannot contend with, what little vegetation can, is the ferocity of the winter gales. These occasionally reach 200 miles an hour on the heights, and 231, a world's record, has been recorded; also a temperature of forty-six degrees below zero. The behavior of the trees near their limit is as it is in the Rockies. "The spaces between the rocks," wrote the Reverend Dr. Manasseh Cutler in 1784, "and on the plain, are filled with spruce and fir, which, perhaps, have been growing ever since the creation, and yet many of them have not attained a greater height than three or four inches, but their spreading tops are so thick and strong as to support the weight of a man without yielding in the smallest degree." (When you think how recently men could believe that a living tree might embrace the entire history of the Cosmos you understand the strain to which scientific discoveries have subjected our culture.) Birds of the Far North nest in the upper reaches of the forest—the brown-capped Boreal chickadee, Olive-backed thrush, Canada (or Gray) jay, the dark, yellow-crowned Three-toed woodpeckers, even the Spruce grouse. Above treeline there is an arctic flora of a dwarf willow and a dwarf birch only six or so inches high, heaths like Lapland rhododendron and Alpine azalea, among other depressed shrubs, and a variety of flowering perennials as in the alpine tundra, including even Moss campion.

In 1642, at a time when climbing mountains had occurred to few persons as a rational thing to do, "one Darby Field," Governor Winthrop wrote, "being accompanied by two Indians, went to the top of the white hill"; the journey took eighteen days. Later the same year two Down-Easterners were inspired to make the same ascent. The capacity of the New England air to nourish the questing, vigorous spirit was early demonstrated. While the White Hill went unattempted again for nearly a century, it seems—there were Indian wars, for one thing—it has cut short many lives since then. The toll it has taken does nothing to diminish the force of its presence—"daunting terrible," an early commentator said of the range. Unprepared climbers are caught above treeline by icy rains, freezing fogs or blizzards and, losing the trail, become lost and die of exposure. There is no record of the number killed on Agiochook, but however many there have been, it has not been enough—enough to save the summit from the weather station, a fancy hotel, an FM radio and television transmitter, and buildings used by the Atomic Energy Commission and the military services. "But," as Stearns Morse interjects quietly, "on the calendar of geologic time these phenomena may be mere ephemera." It seems likely. Meanwhile, at least I am spared them as I have to settle for a run along the highway below the mountain, hearing no sound but the rush of waters alongside that pour downstream into the Androscoggin and the song of a White-throated sparrow, which, for its needle-high pitch, can be equaled by few voices in nature for sweetness.

From here, the highway descends the U-shaped glacial valley called Pinkham Notch, one of the three (Crawford and Franconia Notches being the others) that divide the high Whites into four separate massifs. *It's a wonderful wooded valley with young beeches palely blue in the deepening shadows and the moss and young evergreens forming a carpet on the Ellis River's banks. . . . Getting dark as we go through North Conway, a place of old inns, motor lodges, and antique shops.*

At eleven o'clock I come to a rest area by a toll-gate on the New Hampshire Turnpike and, exhausted, pull off to the side of the road and sleep like the dead until shortly after five in the morning.

· · ·

The foliage, which is halfway out in southern New Hampshire, will be full in Virginia. Apple blossoms, in their prime in Massachusetts, are past it in Connecticut. I note the rocks along Route 128 around Boston, which resemble others I have seen in the forged-rock bases of mountains—and many of them are the Paleozoic granite that bulks large not only in New England east of the

Connecticut River but also through the length and breadth of the Southern Piedmont.* After that I am ready to close down the over-worked tape recorder. . . . But no, there is one thing more: the striking sandstone formations that begin near Hartford, ranging in color from brown to maroon, and build up to parapeted hills several hundred feet high in the neighborhood of Meriden. (Nearly the whole of the Connecticut River Valley up through Massachusetts is occupied by these so-called red sandstones, which also make up a much larger belt that begins at the Hudson River and follows the front of the mountains across northern New Jersey and the corner of Pennsylvania to narrow down into Virginia, passing within five miles of where I live. They are composed of the sediments that washed down from the young Appalachians in the early Mesozoic Period to accumulate along the front of the range to such depths—up to two miles—that the earth's crust evidently sagged beneath them, opening rents into which basaltic magma flowed to harden in sills and dikes. The most famous of these is the Palisades along the western bank of the lower Hudson—the edge of a sill laid bare by erosion.)

The familiar route southward is overlaid in my mind by the scenes of the past three weeks. The exalted beauty of our country; the limitless variety, dramatic or subtle; the sheer physical scope; the nobility! I am left dazed by it, pierced through by, groggy from it. The truth may be—and I think I am repeating myself in this—that persons wanting more security against the terrors of mortal existence and the sense of their failure than they can find in their capacity for iron stoicism are prone to see, for the comfort there is in it, a supreme and unifying conception and consummate resolution in a visible universe that may, in fact, be merely arbitrary, futile, and empty. My solitude during those three weeks of exposure to the unwinding spectacle, and I might also say my gropings through the billions of years of geological history that have accounted for it, have made me more impressionable, obviously. But, having already owned to a view of the Cosmos, when I am pressed by the problem of its ultimate meaning, as an all-encompassing work of art, I must add for what it may be worth that what I have seen has had for me a transcendence about it, as if it were part of a

---

* This may be taken to indicate that a great range once stood just seaward of the then towering Green Mountains and Blue Ridge, of which Katahdin and the White Mountains are the sole lofty remnants.

vision, if a vision of unimaginable origin. All this is by way of confession; anything I may say is subject to discount on the grounds of my infatuation.

That so much remains of the land we have taken over has surprised me. I had underestimated its capacity to absorb punishment. Whether I should feel so had I not avoided the major concentrations of population is another matter. In any case, what one cannot help recognizing is that while some damages we have done the country are being repaired, the omnivorous machine of the American economy is grinding its way relentlessly, on myriad fronts, into what remains of the natural province and that no one of any political consequence is even proposing that it be retarded, let alone arrested.

And for what is aboriginal America being progressively consumed?

I believe I know the answer. It lies in our achievement. And that, surely, is prodigious. We have fashioned a civilization beyond encompassment by the human mind in the multitude and marvel of the engines it commands; in the cataracts of goods it pours forth; in the seas of cropland from which it extracts bumper crops; in the scale of its cities and their intricacy of organization; in the might of its weaponry of war; in the amount of education it provides; in the scope of the benefits in health, comforts, opportunities, mobility, leisure, cultural exhibitions and diversions it affords most of its more than 200 million shareholders and dependents—for it is a noteworthy characteristic of this civilization that its proceeds are devoted neither to empire (now that the nation has acquired for itself the fairer part of the continent) nor to the pomp and vainglory of a minute elect, but more or less to the general welfare, with some even to spare for peoples in other lands victimized by adversity. It is a civilization that, entrenched on earth, is reaching out for the other planets. With the array of skills and insights it enlists, it is a civilization to which, given time, nothing in the way of material achievement would appear impossible.

But what goes with this!

The unspeakable, truly hellish tawdriness with which American communities surround themselves, with which they are permeated, is of course nothing new to anyone who has moved about at all in our country. To feel the full force of the violence America does the senses, however, perhaps it is necessary to run the gamut of it, the sometimes hours-long gamut, again and again, in place after place, day after day, over thousands of miles: the disheveled and disrupted earth, bulldozed and disemboweled; the gas stations, motels, truck depots, food stands ("Burgers Shakes Cones"), drug-, hardware-, and auto-accessory-stores, real-estate and insurance agencies, construction-equipment yards, auto-wreckers, industrial plants, power stations, and countless other manifestations of an insatiable and relentless commercialism making up a chaos of clashing colors and heterogeneous and meaningless structural forms; the blatant, strident, chromatically screaming devices of an all-consuming and pathological hucksterism, and all combined in a patternless and mostly trashy extravaganza as nerve-racking as it is cheap and debasing. You may make all the resolutions in the world to look away from it, not to let it get you, but still you are overpowered.

The truth of the matter is that our society could hardly have produced more ugliness if the production of ugliness had been its prime order of business. The American people, I have come to feel, must be the most sensorily starved, sensorily abused people on earth. No other could be subject to such disintegrative disharmonics.

The sordidness of poverty is not pleasant, but at least it does not preclude remedy; society can strive for its amelioration, and meanwhile the community of the poor is at least a human community. But the monied sordidness of the hard, glaring, sprawling shopping-centers with their huge parking plazas and of the six- or eight-lane expressways running perpetual rivers of extravagant automobiles overweening in brutal, glossy inhumanity—this is sordidness not of pathetic failure but of aggressive success; this is what we *want*. And so it is with the buildings we erect along the commercial streets and highways of the nation, the office buildings, the bank buildings, the department stores. These dominate the portrait we are creating of ourselves, as a people always portrays itself and what it is about in what it builds; and they are crude, crushing, unfeeling, arbitrary assemblages of glass, metal and masonry, posturing in eccentricities of form and garishness of color or standing stark, blank and ominous, pitilessly devoid of grace and charm, alien to every conception of beauty.

If the effect is one of utter soullessness, as it is, how is it to be squared with the impression Americans generally convey of themselves as kind and generous, as solicitous parents, as charitable and given to good works, as helpful and patient with strangers—as I, certainly, have found them to be? The answer might be that a people can be one thing individually, another collectively, as a civilization. That would seem to have been the case with the Germans under the Third Reich, who apparently remained rational and humane through the most demented and brutal excesses of the nation.

As much as by its material achievement you are struck in looking at American society by its being always on the move. Mobility is with us a supreme good. The sixty-billion-dollar Interstate Highway program, leaving mountainsides blasted open and valleys piled with rubble, cities drawn and quartered; the trillion miles we clock yearly on the odometers of our cars; the abandoned farmland, with outbuildings in decay; the frequency with which we move our domiciles: all this testifies to it. Two centuries ago, the Royal Governor of Virginia, Lord Dunmore, observed it when he wrote: "I have learnt from experience that the established Authority of any government in America, and the policy of Government at home, are both insufficient to restrain the Americans; and that they do and will remove as their avidity and restlessness excite them. They acquire no attachment to Place. But wandering about seems engrafted in their Nature; and it is a weakness incident to it, that they should for ever imagine the Lands further off, are still better than those upon which they are already settled." It is a mobility that superficializes, if I may so express it, our relationship with the land.

Abuse followed by neglect: that is what the lands on which we have set our stamp characteristically bespeak. Of the things we have built, you have the impression that most of what is not new, unseasoned, and unassimilated is run-down and deteriorating. Overwhelmingly, it seems, our dwellings are characterless, awkward, subdivision stereotypes fresh-hatched by an uneducated, profit-grabbing builder, and sheet-metal, packing-case, robot-designed "mobile homes," bleak and expressive of transience; or they are drab, shabby houses put up a generation or two or three ago and, by their looks, having had little work and less love invested in them since then. The prevailing aspects of the human occupancy of the country are those of impermanence. "The cluttered transience, the state of perpetual becoming that is the American way": so it is defined by Paul Showers of *The New York Times*, "—a restless, ravaging culture which quickly destroys everything, including itself."

Henry Fairlee, the British journalist, writes in the same vein:

"The Americans, to the outsider, seem to be in a perpetual condition of becoming instead of just being, and I do not think that they yet understand how alarming this is to the rest of the world; how other peoples look across the oceans, from east and west, each day and wonder what the Americans may have become during the night."

If America, in the shapes it is taking, appears soulless, perhaps it is because there is no America—no such entity. The clue may be in the state of the American community—which is to say in its virtual non-existence.

American families move on the average every five years, and since a great number in rural areas and small towns move much less often, it follows that the rest, who largely set the pattern of our national life, move more. They have no time to settle down. *They acquire no attachment to Place.* Predominantly, moreover, they move between suburbs. Ours has become a nation of suburbs. And suburbia represents the negation of community. The indistinguishability of suburbs as between Georgia and New York, Texas and Illinois, is the sign of their artificiality and lack of roots in the locality. Suburbia means the atomization of society—an infinitude of physically separated, individual homes of individual families each self-contained before its television set in its own recreation room, around its barbecue grill in its individual patio, separately mobile in its motorcar and, increasingly, in the powerboat launched from a trailer.

Only a people with ties to the locality as weak as ours could have produced a culture so uniform across so great an area; for what impresses a transcontinental traveler as much as the variety of the natural landscape is the monotony of the human. Throughout a country of three million square miles we erect the same houses and business buildings, drive the same motorcars, read the same magazines, increasingly eat the same food and drink the same cocktails in the same kinds of restaurants and snack-bars, suck the same soft drinks at the same drug-stores, put up at the same motels, see the same motion pictures and television programs, buy the same brands of everything. And the explanation is not, I should argue, that our culture has acquired a strong national, as opposed to local, personality, but that it has been largely denatured of any personality at all. It could be taken on by other peoples, almost any, in place of their own, and increasingly it is being so.

Whatever binding sense of community we had in the past has been very nearly lost. Generally shared antecedents and a common historical experience probably produced a family feeling in Yankee New England. It certainly produced one in the white South. But even in the South the consciousness of community is fast fading. Not for a long time now has there been anything regional the New Englanders could get together on, and this is increasingly true of Southerners. You become even more aware of a lack of family feeling among Americans if you visit England. There, such a feeling seems to underlie much of what is most enviable in that country, including the safety of the streets at night and the pains nearly everyone is at to improve his bit of the landscape with flowers, even if that bit is only a windowsill—for this, when you come to think of it, is a gesture of warmth toward others.

Our insistence on the forms of national identity—our display of the flag, our recital of the oath of allegiance to it, our predilection for loyalty oaths, the invocations of patriotism by our politicians—is probably as symptomatic of the lack of genuine community among us, for which it is an anxious form of unconscious compensation, as the crime and violence that rend us and our flagrant disfigurement of the landscape, in which we reveal our lack of identification with and pride in it. So, I should say, is the evident ethnic consciousness of the diverse elements of our population. A family feeling has long been apparent among Jews and in the past few years it has grown conspicuously among Negroes. It is strong enough among the Irish, Italians, Poles, and Eastern Europeans and I suppose others of the Old World for politicians to have to take close heed of it. Mexican-Americans have taken a name for themselves—Chicanos—and claimed part of the Southwest for their own. The Indians are making their voices heard, *as Indians*. ("I am an American citizen second, a Kiowa first," says Perry Horse.) While such ethnocentrism certainly adds to the strains in the national political organism, its significance is on the whole probably more symptomatic than anything else. Few of us wish to disengage ourselves from America the Provider and the largesse that is the envy of the world. The fact remains that Americans as such are largely denied the comfort and support of a sense of "belonging."

In the remarkable essay I have already quoted from (and shall again), Henry Fairlee goes on to say:

The distemper of America . . . is written in the faces of its peoples. (They must still, if one is to be accurate, be identified as peoples; they are not *one* yet.) Except possibly—and paradoxically—for the Negroes, they are almost never at ease. I know of no other country in which the people are so strained: on buses, on the streets, in their offices, in other people's homes, even in their own homes.

They are a well-meaning people, but almost ashamed to find themselves behaving well. They are a hospitable people, but with an almost complete lack of courtesy. They are more conscious of family than any other pre-dominantly non-Catholic country, but their families have neither a sense of hierarchy nor a sense of real familiarity.

They work hard, but they seem to derive no satisfaction from their work. They play hard, but they seem never to enjoy any leisure. They work at their religion, but they seem to find neither joy nor solace in it. They must be the unhappiest people in the world.

In such a vein are my thoughts running, off and on, in an impressionistic way, as I try to maintain an adjustment to the traffic on the New Jersey Turnpike. They are interrupted by the happy sight of the springtime marshes near the turnpike's end and, just beyond that, by the Delaware Memorial Bridge, which lifts you on high for a stunning view of the bay and a reminder of the world's extent—and of the industrial fumes we are pouring into its canopy of air. Great bridges are thrilling. Sir Denis Brogan is surely right in calling those that span our waters America's most stirring architectural achievement.

The United States, I cannot help thinking, is possessed by that which has become a menace to the world, threatening the progressive impoverishment of the living earth and by the same token—though I cannot altogether explain why I believe it to be the same—the progressive impoverishment of human culture and human life. Or rather—and the thought is even more alarming—perhaps it is possessed by nothing at all and we are seeing a machine consuming its way along to no end but its own perpetuation and self-aggrandizement.

There must be a reason, and one worth trying to get at. Such is my urgent feeling after all the glories I have seen which stand in the path of destruction—glories kept fresh in my mind (not that they need to be) by the green woodland of Maryland, parted by the great Susquehanna leading westward between its steep banks. It is my feeling when I reflect on how much America is a country in which man has expressed himself in beauty as well as in ugliness; for scarcely a community cannot display some acres in which nature has been reworked to advantage in the composition of trees, shrubs, and greensward and in the cultivation of flowers. In few parts of man-made America does one travel many miles without encountering a landscape one could linger long over in contentment. Much of the Piedmont offers more to the eye and spirit and potentially succors a greater variety and abundance of wildlife than it did when it lay in the gloom of solid forest. Here, one is satisfied, we have been not wholly out of tune with the creative principle one seems to see in life. One is surer yet of the best work of our architects and artisans. In any of the older parts of the country are houses that cannot fail to win one over, which accord with and enhance their surroundings and in their felicity of proportion express a vision of harmony and discipline in the society that produced them; for whatever else may be said about our forefathers, they were united in their beliefs in a natural or God-given order that served as a model for man.

Then, on top of all, there is the welcome that awaits me at the doorstep I quitted ninety-six hundred miles before, and the later company of friends, and the warm conviction a stone would come to of the inestimable worthiness and capacities of human nature, which our continuing history instances in abundance.

EPILOGUE:

BACK TO THE ATLANTIC

En dat Virginia quintam!

It was 1619 and the turning point for the colony of Jamestown after the horrors it had barely survived. Some 1,200 new colonists arrived that year, including a shipload of 120 nubile maids "for the making of the men feel at home." John Rolfe, whose marriage with the powerful Powhatan's daughter Pocahontas and introduction of the cultivation of tobacco had saved the colony, now devised a method of curing the leaves that would help create a world-wide demand for the weed and make Virginia a profitable enterprise. A representative assembly was formed, the first in the New World, and, inaugurating a dichotomy that was to rack the new society to the present day, the first cargo of unwilling Africans debarked. (One such African who arrived three years later would become the country's first legally recognized slave-owner.) The first Thanksgiving was held—at Berkeley Plantation. And to signalize its new confidence, the colony adopted a coat of arms. On its escutcheon were quartered the arms appearing on the royal shield—those of England, Scotland, Ireland, and France—above a ringing legend. To the four realms of the Crown—"Behold, Virginia gives the fifth!"

Presumptuous it may have been on the part of a remote young settlement. Yet Virginia—which from a four-hundred-mile section of the Atlantic Coast extended westward, widening progressively, "to the South Sea"—was far vaster than the sum of all the other lands claimed by the English throne, though no one knew it. And

Charles II, thirty-one years later, was not above emblazoning his shield with Virginia's arms. But the salient circumstance was that—though 365 of the colonists were to die in an Indian attack three years later—the English had a secure toe-hold in the New World. They had come to stay, and with them they had brought an idea, quite foreign to the thinking of the Spanish, Portuguese, French, and Dutch, that would make their heirs masters of North America above the Rio Grande. (Seeking more knowledge of what led up to the kind of country I have seen in my travels, I have, as it will appear, been reading history.) Where the others had only trade and gain in view, the English came to work the land. "There were," Charles M. Andrews writes in *The Colonial Period of American History*, "no precedents for plantations, properly so called, in which homes were erected, tillage begun, domestic life cultivated, and the means wherewith to continue a separate social and economic life brought into being." But that is what the English intended.

It had seemed to me that a model tour of America should begin where the continent does, rising out of the Atlantic. And if it were to do so, where better could a beginning be made than where our investment of the continent began, at the cape on which John Smith and his company made their first landing on the way to found a settlement fifty-some miles farther on, up the James River? In that way, two beginnings could be accomplished at once—three, in fact, for in the course of these thoughts, very opportunely, I had been asked by a magazine for an article on my adopted state. If it was too late for me to repair to the Virginia shore for the start of my transcontinental excursion, I could at least do so for a finish, going backward through the past.

It is mid-April when I set out again. To me, this is the best of all times in Tidewater Virginia—by which is meant the coastal plain, through which the rivers flow at sea-level, back and forth with the tides. Not only is it a time when the most flowering trees are in bloom, but it precedes the fullness of spring, and joy is not joy without room for anticipation; over its culmination lies always the shadow of its withdrawal.

From where I live it is two hundred miles to Cape Henry, half the route lying due south to Richmond by the great Eastern trunk highway, Interstate 95. Once you leave the spreading acne of Washington's suburbs you have woods alongside most of the way; Virginia today is over three-fifths in woods. Even in winter these are green with pine, holly, and Mountain laurel. On April fifteenth they are like the forests of the Appalachians two weeks later, each tree a galaxy of little silver-green or tea-colored fairy-flares of budding foliage.

To anyone habituated to old U.S. 1, which parallels 95 a few miles or less away, the change from one to the other is like the dissolution of an embittered marriage. The frenetic discord and visual riot of commercial blight along the older highway, a zone of embattlement giving you the impression of a civilization at terrible odds with the land, has been replaced by peace, but the peace of divorcement. There are simply two worlds along the Interstate. The concrete double race-track goes its way caterwauling with the banshee chorus of the wheeled projectiles it speeds through hill and over vale. Alongside, the tranquil scenes of Nature remain apart. Where there are interconnecting crossroads, the fields and woods are being bulldozed for big new service stations or shopping-centers, and on the highway small mats of fur or feathers show where a possum or a catbird attempted a crossing and failed, but otherwise there is little communication between the two worlds.

But in the countryside along here, however, between Washington and Richmond, less perhaps than in any other part of the nation, was there always such a division of worlds. This is the hundred miles the Army of the Potomac took four blood-soaked years to gain. And there is an intimacy between the foot-soldier and the earth known to few others. The bare, dripping woods, the hot and dusty road, the stinging cold, the darkness and the moon-shadows, the texture and smell of the ground, all apprehended with senses made sharp by fear: these are the foot-soldier's hourly portion.

The war in Virginia is long past, but there is still many a window in Fredericksburg from which marching troops were looked down on in exultance or dread and which shook in its frame to the bombardment; the town changed hands seven times. The older part of Fredericksburg, where once schooners ascending the Rappahannock exchanged cargoes with covered wagons twelve feet tall, is valiantly holding out against engulfment by the present. The noises of motor traffic seem to fall on a cushion of quiet, the old houses sheltered by trees to appeal to the passer-by: "Don't forget us!" Among them the two-hundred-year-old Rising Sun, tavern and stagecoach station, once frequented by Virginia's great, brings home to you how touchingly small-scale and intimate was candlelit Colonial society, how thinly spread over the vast distances of the day.

Nowhere else in the New World is there such a cluster of major battlefields. National Military Parks, consisting largely of long, interconnecting strips, protect the century-old front lines, routes of march and scenes of collision that bring back the engagements of Fredericksburg itself, Chancellorsville, the Wilderness, and Spotsylvania Courthouse. Away from the widening environs of Fredericksburg, however, even the country outside the parks remains much as it must have been when those armies of the young from Massachusetts, New York and Pennsylvania, Texas, Alabama and South Carolina met here to kill and die in the thousands. And when you are alone under a leaden April sky, on the deserted roads that thread the parks, the silence that hangs over all, over the lush green fields, the somber pines, the bare trees coming into leaf, seems to echo to the presence of the youthful legions facing death in the full tide of life. . . . Those now shallow trenches were held by McLaws's brigades; in that tangled declivity Lee and Jackson had their last bivouac; by the overgrown ruins of the iron foundry the 25th Georgia, over-run, fought a rearguard action to the end. The forest seems to stir with troops just beyond the edge of your vision, the marching column to have cleared the ford just before you came, the line of riflemen tense and expectant, chill premonition at their hearts, to be more real than you. And their reality makes the terrible inquiry of the fallen young irresistibly insistent: *why?*

You feel you have to supply an answer, the best you can. Nothing you have read seems to help. All I can say is that suffering must be as integral a part of the life of a society as it is of the life of an individual. If the young of both sides whose lives were cut short here with no second chance did not die in vain it was because of the depth and character we gained as a people through that common ordeal. It was because the four years of that pitiless war, which saw us as a people reduced by shared anguish and tragedy to the essentials of humanity, gave America something—and, again, it may be permissible to attribute the quality of soul to a people—that is lacking in General Motors or the AFL-CIO, the kind of huge, corporate success that after Appomattox the United States set about with all alacrity to become. And perhaps it is from such fields as these, where blood was given to the earth for love of country or for an objective ideal that we derive such title to the land as we possess and such feeling as we may have that it is our home, without which I believe there is no peace of mind for a people.

It is not much of an answer to give those who did not live to realize that for which they gave their lives. On the other side of Richmond, I feel that nothing would serve but joining them in death. There in the quiet woods are the earthworks where the Confederates made their last stand before their capital. It is raining now, with an even persistence, as it was raining often enough then, when there was little to eat, the shelling merciless, the cause lost, and four years of companions slain. . . . One should come to these places alone—or should not. As one wanders on in the rain that falls in the lonely forest, the sadness—it is all so vivid—becomes overpowering. It is almost possible to believe that Nature has healed over with this growth of woods the scenes of shock and tumult as an act of mercy to the dead—or to the living. But there is no escape from the burden of guilt at being alive where so many died so much younger.

"Had trouble?" It is a man getting out of his car by his house, a brick bungalow at the edge of the park, who calls out to me. I tell him I am just walking. The expression on his pleasant, round face is of expecting more, so I repeat, "Thank you all the same." I am tempted to ask what it is like living next to this. But clearly it is nothing you think about much or you could not do it.

State Highway 5, which takes you through the haunted woods from the giant warehouses and railroad yards of Richmond's deepwater port, leads on to the early plantations of the James River and the eighteenth-century mansions of Shirley, Berkeley, and Westover, which are still in occupation, and Chippokes, a State shrine. The countryside around you is a serene one, much of it in forest, its mid-April filigree of luminous green and limpid bronze spangled with the dogwood's ivory blossoms and the redbud's raspberry-ice-cream-colored. Your gaze lingers on the broad fields when you reflect that some were in cultivation when Henry Wriothesley, Earl of Southampton, to whom in his youth Shakespeare had dedicated a "love . . . without end," was Treasurer of the Virginia Company.

At Shirley you might be at an elegant country house of Walpole's day overlooking the estuary of the Thames, of which, indeed, the estuary of the James was virtually an extension when Shirley was begun in the 1720's; ships that loaded in English ports unloaded before the front doors of the Virginia plantation houses. An English mansion of brick planted with England's ivy and England's box and furnished with the work of English cabinetmakers and English silversmiths, Shirley stands for England's ideal, which is Virginia's too, of the landed family anchored in a house proof against the centuries among ancestral fields. And Shirley, nine generations later, is still in the hands of the family that built it—a branch of the great Carter family. I am shown through it by a knowledgeable Negro woman. From her I learn that the pretty little blond boy playing at the feet of a gaunt Negro man who is waxing the floor is one of the Carters' children: the tenth generation. It was a Carter also, who, farther down the James, built a house sometimes called the most beautiful in the nation—the plantation house of Carter's Grove.

Sixty miles from Richmond, Route 5 terminates in the twenty-mile-long Colonial Parkway. This connects the shore on which British empire in the thirteen colonies began and that on which it ended, between them passing the edifice in which it reached its apogee: the strikingly handsome, brick residence, steep-pitched and ballustraded of roof, of the Governors of the Virginia Colony, in Williamsburg.

The historic heart of Warsaw, after it had been leveled by the Luftwaffe in World War II, was rebuilt stone on stone exactly as it had been—under the direction of a Communist government at a time of cruel national want. You are reminded of this extraordinary act of fidelity to the past and to the symbol of the nation's continuity by Colonial Williamsburg. The two-hundred-year-old town, restored to what it was when George Washington, Thomas Jefferson, George Mason, and George Wythe were familiars of the Raleigh Tavern, is one on which the Republic so dotes as to have made it the first point of call for kings and presidents from abroad. It is one that 20 million Americans have visited. The dream that came to possess the Reverend Dr. W. A. R. Goodwin during the long years of his pastorate in the town, when he found himself, as he said, sharing the streets at night with ghosts, has been abundantly vindicated. For this, no thanks are owing to the people's elected representatives either in Congress or in the Virginia Assembly; our legislators are not sentimentalists, like the Polish Communists. The realization of Dr. Goodwin's dream, the rescue of the village—the village where the American Republic's heartbeats were first felt—from the decay and shabby modernity into which it was sunk when he first took up his duties in Bruton Parish Church in 1902, has depended entirely on the public spirit and extraordinary means of one family, John D. Rockefeller, Jr., to whom Dr. Goodwin confided his vision in 1924, and his heirs.

The gift the Rockefellers have made the nation at a cost of $80 million is like a dolls' village magically enlarged to the scale of grown human beings. The heart opens to it straight off. One sees readily how a certain Frederick Jones of North Carolina in 1731 could have considered it "my happy fortune to have had my habitation in that quiet country where there is a great harmony and so great an understanding among all sorts and degrees of people." The harmony is voiced still in the bright clapboard houses and public buildings of soft-hued brick disposed in a friendly proximity but set apart by pampered gardens, along ample streets. That men should spend the best of themselves to give outward form to an inner sense of what is right, simply because it *is* right, goes far to redeem the race, in my judgment. Colonial Williamsburg is the creation of such scruple, such care in execution, on the part of its original artisans and, as well, of the restorers who, through years of detective work, have brought it back into being as it was, as tidy, as happily contrived in design. And among the original artisans I am thinking not only of the builders but the silversmiths, cabinet-makers, paper-makers, gunsmiths, and craftsmen of a score of other callings whose skills are being practiced once more in the village.

What brings so many visitors here? The woman at the information center, on whose open and outgoing nature the monotonous questions of the tourists seem not to weigh, replies, "When I try to pin myself down on an answer to that, I think it comes down to this, that it's the same thing that takes us back to a childhood home. That seems to be the spirit of the people who come here."

She is probably right. The hundreds wandering about the town with you appear even to have recovered a certain gift of childhood, a capacity, one might say, for contentment with the present moment and its novelty. It is how you feel yourself—along with a sense of vicarious triumph: the old town made it back! Dining is a charade, and why not? Those who dine, napkins around the neck, at the revived old inns, whom Negro waiters serve eighteenth-century dishes on Colonial-style tables by candlelight, fall in with it. Whatever brings people here, however, what they find is a town with a special appeal to an age in which the functions of society have been elaborated beyond recognition, fragmented and refragmented and dispersed over thousands of miles, so that hardly anyone can feel that he comprehends it or that his contribution to it makes a particle of difference. In Colonial Williamsburg you return to a relatively self-contained community of human dimensions, one that could be grasped, a society of familiars, almost like a family, in which anyone taken from it would be missed. The eighteenth-century capital of Virginia addresses itself to every people's nostalgia for what has been lost.

But Williamsburg's charm is not only of an irrecoverable past but also of a future we could have if we willed it. It is the charm of a community from which the two influences more responsible than any others for the denigration of the environment and of human nature in our civilization have been excluded. Private motorcars are banned from the Colonial town during daylight and blatant advertising signs even from the commercial quarter at the head of Duke of Gloucester Street, between the restored area and the building constructed for the College of William and Mary, on plans by Sir Christopher Wren, the oldest extant academic building in the country. You see how far without them one could possess one's soul not only in retreats of Nature but in towns among the stimulating and comforting numbers of one's own kind.

Williamsburg is situated about halfway down the peninsula formed by the estuaries of the York and the James. Leaving it by the Colonial Parkway to the east, you pass along the shore of the York and end among rolling green fields high above it, close to its debouchment into Chesapeake Bay. This is the battlefield of Yorktown, or most of it; erosion of the bluff above the river has removed part. The earthen redoubts from which the opposing sides fought have been reconstructed and equipped with the cannon of the day, and by means of signs artfully designed by the National Park Service you can follow the course of the three-week campaign, which saw the American forces under George Washington and the French under the Marquis de Lafayette break through the British defenses. The surrender of General Cornwallis on October 19, 1781, brought a virtual end to a war remarkable in the disparity between the great size of the theater and momentousness of the issue and the paucity of the contending troops; in this conclusive battle, Americans, French, and British each numbered only about eight thousand.

The undulating, grassy battlefield, on which there are only a few other persons, who stay close to their cars in anticipation of more rain, seems high up under a sagging, damp, gray sky. The Revolutionary War is as real to me here as it ever is, but something keeps me from responding to it as an American is supposed to. Perhaps it is the conviction that the war was a terrible misfortune with insufficient reason for it. ("Seldom have two contestants more completely misunderstood each other than the American colonists and British Crown managed to do in the ten years preceding the revolution," say Professors Nevins and Commager in their history.) Had the issue been compromised and the American colonies remained in the fold like the Canadian, to achieve their political liberties as the Canadians did, it seems likely that the carnage and destruction of the Civil War would have been avoided. Even the horrors and disastrous consequences of the two World Wars might have been, had the Central Powers in 1914 and the Axis in 1939 been confronted by a solid British-American partnership.

It would be understandable if the first impression made on you by Jamestown Festival Park were one of regret on Virginia's part for the lost ties with England. A prominent exhibit is made of the inauguration of the park by Queen Elizabeth and Prince Philip on the 350th anniversary of Jamestown's founding, and the present-day British Commonwealth is celebrated in a display quite as if Virginia still gave the fifth realm. And the State still bears, proudly enough, after all, the sobriquet bestowed on it when Charles II, in giving thanks to those who had remained loyal to his house in Cromwell's reign, singled out "my old dominion." For Virginia there is a devastating irony in its having given the independence movement and the young Republic a set of leaders unsurpassed in all history in political genius, including the one man able to carry the Revolution to success, and thus having prepared the doom of the South, which its contribution of another set of leaders, equally unsurpassed in military genius, could not avert. Indeed, the South as a whole has been vitiated by confusion as to what it is ever since the triumph at Appomattox of principles that but for it would never have prevailed at Yorktown.

What the causes of the American Revolution may come down to is that nothing, probably, no form of partnership centered on London, could have contained the expansive, even explosive, force of the American enterprise. In this there was no keener or more far-sighted believer than George Washington himself, aristocratic Virginia planter though he was. Washington's gaze was turned west-ward from the age of fifteen, when he helped survey the upper part of Lord Fairfax's six-million-acre grant at the headwaters of the Potomac. An investor, like Ben Franklin, in western lands, the backer of two canals to promote trade with the upper Ohio, Wash-ington it was too, with his astonishing and unique grasp of the country's potential, who inspired the conception of a federal capital so grand it would take the nation a hundred years to live up to it.

But the belief in America as a country with a special destiny went a long way back. In April 1622, just a year after Plymouth colony had come through its first, ghastly winter, when about half the 145 who had landed were carried off by sickness, the Reverend Dr. Patrick Copland declared in a sermon that "No man can justly say that this country is not capable . . . of all good things that the most opulent part of Christendom do afford, neither are we hope-less that this country may also yield things of better value than any of these." This was the land that looms before us, harsh and drear, in Governor Bradford's sharp and lofty evocation of the dis-embarkation on Cape Cod: "For summer being done, all things stand upon them with a weatherbeaten face; and the whole country, full of woods and thickets, represented a wild and savage hue." Less than eighteen months later this wilderness was seen as prom-ising things of better value than the most opulent part of Christen-dom afforded! But for the start of the vision you have to go back farther still.

Jamestown's site lies at the western end of the Colonial Parkway, which skirts the James at water's edge as it does the York along its eastern portion. You might think that the level land lay spent from the alarms and excursions of history to which it has resounded and now wished only to repose for a century or two beneath the warm southern sun, in the shadow of its woods, half-mesmerized by the vacancy of the plains of water—inland arms of the sea—that form the peninsula. On crossing the causeway to Jamestown Island you have the option—not to be neglected—of taking a five-mile loop road around the island's perimeter, through forest in which the Tidewater evergreens flourish—Loblolly pine, Redbay, Sand-myrtle, holly, and cat-brier—and by reed-grown bays of the estuary. Since this is a National Park you are privileged to gaze upon the forest with the eye of a future when (assuming all goes well) it will have regained the greatness in which the first white men beheld it.

Before crossing to the island, however, it is well to turn off for Jamestown Festival Park. In the pavilion here opened by Queen Elizabeth are excellent exhibits illuminating the colony's background, some with life-like figures of the principals of the drama in their proper settings. Beyond the building is a full-sized reproduction of the original Jamestown, the triangular stockade enclosing the rough-hewn little church and a score of crude huts thatch-roofed with reeds from the inlets; even a few inhabitants are provided in the form of living young men in costume to bring the fort to life, which they do with evident success for the girl tourists. At the shore, lined up at a pier, are sailing replicas of little *Susan Constant,* littler *Goodspeed,* and, littlest, *Discovery,* the vessels that brought the first settlers to the colony—105 of the 144 who had departed from England. It is hard to believe that the small, gaudily painted vessels, which surely would rock like hobby-horses on the most ordinary seas, could have been taken seriously by prospective trans-Atlantic voyagers, least of all by such a number as in fact crowded into them. The death toll says enough of the kind of passage it must have been, with holds and decks swarming with human cargo. And what waited behind Virginia's inscrutable capes was as bad and worse.

The remains of Jamestown lie a mile beyond Festival Park. Here, in a National Parks museum, are additional displays done with admirable verisimilitude, and many artifacts of the early settlement. The land on which the first stockade stood has been engulfed by the James River, however, and nothing survives of the seventeenth-century Colonial capital but the ivy-covered belltower of the church of 1639, a graveyard, and some foundations. Yet this is where the America we know began; you can see your companions of the paths inviting this realization to sink in, as you are doing. Here, beside the broad and tranquil estuary, was where the dreadfully unpropitious start was made.

Reading of the hardships of Jamestown's founders, one wonders how they could have wanted so for food in a land abounding with game, by waters later to be famous for their fishing, floored by beds of oysters for which gourmets would one day outbid one another. But they had come not to learn from the New World or to adapt themselves to it, but to bend it to their will. The adjusting was to be all on the other side. Because the land was what it was and not what it should have been by their lights, they disdained its de-

mands. Sloth and dissension all but worked the settlement's undoing. Half the company were described as gentlemen and only
twelve as laborers. They had come for quick riches. More gentlemen arrived on the next shipment—and goldsmiths. Captain Smith,
one of the few with an appreciation of what they were up against,
spoke out bitterly: "There was now no talk, no hope, no work, but
dig gold, wash gold, refine gold, load gold." This infatuation, which
was all it was, since what looked like gold was not, was very nearly
fatal.

The settlers had a lesson to learn, a lesson Americans have had
repeatedly to be taught and may never have stood more in need of
than today. The third winter was well calculated to drive it home—
the wisdom, that is, of working with and not against, or ignoring,
the character of the land. The Starving Time, as it was called,
followed Smith's return to England for treatment of powder-burns.
It saw the leaderless settlement fall into disorder, work neglected,
and epidemics kill the colonists at the rate of two or three a day—
among other reasons because Jamestown had unwisely been located
on a low-lying, damp and unhealthful peninsula (as the island was
then). Houses and even the logs of the stockade were burned for
fuel and the famished inhabitants, venturing forth to gather acorns
and dig for roots, "dealt mortal wounds with clubs and arrows" by
the Indians, whom some even went to beg of. Of the 490 colonists
in September 1609, 430 died within the next six months. The
abandonment of the colony by the 60 survivors was forestalled by
the arrival of a relief expedition, but even a year later the governor
was writing, "Everie man allmost laments himself of being here."
Seeing little hope of bringing the colony through with "sutch dis-
eased and crased bodies," he expressed the wish that the king would
empty the jails of prisoners awaiting execution and send them to
Virginia, since these at least might be glad "to make this their new
countrie." It would not be long before the king was acting on this
advice, and with a vengeance.

But Jamestown was not all vain fortune-seeking, suicidal indo-
lence or despondency. In 1610 another kind of voice had spoken up
from the colony, the kind with which Dr. Copland would speak
twelve years later at Plymouth. Under the heading *Newes from
Virginia,* those at home were urged to "Be not dismayed at all" and
reassured by the cry:

> Let England knowe our willingness,
> For that our worke is good;
> *Wee hope to plant a nation,*
> *Where none before hath stood.*

A nation, no less! Under the very brow of the wilderness that had just proved its terrors! Whence did such a spirit come?

For that, I found, you must go back even beyond Jamestown.

But I have traveled enough for one day. Stopping the bus by a secluded stretch of woods—easier than pulling all the shades down —I change into clothes less bedraggled than those I have worn through the rain and betake myself back to Williamsburg for a dinner of Brunswick stew in the modest, white-clapboard house occupied by the tavern originally opened by Josiah Chowning in 1766. After that, I have the good luck to find a campground a few miles up the highway, a large field surrounded by woods, empty but for me.

It is still gray and drizzly in the morning when I join the early traffic bearing down on Newport News and Hampton, which occupy the end of the York-James peninsula. From Old Point Comfort, at its tip, a long bridge-with-tunnel crosses the mouth of the James to Norfolk. From this the view to the right is one of the world's great natural harbors and the nation's third busiest—Hampton Roads. Bordering the Roads—actually the lower James—are the Norfolk Naval Base (home port of the Atlantic Fleet) and the huge ship-yards of Newport News and of briny, historic Portsmouth. It was from the latter that there steamed the first iron-clad, *C.S.S. Virginia* (the sunken *Merrimac* refloated and rebuilt), on the afternoon of March 8, 1862, to dispose of five Union warships and render every navy in the world obsolete by sundown—a remarkable twist for the agricultural South to have given history. An aircraft carrier reposes at her berth, the size of part of the city, and several other warships, low and rakish, seem to be straining with belligerent zeal at their moorings. The tooting of lesser craft, the rattle and rumble of dock-side machinery, the smell of a harbor on that damp, drab morning give one's thoughts a new direction; one is almost on shipboard.

And in less than an hour, even by the slow pace of Norfolk's morning traffic, with a turn onto the Chesapeake Bay Bridge-Tun-nel you *are* virtually at sea. Even in fair weather you commit your-self to the bridge, which spans the mouth of the bay, with no other shore in sight and the open Atlantic to your east; it is a startling and exciting experience. Today, neither shore is visible the entire way, going and coming, for a fog lies on the water, adding to the strangeness of the scene. Between the infrequent cars I am alone with a hundred yards of concrete roadway over a vaguely defined disk of restless, glaucous waters. An occasional gull appears out of the mist and vanishes back into it, and several times a fog-horn blares or a bell tolls disconsolately. Twice the highway dips down to a narrow, man-made island of rocks and then, astonishingly, into the mouth of a tunnel, which takes you under a shipping channel. Near the middle, the bridge is widened into a plaza with a restaurant in the center; here you may savor the oddity of your situation and, in fair weather, watch the ships go by. Extending out from it is a fishing-pier from which you may drop a line without being cut off from the piped lounge-music that more and more accompanies Americans (a name I am not sure our forefathers would consider we deserved) on their daily rounds; it comes out of speakers on the lamp-poles. After 17.5 miles, up under the bridge comes the sandy, partly shrub-grown tip of the Great Peninsula, which stands between Chesapeake Bay and the ocean. This is Cape Charles, but the town of that name is ten miles farther up the bay side, beyond the terminus of the bygone Norfolk ferries. It proves to resemble a late nineteenth-century seaside resort, with tidy, substantial houses, each with its greenery, lining wide streets and a boardwalk along the beach—even a gazebo overlooking the bay. It is all singularly quiet. A postman whom I intercept says that the replacement of the ferries by the bridge and the decline in rail traffic have hit the town hard, leaving many of the houses unoccupied.

The bay this morning is still fogbound. But no vista of that unique body of water in even the clearest weather, only days of exploration, can give an idea of its properties. An inland sea two hundred miles long and up to forty wide, it has 5,600 miles of intricately carved shoreline, most of it in beaches, marshes, leafy coves and promontories, and little harbors at the end of village streets, with woods in the background, and fields where gulls follow the plow. A captive salient of the Atlantic taking ocean-going ships up its branches to Richmond, Fredericksburg, Washington, and Baltimore, it is a world in itself for the boatman, a major fishing-ground, home of the nation's last commercial sailing fleet—the oystermen—and winter resort of a still fairly numerous remnant of the ducks, geese, and swans that William Strachey in 1612 found so abundant that "I dare avow it no country in the world may have more." Such, in part, is Chesapeake Bay.

To produce it, some rather special geology was required. The coastal plain, of which it is an indenture, was built up on the ocean floor of sediments washed down from the Appalachians and Piedmont during a period of 80 million years or longer. After the Miocene epoch, which ended some 12 million years ago, it was raised above the surface and thereafter traversed by the rivers that had created it. Of these, the greatest was one having as tributaries the Susquehanna, Patuxent, Potomac, Rappahannock, York, James, and lesser rivers coming in from the east. During the ice-ages, when for tens of thousands of years at a time the diminished ocean lay far back from where it does now and the "fall" of the rivers was increased, the Chesapeake River (if we may call it that) and its tributaries scoured deeper and wider beds in the soft rock of the coastal plain. These, as the ice-sheets melted, the ocean invaded, converting them into a many-pronged bay. Delaware Bay had a comparable origin (Mobile and San Francisco Bays being also flooded river-valleys) and doubtless there would be others to the north were it not that where the ice-sheet reposed the continental bedrock was so depressed beneath its weight that the entire coastal plain north of New York City was inundated by the returning sea.

Crossing the peninsula from Cape Charles, past flat, newly plowed fields of winter-chilled earth steaming in the damp, mild air, I make for the village of Oyster, simply on the strength of its name. I should have hated to miss it. A collection of low houses, small packing-plants and piles of oyster-shells around an inlet filled with little white boats, it is what you might expect on Cape Cod, if the Cape had been overlooked by vacationers. It is strictly a working little port, looking out on one of the islands of sand and marsh that protect this stretch of coast from the seas. A general store and boat-chandler's, I suppose you could call it, at the water's edge has a pier at which half a dozen open craft, piled with wire crab-pots and piloted by hale-looking and talkative fishermen, are awaiting their turn at a gasoline pump. In the little café occupying part of the store, an equal number of their fellows are rallying one another with bursts of horseplay. The sturdily built woman with clear gray eyes behind the counter, who serves me coffee and a doughnut, speaks out with cheerful, full-voiced self-sufficiency and would be a match for any of them, I'd wager. I try not to stare, but unsuccessfully, so taken am I by these booted outdoorsmen, who have been plying the waters for crabs, oysters, clams, and mackerel for two or three hundred years on this side of the ocean and maybe far longer for the bounty of the sea back in England. As untouched by the malaise of our times as by the television set performing off to the side and unable to make itself heard above the boisterous exchanges, they have the robustness that comes from contending with the elements and from nothing else.

There is not much farther to go.

Tourists Florida-bound by the Great Peninsula route may find oleanders at Cape Charles and, along the southern shore of the bay, across the bridge, Live oaks, stunted and with foliage sheered back by the spume-laden winds; the two are outposts of the Deep South. About eight miles east of the end of the bridge, at the mouth of the bay, is Cape Henry. This is where the adventurers of 1607 first landed. The wooden cross they erected at the spot is commemorated by one of stone among the dunes, its base encircled by Virginia creeper, like the great seal of the State. Being well inside a military reservation, it is not easy to find, however.

For six or seven miles to the south, along broad avenues, stretches the resort city of Virginia Beach. But never mind it; at the end of the cross-streets is the beach, and beyond, clear of fog, once again the ocean, glittering, in all its extent, opening your mind with a jolt to the measure of its illimitable waters. The ocean, and nothing but the heaving, falling waves to Europe and Africa. . . . It is some time before I can take myself away. What a tribute to the sea it is, I think, that this procession of expensive hotels and motels—neither term quite right for these glass-walled, balconied, many-colored temples of luxury—interspersed with lodging-houses of a more reserved and less monied time should have formed along here that the affluent may confront the unappeasable wastes before which, of all that is on earth, property and advantage pale to inconsequence. Perhaps all of us livers of soft lives are like those kings of old who among all the sycophants resorted to one they could count on for the truth. . . . And perhaps not, too. Something in the ocean, possibly its own ever-surging vitality, brings out what is vital in us. There is more vigor in the faces of the other strollers on the concrete promenade than you would find in those of pedestrians on a city street.

Thirteen miles after the start of Virginia Beach, a National Wildlife Refuge begins, ending the spread of cottages. (A State park is soon to extend from the Refuge to the North Carolina line.) From here on you have before you open beach backed by dunes and, at a distance behind them, the waters of Back Bay. This is the head of another inland sea, almost comparable in size to Chesapeake Bay, formed principally of Currituck, Albemarle, and Pimlico Sounds. The strand here, in other words, marks the beginning, fifteen miles inside Virginia, of the North Carolina Banks, that chain of long, narrow sand-islands, difficult to account for, that extends for 170 miles and at Cape Hatteras stands 25 miles out at sea.

Wildlife refuge or not, a ramp opens the beach to automobiles. Outboard motors, snowmobiles, trailcycles, dune-buggies, and now all-terrain vehicles: the ordinary American cannot be without his motorized conveyance; it perfectly suits his craving for movement combined with mental and physical passivity. On the beach, the noise of the accursed motorcar coming up behind you is muffled by the rush and hiss of the surf so that it is almost on you before you are aware of it. I am passed by several as I walk on, and well up ahead of me are two others drawn up together with a group of human figures around them. . . . But what is this? Oh joy! They are both sunk and immobilized in the soft sand! Great is Zeus Pater! The situation sorts itself out into an off-white Corvair with a complement of three young men and a gray Jeep in which two girls have evidently attempted their rescue. The Jeep has stalled and its battery is dead. It is given to personable young women— these two are bare-legged and clad in short, loose dresses known, I believe, as shifts—to be appealing. Feeling a traitor to my better self, I come forward with suggestions about the Jeep's extrication and a reasonably strong back, with the result that after considerable shoveling we get it out onto the hard-packed sand and, by dint of energetic shoving, its motor running again. But the Corvair I pronounce hopeless without a towing-truck and leave it, regretting only its being evidently beyond the ocean's reach.

Fifty miles to the south, just inside the Banks, is a long, naturally forested island given the name Roanoke by the Indians. This was the site of the most ambitious early English attempts to colonize the New World, instigated by Sir Walter Raleigh. In 1585, a hundred-odd men were settled on the island by Raleigh's cousin, Sir Richard Grenville; their hardships were such that Sir Francis Drake, calling at the island the next spring on his way home from a foray in the West Indies, acceded to their entreaties and took them back to England. Later that year Grenville landed another fifteen men on the island; these were never seen again. The following year, 1587, Raleigh sent three more ships to Roanoke with 150 settlers, including 17 women and 9 children. Reinforcement and resupply of the colony was delayed for four years, initially by the exigencies of defense against the Spanish Armada, and when relief came it was only to be confronted by an empty fort and the mystery of a lost colony on which no light has ever been thrown.

It was not a beginning to give heart to the colonizers; twenty years were to elapse between the last attempt to settle Roanoke and the precarious establishment of Jamestown. Yet belief in America never died. In 1585, returning from the first expedition to Roanoke, Richard Lane called it "the goodliest and most pleasing Territorie in the World, for the Continent is of a huge and unknown greatness." In 1606, Michael Drayton rallied the spirits of his countrymen for the cause with his *Ode to the Virginia Voyage:*

> And cheerfully at sea,
> Success you still intice,
>   To get the pearl and gold,
> *And ours to hold,*
>   VIRGINIA
> Earth's only Paradise, . . .

Surely it was extraordinary, this conviction that North America, of which the English knew next to nothing, had a promise beyond that of any other land. How was such a blind faith to be accounted for? In a passage early in *The Growth of the American Republic,* by Samuel Eliot Morison and Henry Steele Commager, I felt I had my answer and also that illumination of the genesis of the American enterprise I had unconsciously been seeking since returning from the West. Here it is:

The English were past discouragement. For, underlying all their efforts, the earlier failures as well as later successes, was a powerful drive which thrust them forward no matter what happened; an ideal motive similar to the terrific missionary fervor of the Spanish. This daimon of the English was a burning desire to found a new England, a new society, in which all the best of the past would be conserved, but where life would have a different and better quality from anything then conceivable in Europe. . . . The Utopian ideal for America which was in the mind of every important group of English pioneers from Massachusetts to Georgia, takes off from this *Utopia* of Sir Thomas More, first printed in 1516.

The ideal state envisioned by that Man for All Seasons occupies an island in the New World isolated from aggressive neighbors behind a channel dug by its founder, the fabled King Utopus. It is "full of people, governed by good and wholesome laws." An elected council decides on matters of consequence to the island and chooses a prince to reign over all, while each group of thirty families has its own head, elected annually. The towns, separated by large rural areas, are no more than a day's walk apart. Exceptionally gifted persons are trained for an academy of learning. All others work six hours a day—no more—at a trade or craft, except that each must do a two-year stint on a cooperative farm outside his city. However, "often it chanceth that a handicraftsman doth so earnestly bestow his vacant and spare hours in learning, and through diligence so profiteth therein, that he is taken from his handy occupation, and promoted to the company of the learned." Labor is lightened by oxen for the heavy work and technology has advanced to incubators for raising chickens. The Utopians share alike in the fruits of production, none desiring more than his neighbors. To ensure contempt for ostentation, jewels are given to children to play with, gold and silver used for chains for criminals, who are employed as slaves instead of being put to death, as they were by Sir Thomas More's contemporaries. Young and old together, except children under five, dine by choice in great halls, all joining in refreshing conversation and afterward listening to debates and music. Education is compulsory and extended by evening lectures for adults, for great store is set by "free liberty of the mind, and the garnishing the same." Along the "very commodious and handsome streets," twenty feet wide, are houses of "fair and gorgeous building," fireproof, well supplied with windows and provided with gardens, which the Utopians cultivate for pleasure, preferring such labors to dicing and gambling. In each quarter of the city are commodious hospitals in which patients are tended free of charge. Because the family is the basic unit of society, its welfare is a concern of the state. While war is regarded "as a thing very beastly," there is compulsory military training for both sexes, and "engines for war they devise and invent wonders wittily." The Utopians work to enrich the state so that it will have the means of obtaining immunity from attack, and such wars as they have fought have been in defense of friendly states standing between them and aggressive tyrants. They are a religious people but enjoy a freedom of worship quite unknown in Catholic England when More was writing. Many are Christians, many practice other forms of religion. Atheism is outlawed and so is militant sectarianism, the Utopians judging it "extreme madness to follow sharp and painful virtue, and . . . banish the pleasure of life." Their ideal is "life ordered according to nature."

More's beguiling vision evokes for Morison and Commager "the American dream."

One can certainly see the American dream *in* it—no less the Communist dream. And if Communists, where they have achieved national power, have travestied the *Utopia* by expanding the role of the commune out of all conscience at the expense of that of the individual, we have betrayed it by making the individual the be-all and end-all and largely ignoring the communal character Utopia was to have had.

If one thinks of the United States and the Soviet Union as Utopias-Aspirant, one may perhaps better understand them. Neither is a nation, which is a family of people. There is no name for the nationality of their citizens because they do not constitute a nationality. It was not intended that they should. The United States and the Soviet Union started as political experiments—lessons for mankind, if you like—and so they remain. Rather than nations, they are open-ended political organizations susceptible of indefinite extension. The Soviet Union could as well incorporate Mongolia and Iran as not, Mexico be as readily added to the United States as Hawaii and Puerto Rico have been.

Both countries are in fact collections of nationalities. The United States was to have proved itself to be a melting-pot, but the Sioux writer Vine Deloria, Jr. is probably justified in pronouncing the theory dead, killed by the realization of the minorities that for them "integration was group suicide in the truest sense of the word." We can hardly expect the grandson of Italian immigrants to feel closer to Thomas Jefferson and Herman Melville than to Giuseppe Garibaldi and Giuseppe Verdi, a Jew because he is American to feel no

different because of the ancient history of his people and their long
endurance and cohesion under alien tyrannies, a Navajo to accept
among his heroes men distinguished for killing Indians, a Negro
to feel his past adequately dealt with in histories of Southern slave-
holders and Yankee traffickers in Africans. (I myself should have
to be more liberated from my origins than I am not to feel stirred
by the victory of Lee and Jackson at Chancellorsville or not to have
a special regard for England.) And the cultural cross-fertilization we
like to think of is as likely to prove cross-sterilization. The only
common denominator of diverse traditions is no tradition.

To feel a need for reassurance as to one's roots—one's moorings—
seems to me very natural. And I fear there is much force in Enoch
Powell's charge that "All the wealth, all the success, all the accumu-
lation of treasure and learning in the United States have not availed
to make it metropolitan. . . . It is still a colony, planted in a
strange land where it did not grow." We are all—all but the Indians
—still in a sense colonists and still without a feeling of identity with
the land. "Modern American civilization did not evolve organically
out of this continent's soil or historical past," as René Dubos has
observed, but from "conquest, the enemy being Nature itself"—
the continent. The fatherland, the motherland: would it ever occur
to us to speak of the United States as such?

Insecurely rooted, if rooted at all, in the land they inhabit, heterogeneous, largely without a family feeling as Americans, the peoples
of our country have yet to a remarkable degree been able to act
as a united nation. What has given the United States its unity has
been the force of an idea. To the American version of the Utopian
ideal every significant political group in the country and every
ethnic group but one has subscribed—and that one, the Indians, is
coming around to it, it appears. The Negroes were converts long
before they had much chance to pursue it, and as for the rest of us,
it was what brought us here to begin with. The American dream of
individual freedom, political equality, social justice, universal education and opportunity for advancement, and continuous progress
in the material betterment of all has been a potent vision indeed.
The fulfillment of the dream from the landing on Roanoke to the
landing on the moon is matched by few epics in human history. And
the magnetism of the vision has by no means worked on us alone.
What we have gained for ourselves by its inspiration is what the
overwhelming preponderance of mankind wants for itself. In free

competition with the Communist version of Utopia ours has almost everywhere prevailed. If not the most incendiary idea ever loosed on mankind, no other has ever demonstrated an appeal at once so powerful and so nearly universal.

But for us the American dream has about run out. That, as I see it, is the meaning of the evidently deepening crisis in American civilization. We have never, to my knowledge, been more confused as to what we are about or more ridden by anxiety and never since the Civil War been more racked by dissension. The dream is running out, for one thing, because we have largely attained it. It is true that substantial pockets of poverty remain among us as do some denials of full and fair opportunities for Negroes, Indians, and Chicanos. But anyone who believes that all will be well with us when anyone willing to exert himself sufficiently can win a 4-bedrm, Split or Colonial w/firepl, gas air cond., deluxe kit and fam. rm. on lge. corner lot, 5 mins from Beltway and lge. shop. cent. with color television, two late-model automobiles in the carport, and a cottage at the beach is, I think, misjudging what is amiss with us. Indeed, in the face of the enormous improvement in the lot of the deprived minorities in recent years and of the fact that they are far better off than five-sixths of the human race and have every expectation of continuing to do better, the suspicion arises that the emotion-charged issue idealists have made of their plight is a device for avoiding recognition of the crucial flaw in the vision that has given us national unity and direction and an unheard-of abundance of goods. It is a flaw none of us is eager to acknowledge.

The preoccupation of the American dream with the deserts of the individual to an extent that would have shocked Sir Thomas More, which has been its strength, is also its weakness. The bounty of the earth, the nation, and even God himself has no higher function in our eyes, one would suppose, than to serve the individual and promote his individual satisfactions. This view has made us a nation of go-getters and has put the national patrimony pretty much at the disposal of the acquisitive—to be gone at and got. The enterprising, from whom our manifold material blessings flow, but largely as the mere by-product of their profit-seeking, have been accorded the supreme sanction; the English Puritan divines, frowning on idleness and eschewing mysticism, Professors Morison and Commager tell us, "taught that a good businessman served God quite as well as a good clergyman, provided he were honest," and the teaching fell on receptive ground.

All power to the individual: that has been our doctrine, and the result has been a gross national product unmatched in the world and a continent ravaged with a dispatch unmatched in history. While continuing to exploit our natural riches with inexhaustible drive, our entrepreneurs have with increasing vigor been exploiting us, the market for their product. From sea to shining sea we are at the mercy of a commercialism that appalls us with its aggressiveness and vulgarity, its denigration of all but the most debased and trivial standards. Whether we can take much more abuse of our senses and disintegrative violence to our inner order, I do not pretend to know; the nihilistic direction the arts have taken is sufficient warning of the direction of our civilization. It is evident, however, that our homeland cannot stand forever the pillaging it takes at our hands, the medium of our existence much more prostitution. In the past few years it has become plain to all that civilized man's mounting requirements of the earth threaten his undoing. For this the United States must bear a heavy responsibility both in the example it has set and in its own demands on the common environment; it consumes forty percent of the raw materials taken from the earth and produces probably an equivalent proportion of the pollutants visited upon it.

And what are the rewards of our costly triumphs? A material abundance and an intoxicating mobility, yes; but have these seen us achieve a sense of fulfillment and our hearts fill with joy? Henry Fairlee's judgment that we must be the unhappiest people in the world does not seem to me far-fetched; and I am impressed by the reason he finds for it: "The distemper of America is a daily strain which sets men against men, and each man against himself; the virus which causes this distemper is the pressure to achieve, the achievement calculated in terms of money; the system in which this virus is bred is capitalism"—the economic expression of individualism.

That is the price we pay for making our national life a free-for-all in which we can feel our existences justified only as we win success—wealth or acclaim. But the cost—on top of the degradation of our environment—does not stop there.

If you would render a child's life empty, give him everything he wants; and if you would deprive the individual's life of meaning, tell him that it is all that has meaning. If life has no point beyond what I can get out of it and what other human beings, essentially like me, can get out of it, I am not going to be reconciled to my lot or sustained when what I am getting out of it is not very much—which is bound to be a good deal of the time—and when I see extinction as the end of it all. A substantial portion of Americans, admittedly, profess a belief in an after-life, but probably most, even of these, look for a justification of life in the here and now. In the roll of Other-Worldly societies ours would hardly lead all the rest; and one guided less by the Christian injunction to "Lay not up for yourselves treasures upon earth" would be difficult to imagine. We make much of the ideal of service to others, and rightly so, for a noble and civilizing ideal it is, and we may take great credit to ourselves that we are on the whole a humane people. But if the ultimate purpose is for everyone to advance the cause of others intrinsically no different from himself, we have a dispensation perilously close to everyone's taking in everyone else's washing. In the end we cannot be satisfied with that.

If we are to have the strength life requires of us, we have to see something beyond the mere collection of highly imperfect specimens of our kind that meets the eye. We have to feel that our brief and paltry existences are redeemed and given meaning by their association with that which transcends them in significance and duration. We need to be identified with something greater than we are. Traditionally, that something has been the larger organism of the community or society, which has its own being and personality, its honor and its glory, and which is enduring far beyond the brevity of individual lives, so that the more at one with it we are, the more we share its consciousness, and the more we can contribute to it, the more we partake of its continuity.

There has been another something, too, and that is an idea that possesses society, expressing society's view of what life is about, giving it a structure, a sense of purpose, and a discipline, and inspiring its arts. Moreover, the general acceptance of this idea, or body of myth, in itself increases the cohesion of society and its vitality and consequently also the value to its members of the sense of belonging. But to this rule there has been one exception: the idea that has animated our own society. The American idea, the American dream, by thrusting the individual to the center of the stage, by inciting to individual self-awareness and self-centeredness and by ever increasing the individual's geographical and social mobility, as by dispersing the city, has atomized society. Charles A. Reich is surely warranted in calling the United States a great anti-community.

It is an anti-society and as such an anti-culture. That is why the American dream, to which other peoples seem helplessly susceptible, has become a menace to mankind. Unless the expansion of Americanism can be arrested, every culture, given time, will succumb, and we shall end with a universal and uniform non-culture of vast airports, huge, cubistical, glass-walled building-warrens, super-shopping-centers, cities—the communities heretofore inseparable from civilization—destroyed by the motorcar, the countryside given over to multi-lane expressways, the rootless population seeking in sensation or opiates what is missing from life. Because almost anything would seem preferable, I feel not dismayed but relieved, with Vine Deloria, Jr., that the great discovery of the civil-rights movement was, as he puts it, "that blacks continued to be black, even though the legislation promised that they would be the same as whites." If the growth of the great national non-culture can be combated only by sub-national true cultures, then, I say, by all means let us have them.

We Americans have always been prone to assure ourselves that what is best for the individual is best for society. This is no more necessarily true than that what is best for the individual is best for the species. Without individuals the species would not exist, of course, but every species has achieved its evolution, man not excepted, through the ruthless elimination of individuals impeding that evolution. We recognize readily enough in war that society's vital interests may require the unreckoning sacrifice of individual lives, but for the rest it goes thoroughly against our grain to acknowledge how far the ultimate good may depend on the subordination of individual interests to those of the whole.

Writing of the building of the wonderful cathedral at Chartres, Sir Kenneth Clark recalls in *Civilisation* that "In the year 1144, they say, when the towers seemed to be rising as if by magic, the faithful harnessed themselves to the carts which were bringing stone, and dragged them from the quarry to the cathedral. The enthusiasm spread throughout France. Men and women came from far away carrying heavy burdens of provisions for the workmen— wine, oil, corn. Amongst them were lords and ladies, pulling carts with the rest. There was perfect discipline, and a most profound silence and each man forgave his enemies." Had the participants in the great work devoted themselves each to the improvement of his dwelling, or all together to public housing, the sum of physical comforts in that comfortless age would surely have been increased far more. But would as much have been done for the lives of those who took part as by this soaring edifice and the witness it gives "of dedication to a great civilising ideal"?

And it has been the same with every great cultural creation, we may be sure: the Parthenon, the temples of the Forbidden City, the Shwe Dagon Pagoda, the Potala, the Taj Mahal, the Louvre, Saint Peter's, Saint Paul's. Every one of them was purchased by the sacrifice, willing or unwilling, of the population's physical comforts, and each elevated and gave focus to society and to the individual lives of which society is woven. In each case the tangible rewards accorded to men were curtailed in order that the stature of Man might be enhanced. What can be done for one tends always to limit what can be done for the other. *"A mesure que l'humanité se perfectionne, l'homme se dégrade":* the sum of Gustave Flaubert's convictions "is in this chilling sentence," Lewis Galantiere writes in the *New York Times Book Review,* "of which a feeble translation would be: 'The more humanity advances, the more man is degraded.' "

There was a saying when men shipped before the mast and had to climb on swaying spars in gales to take in canvas, and it strikes me as most apposite: "One hand for the ship, one for yourself." I think it an evil when men are required to give society the use of one hand and four-fifths that of the other, but the penalties of an equal but opposite imbalance are only too plain in the pass to which our country has been brought. It is one at which an intelligent and respected critic, Brooks Atkinson, can declare that "Life could not be more ugly or futile than it is in America at the moment." The point is that it is bound to be to the degree that self-gratification is the ultimate aim and the means are available to achieve it.

We have come close enough to a common material abundance to perceive that it does not supply the answer to the needs of the human spirit. On top of that, we can see that by pursuing it we have wasted and debased the earth on which we depend for physical and spiritual sustenance. The national purpose has been found critically wanting, and we have no other. At the same time, we are without a deeply rooted and well-knit society through being part of which we should have a sense of a place in the world and of counting for something not wholly limited by the terms of our mortality; we lack the communal bonds that are the traditional support of morale. Probably among no other peoples is there such loneliness as among Americans, and most of all among older Americans, whose world has been left behind by the pace of change. Society, like our physical environment, has been a casualty of the drive for the American dream. And what makes our situation perilous as well as painful is that only a strong society with a commanding voice would seem to be able to stay us in our ravagement of that environment and preserve us from the fate we are preparing for ourselves.

Public concern has, to be sure, been aroused. Certain measures of conservation are being taken and more will be. More energetic actions against pollution may be anticipated. But what is called for is almost a reversal of the current of our national character; and that, to say the least, is not in prospect. While "here and there, the gopsel is being questioned," as Colman McCarthy expresses it in *The Washington Post,* "America is in no danger of committing heresy against its sacred doctrine of maximum production and maximum consumption."

This doctrine is given precise expression. It calls for a rate of economic growth of not less than four percent a year in dollars of constant value. "At such a rate of increase, the Gross National Product (GNP) would double nearly six times a century," Rufus E. Miles points out. "In two centuries the United States would have a GNP of more than $2,500 trillion—over 2,500 times (in non-inflated dollars) our present GNP. Virtually everybody would be a millionaire." What that would do to the earth may be imagined. Writing in 1970, Edwin L. Dale, Jr., an economist with *The New York Times,* observed that "the real output of goods and services in the United States has grown as much since 1950 as it grew in the entire period from the landing of the Pilgrims in 1620"; such is the meaning of the law of compound interest. The prospect "of an annual rate of real growth of about 4 percent, compounded," he declared, "is terrifying." But the rate is holy dogma. And we are nearly all implicated; all are hungry for that continuing betterment in circumstances that only unslackening economic growth can supply, and there are more of us all the time.

To deflect us from our course would take an idea as potent as the American dream has been. Men have shown that they can be lifted out of themselves by a vision of a redeeming order to which they may aspire, for which they may toil and sacrifice and which will justify their toil and sacrifice. The American dream was itself just such a vision, and it was impelling as much because of as in spite of the fact that its realization lay beyond the lifetimes of those who dreamed it, in a world of the future. "The pursuit of a remote and ideal object which captivates the imagination by its splendor and the reason by its simplicity," Lord Acton wrote, "evokes an energy which would not be inspired by a rational, possible end, limited by many antagonistic claims, and confined to what is reasonable, practicable and just."

It is in the pursuit of such an ideal that society finds cohesion and unity and the conviction to make the demands of its members that are going to have to be made of us if we are to be saved. These will be stringent demands indeed. For: "An element in man's nature has become swollen out of all proportion; and there is no harmony within him," as E. J. Mishan of the London School of Economics writes. "Greed pulses through our psyche as naturally as blood through our veins. Whether it is the public man for office, the private man for money, the scientist for status, the hippie for pleasure [or, he might have added, the parent for multiple offspring], our greed is unbridled, and we push on ruthlessly in quest of gratification." We think this is freedom. In fact it is bondage. Saint Exupéry expressed the exact truth when he exclaimed, "No man can draw a free breath who does not share with other men a common and disinterested ideal. Life has taught us that love does not consist in gazing at each other but in looking outward together in the same direction. There is no comradeship except through union in the same high effort."

As I come now to the point I recognize I have had in mind on every page of this recital, my voice almost fails; so it is quite likely to happen that on venturing out upon a stage the presumption of which one suddenly perceives oneself guilty saps one's confidence in one's message. Yet I believe it worth offering. It is this: that if I were granted a wish for the American people it would be for them truly to discover the continent they have made theirs, to see it fully as the work of almighty creation it is, with a comprehension of all that has gone into it in four billion years. In doing so they would see that preserving its noble features, its beauty in the variety of forms, great and small, in which it shines forth, and its procreative powers, husbanding, cherishing, and cultivating it, and in the work of their own hands creating to match, so to speak, is a mission to command the best that is in them.

When, in the late Middle Ages and Renaissance, Italy held the position of the United States today as the wealthiest country in the world, says Bertrand de Jouvenel of the University of Paris, "she gave the world what is still our richest patrimony. Is it not time for her heirs to emulate her?" And here I think we should heed the testimony of an eminent German art-historian. Speaking of one of the centers of the Renaissance, Wolfgang Braunfels writes, "Siena would never have become the city we see today without, *first*, the belief that the ordering of the town was a mirror of the cosmos and so of life itself, *secondly*, that this order could be manifested in symbolic form and, *thirdly*, that it was incumbent on every citizen to collaborate in the establishment of this order." An Office for Beauty served to prevent violations of the *decor publicus;* and inasmuch as the Sienese conception of beauty was an evolving one, he explains, "we have a living city," the product of "a long and sustained effort to reach a Utopian perfection" with "at every stage . . . new impetuses for art."

Our continent is steadily deteriorating. The most powerful forces among and within us are bent on debauching it for the greater opulence of a swarming, hedonistic population and the proliferation of an awesome and inhuman ugliness. In the circumstances, it may seem hopelessly naive to speak of aiming at a garden that will harmonize the best of nature and of man, mirroring and symbolizing the cosmic order as science and an awareness of the consummate artistry of Creation reveal it to us. And it is hopelessly naive. To arrest the blight man is spreading across the earth, in the view of Claude Lévi-Strauss, the French anthropologist, "would take a spiritual revolution as great as that which led to the advent of Christianity," and he may well be right. But having made these acknowledgments, one may point out, for what it may be worth, that the highest beliefs we profess plead the continent's cause. If we have any feeling for our country, which by our fervent expressions of patriotism we would have it thought we have, we should not tolerate the desecration of those scenes, natural or human in origin, which have entered the warp and woof of the nation's character and brought out or exemplify the best in the American people. The country in its appearance will faithfully mirror our regard for it, whether this be one of mercenary indifference or of respect and love. Only as we treat it as a home will it provide one.

The other feeling is the religious one. How much it enters into most church-going and the ready invocations of God so common among us is a matter of opinion, but surely the feeling is real enough. To me, the one worthy refuge of the human spirit that is proof against the vicissitudes of existence, as far as any can be, lies in a consciousness of and response to the Universal—the Creator, if one prefers, or, as I should say, agnostic that I am, the Genius of Creation—revealed in the great Cosmos and, for us as a people, in the portion of the earth in our keeping. As we prove ourselves worthy or unworthy of that we shall show how far, if at all, we can be moved by reverence.

What seems to me evident is that if the sacrifice of our homeland to its inhabitants' pursuit of self-gratification is ever halted it will be because its degradation or destruction to that end incurs the spontaneous condemnation visited upon the sacrilegious and upon acts of national betrayal.

In some of our literature and painting, in the best of our building, in the care we have taken of some of our land, in the battle for its preservation that some of us have fought valiantly, in countless attestations of love for it, we have shown that as a people we are not incapable of the kind of idealism that led to the building of the cathedral of Chartres. But what seems to me most likely for the future is that we shall take scant counsel of religion or patriotism but shall continue to rest our faith in technology. And one should not underrate technology's capacities. Perhaps we can go on indefinitely, compensated by luxuries for the intangibles of life we shall be without, inured by habit to the ugliness and cacophony we spread, sloughing off from the species as unfit for survival those persons who sicken at our impoverishment of the earth. Perhaps mankind will be united at last, and in the naked enterprise of subjugating and exploiting Nature.

But I doubt that it will work. Technology is vital to us; but to rely on technology to save us from the ills it brings in train is to me like resorting to fire-hoses to thrust back flood waters. And I am impressed by how consistently men have shown a need for something to believe in, for a meaning external to themselves to

bring them together and vindicate their lives. In default of a worthy
and constructive purpose they can and will find other kinds pur-
veyed by the fanatics who are always waiting in the wings. Or, in
the spirit of one who bites on a tooth tormenting him with pain,
they may avenge themselves by destructiveness on the society that
fails to provide their lives with meaning.

Those who conquer or escape from Nature, moreover, had better
be prepared to find their victory in the long run illusory. The fate
of other groups of men, small and great, which by the amassing of
wealth—power—have been able to separate themselves from the
land as we have is not encouraging. One has the impression that
the more we succeed in subduing Nature and eliminating it from
the sphere of our lives, the less of Nature remains in us to give us
life. Or perhaps it is that life arises in response to hardship and danger, to challenge, and that as we exchange these for ease, comfort
and security, it fails within us.

But if one despairs of the monster we are creating in the name
of civilization, one does not despair when one is out from under it.
Life—natural life—buoys us up. "Ever since it has existed on earth,"
as Charles de Gaulle observed, "life has waged a battle it has never
lost." And: "Old Earth," he exclaims, "worn by the ages, wracked
by rain and storm, exhausted yet ever ready to produce what life
must have to go on!"

Old Earth! Earth and Mystery! I feel close to both watching
the waves roll in on the Virginia shore as they roll in inexhaustibly
on all the shores of the planet, and will roll, let man do what he
may. Sea and mountains: a week later I finish my tour of Virginia
along the same road on which I had set out for the West, beside the
crest of the Blue Ridge. The old hills appear to grow more massive
as the darkness steals up them from the Piedmont and the Shenandoah Valley, where the lights have come on in shimmering constellations of minute but brilliant jewels. . . . One is not only one's
society; one is also oneself, to render the Universal, the Great Spirit,
whatever observance one has it in one to give.

And in return? The mountains looming around me, still in their
drab winter coat of naked forest, full of their own being in the
faintly luminous darkness, give an answer. In return there is the
knowledge that whatever is, is unimaginably great and—relieving
us of the burden of need to come to ultimate conclusions about life
—unknowable. There is the peace of mind that comes in accepting

the limitations of one's poor powers and recognizing that as far as the farthest galaxy, as near as the heart of the flower at one's feet, there is mystery, mystery our science may refine but can never penetrate, mystery ever meeting our searching gaze.

SOURCE NOTES

8 *The War Memoirs of Charles de Gaulle,* Vol. III. Simon and Schuster. New York. 1960.

20 S. Herbert Evison. "Finding a Route for the Blue Ridge Parkway." *National Parks Magazine.* Washington, D.C. September 1969.

23 D. H. Lawrence. *Etruscan Places.* Viking Press. New York. 1932.

33 *John and William Bartram's America.* Edited by Helen G. Cruickshank, Devin-Adair. 1957.

33 Henry Steele Commager. *Documents of American History.* Appleton-Century-Crofts. New York. 1948.

33 Ray Allen Billington. *Westward Expansion.* Macmillan. New York. 1967.

33 Samuel Eliot Morison and Henry Steele Commager. *The Growth of the American Republic.* Oxford University Press. New York. 1956.

35 Allan Nevins and Henry Steele Commager. *The Pocket History of the United States.* Pocket Books. New York. 1942.

35 *Op. cit.*

44 Antoine de Saint Exupéry. *Wind, Sand and Stars.* Translated by Lewis Galantière. Bantam Books. New York. 1945.

44 O. Henry. *A Municipal Report. Strictly Business.* Doubleday, Doran & Co. New York. 1909.

45 A. W. Küchler. *Potential Natural Vegetation of the Coterminous United States.* Special Publication No. 36. American Geographical Society. New York. 1964.

46 Conrad Richter. *The Trees.* Alfred A. Knopf. New York. 1940.

50 Mark Twain. *Life on the Mississippi.* Harper & Bros. New York. 1951.

51 *Op. cit.*

55 *Audubon's America: The Narratives and Experiences of John James Audubon.* Edited by Donald Culross Peattie. Houghton Mifflin. Boston. 1940.

56 *Op. cit.*

57 *Op. cit.*

57 *Op. cit.*

62 *Journals of Lewis and Clark.* Edited by Bernard DeVoto. Houghton Mifflin. Boston. 1953.

63 Thomas D. Clark. *Frontier America.* Charles Scribner's Sons. New York. 1959.

83 Arnold J. Toynbee. "The Desert Hermits." *Horizon*. New York. Spring 1970.

94 Kenneth Clark. *Civilisation: A Personal View*. British Broadcasting Company. London. 1969.

97 Weldon F. Heald. "A Guadalupe Mountains National Park." *National Parks Magazine*. Washington, D.C. September 1965.

105 Ivan Turgeniev. *Fathers and Children*. Charles Scribner's Sons. New York. 1921.

110 Descriptive folder on Grand Canyon National Park. National Park Service, Department of the Interior. Washington, D.C. 1966.

111 François Leydet. *Time and the River Flowing: Grand Canyon*. Sierra Club. 1964.

111 *Congressional Quarterly*. Washington, D.C. November 1, 1968.

112 François Leydet. *Time and the River Flowing: Grand Canyon*. Sierra Club. 1964.

114 *Op. cit.*

115 *Op. cit.*

115 Joseph Conrad. *Heart of Darkness; Youth*. Doubleday, Doran & Co. New York. 1928.

122 John A. Hawgood. *America's Western Frontiers*. Alfred A. Knopf. New York. 1967.

126 Rodman W. Paul. *Mining Frontiers of the Far West, 1848–1880*. Henry Holt. New York. 1963.

128 *Op. cit.*

128 *Op. cit.*

128 *Op. cit.*

129 *Op. cit.*

130 Rodman W. Paul. *Mining Frontiers of the Far West, 1848–1880*. Henry Holt. New York. 1963.

131 Mark Twain. *Roughing It*. Harper and Bros. New York. 1913.

147 John Muir. *The Mountains of California*. Anchor Books. Doubleday & Company. 1961.

149 *Op. cit.*

150 Edwin Way Teale. *The Wilderness World of John Muir*. Houghton Mifflin. Boston. 1954.

150 *Op. cit.*

151 H. Munro Fox. *The Personality of Animals*. Pelican Books. London. 1940.

152 John Muir, *The Mountains of California*. Anchor Books. Doubleday & Company. New York. 1961.

152 John Muir. *Our National Parks*. Houghton Mifflin. Boston. 1901.

152 John Muir. *The Mountains of California*. Anchor Books. Doubleday & Company. New York. 1961.

152 Edwin Way Teale. *The Wilderness World of John Muir*. Houghton Mifflin. Boston. 1954.

153 John Muir. *The Mountains of California*. Anchor Books. Doubleday & Company. New York. 1961.

153 Edwin Way Teale. *The Wilderness World of John Muir*. Houghton Mifflin. Boston. 1954.

154 *Op. cit.*

154 John Muir. *The Mountains of California*. Anchor Books. Doubleday & Company. New York. 1961.

154 Robert Louis Stevenson. "Aes Triplex," in *Virginibus Puresque*. Charles Scribner's Sons. New York. 1925.

155 Edwin Way Teale. *The Wilderness World of John Muir*. Houghton Mifflin. Boston. 1954.

155 John Muir. *The Mountains of California*. Anchor Books. Doubleday & Company. New York. 1961.

157 *California: A Guide to the Golden State.* Works Progress Administration. Hastings House. New York. 1939.

164 Philip B. King. *Evolution of North America.* Princeton University Press. 1959.

173 Lynn White, Jr. "The Historical Roots of Our Ecologic Crisis." *Science.* March, 1966.

174 *Op. cit.*

184 *The American Heritage Book of Natural Wonders.* Edited by Alvin M. Josephy, Jr. American Heritage Publishing Co. New York. 1963.

187 Konrad Lorenz in interview with Frédéric de Towarnicki. *New York Times Magazine.* July 5, 1970.

191 Freeman Tilden. *The National Parks.* Alfred A. Knopf. New York. 1968.

199 *Wyoming; A Guide to Its History, Highways, and People.* Works Progress Administration. Oxford University Press. New York. 1941.

200 *Op. cit.*

202 *Op. cit.*

203 *Op. cit.*

204 John A. Hawgood. *America's Western Frontiers.* Alfred A. Knopf. New York. 1967.

211 Albert Speer. *Inside the Third Reich: Memoirs.* Macmillan Co. New York. 1970.

215 Calvin Tomkins. *The Lewis and Clark Trail.* Harper and Row. New York. 1965.

215 Russell T. Rutter and Douglas H. Pimlott. *The World of the Wolf.* J. B. Lippincott Co. Philadelphia and New York. 1968.

216 Marie Sandoz. *Love Song to the Plains.* Harper & Bros. New York. 1961.

217 Peter Farb. *Man's Rise to Civilization.* E. P. Dutton & Co. New York. 1968.

218 John A. Hawgood. *America's Western Frontiers.* Alfred A. Knopf. New York. 1967.

218 *Op. cit.*

219 *Time.* New York. September 14, 1970.

225 Gustave Flaubert. *Madame Bovary.* Translated by Francis Steegmuller. Random House. New York. 1957.

226 *Encyclopaedia Britannica.* Eleventh Edition. New York. 1910.

227 Antoine de Saint Exupéry. *Wind, Sand and Stars.* Translated by Lewis Galantière. Bantam Books. New York. 1945.

229 Peter Farb. *Man's Rise to Civilization.* E. P. Dutton & Co. New York. 1968.

232 Sigurd F. Olson. *The Singing Wilderness.* Alfred A. Knopf. New York. 1956.

234 D. H. Lawrence. *Etruscan Places.* Viking Press. New York. 1932.

239 Bernard DeVoto. *The Course of Empire.* Houghton Mifflin Co. Boston. 1952.

239 *Op. cit.*

244 John A. Hawgood. *America's Western Frontiers.* Alfred A. Knopf. New York. 1967.

244 Charles M. Andrews. *The Colonial Period of American History.* Yale University Press. 1964.

249 Joseph Conrad. Preface to *A Personal Record.* Doubleday, Doran & Co. New York. 1928.

251 Robert Carter. *Picturesque America; Or the Land we Live In.* Edited by William Cullen Bryant. D. Appleton & Co. New York. 1872.

252 Samuel Franklin Emmons. Biographical Memoire of Clarence King. Read at National Academy of Sciences, April 23, 1903. Judd and Detweiler, Printers. Washington, D.C. 1907.

253 Robert H. Boyle. *The Hudson River.* W. W. Norton & Co. New York. 1969.

253 *Op. cit.*

254 "The Adirondacks." *American Heritage.* New York. August 1969.

254 Robert H. Boyle. *The Hudson River.* W. W. Norton & Co. New York. 1969.

254 J. T. Cunningham. "Forever Wild?" *Audubon Magazine.* New York. March 1967.

259 Stearns Morse. *Some White Mountains History. A Brief Guide to the Natural History of the White Mountains.* New Hampshire Audubon Society. Concord, N.H.

261 *New Hampshire: A Guide to the Granite State.* Works Progress Administration. Houghton Mifflin Company. Boston. 1938.

261 Robert S. Monahan. *Trees of the White Mountains. A Brief Guide to the Natural History of the White Mountains.* New Hampshire Audubon Society. Concord, N.H.

261 *New Hampshire: A Guide to the Granite State.* Works Progress Administration. Houghton Mifflin Co. Boston. 1938.

262 *Op. cit.*

266 Samuel Eliot Morison and Henry Steele Commager. *The Growth of the American Republic.* Oxford University Press. New York. 1956.

266 Paul Showers. Review of *American Album. New York Times Book Review.* September 8, 1968.

267 Henry Fairlee. Excerpts from an article in *Interplay* magazine. *The Washington Post.* December 7, 1969.

268 John Corry. "A Man Called Perry Horse." *Harper's Magazine.* New York. October 1970.

269 *Op. cit.*

272 Charles M. Andrews. *The Colonial Period of American History.* Yale University Press. 1964.

277 ". . . A Unique and Irresistible Appeal." The President's Report. Colonial Williamsburg. Williamsburg, Va.

279 Allan Nevins and Henry Steele Commager. *The Pocket History of the United States.* Pocket Books. New York. 1942.

282 R. V. Coleman. *The First Frontier.* Charles Scribner's Sons. New York. 1948.

282 Charles M. Andrews. *The Colonial Period of American History.* Yale University Press. 1964.

285 National Park Service sign on Jamestown Island circumferential road.

288 Charles M. Andrews. *The Colonial Period of American History.* Yale University Press. 1964.

288 Samuel Eliot Morison and Henry Steele Commager. *The Growth of the American Republic.* Oxford University Press. New York. 1956.

289 *Op. cit.*

290 Vine Deloria, Jr. Talk at Smithsonian Institution Symposium. November 18, 1970.

291 Frank Melville. "One Visit to America." *New York Times Magazine.* December 15, 1968.

291 René Dubos. *Man and His Environment; The Fitness of Man's Environment.* Smithsonian Press. Washington, D.C. 1967.

293 *Op. cit.*

293 *Op. cit.*

295 *Op. cit.*

296 Kenneth Clark. *Civilisation: A Personal View.* British Broadcasting Company. London. 1969.

296 Lewis Galantière. *New York Times Book Review.* November 19, 1967.

297 Colman McCarthy. *The Washington Post.* Washington, D.C. November 8, 1970.

297 Rufus E. Miles, Jr. "The Population Challenge of the '70's." *Population Bulletin.* Population Reference Bureau. Washington, D.C. February 1970.

297 Edwin L. Dale, Jr. "The Economics of Pollution." *New York Times Magazine*. April 19, 1970.

298 E. J. Mishan. *Futurism and the Worse That Is Yet to Come*. Inaugural address, American University, Washington, D.C. May 19, 1970.

298 Antoine de Saint Exupéry. *Wind, Sand and Stars*. Translated by Lewis Galantière. Bantam Books. New York. 1945.

299 Bertrand de Jouvenel. *The Stewardship of the Earth*. *The Fitness of Man's Environment*. Smithsonian Press. Washington, D.C. 1967.

299 Wolfgang Braunfels. *Institutions and Their Corresponding Ideals; The Fitness of Man's Environment*. Smithsonian Press. Washington, D.C. 1967.

299 Claude Lévi-Strauss. Interview with John L. Hess. *New York Times*. December 31, 1969.

301 *The War Memoirs of Charles de Gaulle*, Vol. III. Simon and Schuster. New York. 1960.

INDEX

NORTHERN ROCKY MTS.

COLUMBIA-SNAKE

PLATEAU

G
R
E
A
T

P

CASCADE MTS.

R
A
N
G
E

CENTRAL ROCKY MTS.

GREAT

BASIN

WASATCH MTS.

SIERRA NEVADA MTS.

COLORADO

BASIN-AND-RANGE PROVINCE

PLATEAU

SOUTHERN ROCKY MTS.

P
L
A
I
N
S

C
O
A
S
T

PACIFIC

OCEAN

SIERRA MADRE OCCIDENTAL

TOPOGRAPHICAL MAP